A little while ago, when they
held the character popularity
poll, I got a Black Bulls robe
bouquet addressed to Luck.
Incredible workmanship! That
battle maniac is one lucky guy.
Thank you very much!!

— *Yūki Tabata, 2017*

YŪKI TABATA

was born in Fukuoka Prefecture
and got his big break in the 2011
Shonen Jump Golden Future Cup
with his winning entry, *Hungry
Joker*. He started the magical fantasy
series *Black Clover* in 2015.

BLACK CLOVER
VOLUME 13
SHONEN JUMP Manga Edition

Story and Art by YŪKI TABATA

Translation ✽ TAYLOR ENGEL,
HC LANGUAGE SOLUTIONS, INC.

Touch-Up Art & Lettering ✽ ANNALIESE CHRISTMAN

Design ✽ SHAWN CARRICO

Editor ✽ ALEXIS KIRSCH

First published in Japan in 2015 by SHUEISHA Inc., Tokyo.
English translation rights arranged by SHUEISHA Inc.

Printed in the U.S.A.

Published by VIZ Media, LLC
P.O. Box 77010
San Francisco, CA 94107

10 9 8 7 6 5 4 3 2 1
First printing, November 2018

SHONEN JUMP MANGA

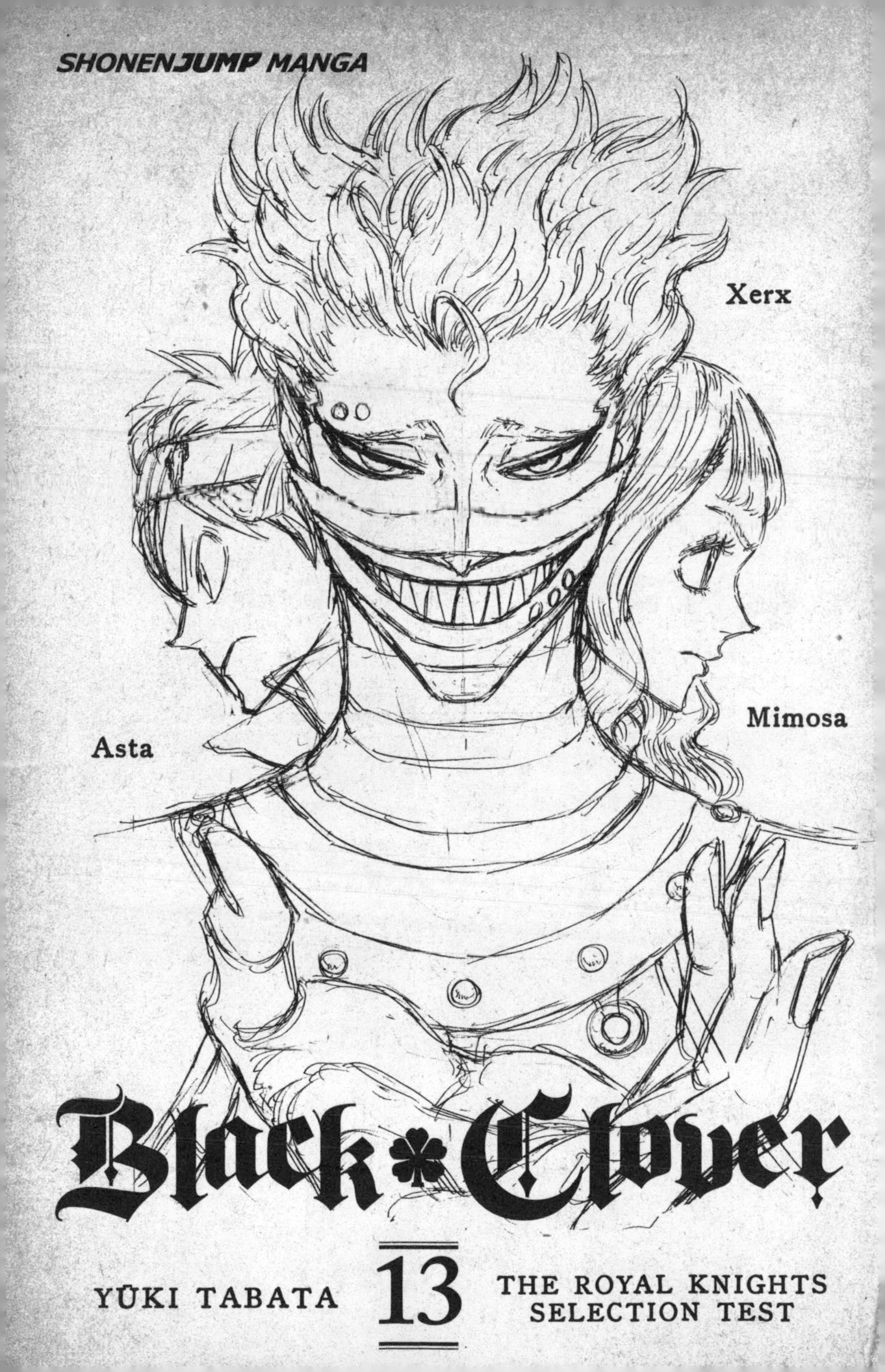

Xerx
Mimosa
Asta

Black Clover

YŪKI TABATA

13

THE ROYAL KNIGHTS SELECTION TEST

Characters

Yuno

Member of: The Golden Dawn

Magic: Wind

Asta's best friend, and a good rival who's also been working to become the Wizard King. He controls Sylph, the spirit of wind.

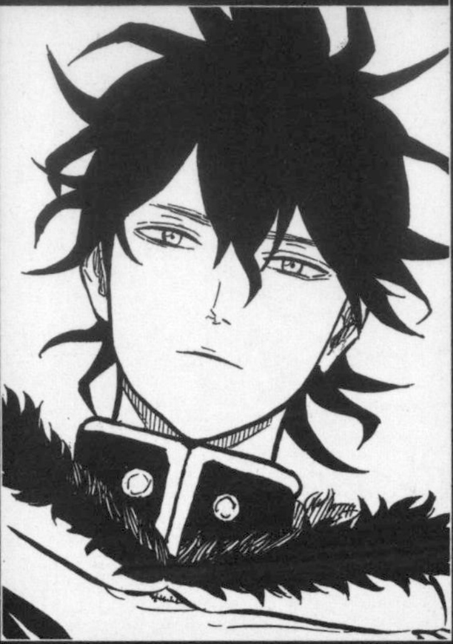

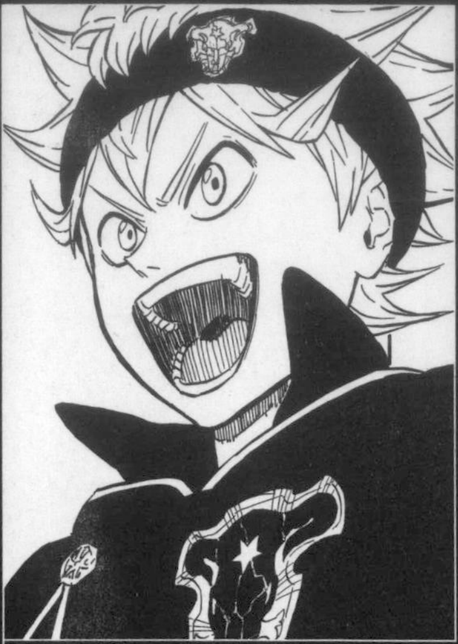

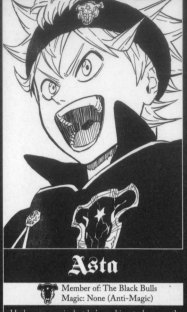

Asta

Member of: The Black Bulls

Magic: None (Anti-Magic)

He has no magic, but he's working to become the Wizard King through sheer guts and his well-trained body. He fights with an anti-magic sword.

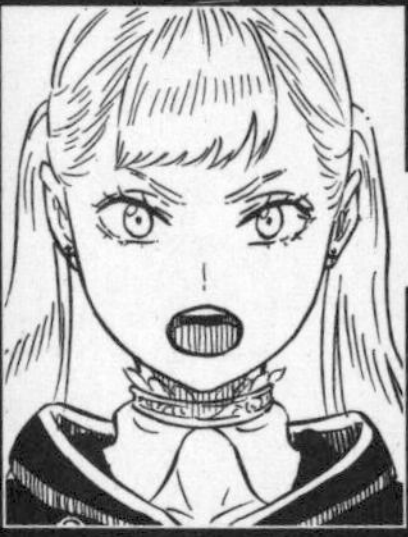

Noelle Silva

Member of: The Black Bulls

Magic: Water

A royal. She feels inferior to her brilliant siblings. Her latent abilities are an unknown quantity.

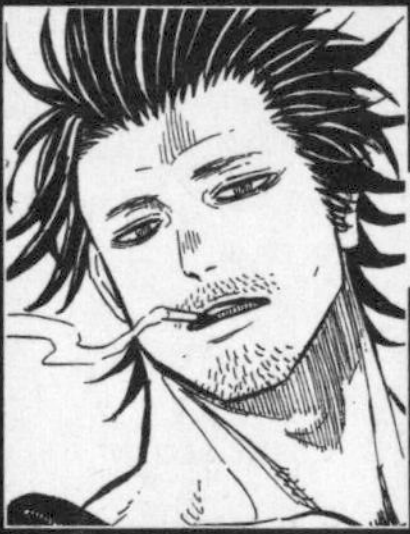

Yami Sukehiro

Member of: The Black Bulls

Magic: Dark

A captain who looks fierce and has a hot temper, but is very popular with his brigade. A heavy smoker.

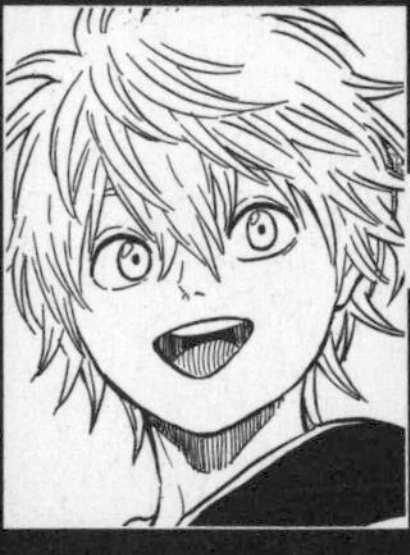

Luck Voltia

Member of: The Black Bulls

Magic: Lightning

A battle maniac. Once he starts fighting, he gets totally absorbed in it. Smiles constantly.

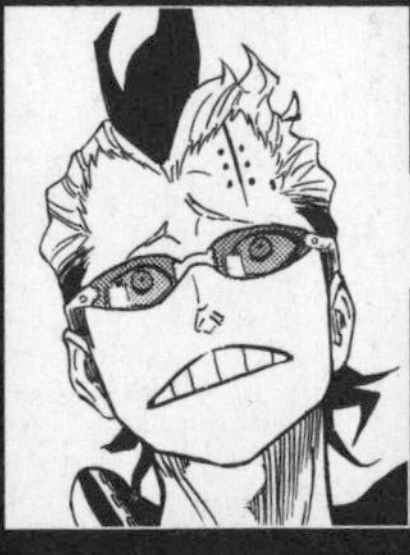

Magna Swing

Member of: The Black Bulls

Magic: Flame

He has the temperament of a delinquent, but he's quite courageous and does the right thing. Good at taking care of his companions.

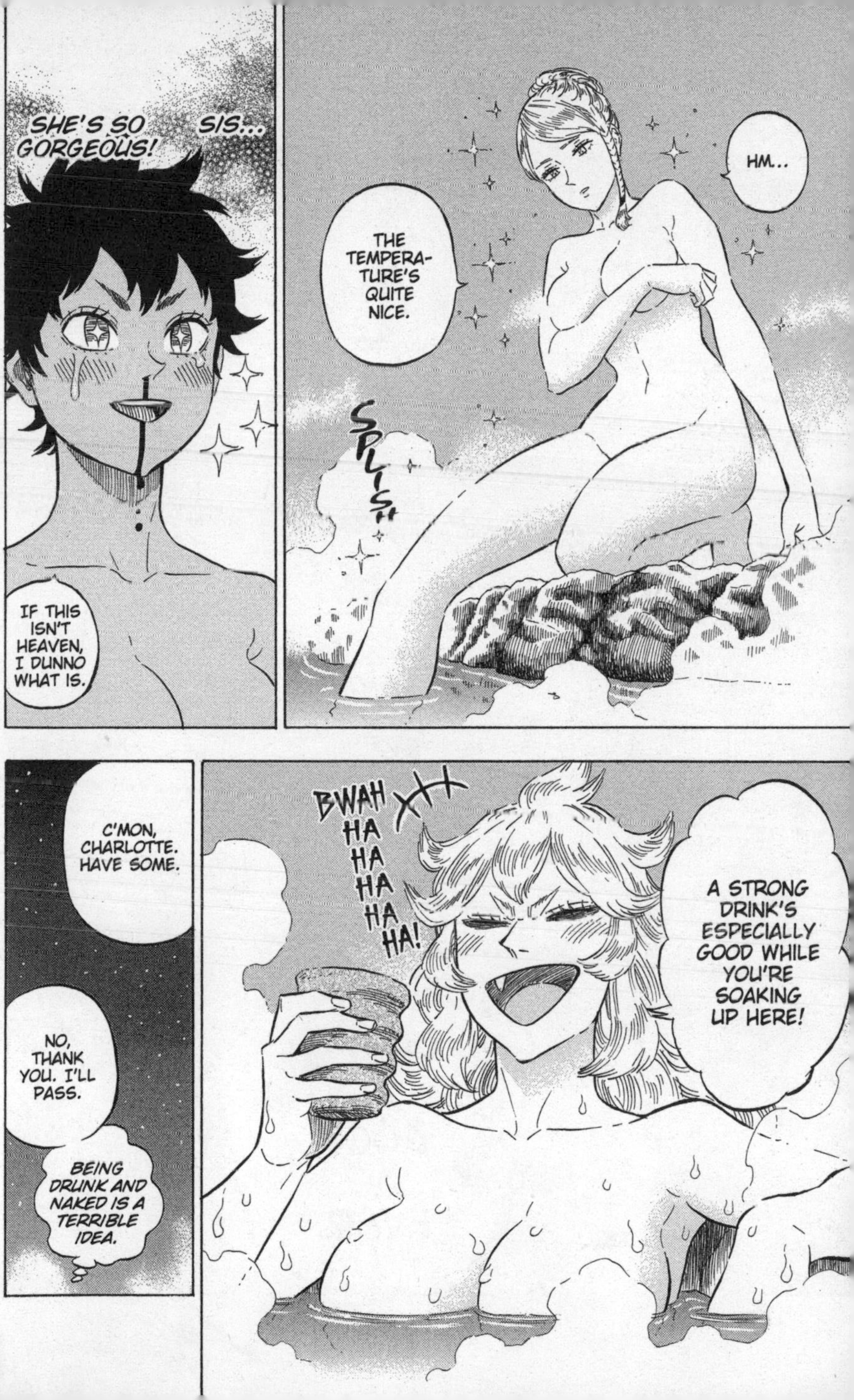
HM...
THE TEMPERA-TURE'S QUITE NICE.
SPLISH
SIS...
SHE'S SO GORGEOUS!
IF THIS ISN'T HEAVEN, I DUNNO WHAT IS.
BWAH HA HA HA HA HA!
A STRONG DRINK'S ESPECIALLY GOOD WHILE YOU'RE SOAKING UP HERE!
C'MON, CHARLOTTE. HAVE SOME.
NO, THANK YOU. I'LL PASS.
BEING DRUNK AND NAKED IS A TERRIBLE IDEA.

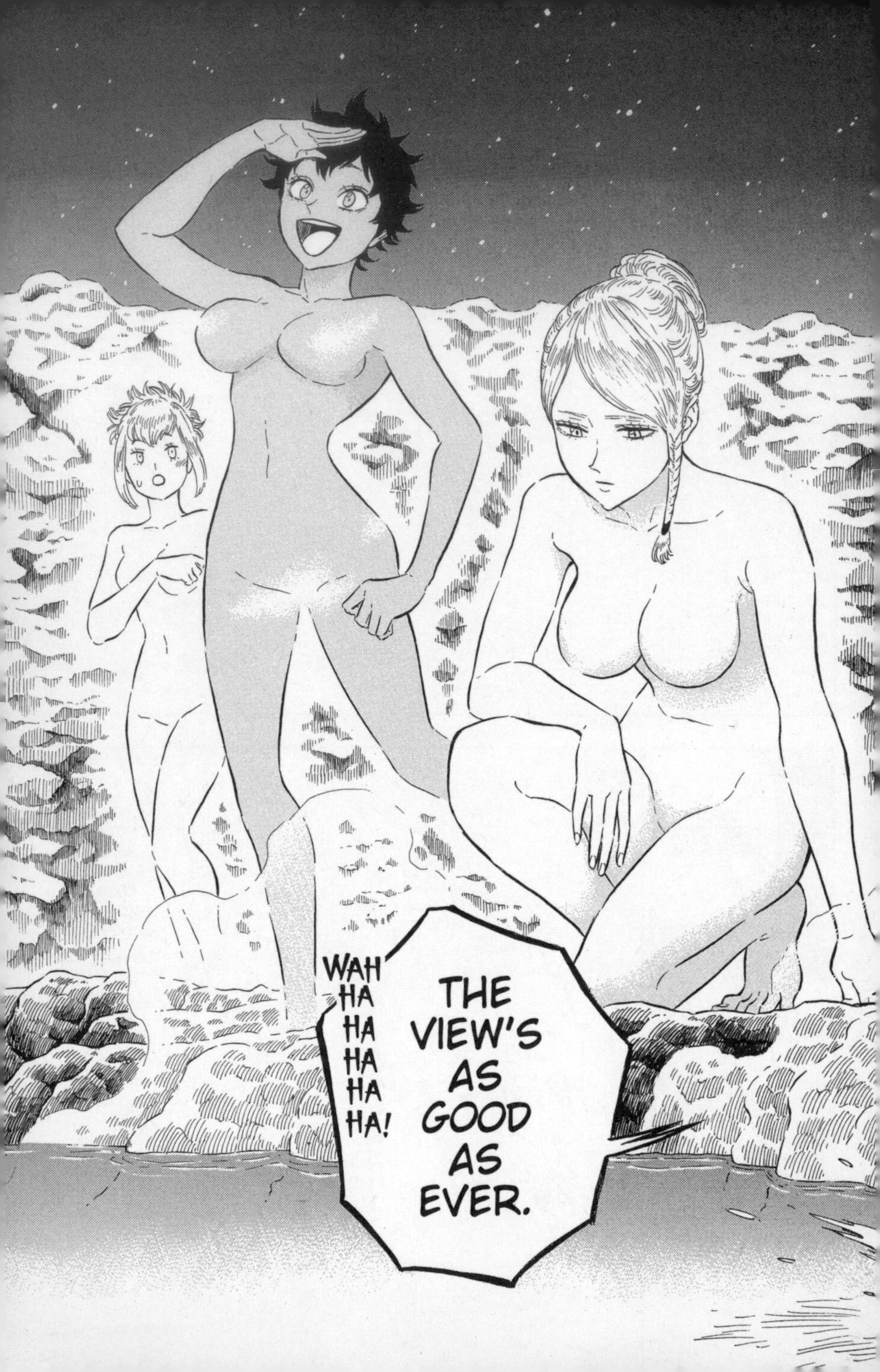
THE VIEW'S AS GOOD AS EVER.
WAH HA HA HA HA HA!

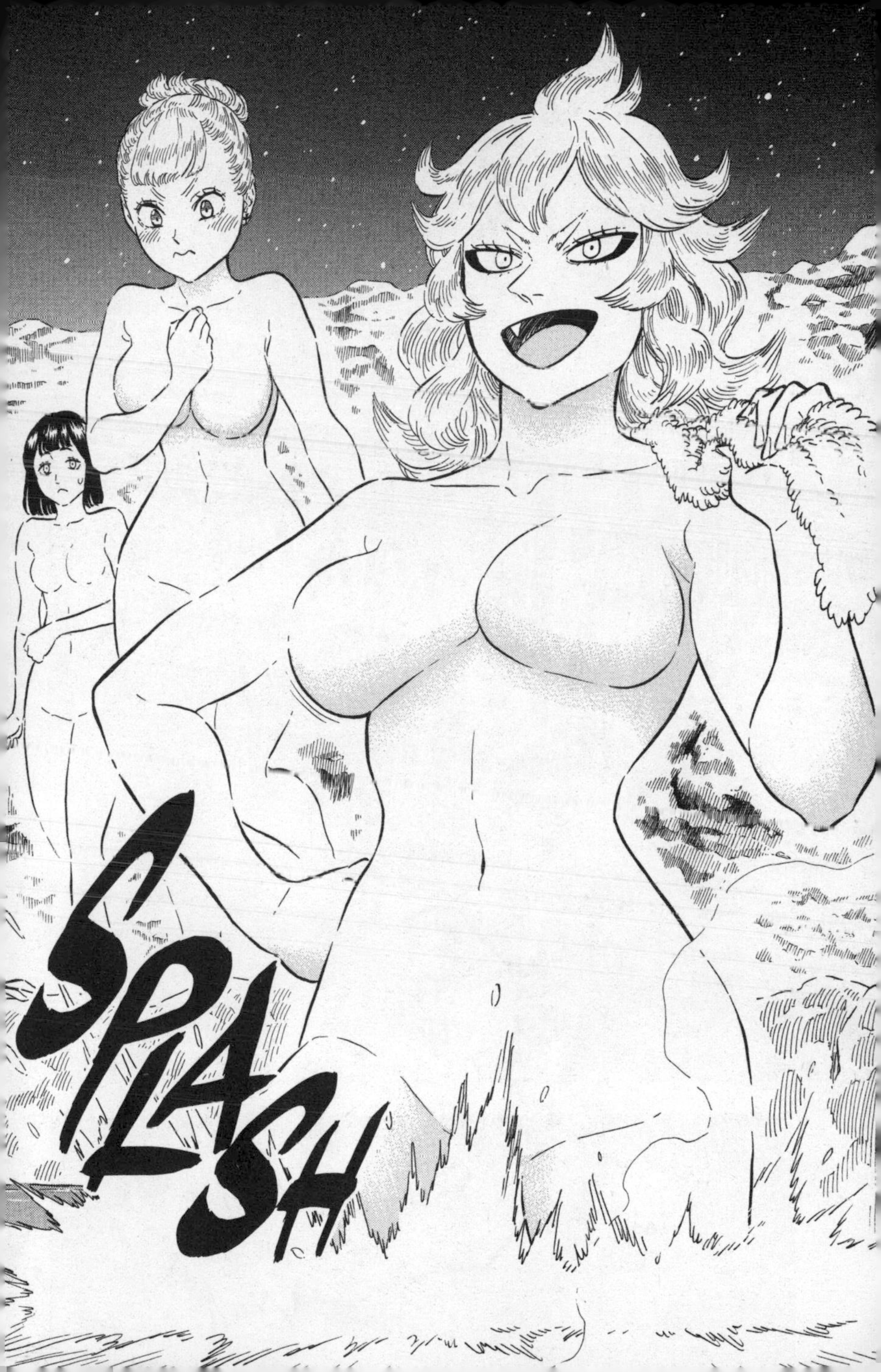
SPLASH

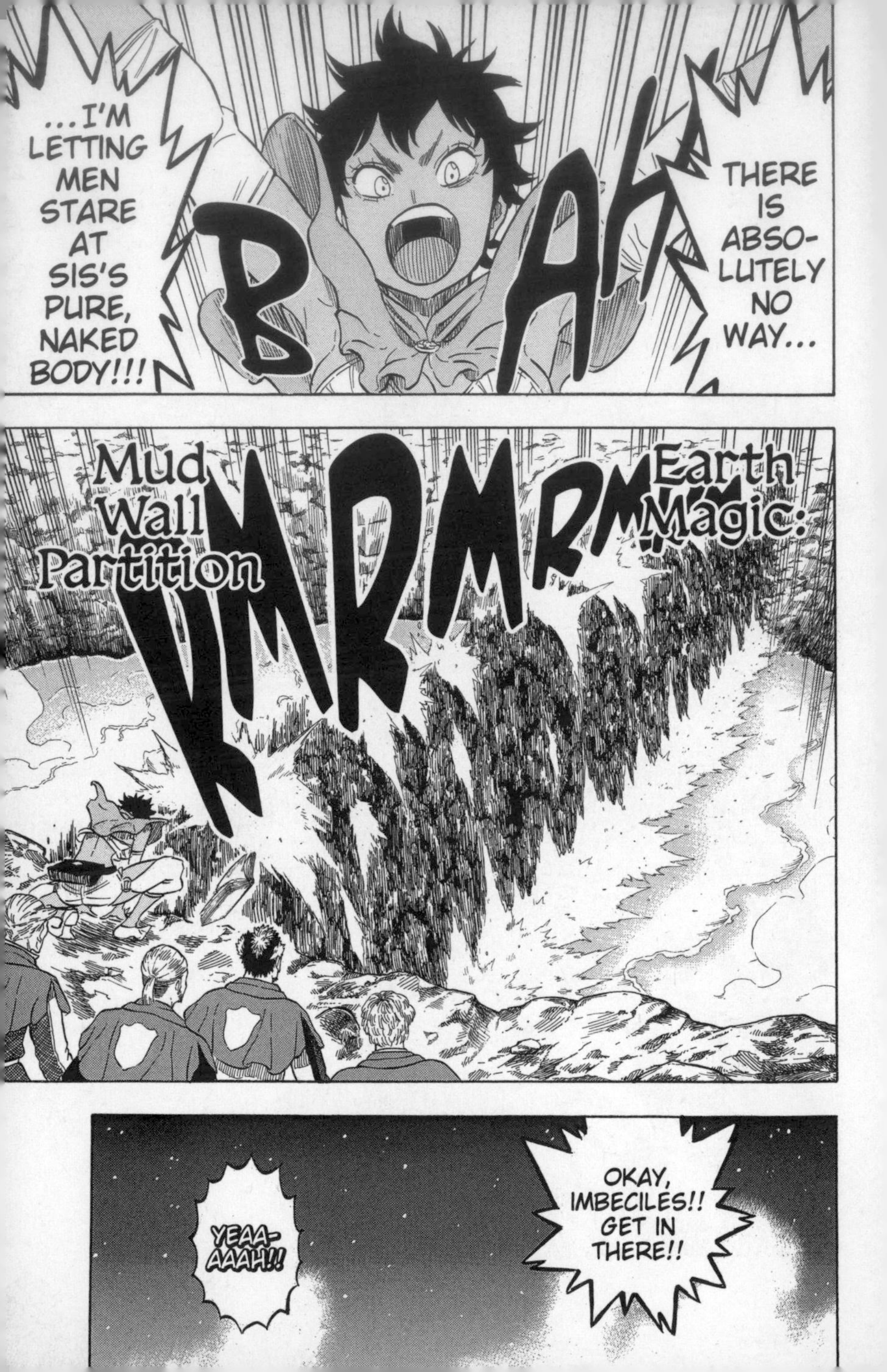
THERE IS ABSOLUTELY NO WAY...
BAH
...I'M LETTING MEN STARE AT SIS'S PURE, NAKED BODY!!!
Earth Magic:
Mud Wall Partition
OKAY, IMBECILES!! GET IN THERE!!
YEAAAAAH!!

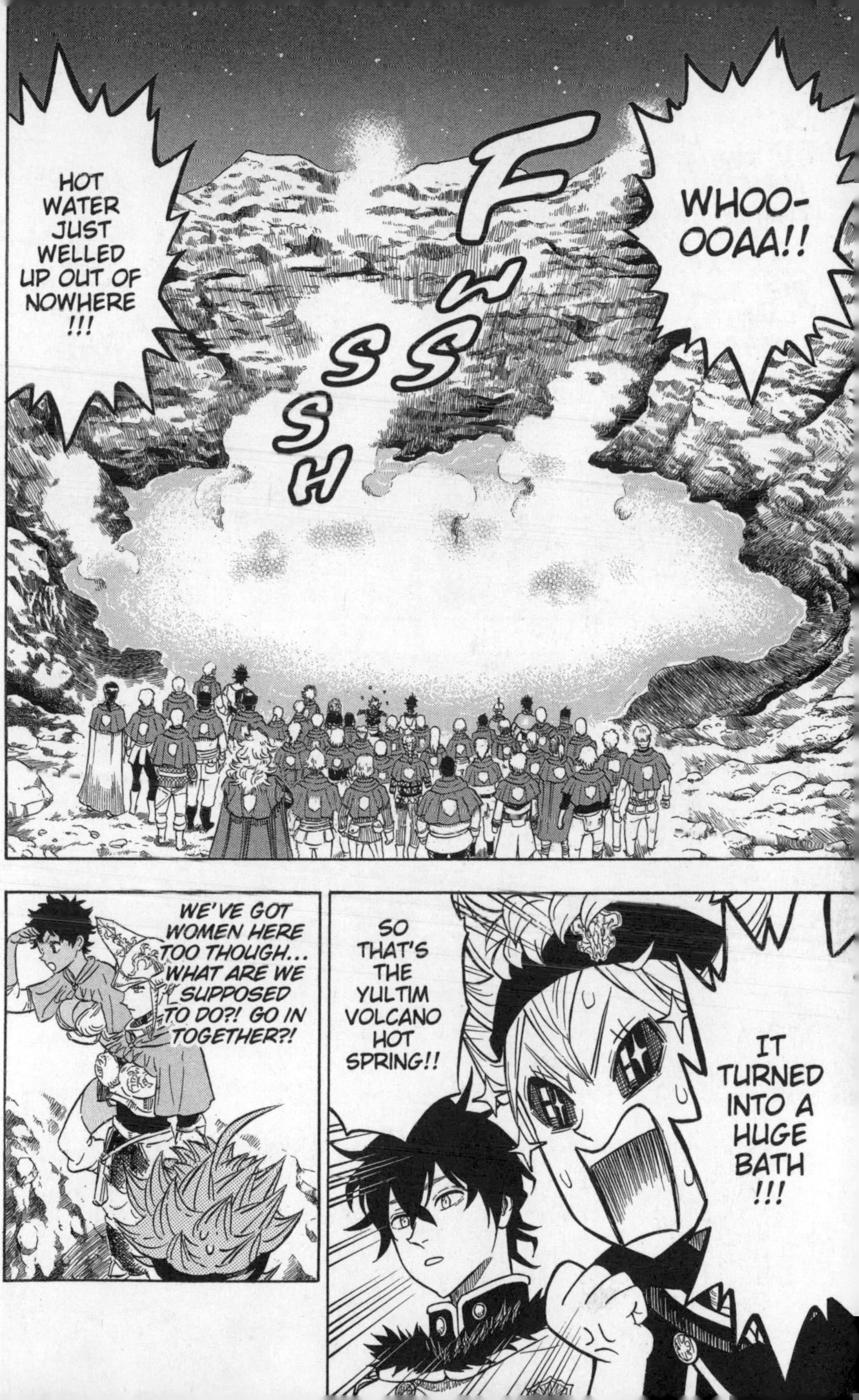
WHOO-OOAA!!
FWSSSH
HOT WATER JUST WELLED UP OUT OF NOWHERE!!!
IT TURNED INTO A HUGE BATH!!!
SO THAT'S THE YULTIM VOLCANO HOT SPRING!!
WE'VE GOT WOMEN HERE TOO THOUGH... WHAT ARE WE SUPPOSED TO DO?! GO IN TOGETHER?!

Page 111: Into the Hot Spring

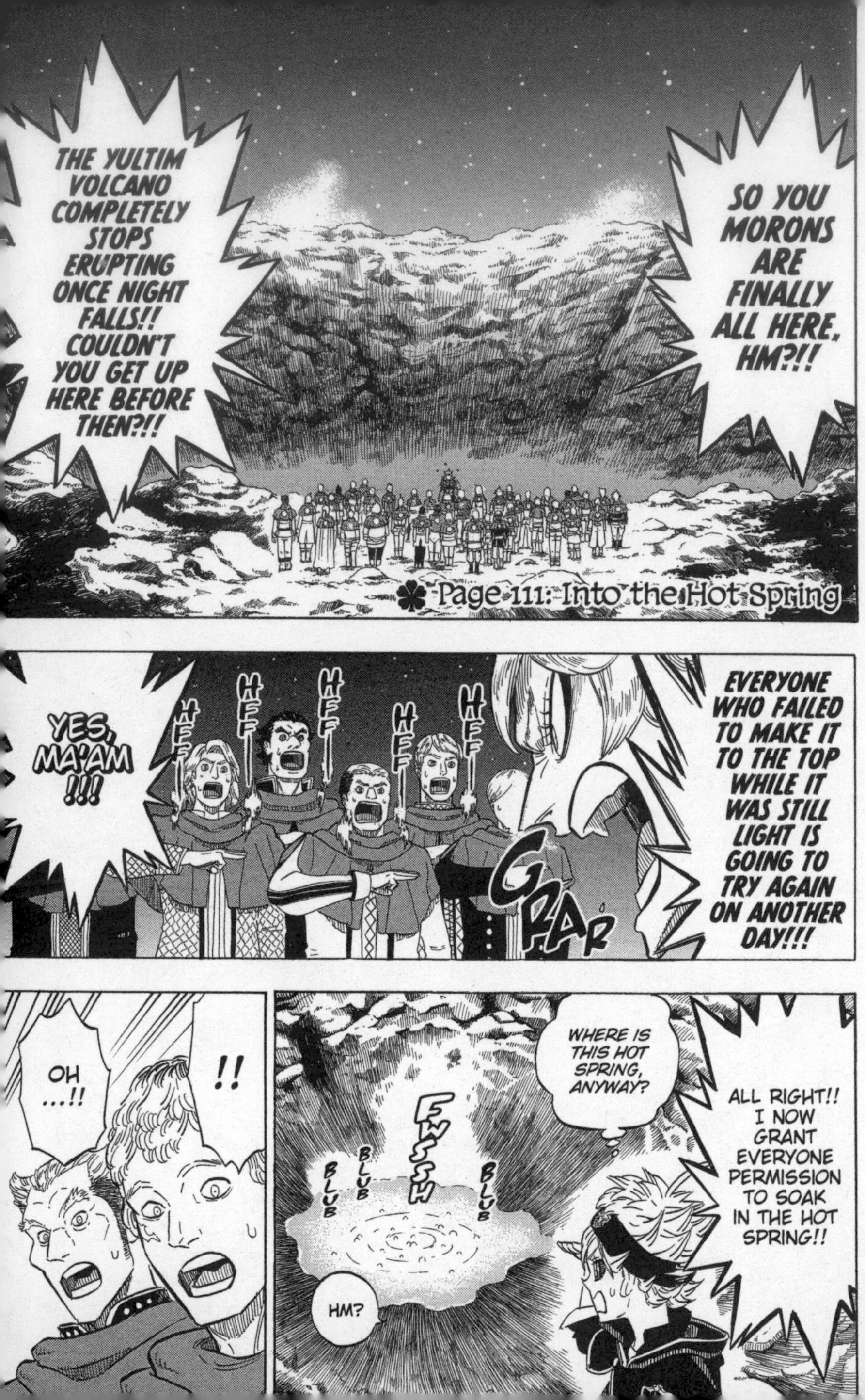
SO YOU MORONS ARE FINALLY ALL HERE, HM?!!
THE YULTIM VOLCANO COMPLETELY STOPS ERUPTING ONCE NIGHT FALLS!! COULDN'T YOU GET UP HERE BEFORE THEN?!!
EVERYONE WHO FAILED TO MAKE IT TO THE TOP WHILE IT WAS STILL LIGHT IS GOING TO TRY AGAIN ON ANOTHER DAY!!!
GRAR
HEFF
HEFF
HEFF
HEFF
HEFF
YES, MA'AM!!!
ALL RIGHT!! I NOW GRANT EVERYONE PERMISSION TO SOAK IN THE HOT SPRING!!
WHERE IS THIS HOT SPRING, ANYWAY?
FWSSH
BLUB
BLUB
BLUB
HM?
!!
OH ...!!

CONTENTS

BLACK ❀ CLOVER

13

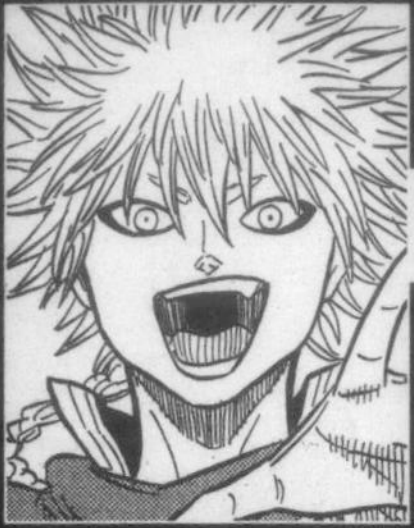

Leopold Vermilion

Member of: The Crimson Lion Kings
Magic: Flame

The younger brother of the brigade captain Fuegoleon. Considers Asta his rival.

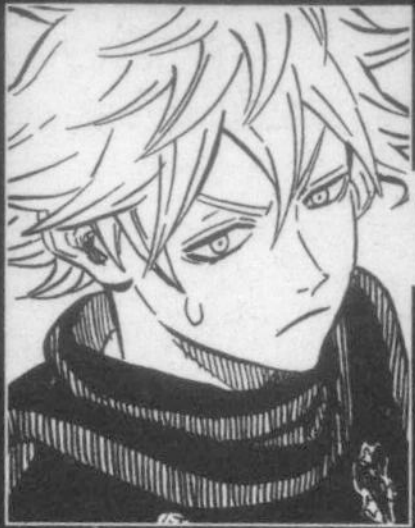

Finral Roulacase

Member of: The Black Bulls
Magic: Spatial

A flirt who immediately chats up any woman he sees. He can't attack, but he has high-level abilities.

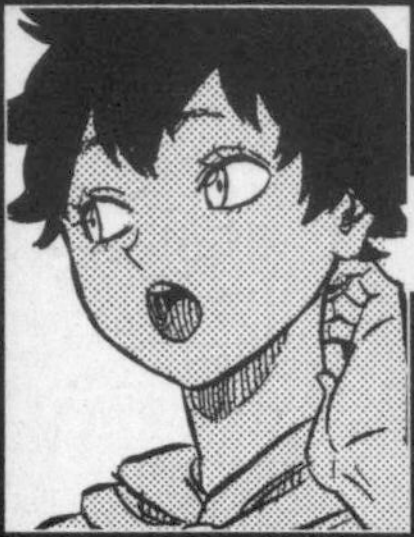

Sol Marron

Member of: The Blue Rose Knights
Magic: Earth

Spirited, freewheeling and exceptionally energetic. Adores her captain and calls her "Sis."

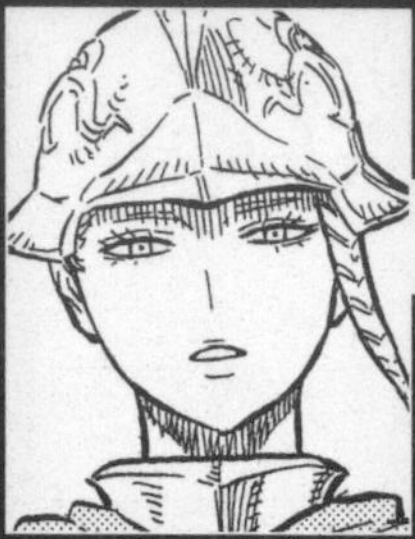

Charlotte Roselei

Member of: The Blue Rose Knights
Magic: Briar

Has a cool personality. As a rule, she doesn't like men, but she seems to make an exception for Yami…

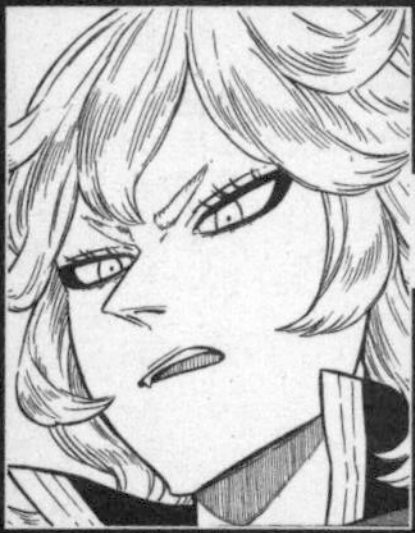

Mereoleona Vermilion

Member of: The Crimson Lion Kings
Magic: Flame

A brand-new captain. She has a stormy personality, but her combat abilities are legit.

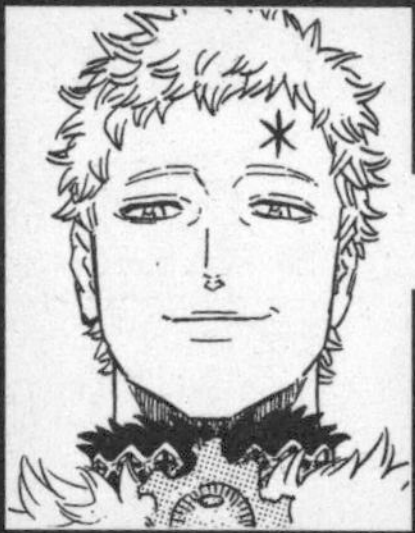

Julius Novachrono

Wizard King

The strongest man in the Clover Kingdom. Also a peerless magic fanatic. Hugely popular with the kingdom's citizens.

STORY

In a world where magic is everything, Asta and Yuno are both found abandoned on the same day at a church in the remote village of Hage. Both dream of becoming the Wizard King, the highest of all mages, and they spend their days working toward that dream.

The year they turn 15, both receive grimoires, magic books that amplify their bearer's magic. They take the entrance exam for the Magic Knights, nine groups of mages under the direct control of the Wizard King. Yuno, whose magic is strong, joins the Golden Dawn, an elite group, while Asta, who has no magic at all, joins the Black Bulls, a group of misfits. With this, the two finally take their first step toward becoming the Wizard King…

A Royal Knights selection test is created in order to assemble the ultimate brigade to put down the Eye of the Midnight Sun. Asta, Yuno and the others end up participating in a hot-spring training camp that the Crimson Lion Kings hold to prepare for the exam. After they make it through Mereoleona's harsh training, the much-anticipated hot spring turns out to be…

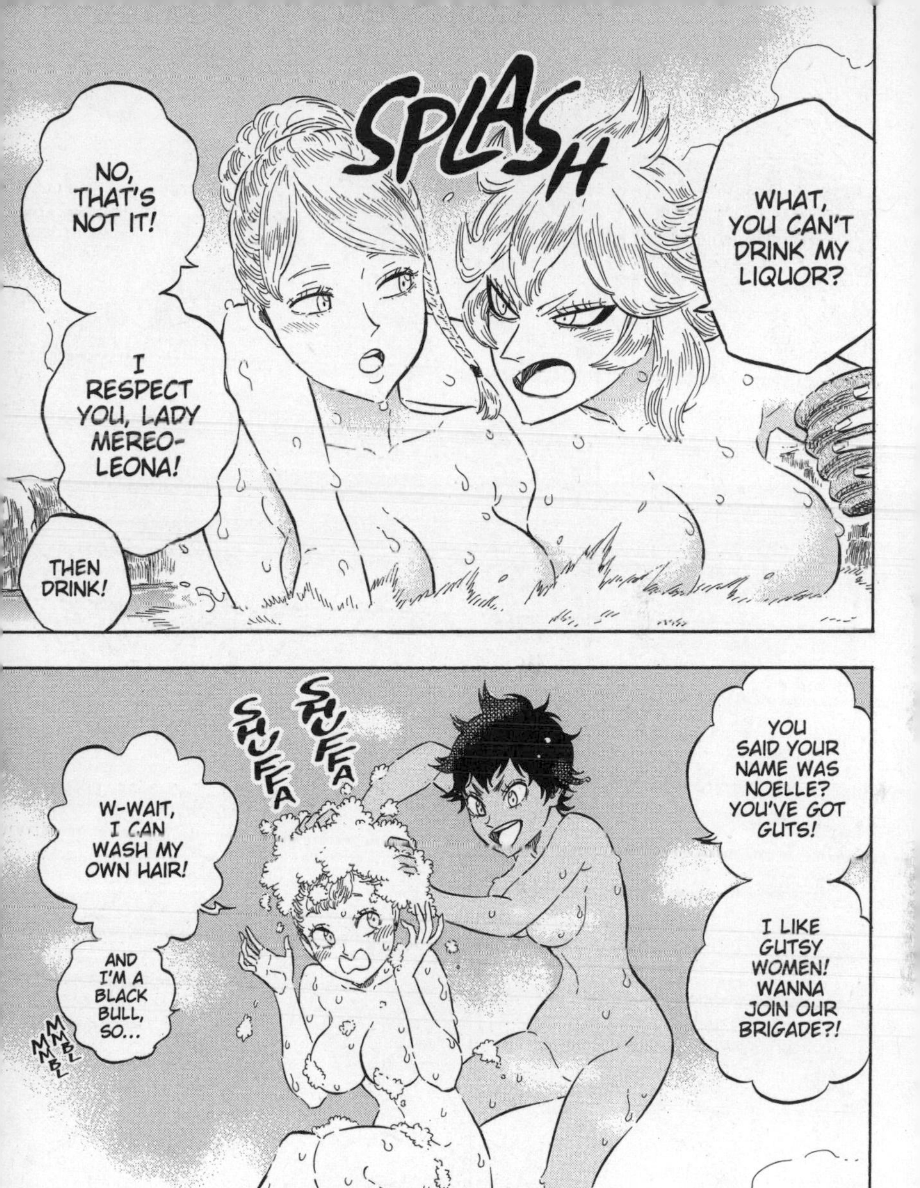
WHAT, YOU CAN'T DRINK MY LIQUOR?
SPLASH
NO, THAT'S NOT IT!
I RESPECT YOU, LADY MEREO-LEONA!
THEN DRINK!
YOU SAID YOUR NAME WAS NOELLE? YOU'VE GOT GUTS!
I LIKE GUTSY WOMEN! WANNA JOIN OUR BRIGADE?!
SHUFFA
SHUFFA
W-WAIT, I CAN WASH MY OWN HAIR!
AND I'M A BLACK BULL, SO...
MMBL MMBL

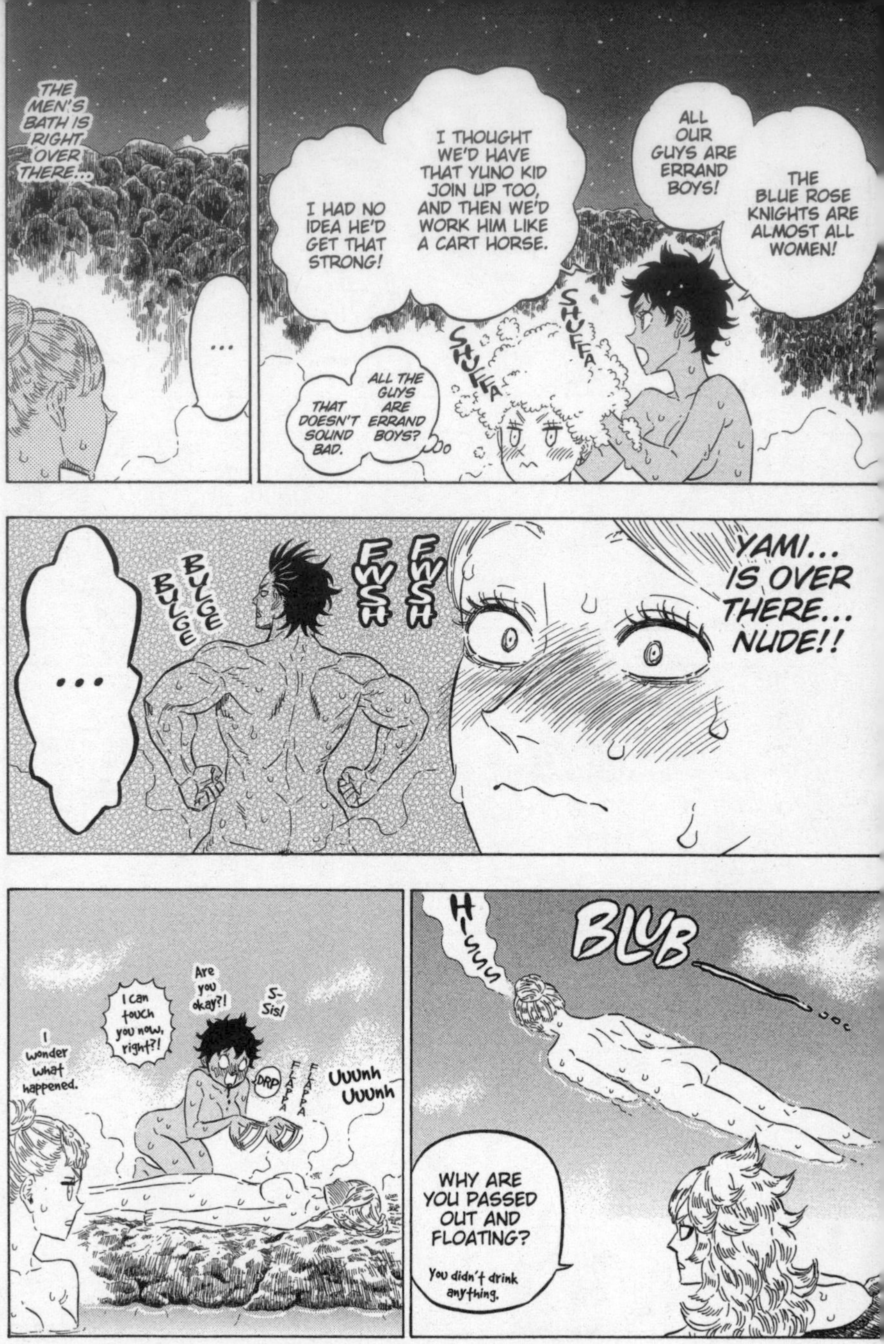

THE BLUE ROSE KNIGHTS ARE ALMOST ALL WOMEN!
ALL OUR GUYS ARE ERRAND BOYS!
I THOUGHT WE'D HAVE THAT YUNO KID JOIN UP TOO, AND THEN WE'D WORK HIM LIKE A CART HORSE.
I HAD NO IDEA HE'D GET THAT STRONG!
SHUFFA
SHUFFA
ALL THE GUYS ARE ERRAND BOYS?
THAT DOESN'T SOUND BAD.
THE MEN'S BATH IS RIGHT OVER THERE...
...
YAMI... IS OVER THERE... NUDE!!
FWSH
FWSH
BULGE
BULGE
...
BLUB
HISSSS
WHY ARE YOU PASSED OUT AND FLOATING?
You didn't drink anything.
S-Sis!
Are you okay?!
I can touch you now, right?!
Uuunh Uuunh
FLAPPA
FLAPPA
DRP
I wonder what happened.

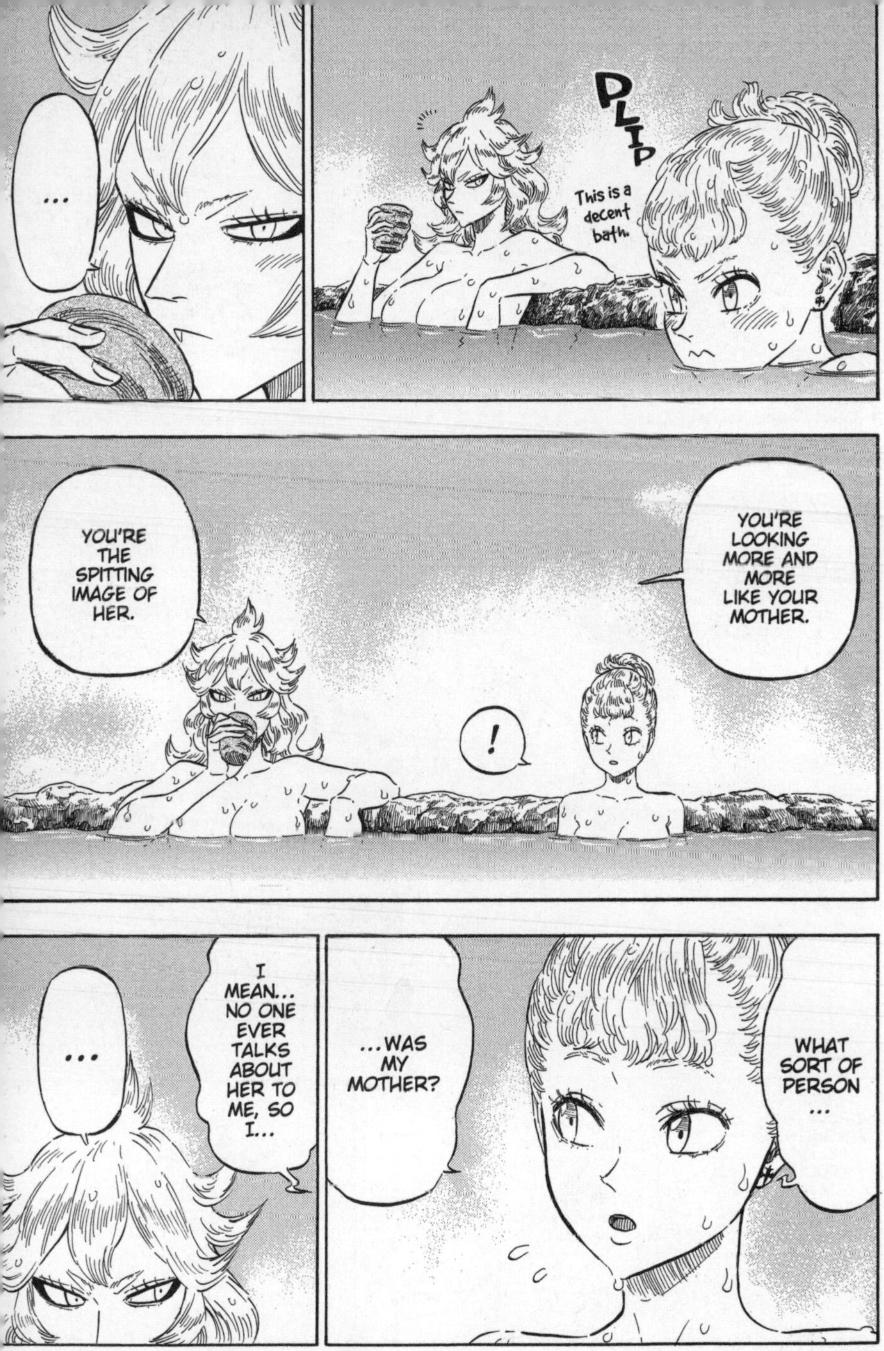
PLIP
This is a decent bath.
...
YOU'RE LOOKING MORE AND MORE LIKE YOUR MOTHER.
YOU'RE THE SPITTING IMAGE OF HER.
!
WHAT SORT OF PERSON ...
...WAS MY MOTHER?
I MEAN... NO ONE EVER TALKS ABOUT HER TO ME, SO I...
...

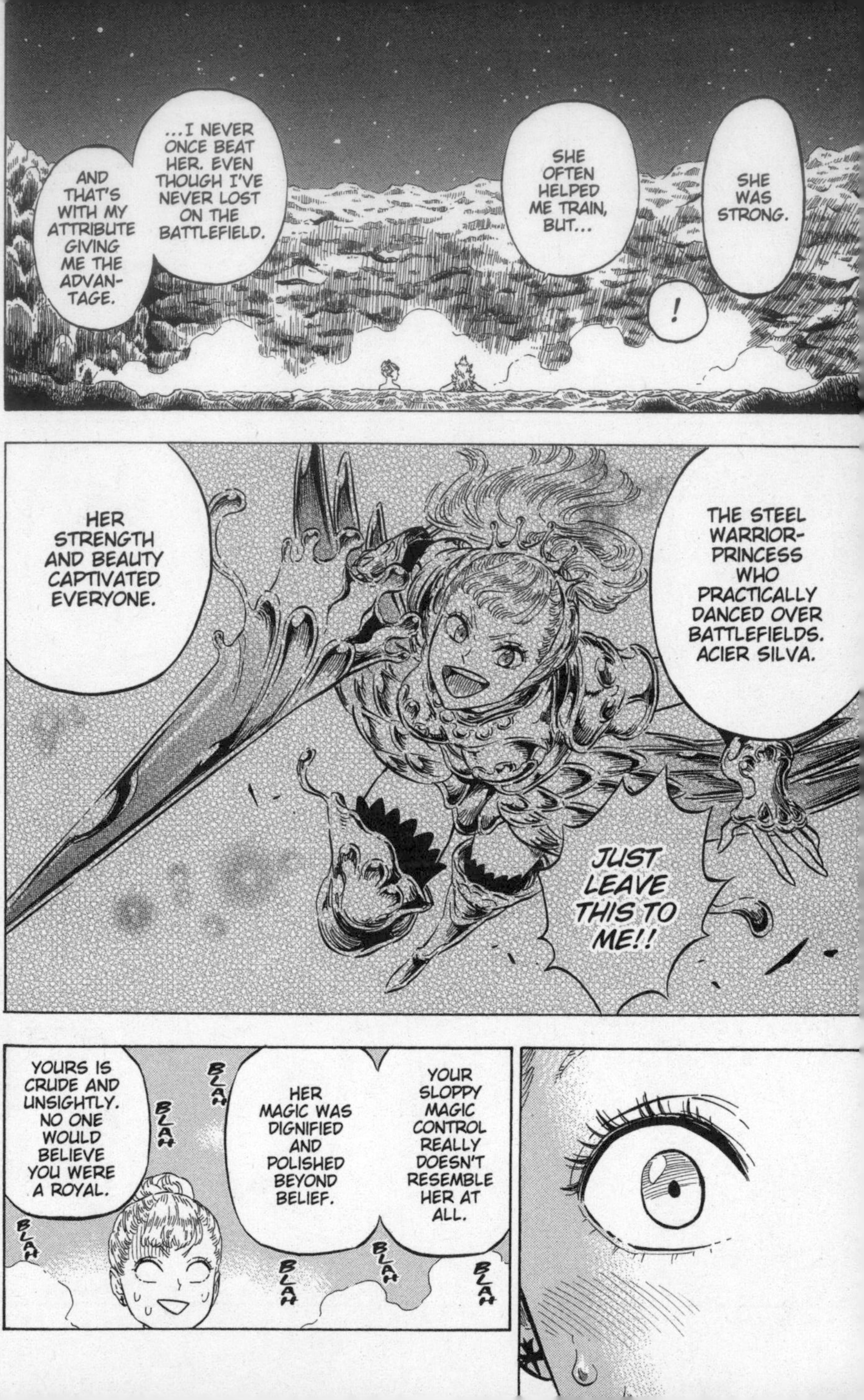
SHE WAS STRONG.
!
SHE OFTEN HELPED ME TRAIN, BUT...
...I NEVER ONCE BEAT HER. EVEN THOUGH I'VE NEVER LOST ON THE BATTLEFIELD.
AND THAT'S WITH MY ATTRIBUTE GIVING ME THE ADVAN-TAGE.
THE STEEL WARRIOR-PRINCESS WHO PRACTICALLY DANCED OVER BATTLEFIELDS. ACIER SILVA.
HER STRENGTH AND BEAUTY CAPTIVATED EVERYONE.
JUST LEAVE THIS TO ME!!
YOUR SLOPPY MAGIC CONTROL REALLY DOESN'T RESEMBLE HER AT ALL.
BLAH
BLAH
HER MAGIC WAS DIGNIFIED AND POLISHED BEYOND BELIEF.
BLAH
BLAH
BLAH
YOURS IS CRUDE AND UNSIGHTLY. NO ONE WOULD BELIEVE YOU WERE A ROYAL.
BLAH

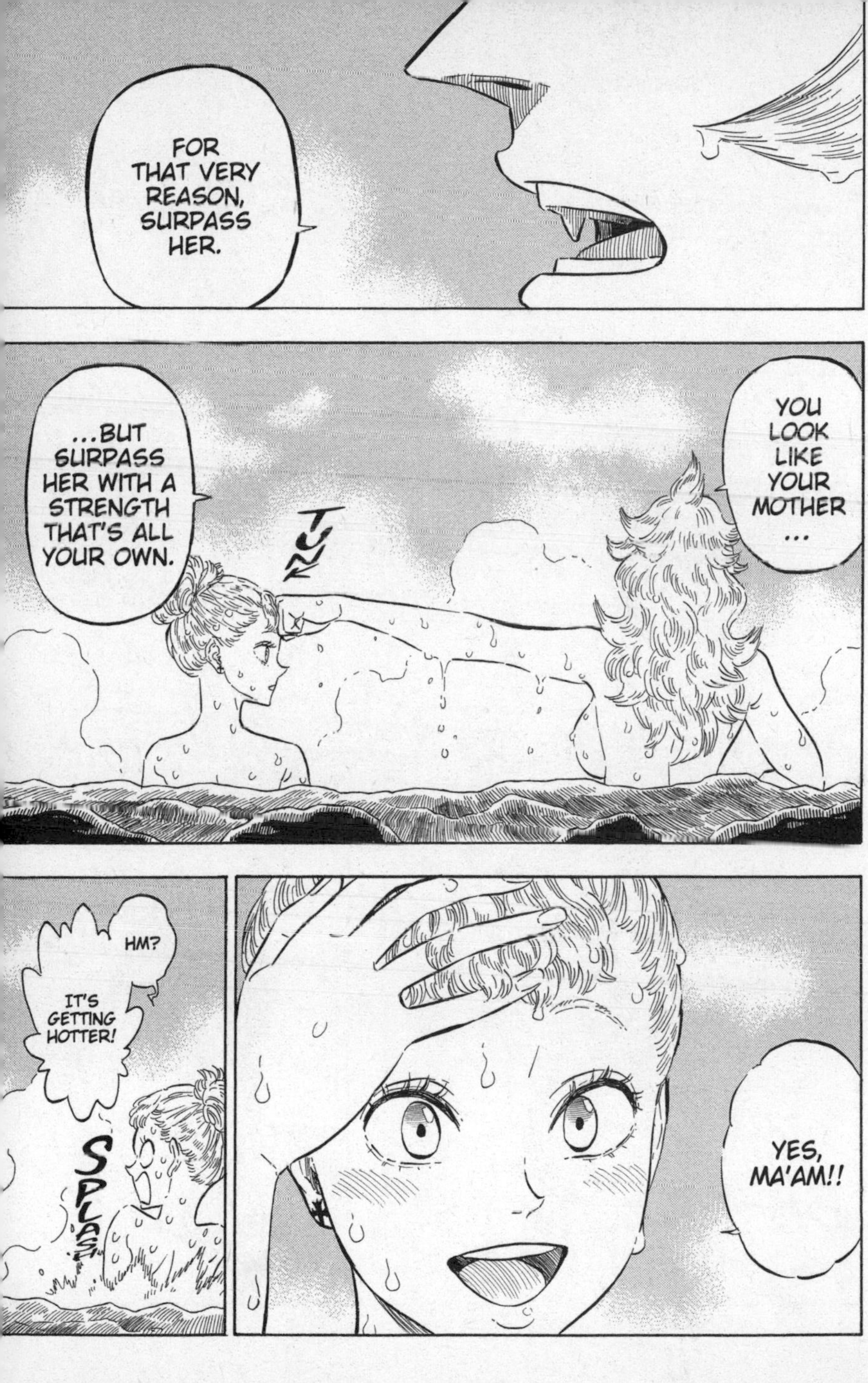
FOR THAT VERY REASON, SURPASS HER.
YOU LOOK LIKE YOUR MOTHER ...
TUNK
...BUT SURPASS HER WITH A STRENGTH THAT'S ALL YOUR OWN.
YES, MA'AM!!
HM?
IT'S GETTING HOTTER!
SPLASH!

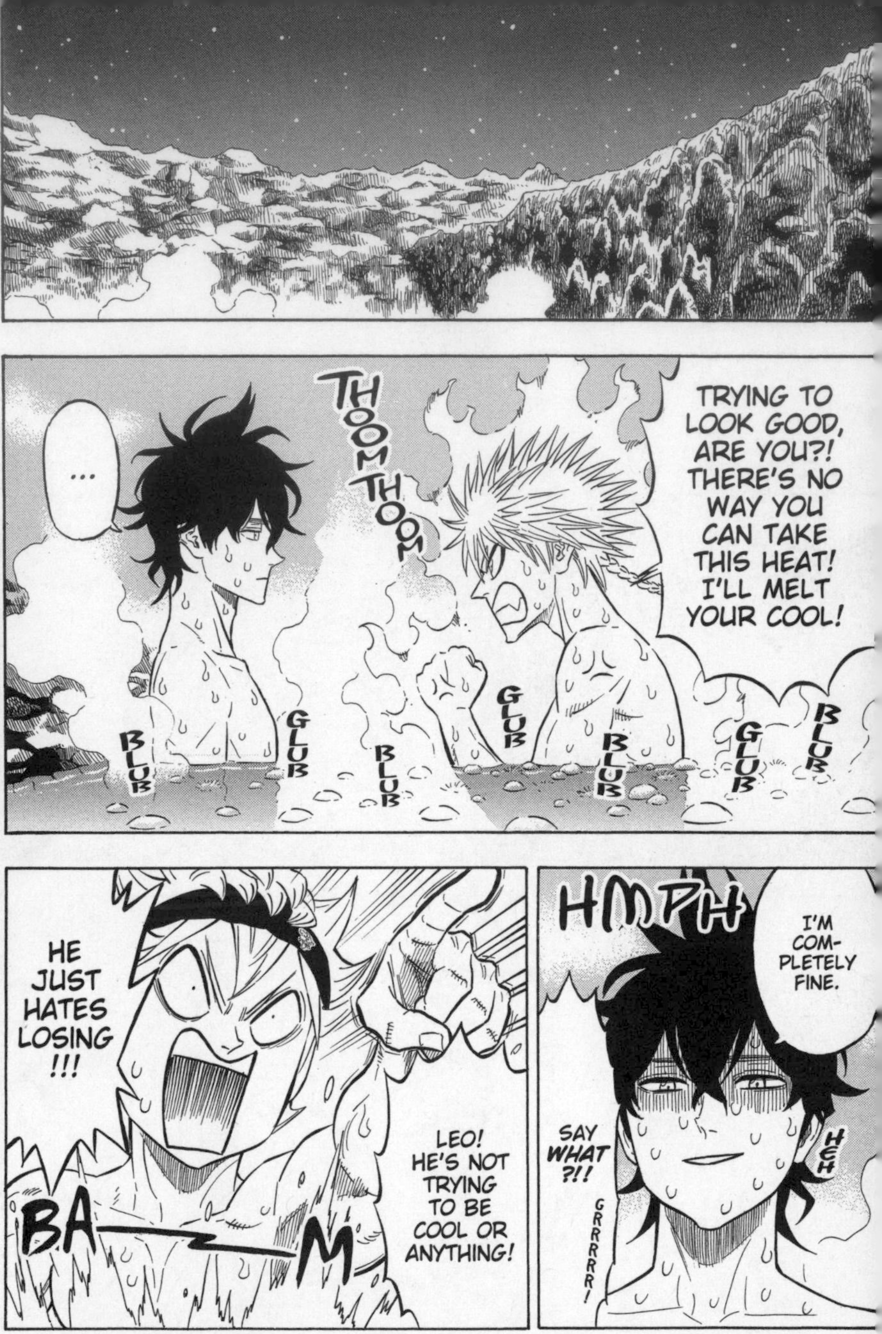

TRYING TO LOOK GOOD, ARE YOU?! THERE'S NO WAY YOU CAN TAKE THIS HEAT! I'LL MELT YOUR COOL!
THOOM THOOM
...
BLUB
GLUB
BLUB
GLUB
BLUB
GLUB
BLUB
HMPH
I'M COM-PLETELY FINE.
HEH
SAY WHAT ?!!
GRRRRR!
LEO! HE'S NOT TRYING TO BE COOL OR ANYTHING!
HE JUST HATES LOSING !!!
BA—M

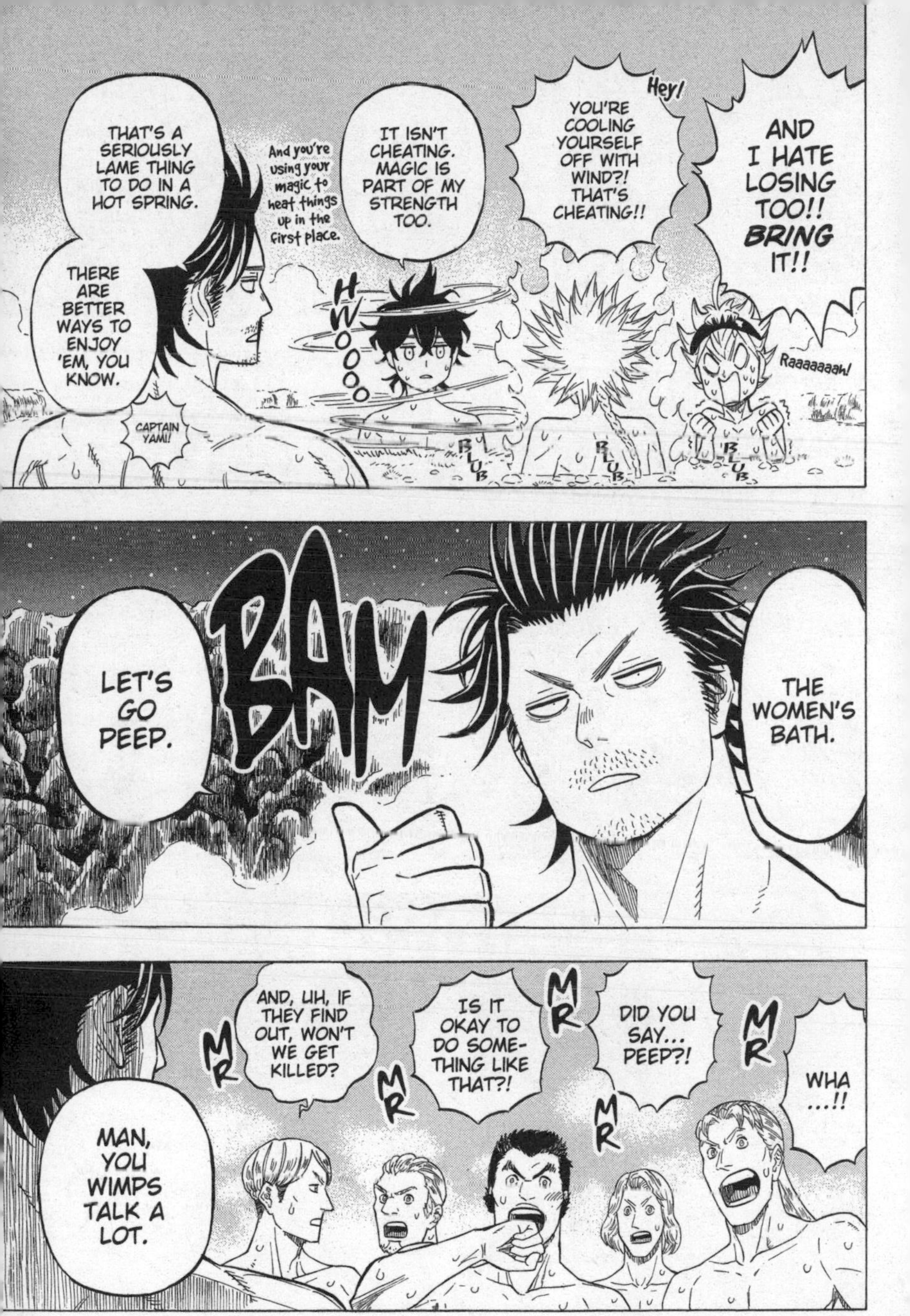
AND I HATE LOSING TOO!! BRING IT!!
Raaaaaaah!
Hey!
YOU'RE COOLING YOURSELF OFF WITH WIND?! THAT'S CHEATING!!
IT ISN'T CHEATING. MAGIC IS PART OF MY STRENGTH TOO.
And you're using your magic to heat things up in the first place.
HWOOOOO
THAT'S A SERIOUSLY LAME THING TO DO IN A HOT SPRING.
THERE ARE BETTER WAYS TO ENJOY 'EM, YOU KNOW.
CAPTAIN YAMI!
BLUB
BLUB
BLUB
THE WOMEN'S BATH.
BAM
LET'S GO PEEP.
WHA ...!!
MR
DID YOU SAY... PEEP?!
MR
MR
IS IT OKAY TO DO SOMETHING LIKE THAT?!
MR
AND, UH, IF THEY FIND OUT, WON'T WE GET KILLED?
MR
MAN, YOU WIMPS TALK A LOT.

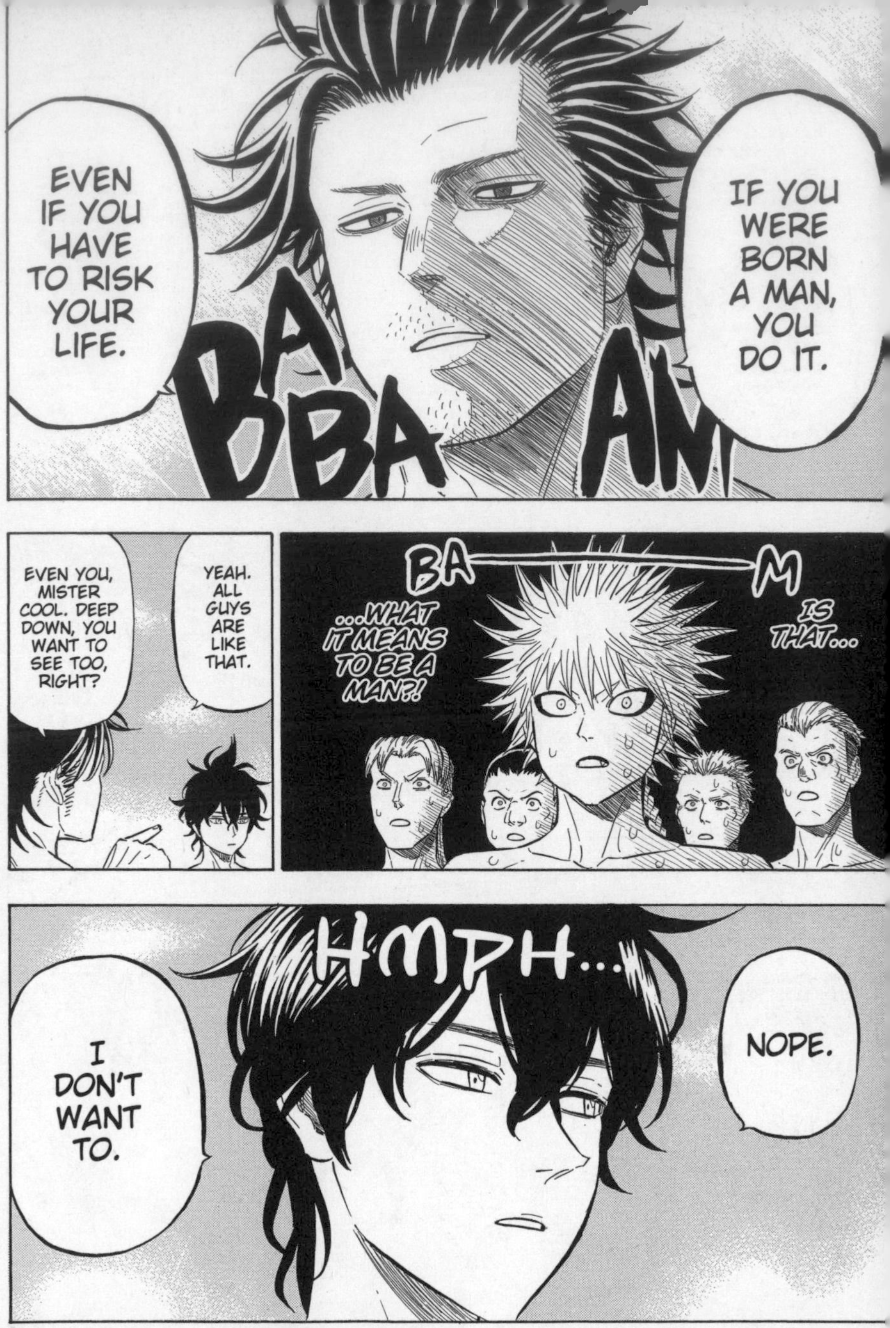
IF YOU WERE BORN A MAN, YOU DO IT.
BADBAAM
EVEN IF YOU HAVE TO RISK YOUR LIFE.
BA—M
IS THAT...
...WHAT IT MEANS TO BE A MAN?!
YEAH. ALL GUYS ARE LIKE THAT.
EVEN YOU, MISTER COOL. DEEP DOWN, YOU WANT TO SEE TOO, RIGHT?
HMPH...
NOPE.
I DON'T WANT TO.

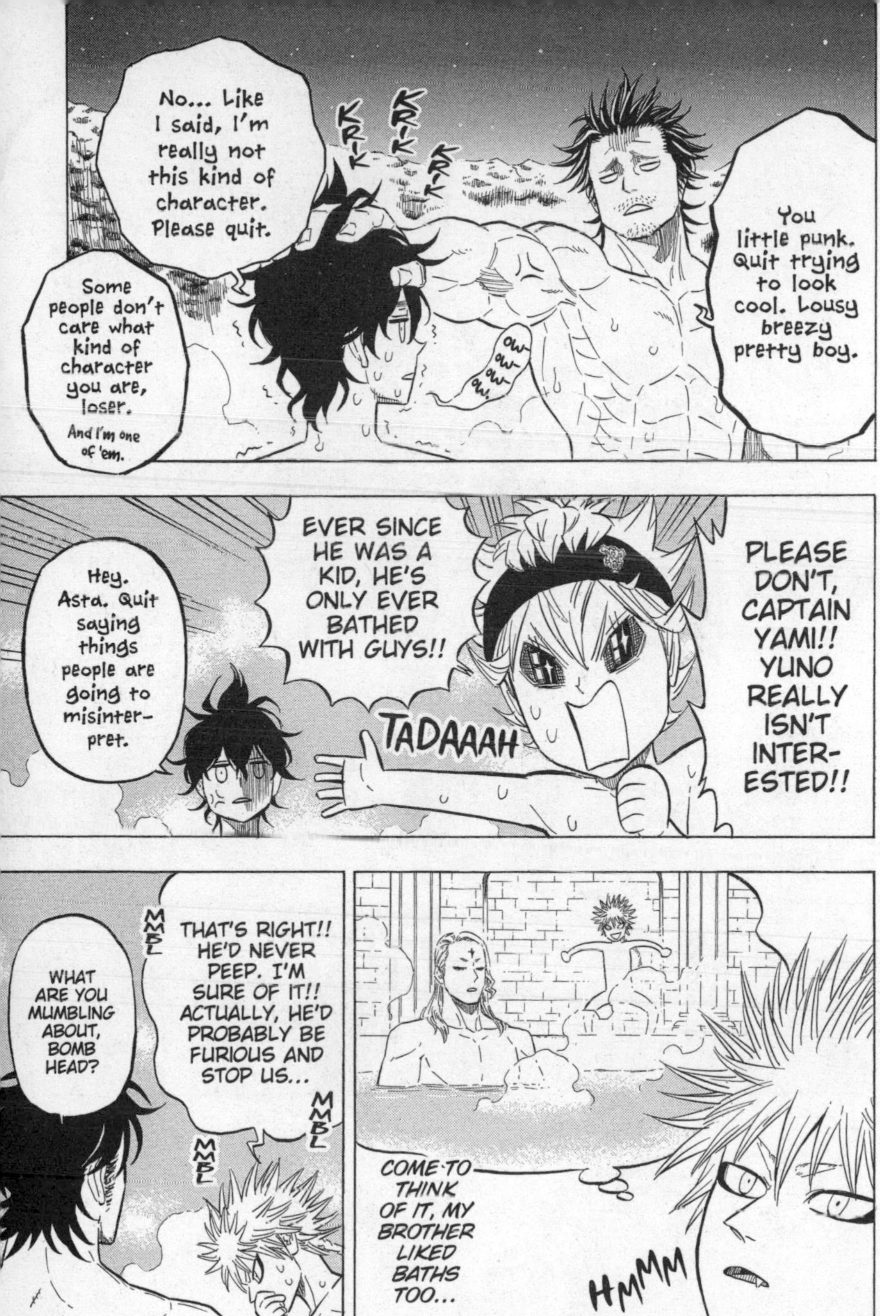
You little punk. Quit trying to look cool. Lousy breezy pretty boy.
KRIK KRIK KRIK
No... Like I said, I'm really not this kind of character. Please quit.
ow-ow-ow-ow!
Some people don't care what kind of character you are, loser.
And I'm one of 'em.
PLEASE DON'T, CAPTAIN YAMI!! YUNO REALLY ISN'T INTERESTED!!
EVER SINCE HE WAS A KID, HE'S ONLY EVER BATHED WITH GUYS!!
TADAAAH
Hey. Asta. Quit saying things people are going to misinterpret.
HMMM
COME TO THINK OF IT, MY BROTHER LIKED BATHS TOO...
THAT'S RIGHT!! HE'D NEVER PEEP. I'M SURE OF IT!! ACTUALLY, HE'D PROBABLY BE FURIOUS AND STOP US...
MMBL
MMBL
MMBL
WHAT ARE YOU MUMBLING ABOUT, BOMB HEAD?

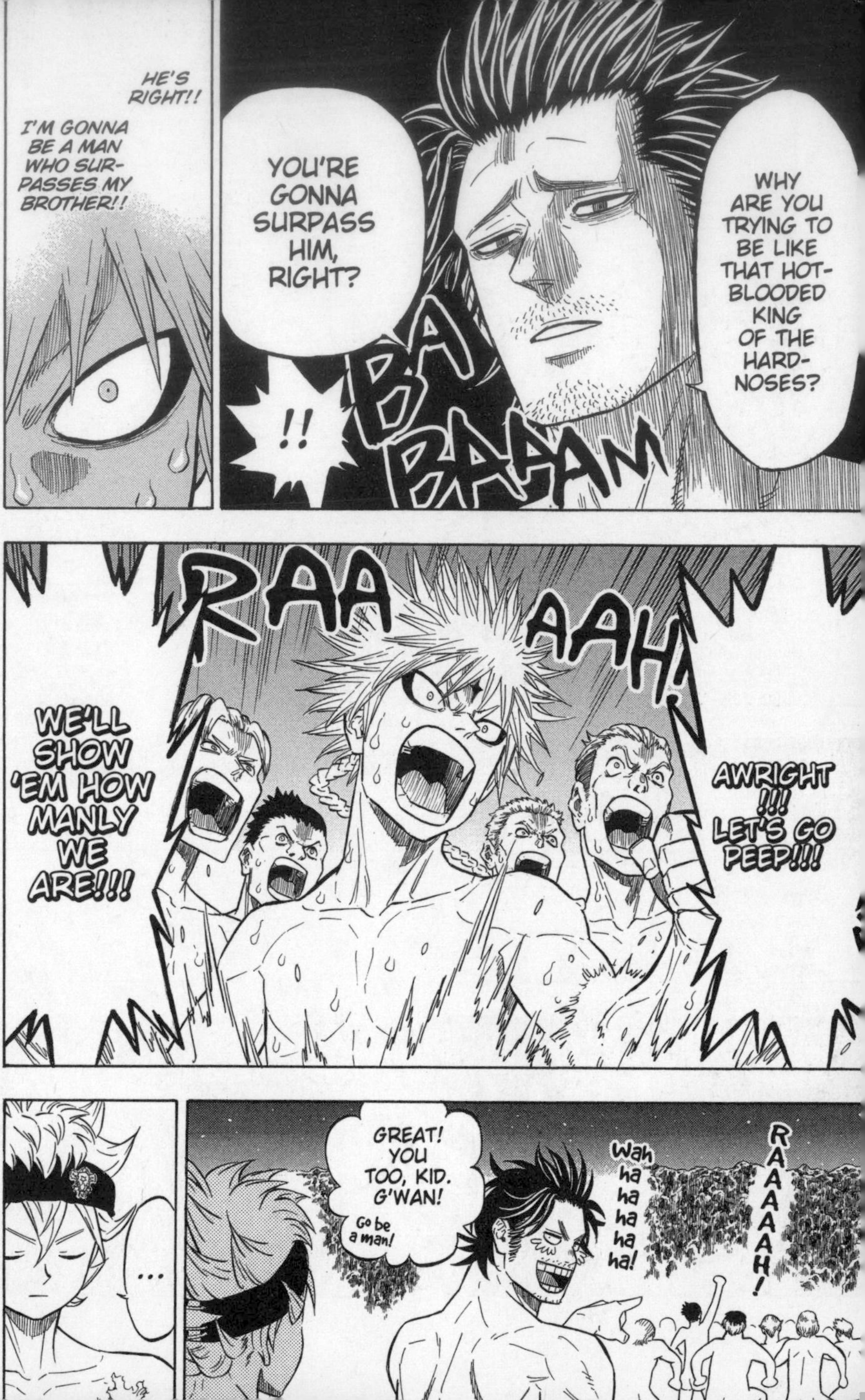
WHY ARE YOU TRYING TO BE LIKE THAT HOT-BLOODED KING OF THE HARD-NOSES?
YOU'RE GONNA SURPASS HIM, RIGHT?
BA BRAAM
!!
HE'S RIGHT!!
I'M GONNA BE A MAN WHO SURPASSES MY BROTHER!!
RAA AAH!
AWRIGHT!!! LET'S GO PEEP!!!
WE'LL SHOW 'EM HOW MANLY WE ARE!!!
RAAAAAH!
Wah ha ha ha ha ha!
GREAT! YOU TOO, KID. G'WAN!
Go be a man!
...

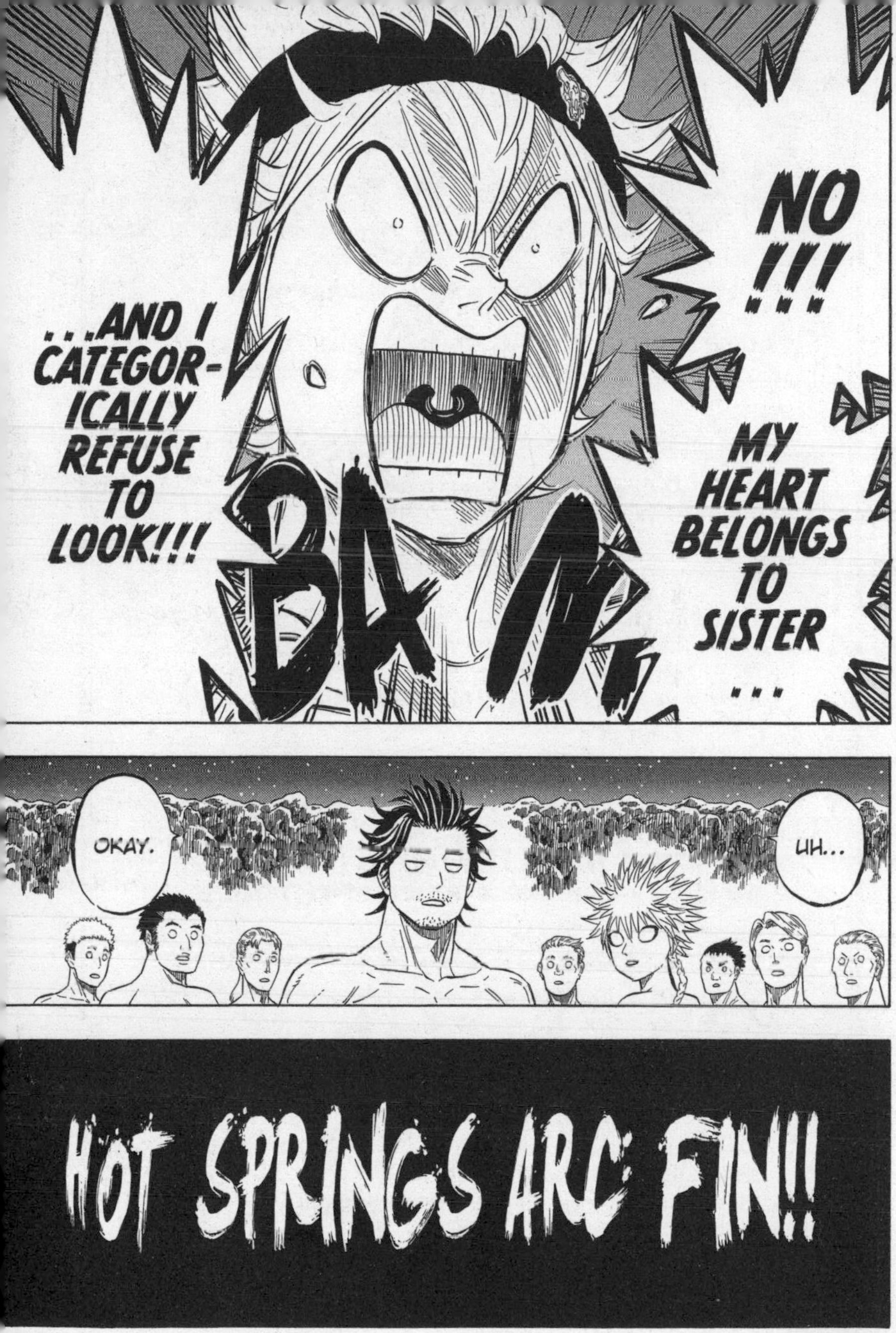
NO!!! MY HEART BELONGS TO SISTER...
...AND I CATEGOR-ICALLY REFUSE TO LOOK!!!
UH...
OKAY.
HOT SPRINGS ARC FIN!!

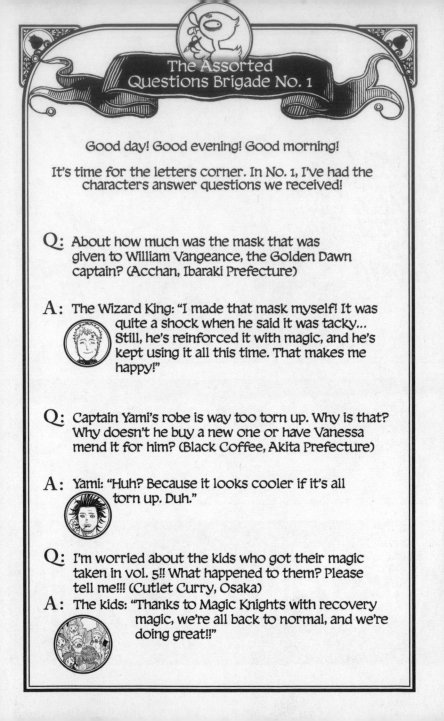

The Assorted Questions Brigade No. 1

Good day! Good evening! Good morning!

It's time for the letters corner. In No. 1, I've had the characters answer questions we received!

Q: About how much was the mask that was given to William Vangeance, the Golden Dawn captain? (Acchan, Ibaraki Prefecture)

A: The Wizard King: "I made that mask myself! It was quite a shock when he said it was tacky... Still, he's reinforced it with magic, and he's kept using it all this time. That makes me happy!"

Q: Captain Yami's robe is way too torn up. Why is that? Why doesn't he buy a new one or have Vanessa mend it for him? (Black Coffee, Akita Prefecture)

A: Yami: "Huh? Because it looks cooler if it's all torn up. Duh."

Q: I'm worried about the kids who got their magic taken in vol. 5!! What happened to them? Please tell me!!! (Cutlet Curry, Osaka)

A: The kids: "Thanks to Magic Knights with recovery magic, we're all back to normal, and we're doing great!!"

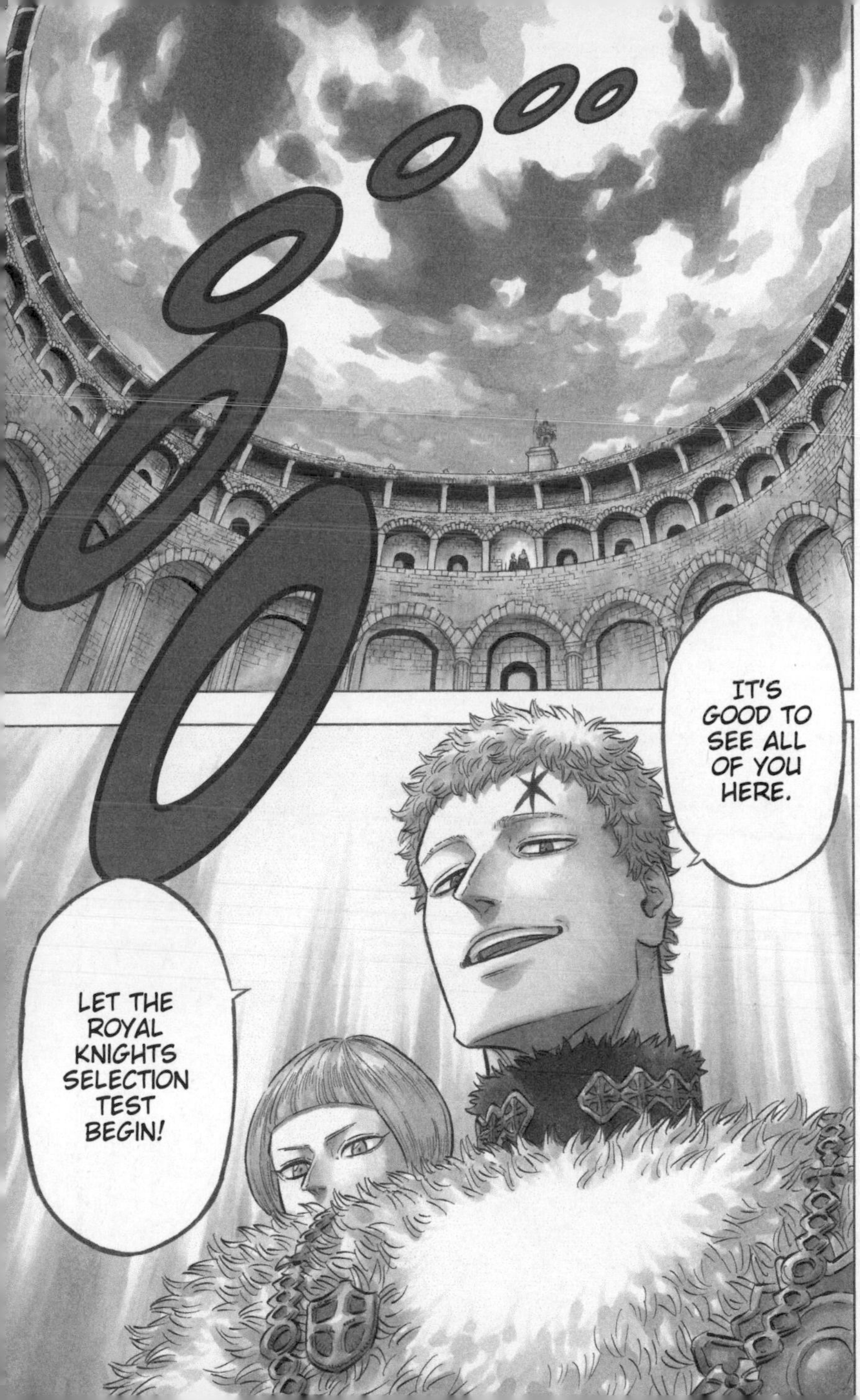
IT'S GOOD TO SEE ALL OF YOU HERE.
LET THE ROYAL KNIGHTS SELECTION TEST BEGIN!

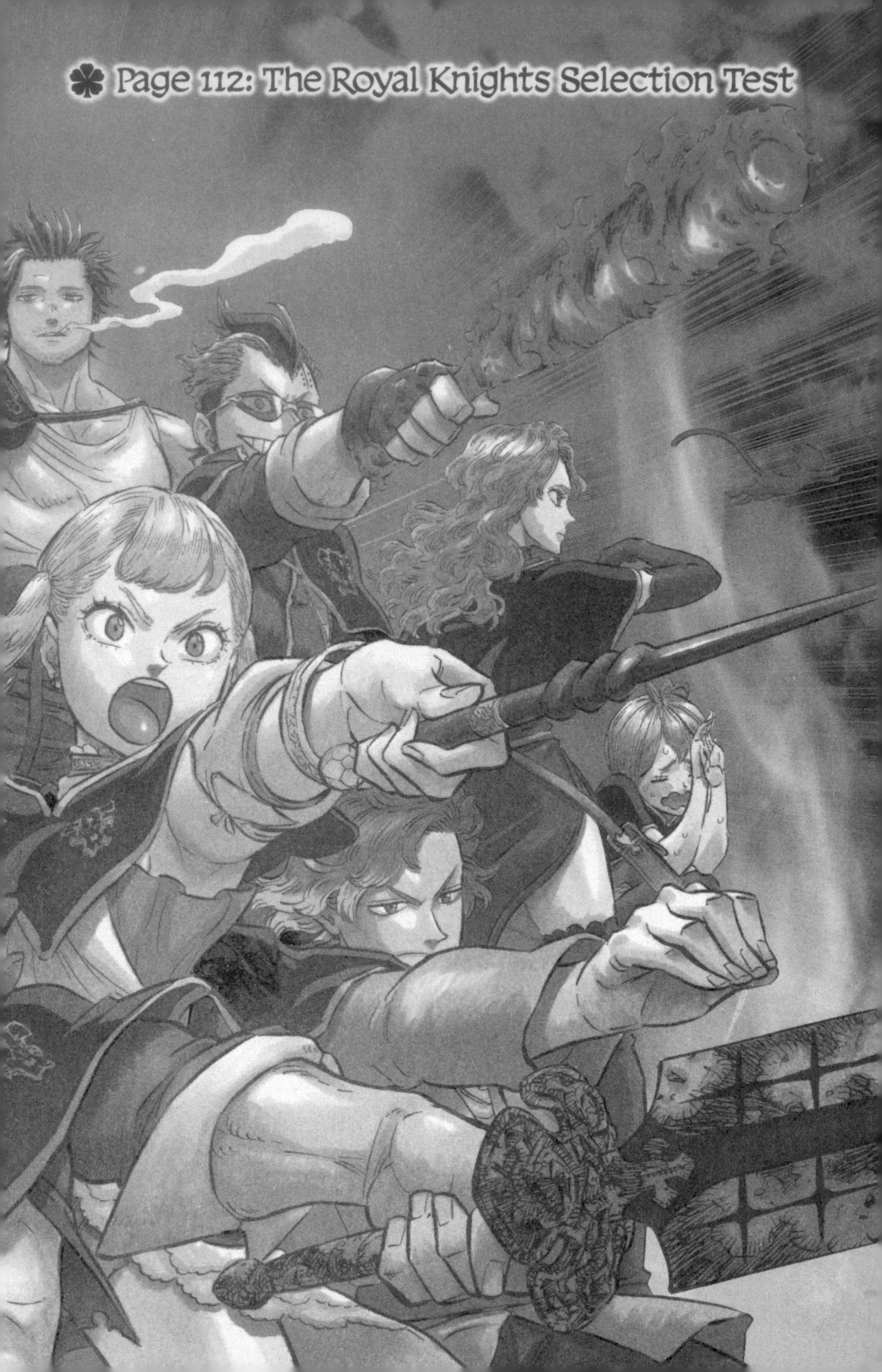
Page 112: The Royal Knights Selection Test

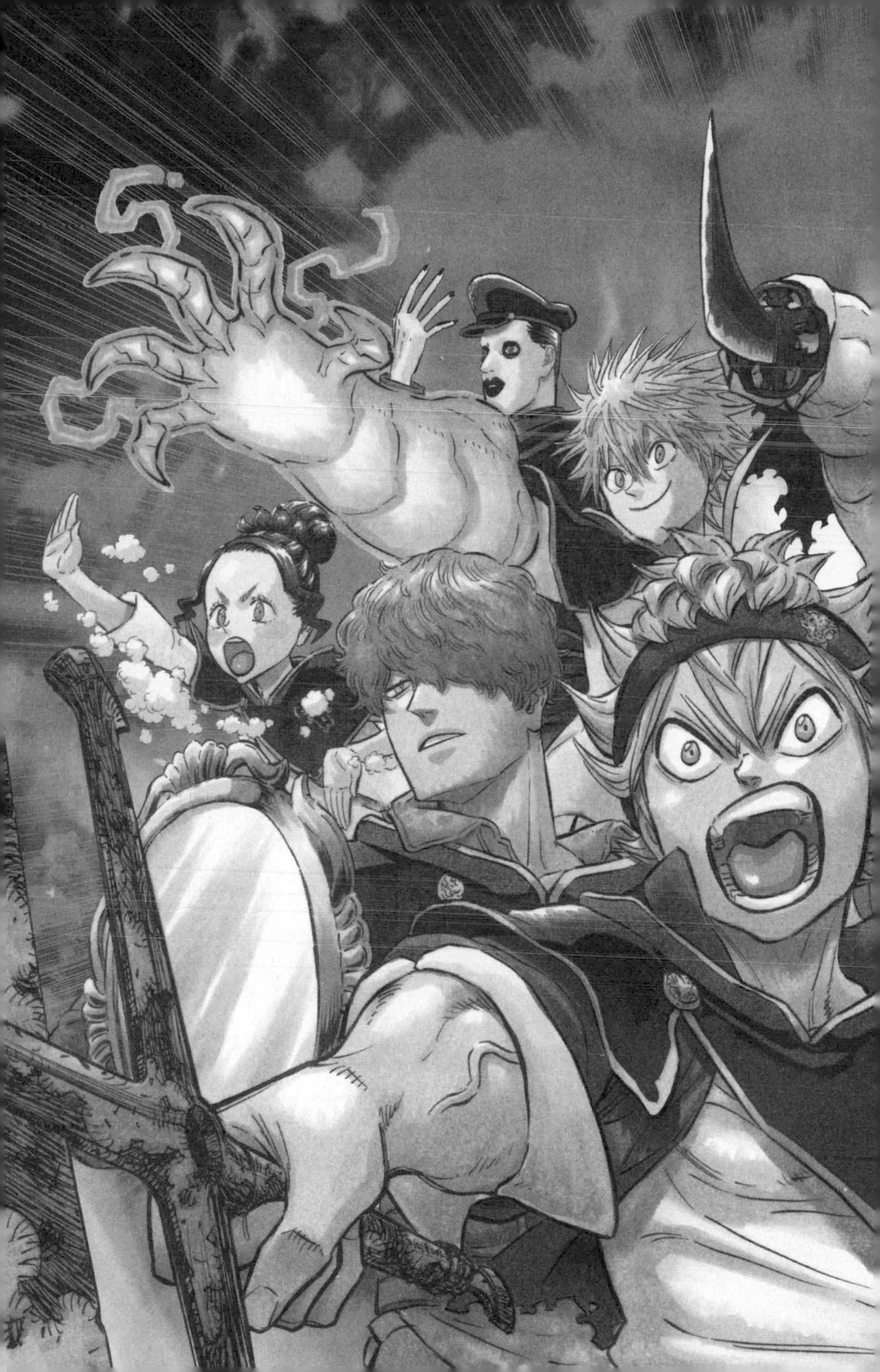

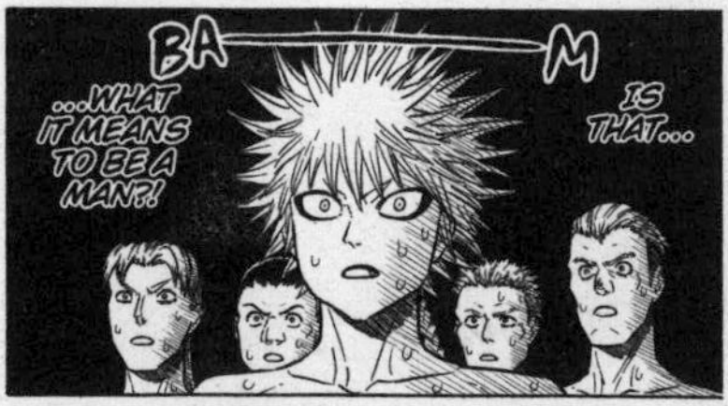
BA——M
IS THAT...
...WHAT IT MEANS TO BE A MAN?!

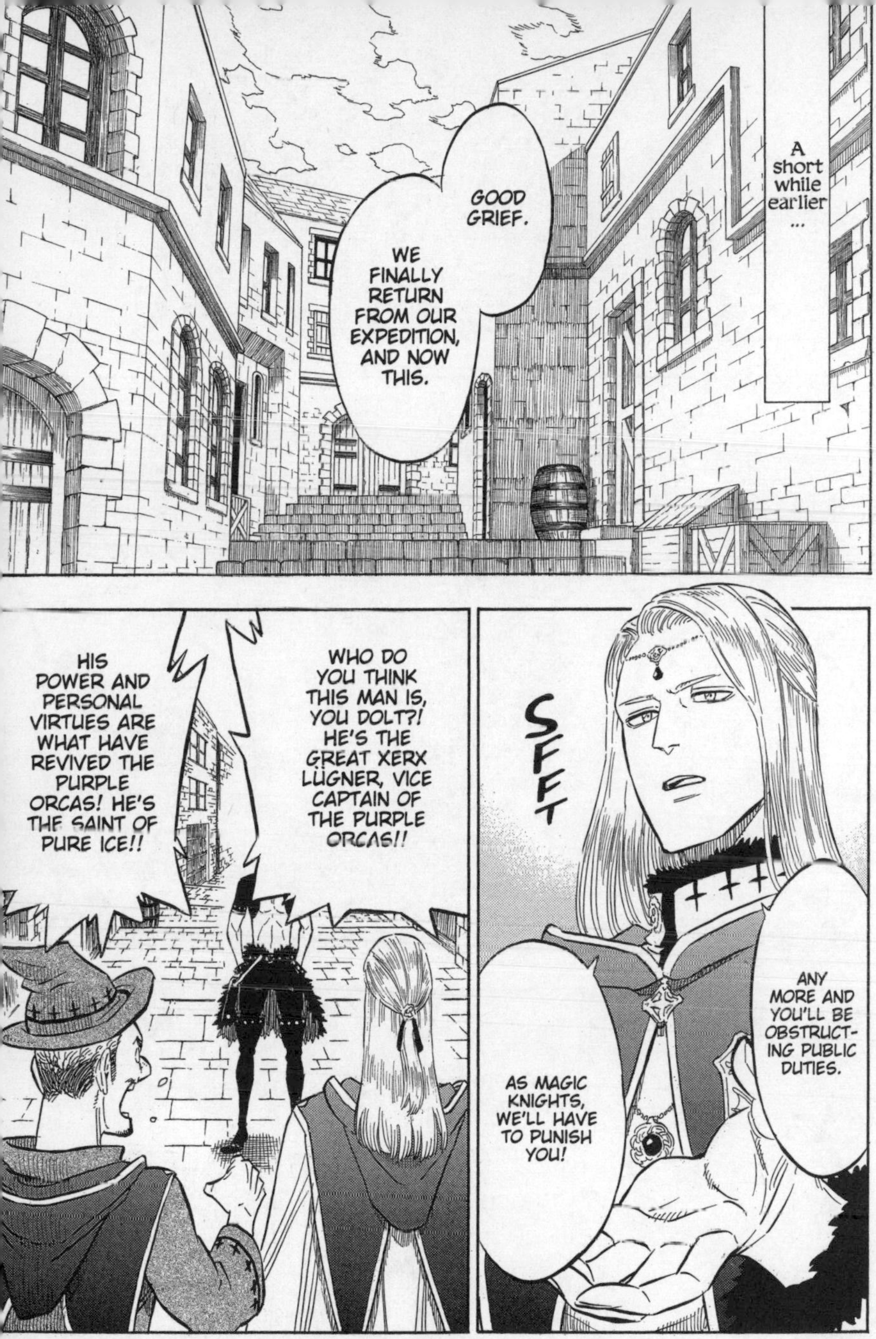
A short while earlier...
GOOD GRIEF.
WE FINALLY RETURN FROM OUR EXPEDITION, AND NOW THIS.
SFFT
ANY MORE AND YOU'LL BE OBSTRUCTING PUBLIC DUTIES.
AS MAGIC KNIGHTS, WE'LL HAVE TO PUNISH YOU!
WHO DO YOU THINK THIS MAN IS, YOU DOLT?! HE'S THE GREAT XERX LÜGNER, VICE CAPTAIN OF THE PURPLE ORCAS!!
HIS POWER AND PERSONAL VIRTUES ARE WHAT HAVE REVIVED THE PURPLE ORCAS! HE'S THE SAINT OF PURE ICE!!

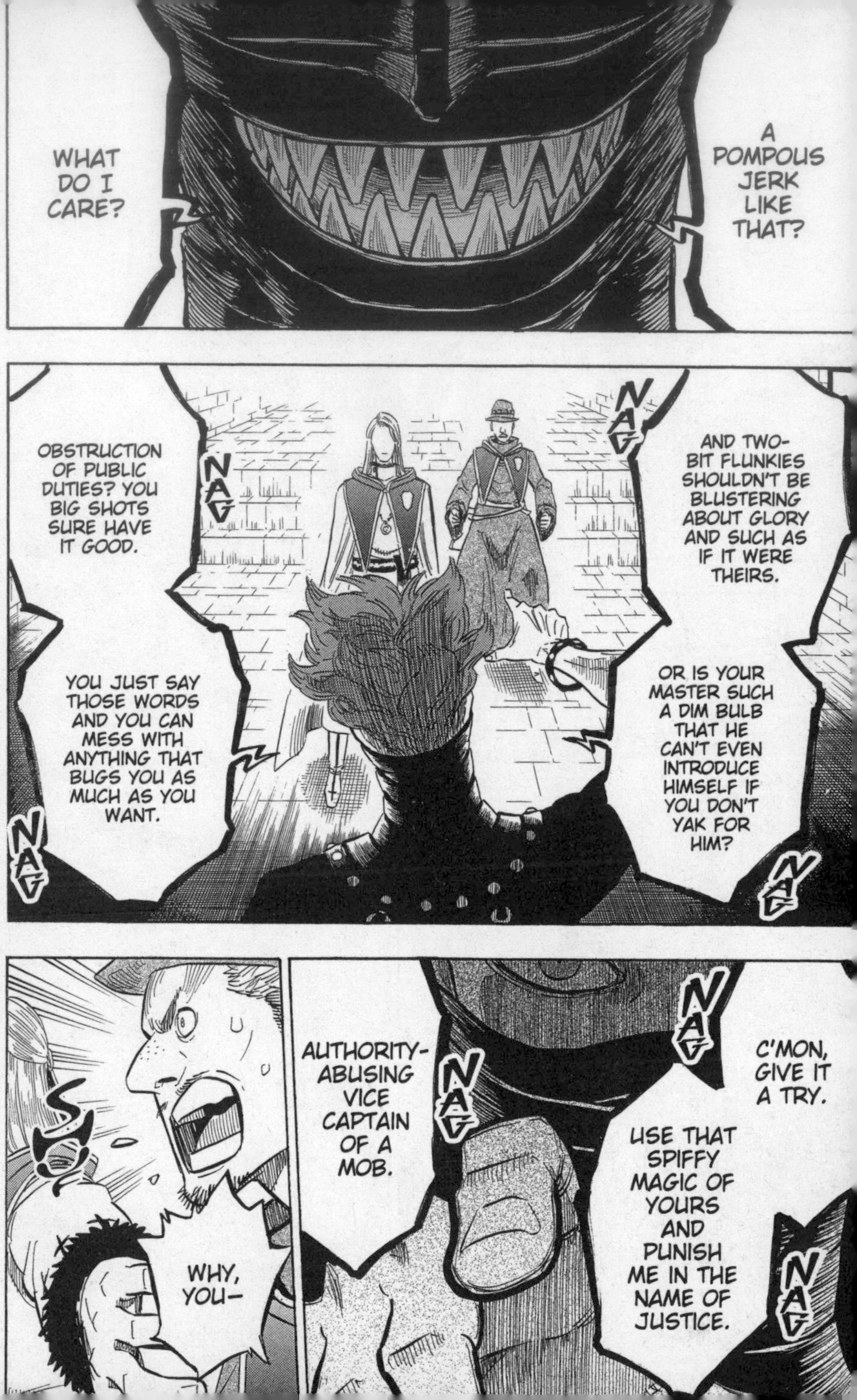
A POMPOUS JERK LIKE THAT?
WHAT DO I CARE?
NAG NAG
AND TWO-BIT FLUNKIES SHOULDN'T BE BLUSTERING ABOUT GLORY AND SUCH AS IF IT WERE THEIRS.
NAG NAG
OBSTRUCTION OF PUBLIC DUTIES? YOU BIG SHOTS SURE HAVE IT GOOD.
OR IS YOUR MASTER SUCH A DIM BULB THAT HE CAN'T EVEN INTRODUCE HIMSELF IF YOU DON'T YAK FOR HIM?
YOU JUST SAY THOSE WORDS AND YOU CAN MESS WITH ANYTHING THAT BUGS YOU AS MUCH AS YOU WANT.
NAG NAG
NAG NAG
C'MON, GIVE IT A TRY.
NAG NAG
USE THAT SPIFFY MAGIC OF YOURS AND PUNISH ME IN THE NAME OF JUSTICE.
NAG NAG
AUTHORITY-ABUSING VICE CAPTAIN OF A MOB.
NAG NAG
WHY, YOU-

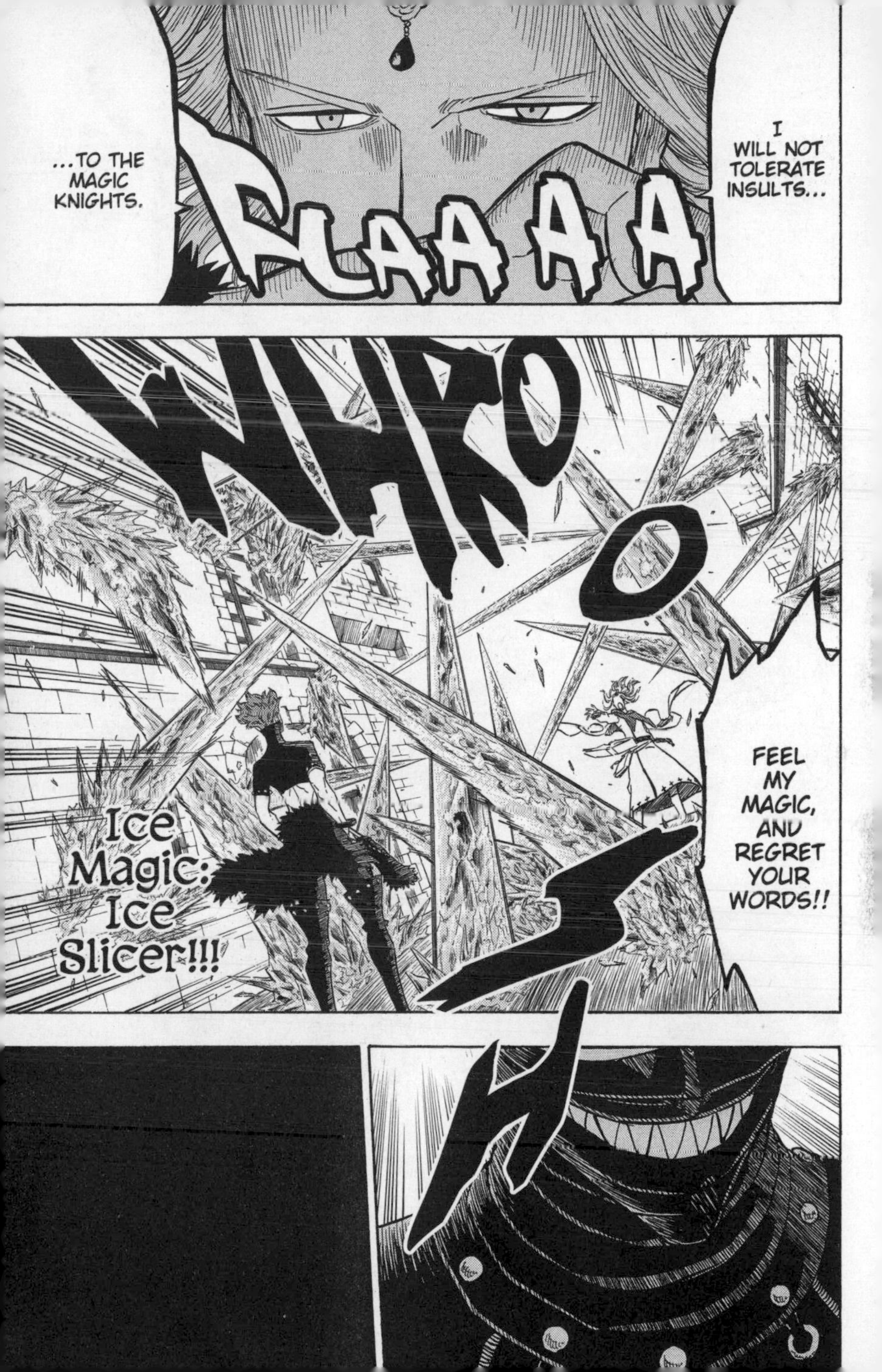
I WILL NOT TOLERATE INSULTS...
...TO THE MAGIC KNIGHTS.
FLAAAA
FEEL MY MAGIC, AND REGRET YOUR WORDS!!
Ice Magic: Ice Slicer!!!

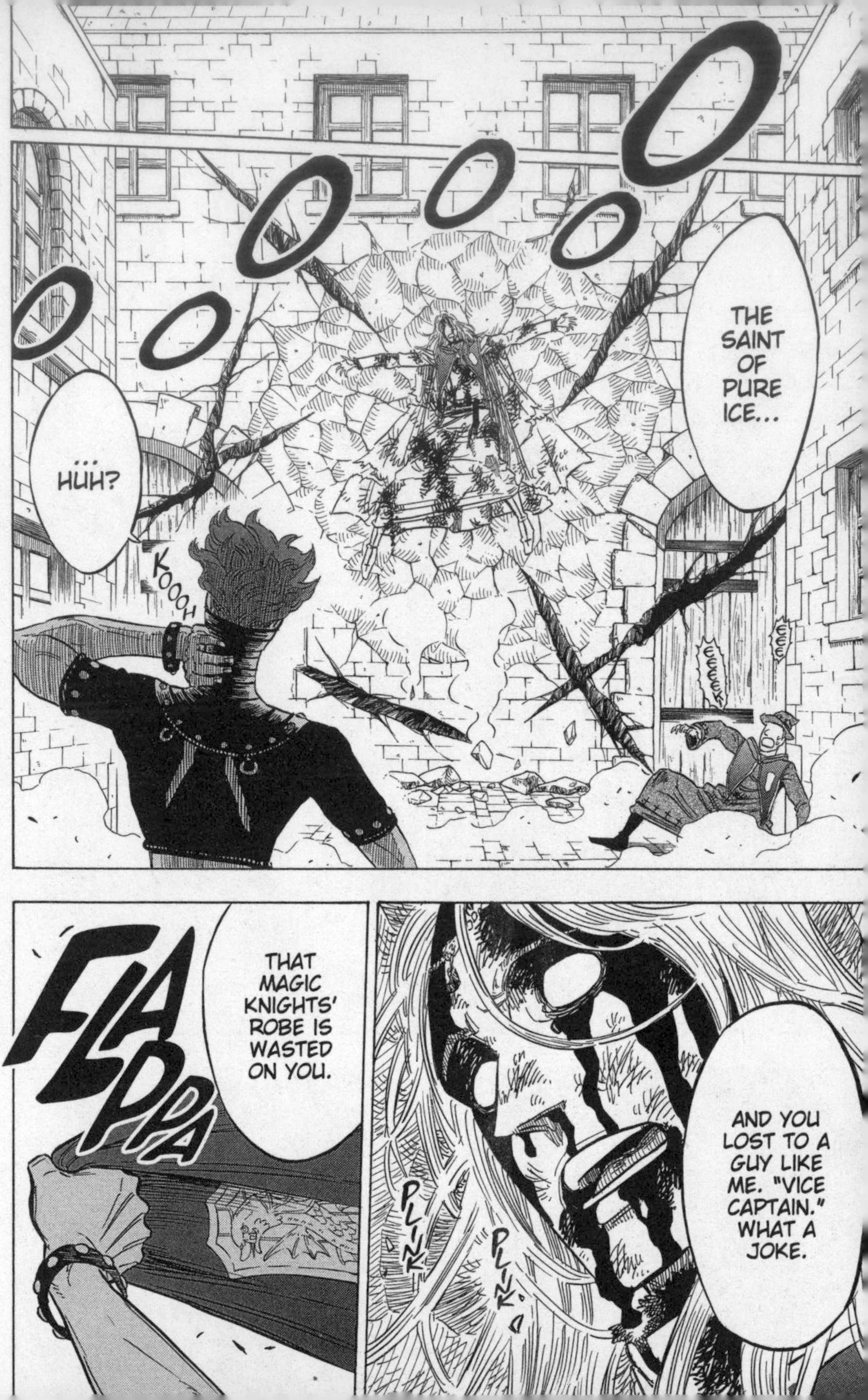
THE SAINT OF PURE ICE...
...HUH?
KOOOH
EEEEEK
EEE
AND YOU LOST TO A GUY LIKE ME. "VICE CAPTAIN." WHAT A JOKE.
PLINK
PLINK
THAT MAGIC KNIGHTS' ROBE IS WASTED ON YOU.
FLAPPA

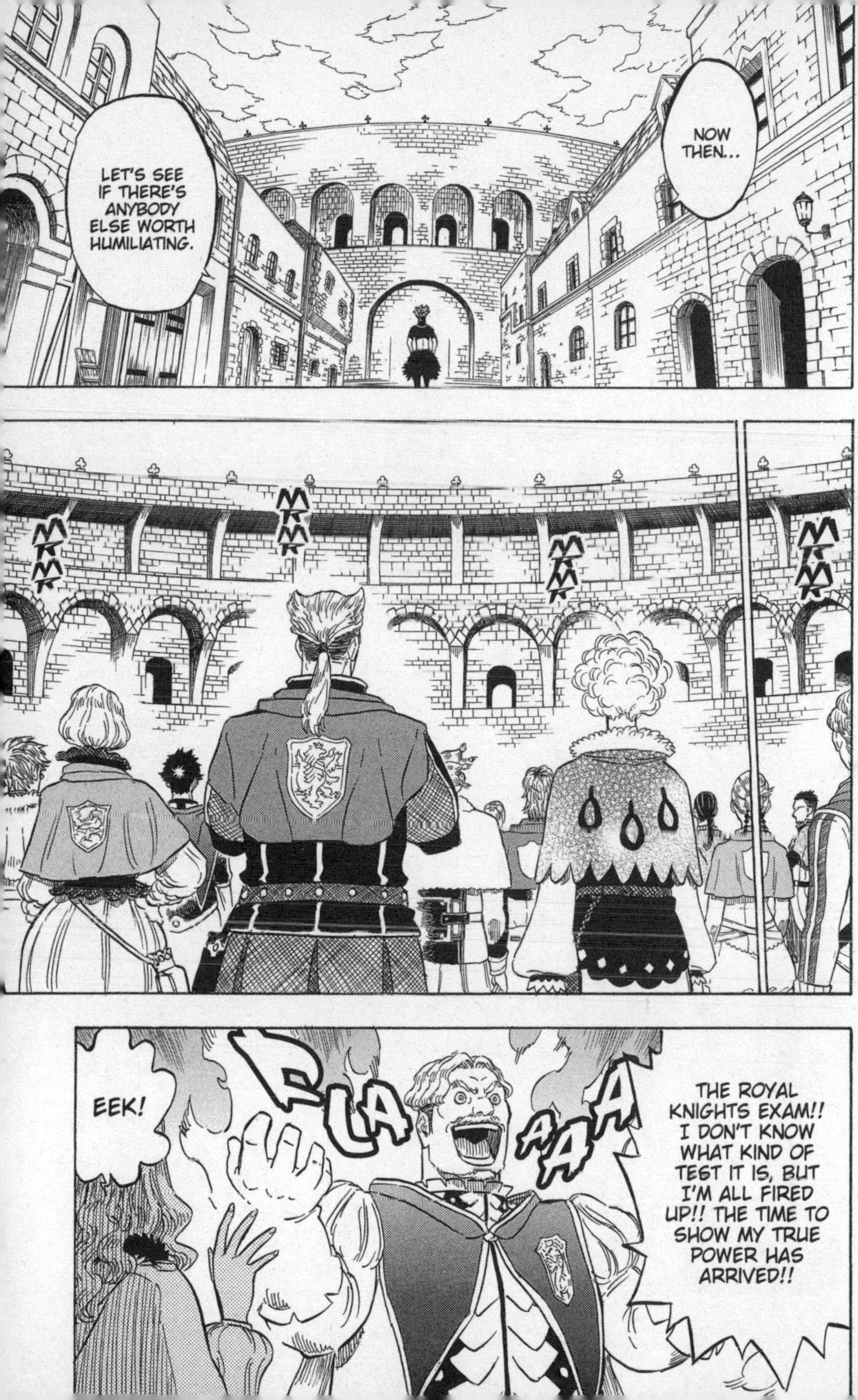
NOW THEN...
LET'S SEE IF THERE'S ANYBODY ELSE WORTH HUMILIATING.
MRMR
MRMR
MRMR
MRMR
THE ROYAL KNIGHTS EXAM!! I DON'T KNOW WHAT KIND OF TEST IT IS, BUT I'M ALL FIRED UP!! THE TIME TO SHOW MY TRUE POWER HAS ARRIVED!!
LAAAA
EEK!

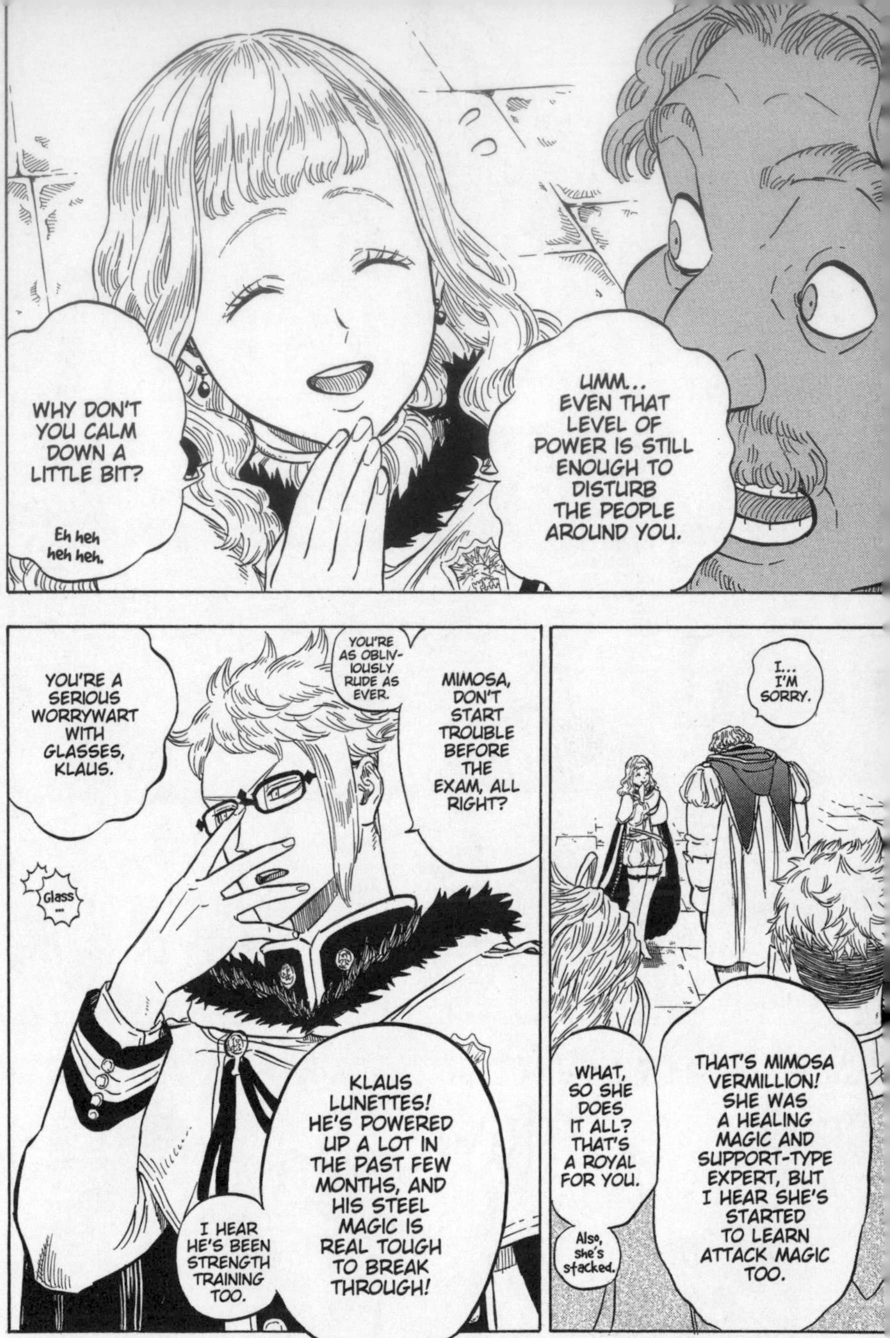
UMM... EVEN THAT LEVEL OF POWER IS STILL ENOUGH TO DISTURB THE PEOPLE AROUND YOU.
WHY DON'T YOU CALM DOWN A LITTLE BIT?
Eh heh heh heh.
I... I'M SORRY.
THAT'S MIMOSA VERMILLION! SHE WAS A HEALING MAGIC AND SUPPORT-TYPE EXPERT, BUT I HEAR SHE'S STARTED TO LEARN ATTACK MAGIC TOO.
WHAT, SO SHE DOES IT ALL? THAT'S A ROYAL FOR YOU.
Also, she's stacked.
MIMOSA, DON'T START TROUBLE BEFORE THE EXAM, ALL RIGHT?
YOU'RE AS OBLIVIOUSLY RUDE AS EVER.
YOU'RE A SERIOUS WORRYWART WITH GLASSES, KLAUS.
Glass...
KLAUS LUNETTES! HE'S POWERED UP A LOT IN THE PAST FEW MONTHS, AND HIS STEEL MAGIC IS REAL TOUGH TO BREAK THROUGH!
I HEAR HE'S BEEN STRENGTH TRAINING TOO.

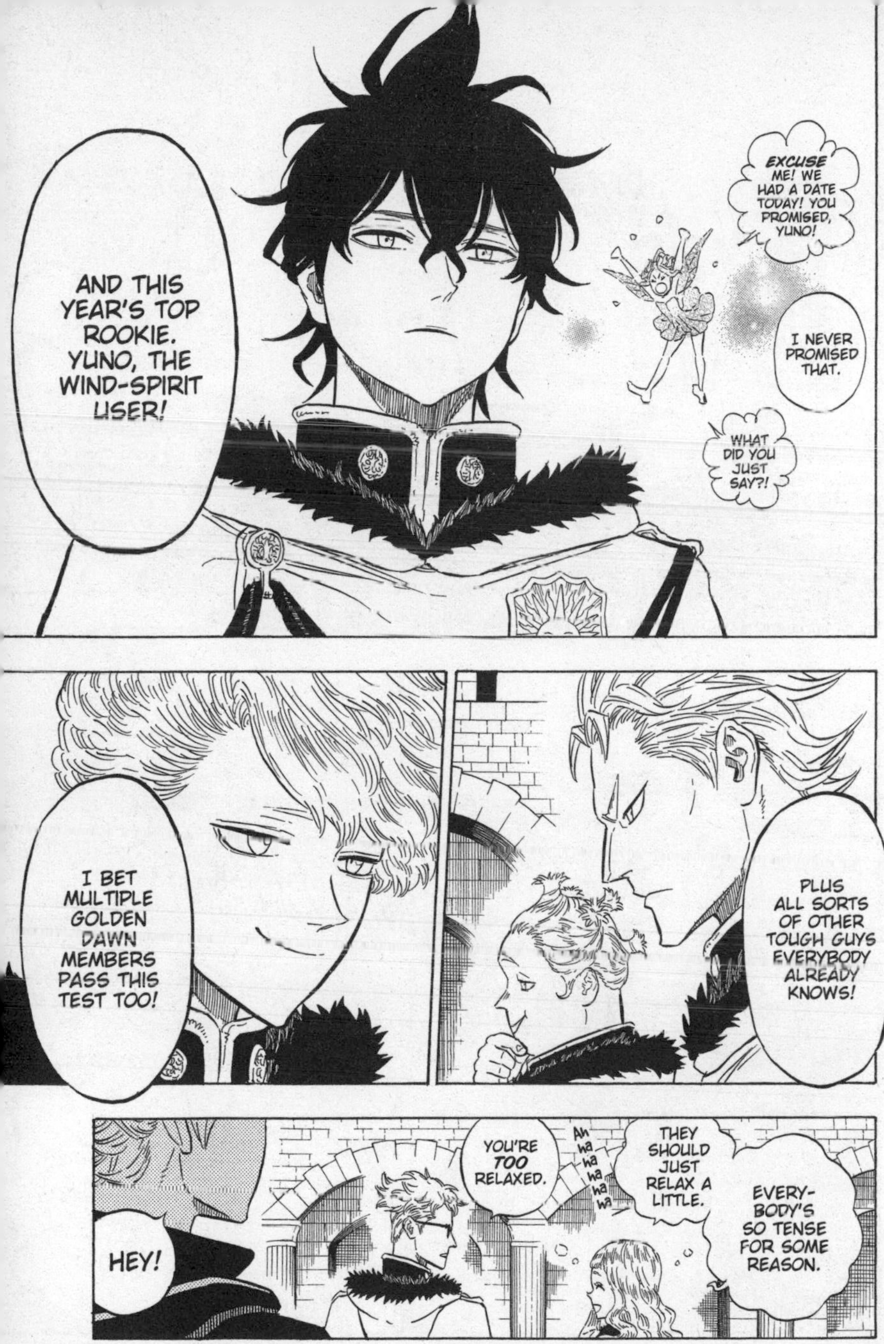
EXCUSE ME! WE HAD A DATE TODAY! YOU PROMISED, YUNO!
I NEVER PROMISED THAT.
WHAT DID YOU JUST SAY?!
AND THIS YEAR'S TOP ROOKIE. YUNO, THE WIND-SPIRIT USER!
PLUS ALL SORTS OF OTHER TOUGH GUYS EVERYBODY ALREADY KNOWS!
I BET MULTIPLE GOLDEN DAWN MEMBERS PASS THIS TEST TOO!
EVERY-BODY'S SO TENSE FOR SOME REASON.
THEY SHOULD JUST RELAX A LITTLE.
Ahahahahaha
YOU'RE TOO RELAXED.
HEY!

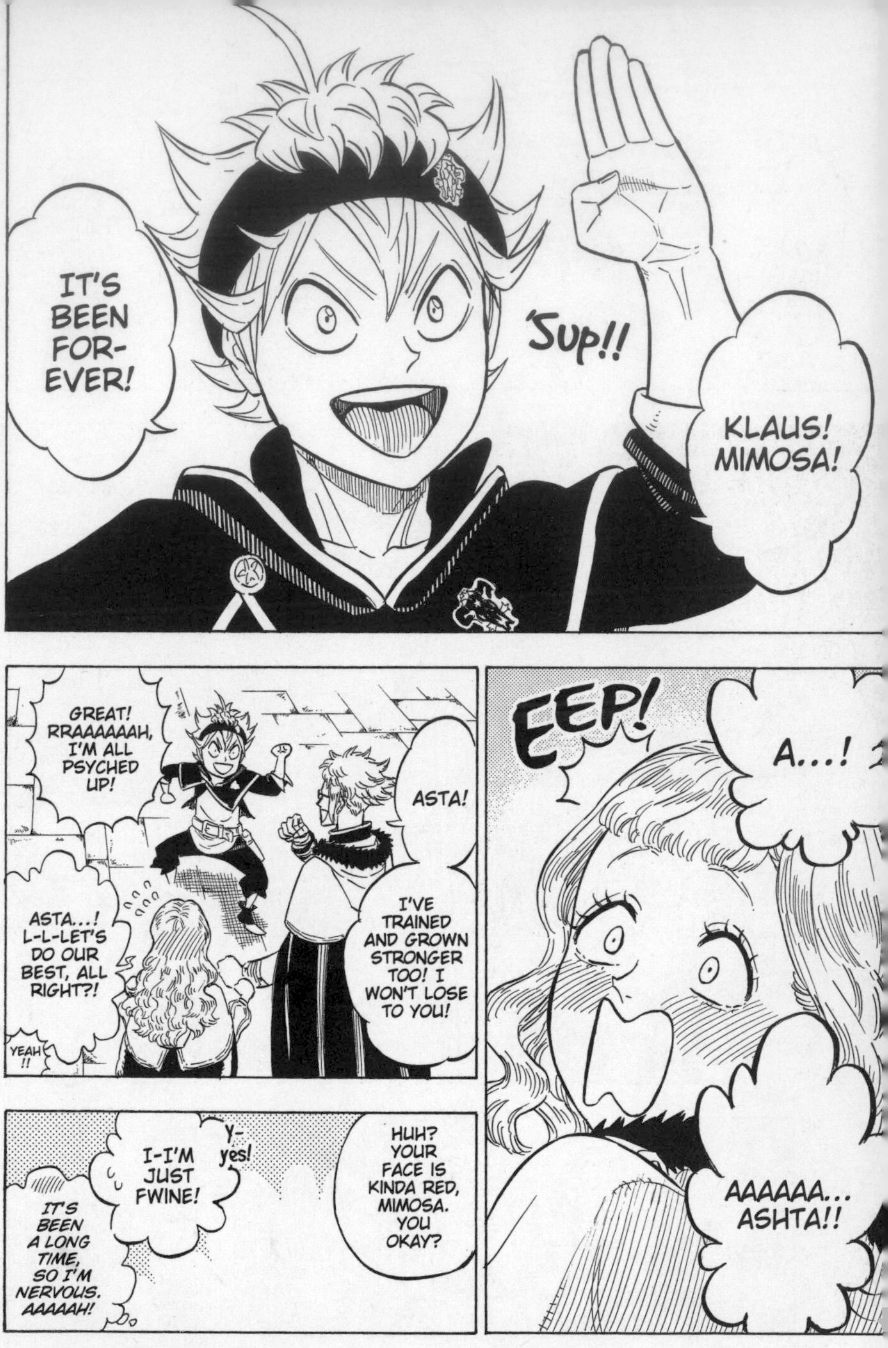
'Sup!!
KLAUS! MIMOSA!
IT'S BEEN FOR-EVER!
EEP!
A...!
AAAAAA... ASHTA!!
ASTA!
I'VE TRAINED AND GROWN STRONGER TOO! I WON'T LOSE TO YOU!
GREAT! RRAAAAAAH, I'M ALL PSYCHED UP!
ASTA...! L-L-LET'S DO OUR BEST, ALL RIGHT?!
YEAH!!
HUH? YOUR FACE IS KINDA RED, MIMOSA. YOU OKAY?
Y-yes!
I-I'M JUST FWINE!
IT'S BEEN A LONG TIME, SO I'M NERVOUS. AAAAAH!

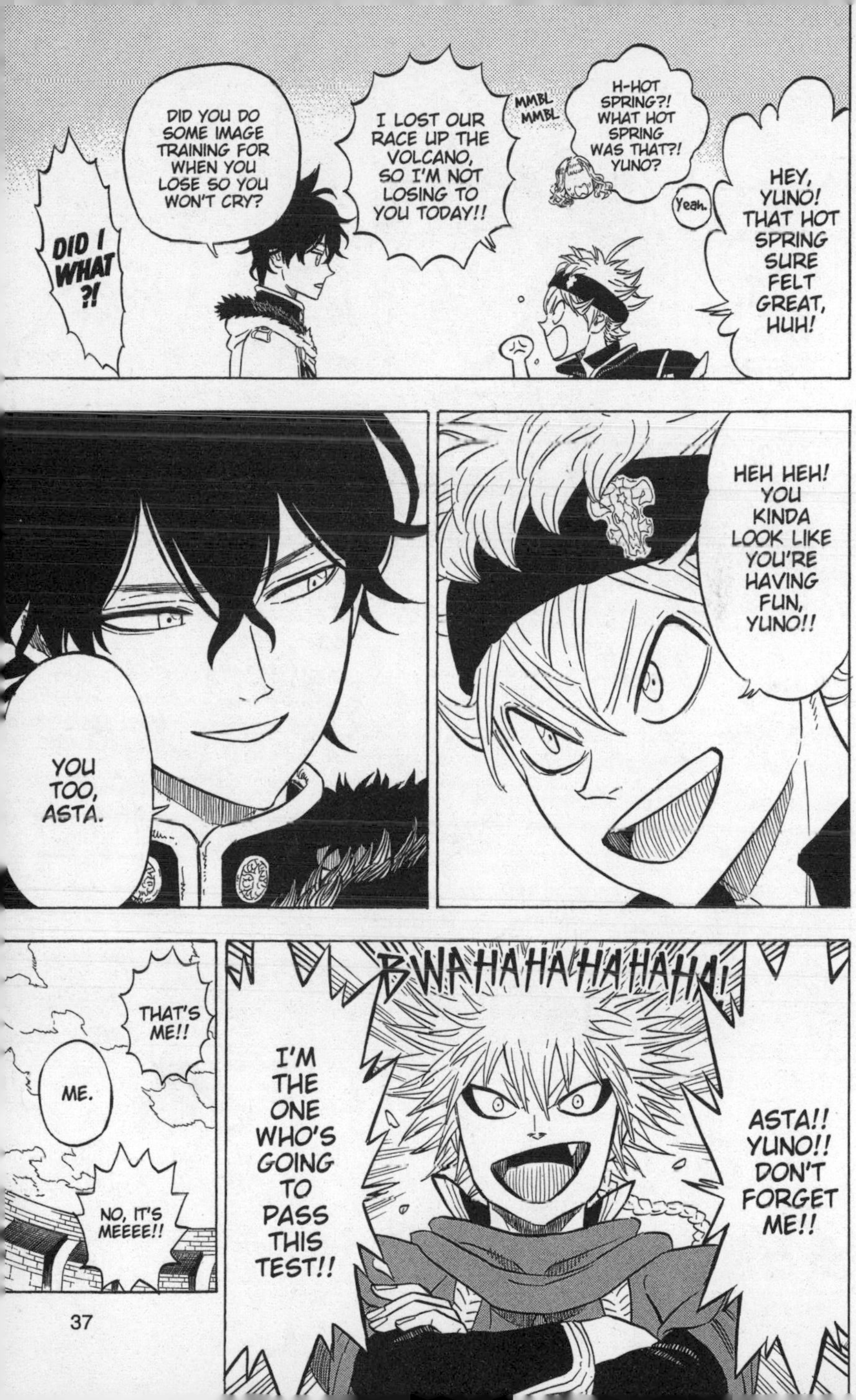
HEY, YUNO! THAT HOT SPRING SURE FELT GREAT, HUH!
Yeah.
H-HOT SPRING?! WHAT HOT SPRING WAS THAT?! YUNO?
MMBL MMBL
I LOST OUR RACE UP THE VOLCANO, SO I'M NOT LOSING TO YOU TODAY!!
DID YOU DO SOME IMAGE TRAINING FOR WHEN YOU LOSE SO YOU WON'T CRY?
DID I WHAT?!
HEH HEH! YOU KINDA LOOK LIKE YOU'RE HAVING FUN, YUNO!!
YOU TOO, ASTA.
BWAHAHAHAHAHAHA!
ASTA!! YUNO!! DON'T FORGET ME!!
I'M THE ONE WHO'S GOING TO PASS THIS TEST!!
THAT'S ME!!
ME.
NO, IT'S MEEEE!!

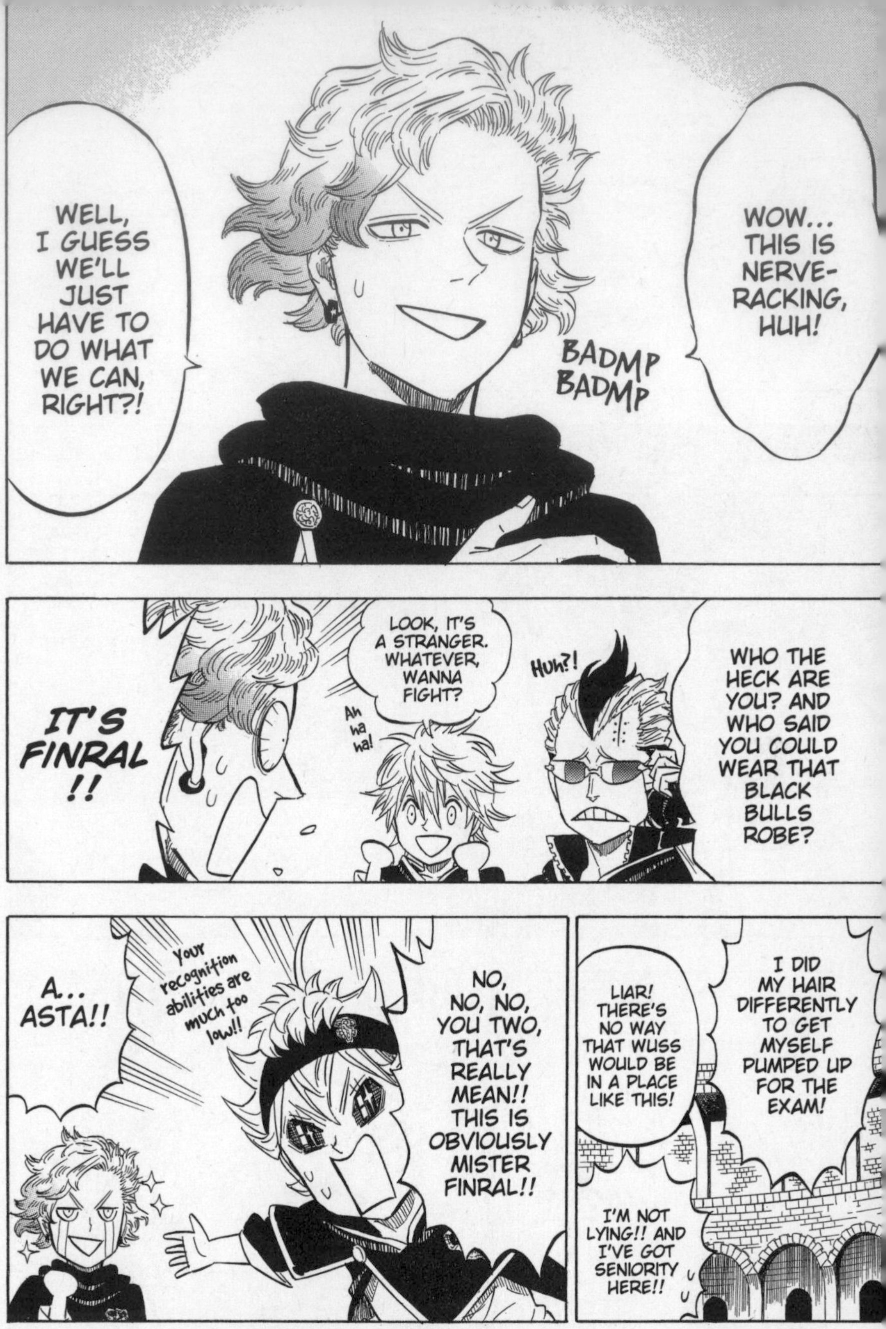
WOW... THIS IS NERVE-RACKING, HUH!
BADMP BADMP
WELL, I GUESS WE'LL JUST HAVE TO DO WHAT WE CAN, RIGHT?!
WHO THE HECK ARE YOU? AND WHO SAID YOU COULD WEAR THAT BLACK BULLS ROBE?
Huh?!
LOOK, IT'S A STRANGER. WHATEVER, WANNA FIGHT?
Ah ha ha!
IT'S FINRAL!!
I DID MY HAIR DIFFERENTLY TO GET MYSELF PUMPED UP FOR THE EXAM!
LIAR! THERE'S NO WAY THAT WUSS WOULD BE IN A PLACE LIKE THIS!
I'M NOT LYING!! AND I'VE GOT SENIORITY HERE!!
NO, NO, NO, YOU TWO, THAT'S REALLY MEAN!! THIS IS OBVIOUSLY MISTER FINRAL!!
Your recognition abilities are much too low!!
A... ASTA!!

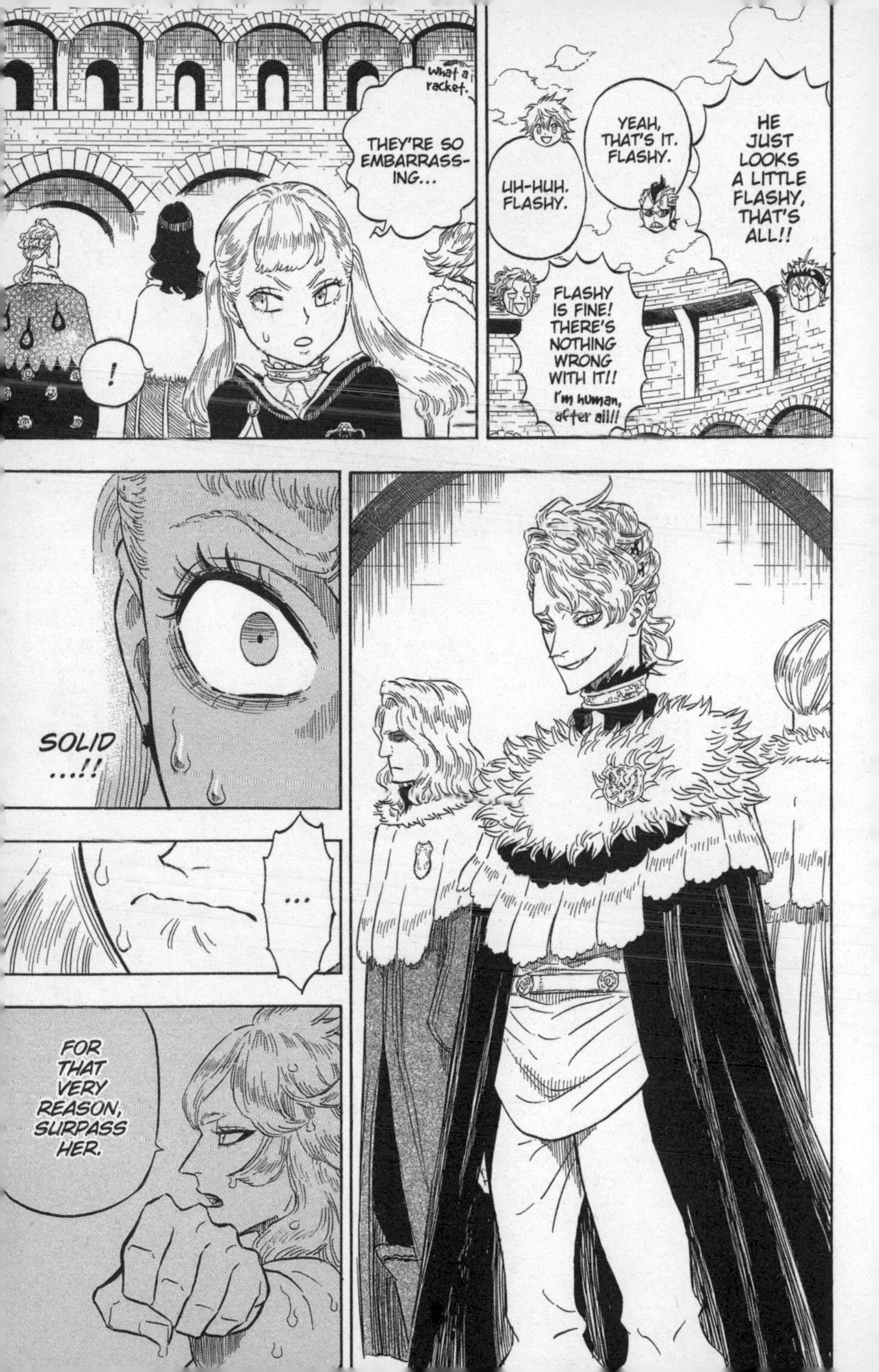
HE JUST LOOKS A LITTLE FLASHY, THAT'S ALL!!
YEAH, THAT'S IT. FLASHY.
UH-HUH. FLASHY.
FLASHY IS FINE! THERE'S NOTHING WRONG WITH IT!!
I'm human, after all!!
what a racket.
THEY'RE SO EMBARRASS-ING...
!
SOLID ...!!
...
FOR THAT VERY REASON, SURPASS HER.

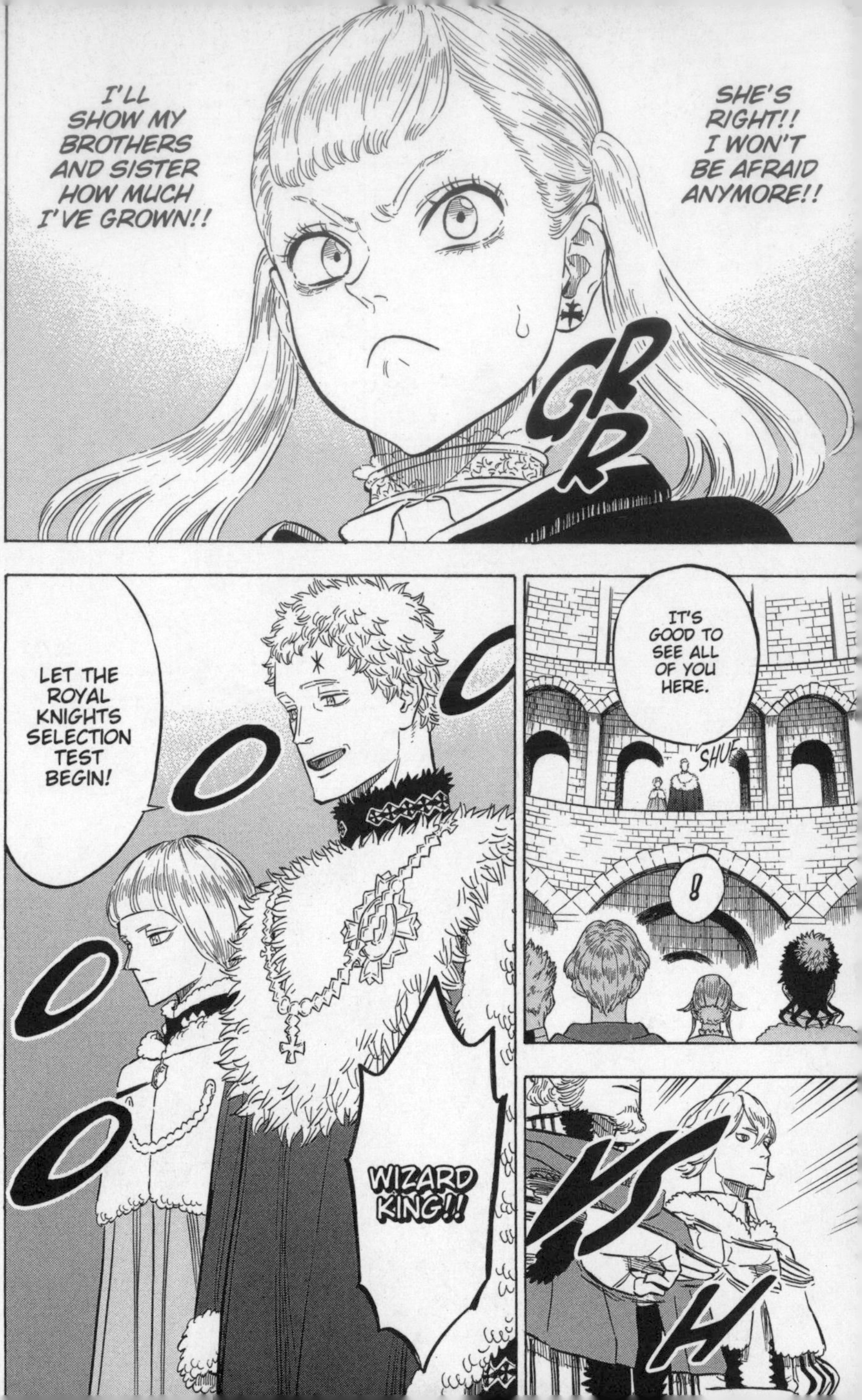
SHE'S RIGHT!! I WON'T BE AFRAID ANYMORE!!
I'LL SHOW MY BROTHERS AND SISTER HOW MUCH I'VE GROWN!!
GRR
IT'S GOOD TO SEE ALL OF YOU HERE.
SHUF
!
LET THE ROYAL KNIGHTS SELECTION TEST BEGIN!
WIZARD KING!!

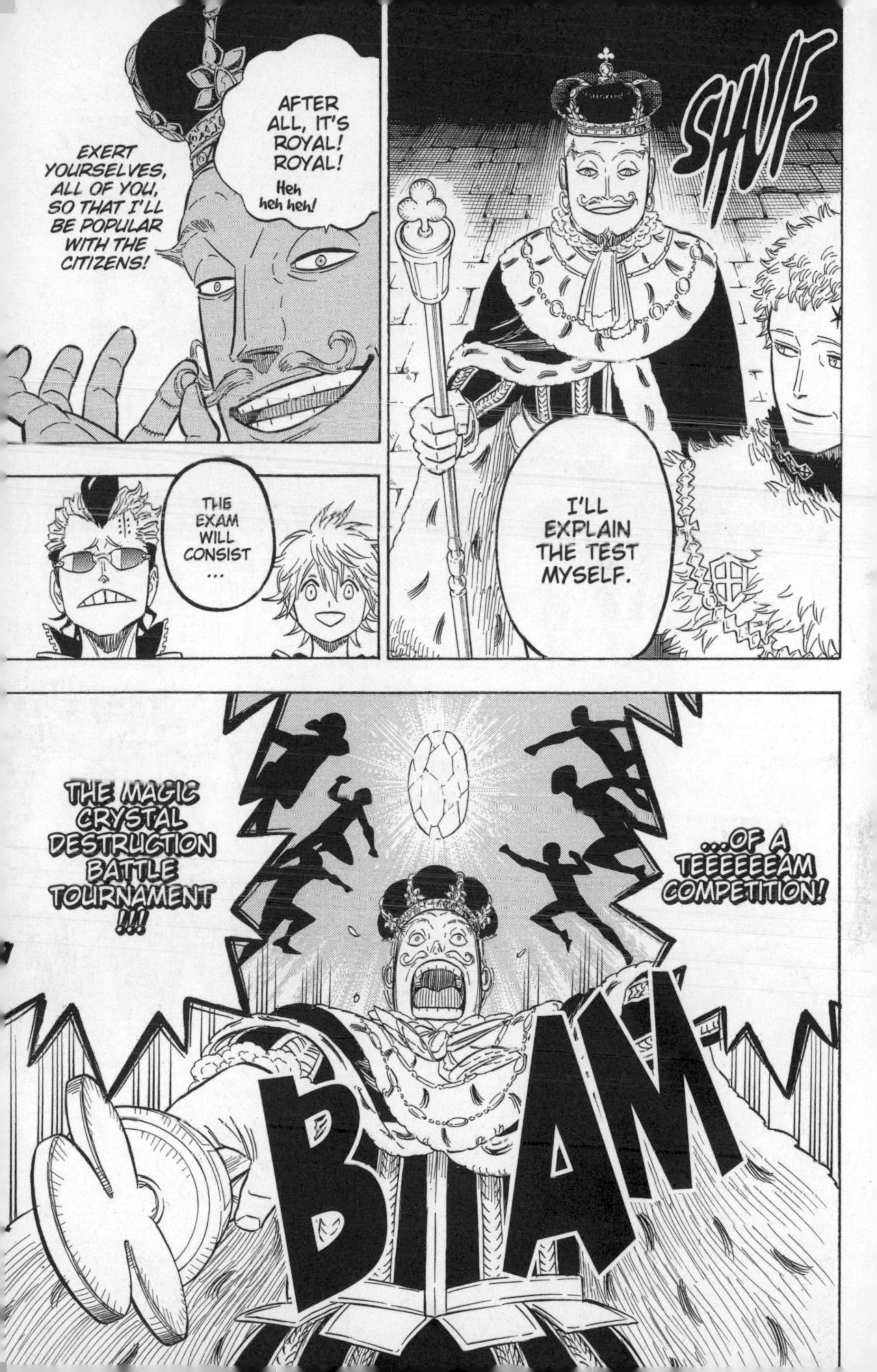
SHUF
I'LL EXPLAIN THE TEST MYSELF.
AFTER ALL, IT'S ROYAL! ROYAL!
Heh heh heh!
EXERT YOURSELVES, ALL OF YOU, SO THAT I'LL BE POPULAR WITH THE CITIZENS!
THE EXAM WILL CONSIST ...
...OF A TEEEEEEAM COMPETITION!
THE MAGIC CRYSTAL DESTRUCTION BATTLE TOURNAMENT!!!
BLAM

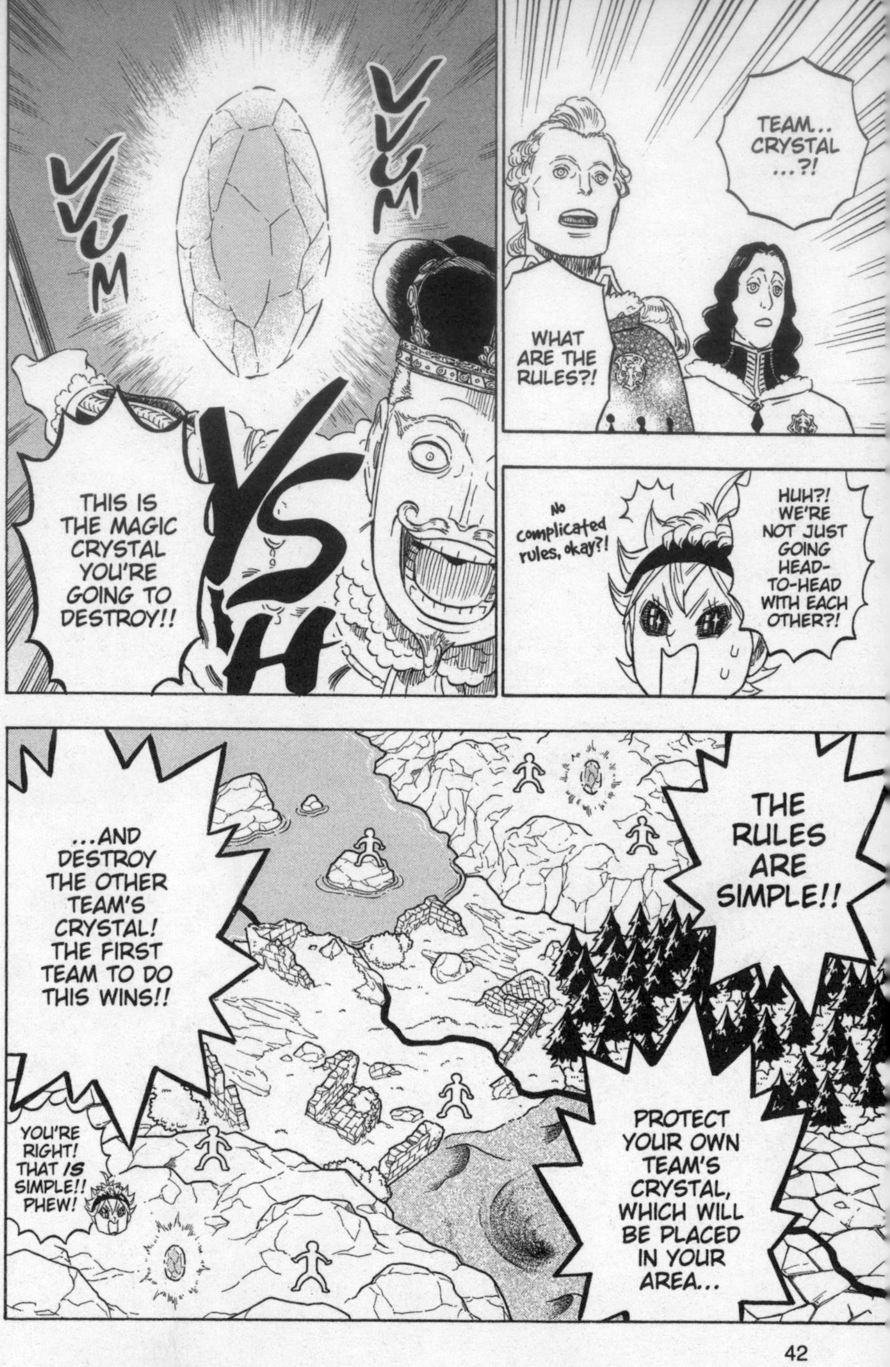
TEAM... CRYSTAL ...?!
WHAT ARE THE RULES?!
HUH?! WE'RE NOT JUST GOING HEAD-TO-HEAD WITH EACH OTHER?!
No complicated rules, okay?!
VVUM
VVUM
THIS IS THE MAGIC CRYSTAL YOU'RE GOING TO DESTROY!!
VSH
THE RULES ARE SIMPLE!!
PROTECT YOUR OWN TEAM'S CRYSTAL, WHICH WILL BE PLACED IN YOUR AREA...
...AND DESTROY THE OTHER TEAM'S CRYSTAL! THE FIRST TEAM TO DO THIS WINS!!
YOU'RE RIGHT! THAT *IS* SIMPLE!! PHEW!

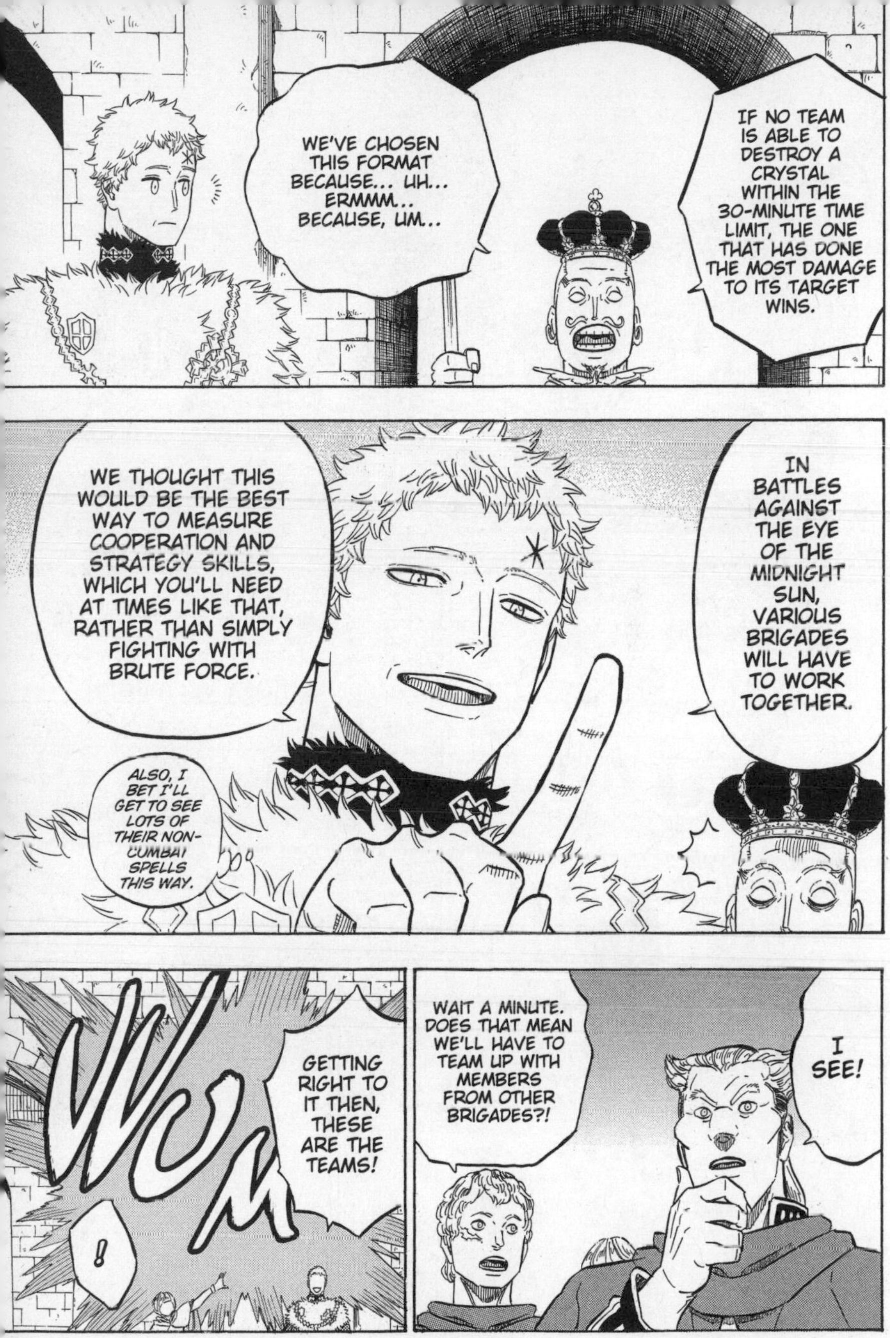
IF NO TEAM IS ABLE TO DESTROY A CRYSTAL WITHIN THE 30-MINUTE TIME LIMIT, THE ONE THAT HAS DONE THE MOST DAMAGE TO ITS TARGET WINS.
WE'VE CHOSEN THIS FORMAT BECAUSE... UH... ERMMM... BECAUSE, UM...
IN BATTLES AGAINST THE EYE OF THE MIDNIGHT SUN, VARIOUS BRIGADES WILL HAVE TO WORK TOGETHER.
WE THOUGHT THIS WOULD BE THE BEST WAY TO MEASURE COOPERATION AND STRATEGY SKILLS, WHICH YOU'LL NEED AT TIMES LIKE THAT, RATHER THAN SIMPLY FIGHTING WITH BRUTE FORCE.
ALSO, I BET I'LL GET TO SEE LOTS OF THEIR NON-COMBAT SPELLS THIS WAY.
I SEE!
WAIT A MINUTE. DOES THAT MEAN WE'LL HAVE TO TEAM UP WITH MEMBERS FROM OTHER BRIGADES?!
GETTING RIGHT TO IT THEN, THESE ARE THE TEAMS!
!

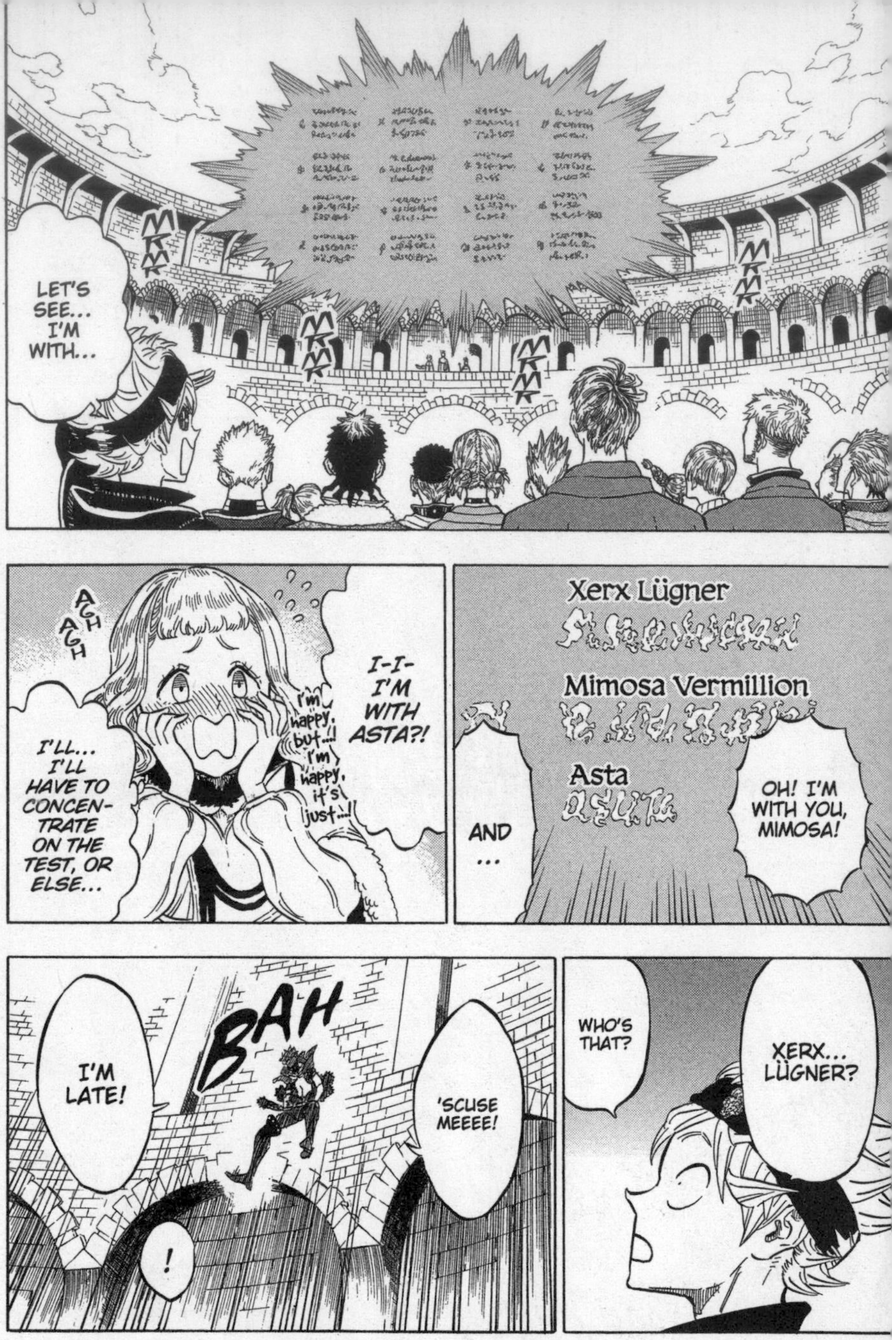
MKMK
MKMK
MKMK
MKMK
LET'S SEE... I'M WITH...
Xerx Lügner
Mimosa Vermillion
Asta
OH! I'M WITH YOU, MIMOSA!
AND ...
I-I-I'M WITH ASTA?!
I'm happy, but...! I'm happy, it's just...!
AGH AGH
I'LL... I'LL HAVE TO CONCEN-TRATE ON THE TEST, OR ELSE...
XERX... LÜGNER?
WHO'S THAT?
'SCUSE MEEEE!
BAH
I'M LATE!
!

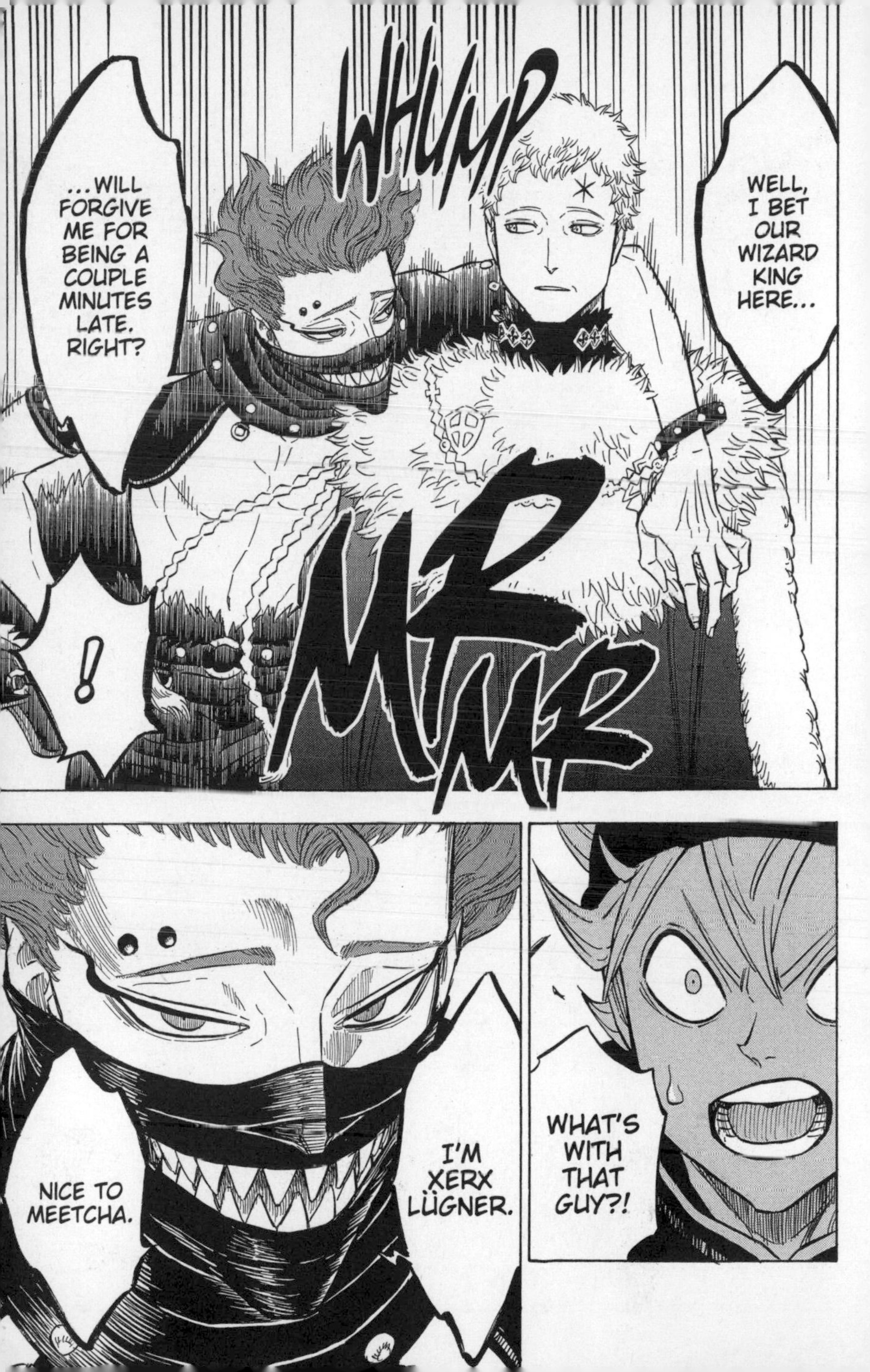
WELL, I BET OUR WIZARD KING HERE...
WHUMP
...WILL FORGIVE ME FOR BEING A COUPLE MINUTES LATE. RIGHT?
!
WHAT'S WITH THAT GUY?!
I'M XERX LÜGNER.
NICE TO MEETCHA.

Solid Silva

Age: 18
Height: 169 cm
Birthday: February 26
Sign: Pisces
Blood Type: B
Likes: Grilled lamb chops, being sarcastic

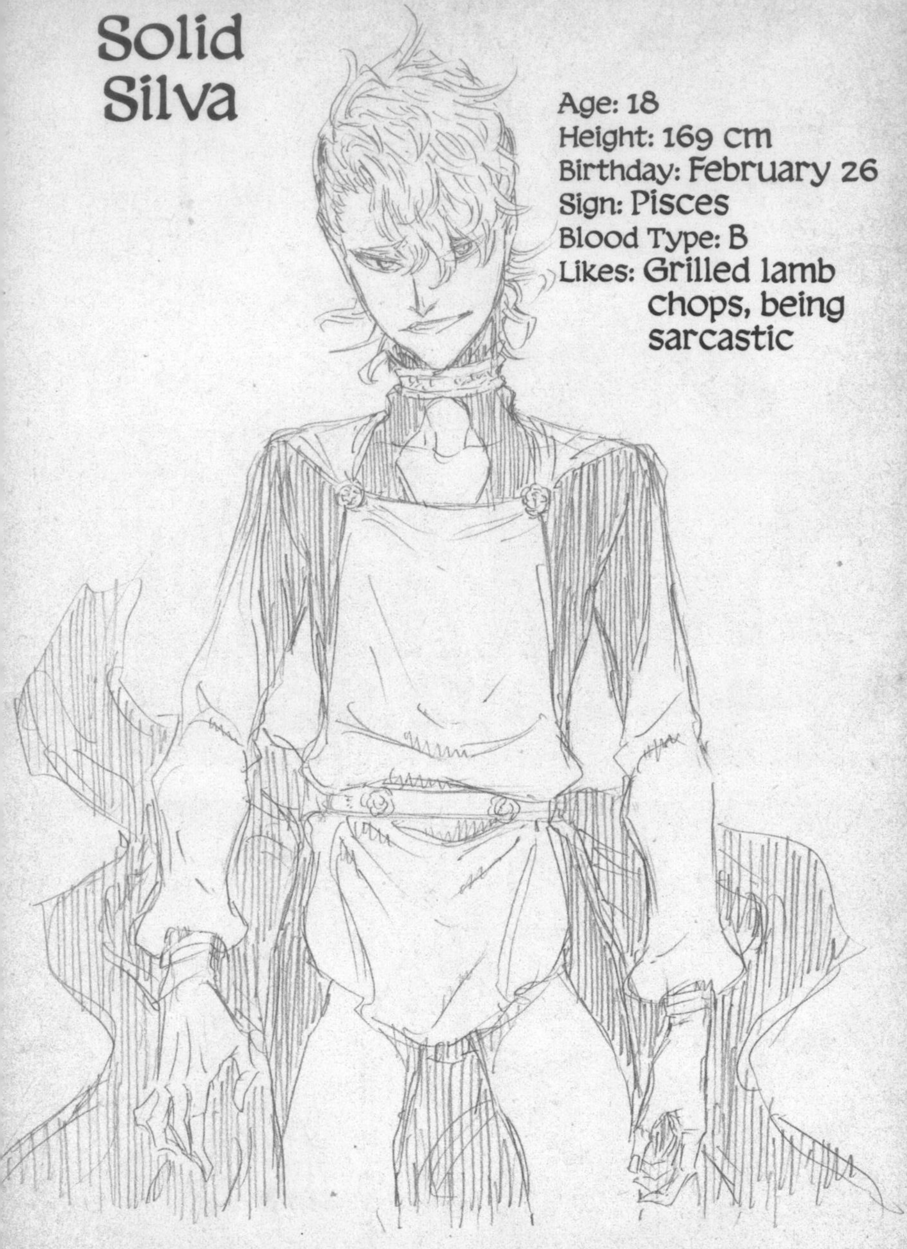

Character Profile

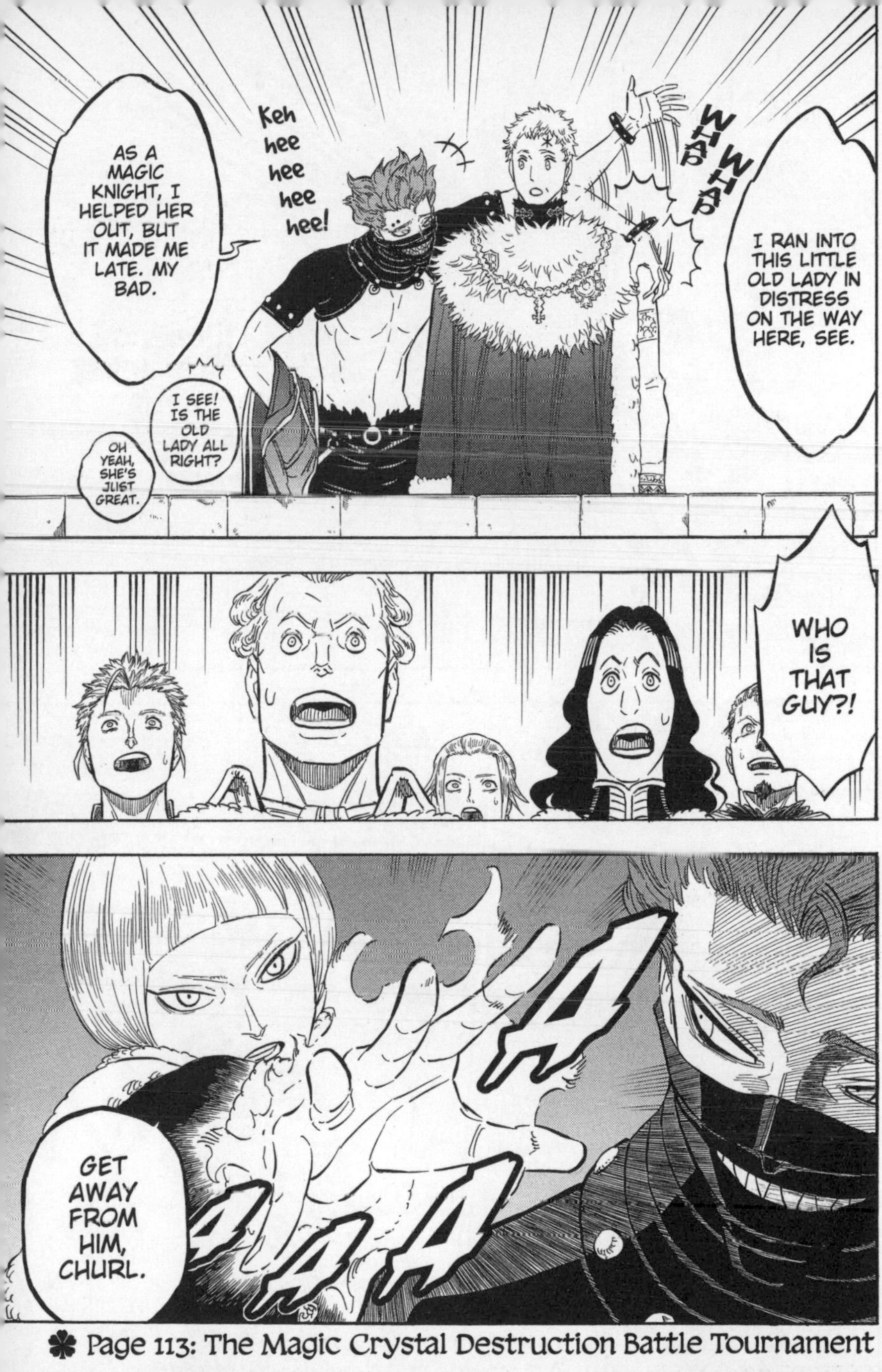
I RAN INTO THIS LITTLE OLD LADY IN DISTRESS ON THE WAY HERE, SEE.
WHAP WHAP
Keh hee hee hee hee!
AS A MAGIC KNIGHT, I HELPED HER OUT, BUT IT MADE ME LATE. MY BAD.
I SEE! IS THE OLD LADY ALL RIGHT?
OH YEAH, SHE'S JUST GREAT.
WHO IS THAT GUY?!
GET AWAY FROM HIM, CHURL.

Page 113: The Magic Crystal Destruction Battle Tournament

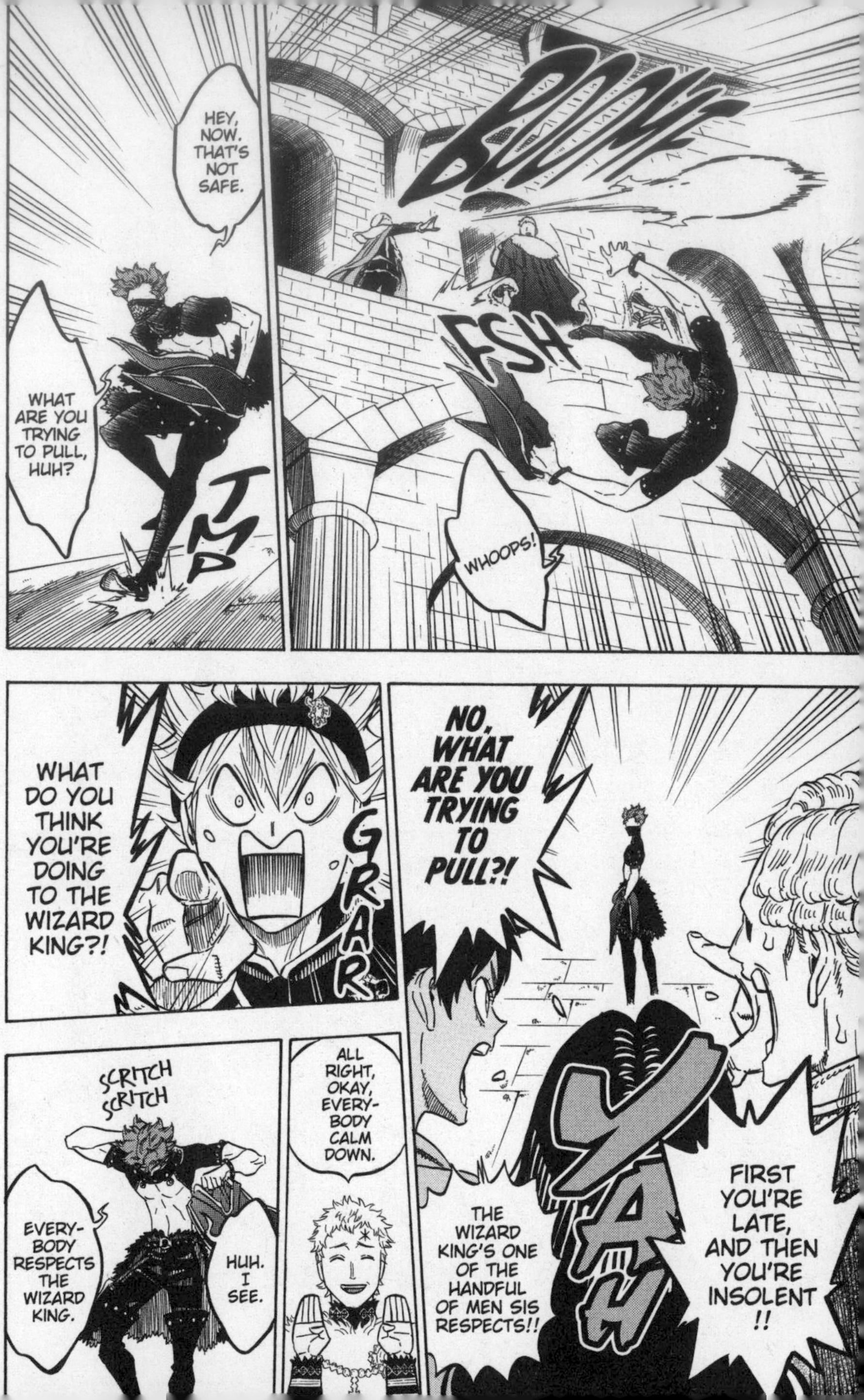
BOOM
FSH
WHOOPS!
HEY, NOW. THAT'S NOT SAFE.
WHAT ARE YOU TRYING TO PULL, HUH?
TMP
NO, WHAT ARE YOU TRYING TO PULL?!
YAH
FIRST YOU'RE LATE, AND THEN YOU'RE INSOLENT!!
THE WIZARD KING'S ONE OF THE HANDFUL OF MEN SIS RESPECTS!!
WHAT DO YOU THINK YOU'RE DOING TO THE WIZARD KING?!
GRAR
ALL RIGHT, OKAY, EVERY-BODY CALM DOWN.
SCRITCH SCRITCH
EVERY-BODY RESPECTS THE WIZARD KING.
HUH. I SEE.

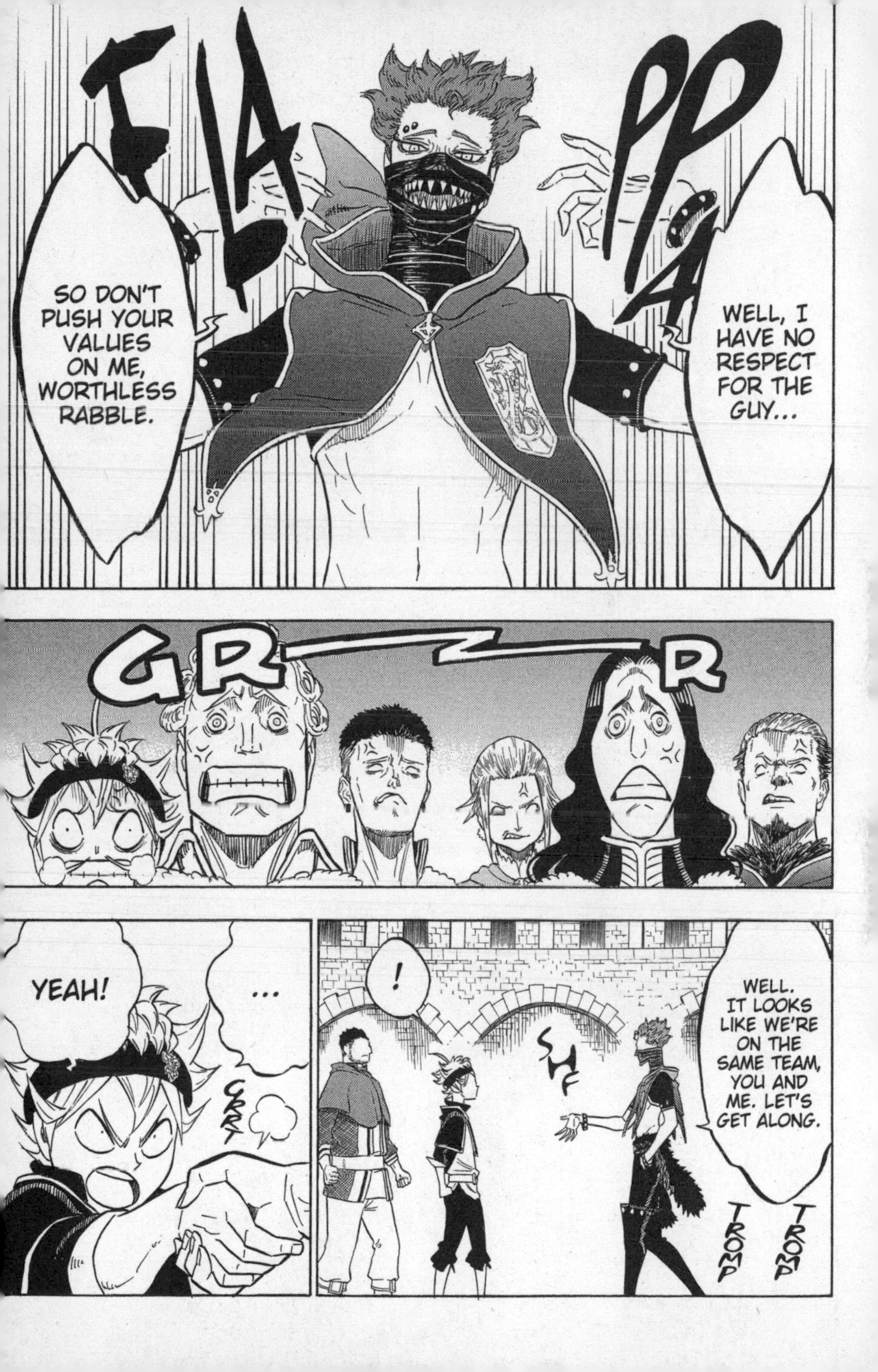
FLAPPA
WELL, I HAVE NO RESPECT FOR THE GUY...
SO DON'T PUSH YOUR VALUES ON ME, WORTHLESS RABBLE.
GRRR
WELL. IT LOOKS LIKE WE'RE ON THE SAME TEAM, YOU AND ME. LET'S GET ALONG.
!
SHF
TROMP
TROMP
...
YEAH!
GRRT

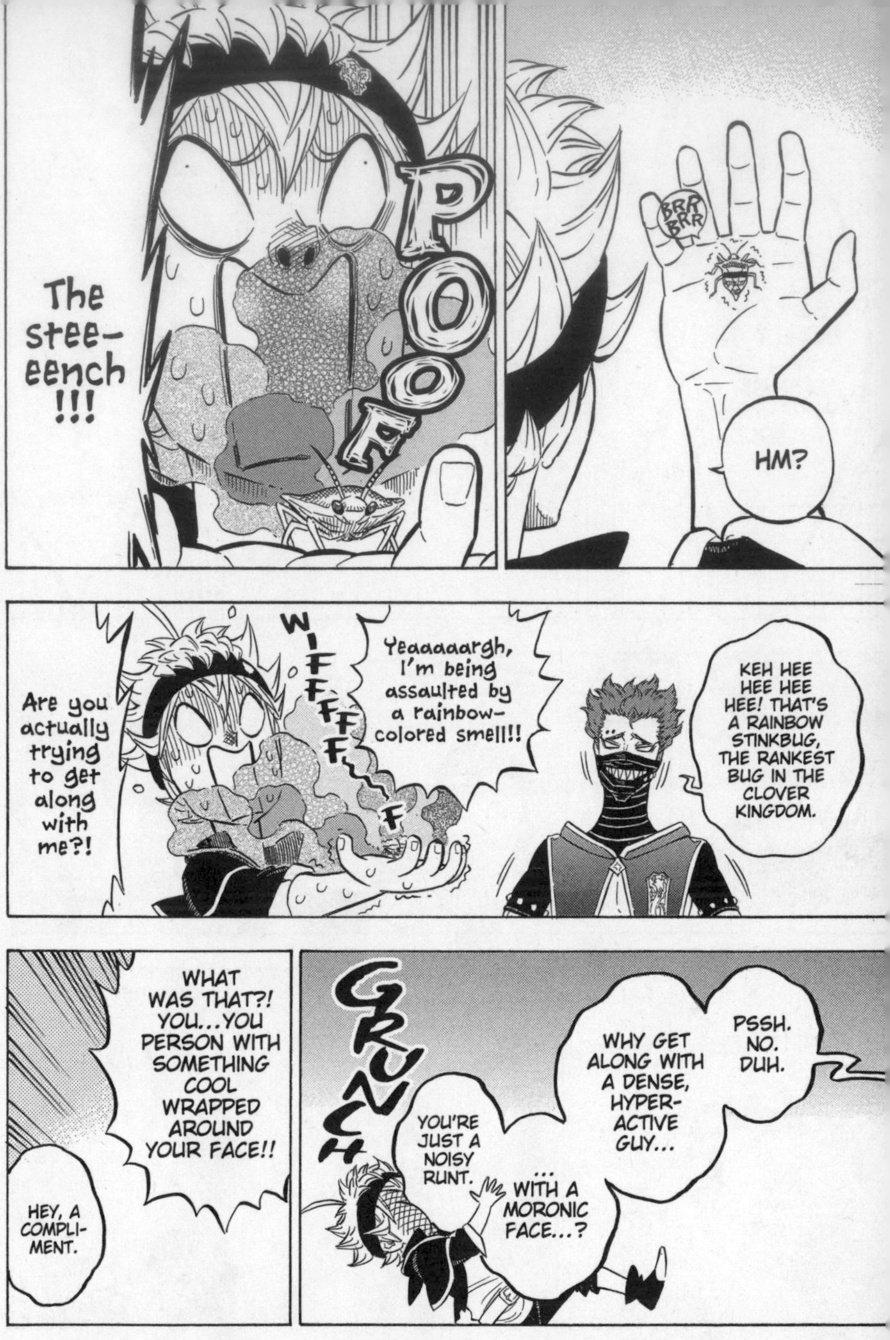
BRR BRR
HM?
POOF
The steee-eench!!!
KEH HEE HEE HEE HEE! THAT'S A RAINBOW STINKBUG, THE RANKEST BUG IN THE CLOVER KINGDOM.
Yeaaaaargh, I'm being assaulted by a rainbow-colored smell!!
WIFFFFFF
Are you actually trying to get along with me?!
PSSH. NO. DUH.
WHY GET ALONG WITH A DENSE, HYPER-ACTIVE GUY...
GRUNCH
YOU'RE JUST A NOISY RUNT.
...WITH A MORONIC FACE...?
WHAT WAS THAT?! YOU...YOU PERSON WITH SOMETHING COOL WRAPPED AROUND YOUR FACE!!
HEY, A COMPLI-MENT.

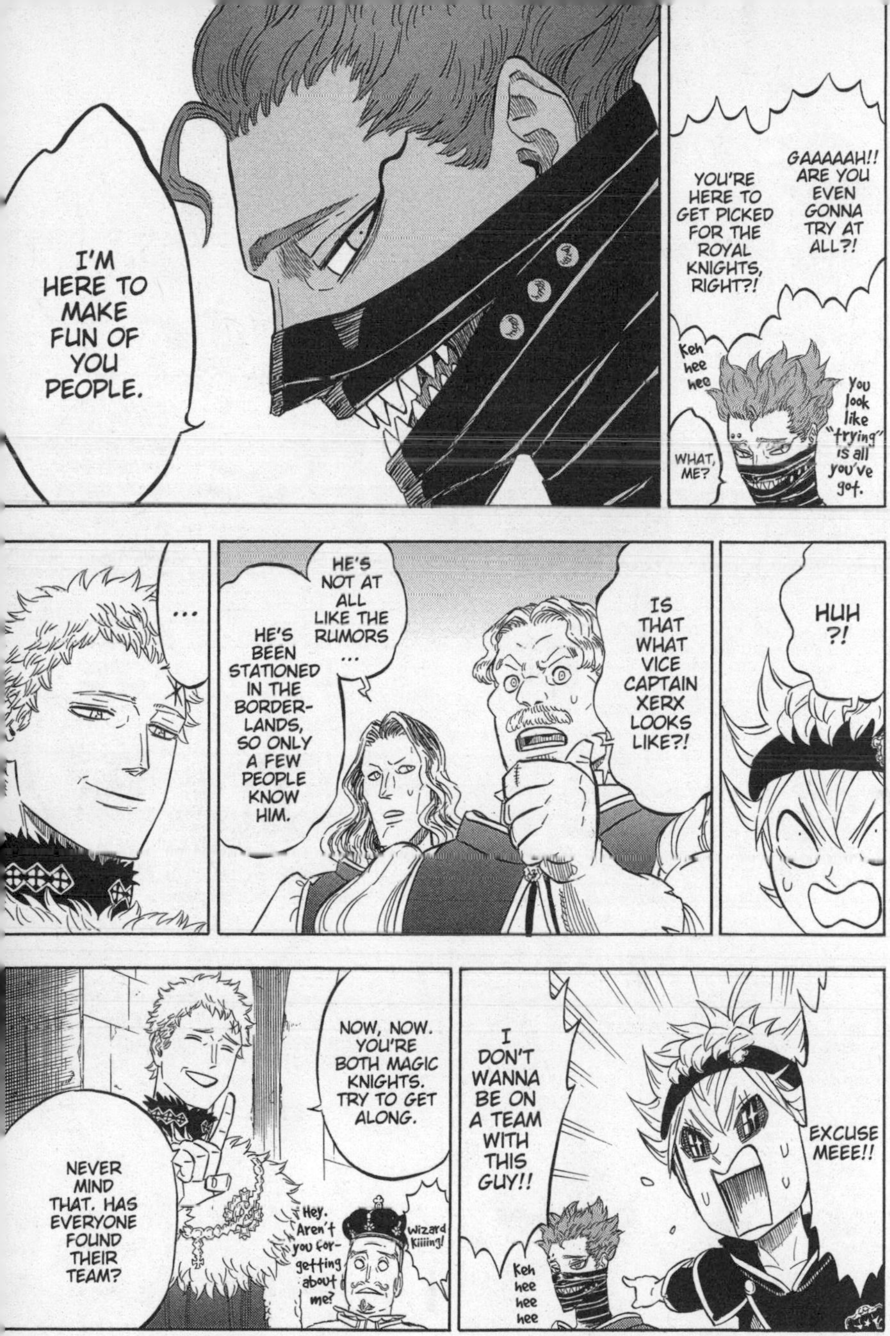
GAAAAAH!! ARE YOU EVEN GONNA TRY AT ALL?!
YOU'RE HERE TO GET PICKED FOR THE ROYAL KNIGHTS, RIGHT?!
Keh hee hee
You look like "trying" is all you've got.
WHAT, ME?
I'M HERE TO MAKE FUN OF YOU PEOPLE.
HUH?!
IS THAT WHAT VICE CAPTAIN XERX LOOKS LIKE?!
HE'S NOT AT ALL LIKE THE RUMORS...
HE'S BEEN STATIONED IN THE BORDER-LANDS, SO ONLY A FEW PEOPLE KNOW HIM.
...
EXCUSE MEEE!!
I DON'T WANNA BE ON A TEAM WITH THIS GUY!!
Keh hee hee hee
NOW, NOW. YOU'RE BOTH MAGIC KNIGHTS. TRY TO GET ALONG.
Wizard Kiiiing!
Hey. Aren't you for-getting about me?
NEVER MIND THAT. HAS EVERYONE FOUND THEIR TEAM?

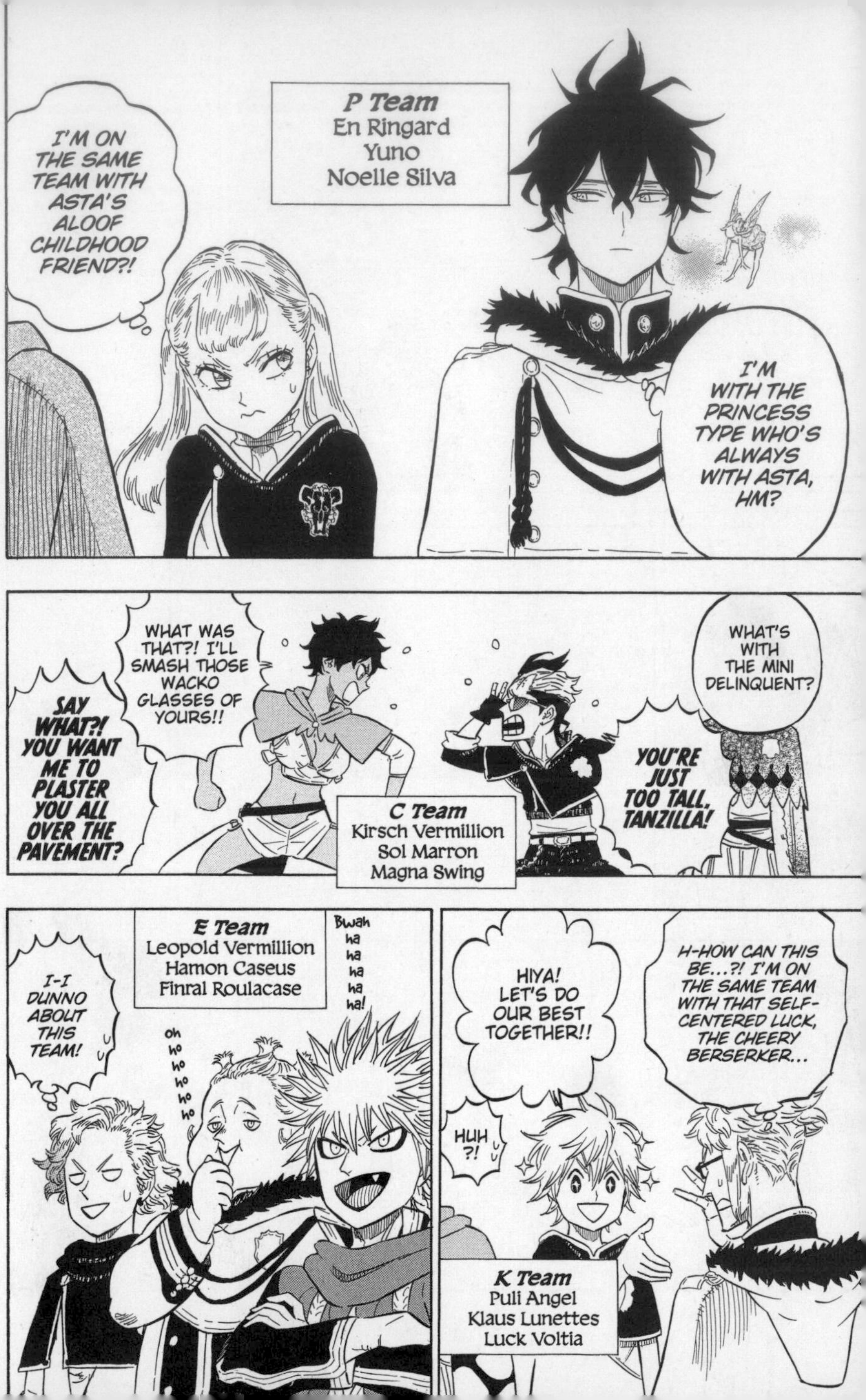
P Team
En Ringard
Yuno
Noelle Silva
I'M ON THE SAME TEAM WITH ASTA'S ALOOF CHILDHOOD FRIEND?!
I'M WITH THE PRINCESS TYPE WHO'S ALWAYS WITH ASTA, HM?
WHAT'S WITH THE MINI DELINQUENT?
YOU'RE JUST TOO TALL, TANZILLA!
WHAT WAS THAT?! I'LL SMASH THOSE WACKO GLASSES OF YOURS!!
SAY WHAT?! YOU WANT ME TO PLASTER YOU ALL OVER THE PAVEMENT?
C Team
Kirsch Vermillion
Sol Marron
Magna Swing
H-HOW CAN THIS BE...?! I'M ON THE SAME TEAM WITH THAT SELF-CENTERED LUCK, THE CHEERY BERSERKER...
HIYA! LET'S DO OUR BEST TOGETHER!!
HUH ?!
K Team
Puli Angel
Klaus Lunettes
Luck Voltia
E Team
Leopold Vermillion
Hamon Caseus
Finral Roulacase
Bwah ha ha ha ha ha!
I-I DUNNO ABOUT THIS TEAM!
oh ho ho ho ho ho ho

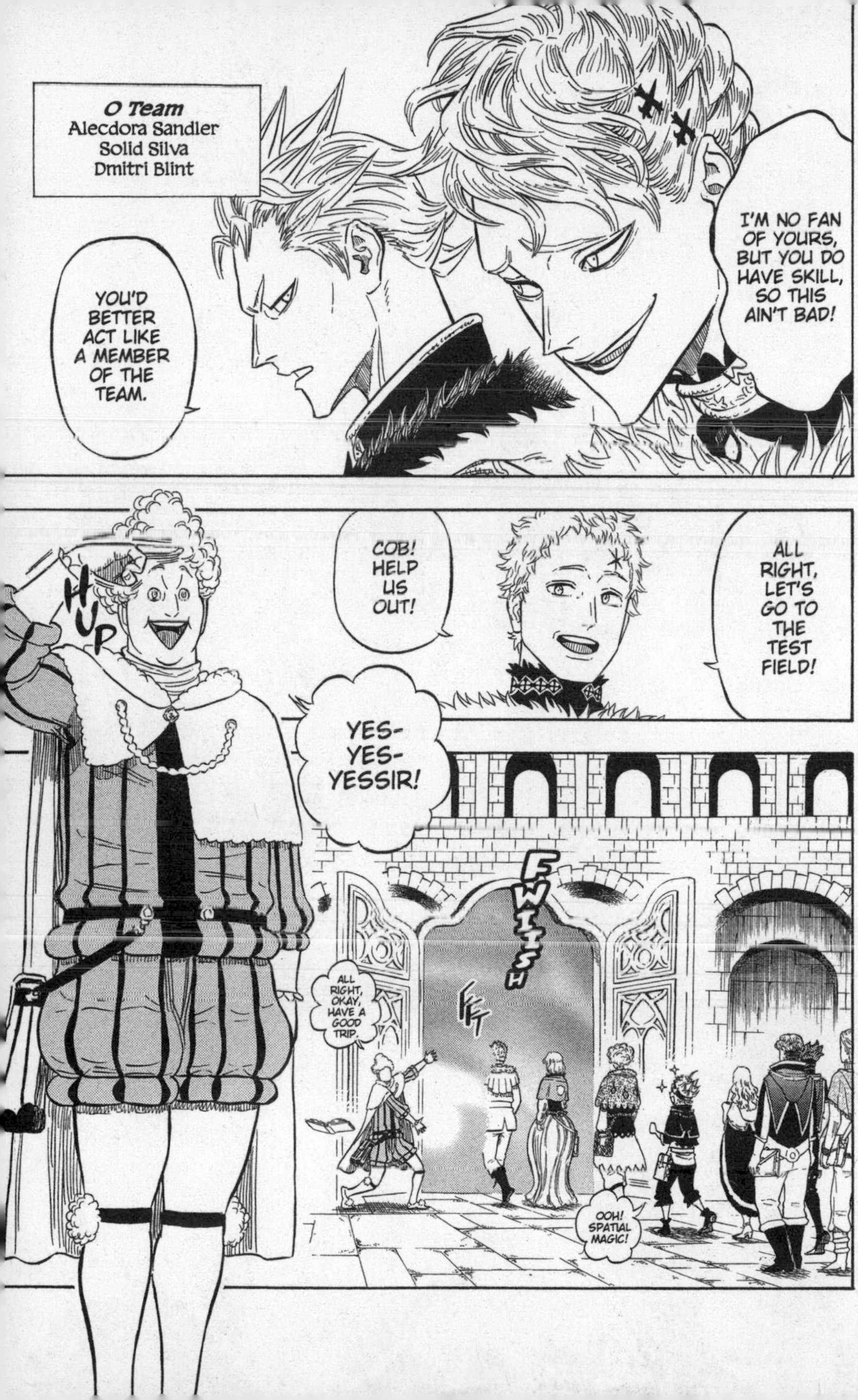
O Team
Alecdora Sandler
Solid Silva
Dmitri Blint
I'M NO FAN OF YOURS, BUT YOU DO HAVE SKILL, SO THIS AIN'T BAD!
YOU'D BETTER ACT LIKE A MEMBER OF THE TEAM.
ALL RIGHT, LET'S GO TO THE TEST FIELD!
COB! HELP US OUT!
FWISH
FFT
OOH! SPATIAL MAGIC!
ALL RIGHT, OKAY, HAVE A GOOD TRIP.
HUP
YES-YES-YESSIR!

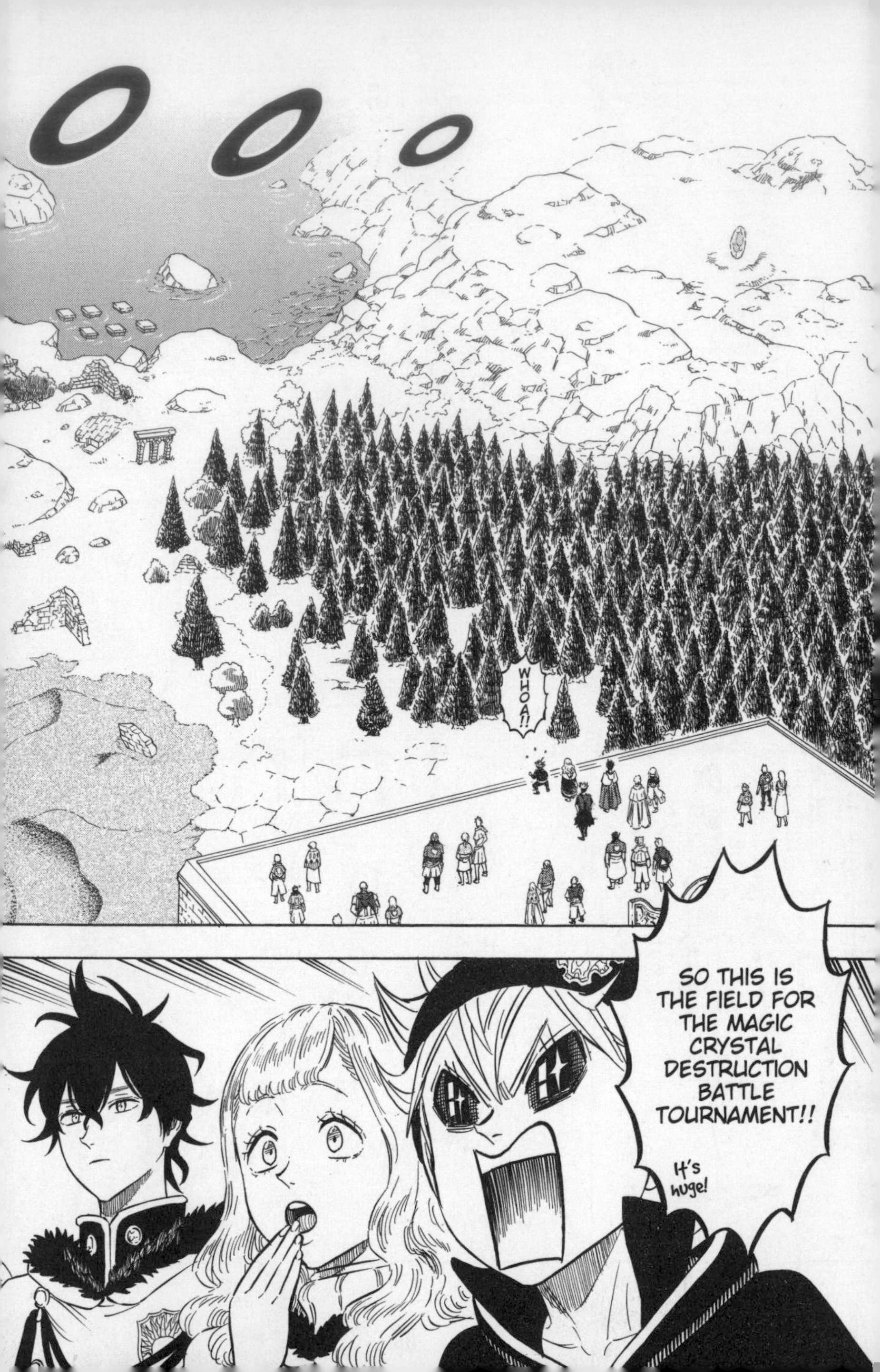
WHOA!!
SO THIS IS THE FIELD FOR THE MAGIC CRYSTAL DESTRUCTION BATTLE TOURNAMENT!!
It's huge!

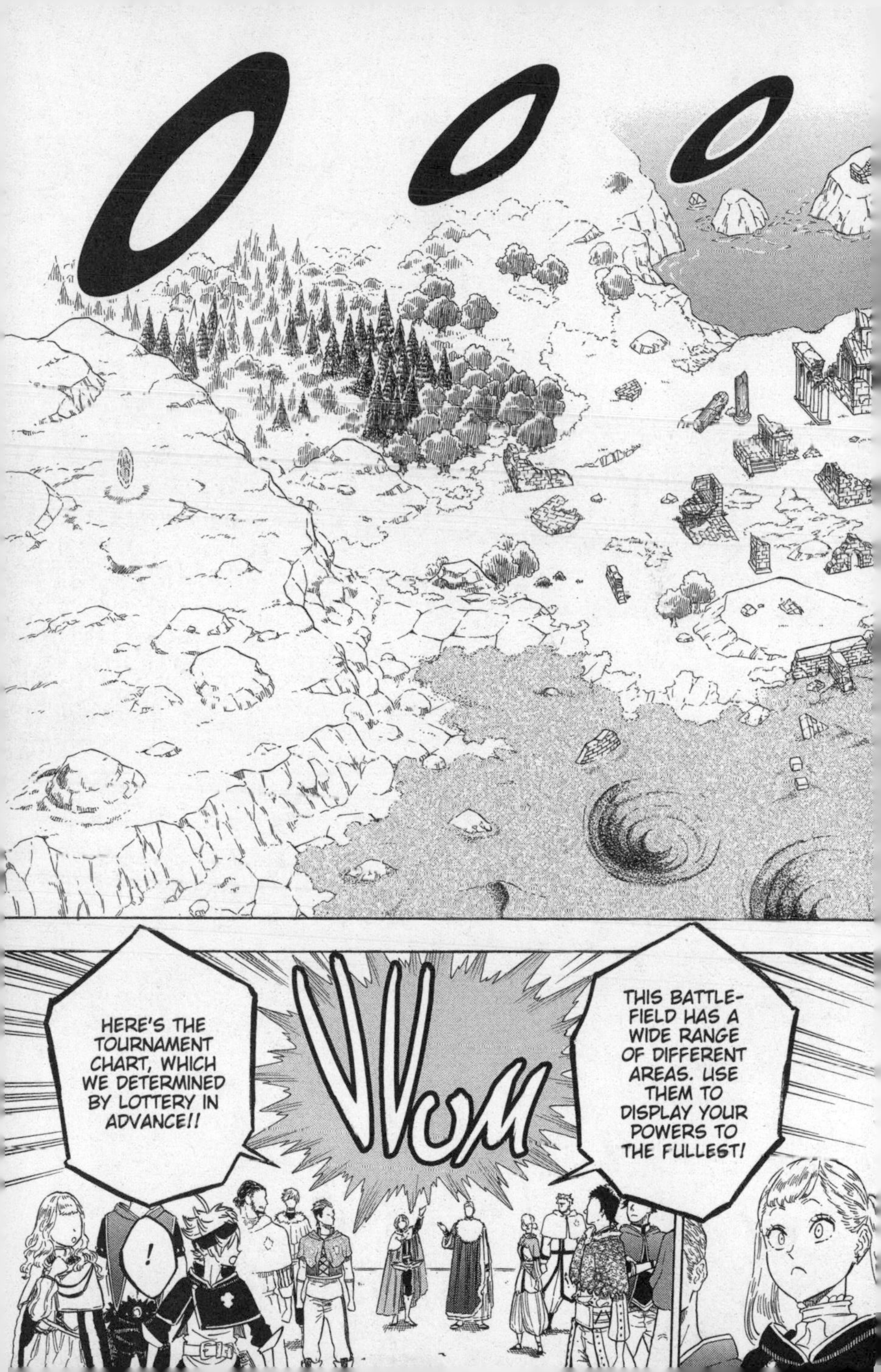
THIS BATTLE-FIELD HAS A WIDE RANGE OF DIFFERENT AREAS. USE THEM TO DISPLAY YOUR POWERS TO THE FULLEST!
HERE'S THE TOURNAMENT CHART, WHICH WE DETERMINED BY LOTTERY IN ADVANCE!!
!

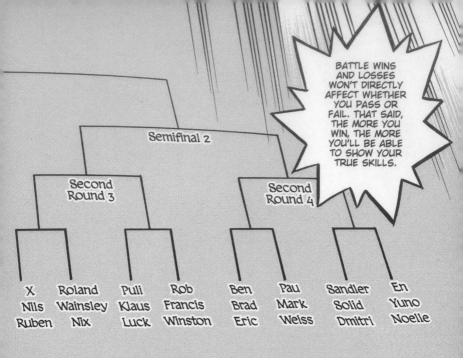

BATTLE WINS AND LOSSES WON'T DIRECTLY AFFECT WHETHER YOU PASS OR FAIL. THAT SAID, THE MORE YOU WIN, THE MORE YOU'LL BE ABLE TO SHOW YOUR TRUE SKILLS.

Semifinal 2

Second Round 3

Second Round 4

X
Nils
Ruben

Roland
Wainsley
Nix

Puli
Klaus
Luck

Rob
Francis
Winston

Ben
Brad
Eric

Pau
Mark
Weiss

Sandler
Solid
Dmitri

En
Yuno
Noelle

...

I'M FACING SOLID'S TEAM RIGHT AWAY!!

!!

I'LL FINISH YOU OFF MYSELF, NOELLE!!

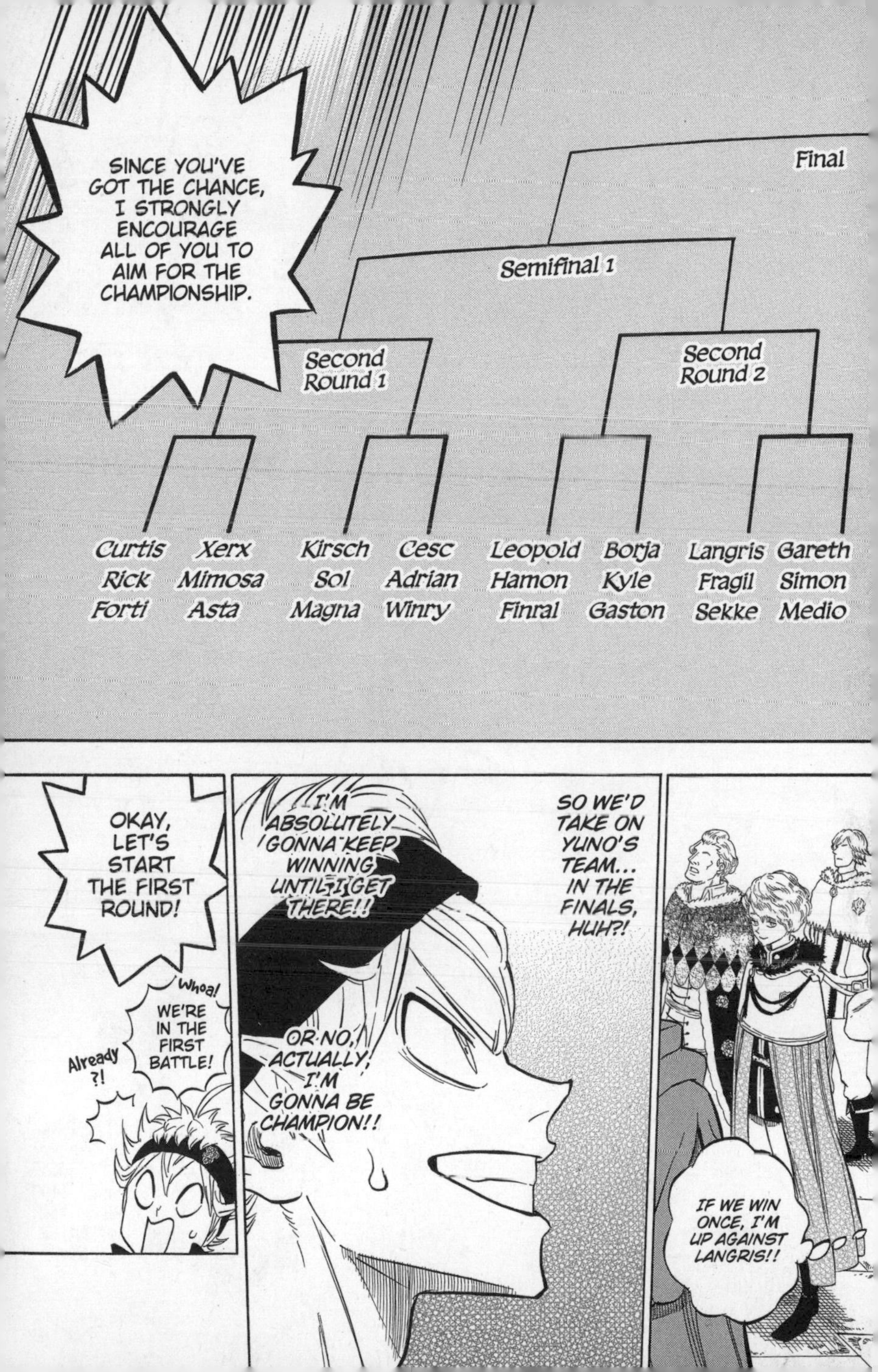
SINCE YOU'VE GOT THE CHANCE, I STRONGLY ENCOURAGE ALL OF YOU TO AIM FOR THE CHAMPIONSHIP.
Final
Semifinal 1
Second Round 2
Second Round 1
Curtis Rick Forti
Xerx Mimosa Asta
Kirsch Sol Magna
Cesc Adrian Winry
Leopold Hamon Finral
Borja Kyle Gaston
Langris Fragil Sekke
Gareth Simon Medio
IF WE WIN ONCE, I'M UP AGAINST LANGRIS!!
SO WE'D TAKE ON YUNO'S TEAM... IN THE FINALS, HUH?!
I'M ABSOLUTELY GONNA KEEP WINNING UNTIL I GET THERE!!
OR NO, ACTUALLY, I'M GONNA BE CHAMPION!!
OKAY, LET'S START THE FIRST ROUND!
Whoa!
WE'RE IN THE FIRST BATTLE!
Already?!

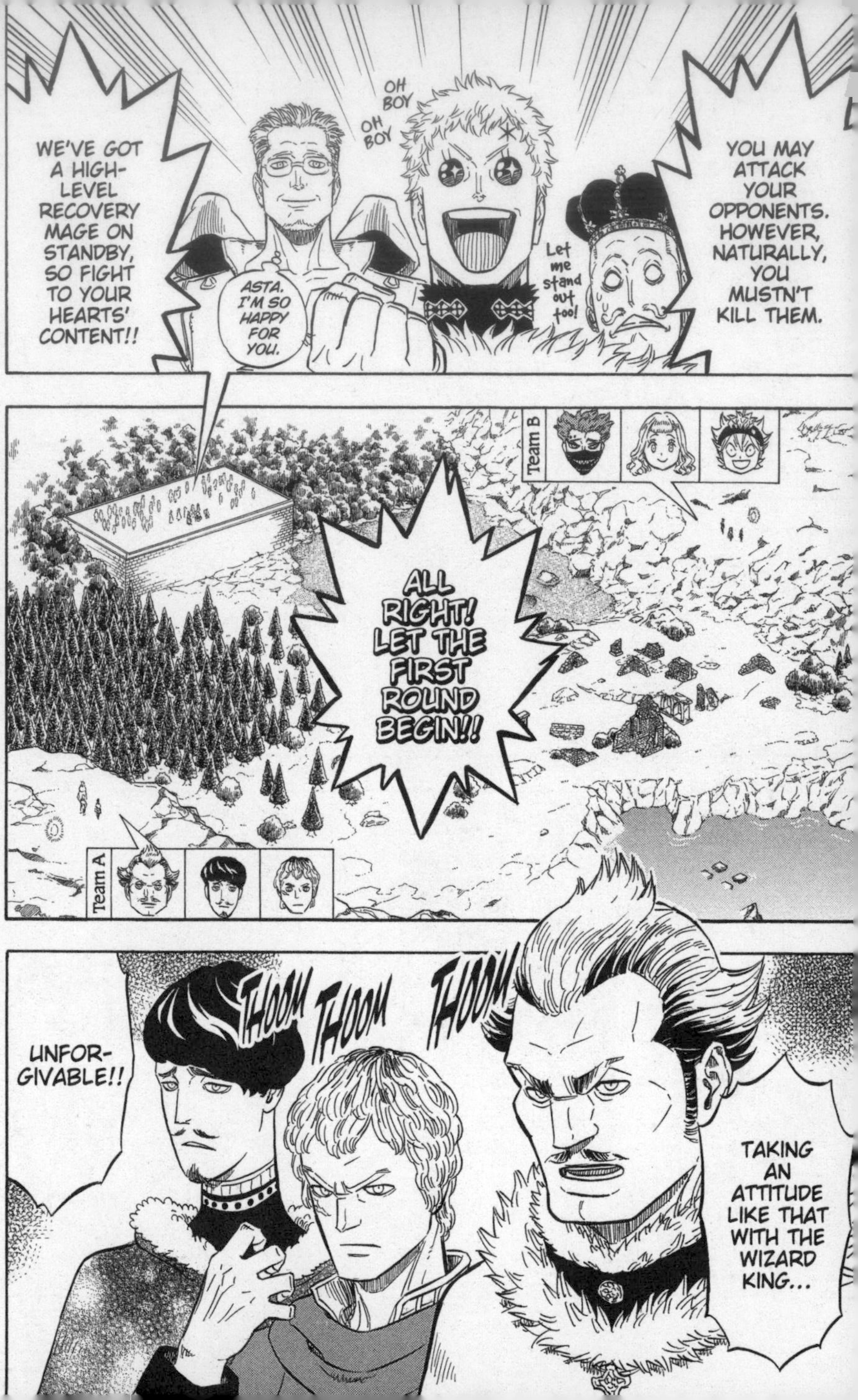
YOU MAY ATTACK YOUR OPPONENTS. HOWEVER, NATURALLY, YOU MUSTN'T KILL THEM.
Let me stand out too!
OH BOY OH BOY
WE'VE GOT A HIGH-LEVEL RECOVERY MAGE ON STANDBY, SO FIGHT TO YOUR HEARTS' CONTENT!!
ASTA. I'M SO HAPPY FOR YOU.
Team B
ALL RIGHT! LET THE FIRST ROUND BEGIN!!
Team A
THOOM THOOM THOOM
TAKING AN ATTITUDE LIKE THAT WITH THE WIZARD KING...
UNFORGIVABLE!!

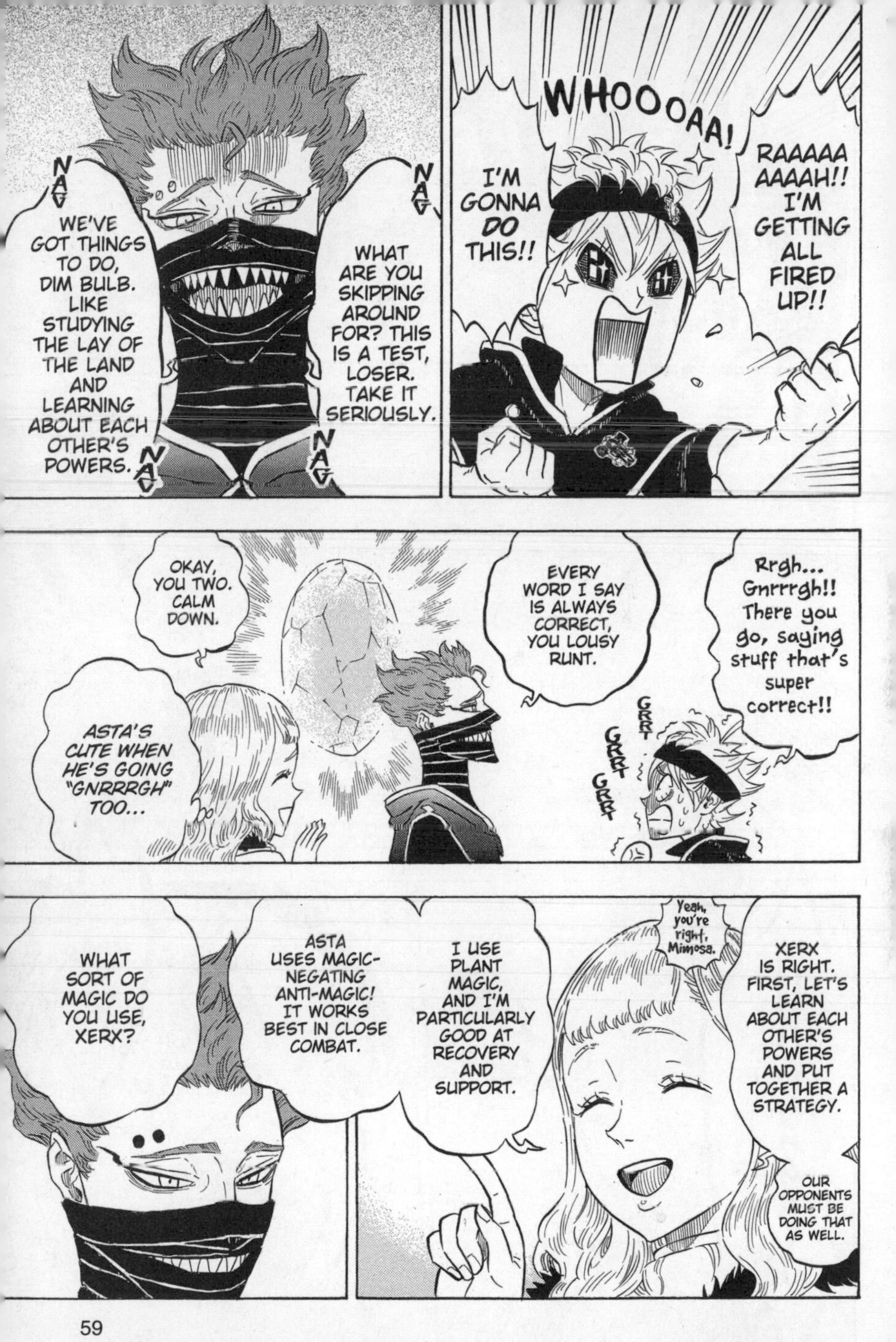
WHOOOOAA!
RAAAAA AAAAH!! I'M GETTING ALL FIRED UP!!
I'M GONNA DO THIS!!
NAG
WHAT ARE YOU SKIPPING AROUND FOR? THIS IS A TEST, LOSER. TAKE IT SERIOUSLY.
NAG
WE'VE GOT THINGS TO DO, DIM BULB. LIKE STUDYING THE LAY OF THE LAND AND LEARNING ABOUT EACH OTHER'S POWERS.
NAG
NAG
Rrgh... Gnrrrgh!! There you go, saying stuff that's super correct!!
GRRT GRRT GRRT
EVERY WORD I SAY IS ALWAYS CORRECT, YOU LOUSY RUNT.
OKAY, YOU TWO. CALM DOWN.
ASTA'S CUTE WHEN HE'S GOING "GNRRRGH" TOO...
XERX IS RIGHT. FIRST, LET'S LEARN ABOUT EACH OTHER'S POWERS AND PUT TOGETHER A STRATEGY.
Yeah, you're right, Mimosa.
OUR OPPONENTS MUST BE DOING THAT AS WELL.
I USE PLANT MAGIC, AND I'M PARTICULARLY GOOD AT RECOVERY AND SUPPORT.
ASTA USES MAGIC-NEGATING ANTI-MAGIC! IT WORKS BEST IN CLOSE COMBAT.
WHAT SORT OF MAGIC DO YOU USE, XERX?

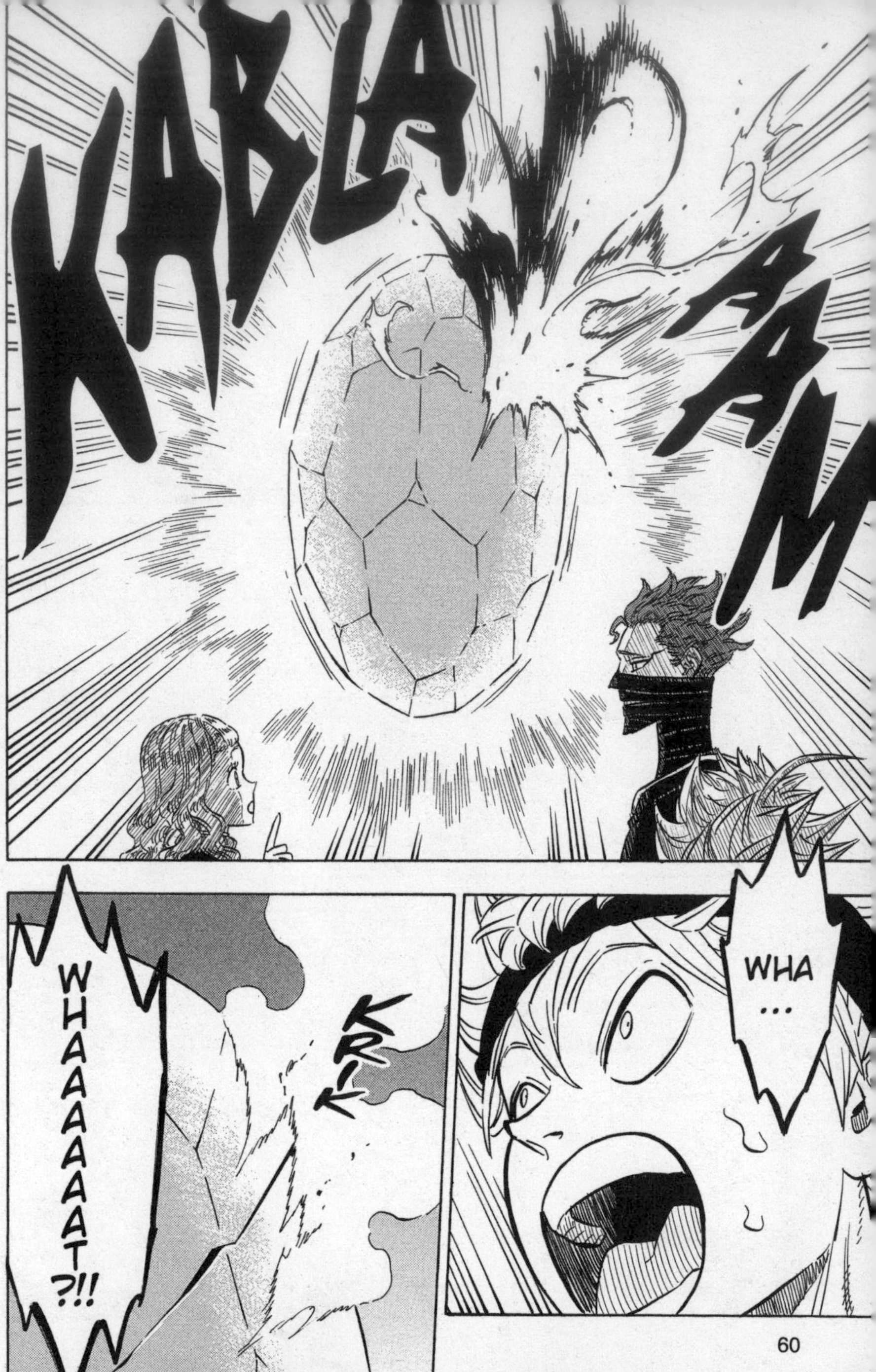
KABLAAAM
WHA ...
KRIK
WHAAAAAAT?!!

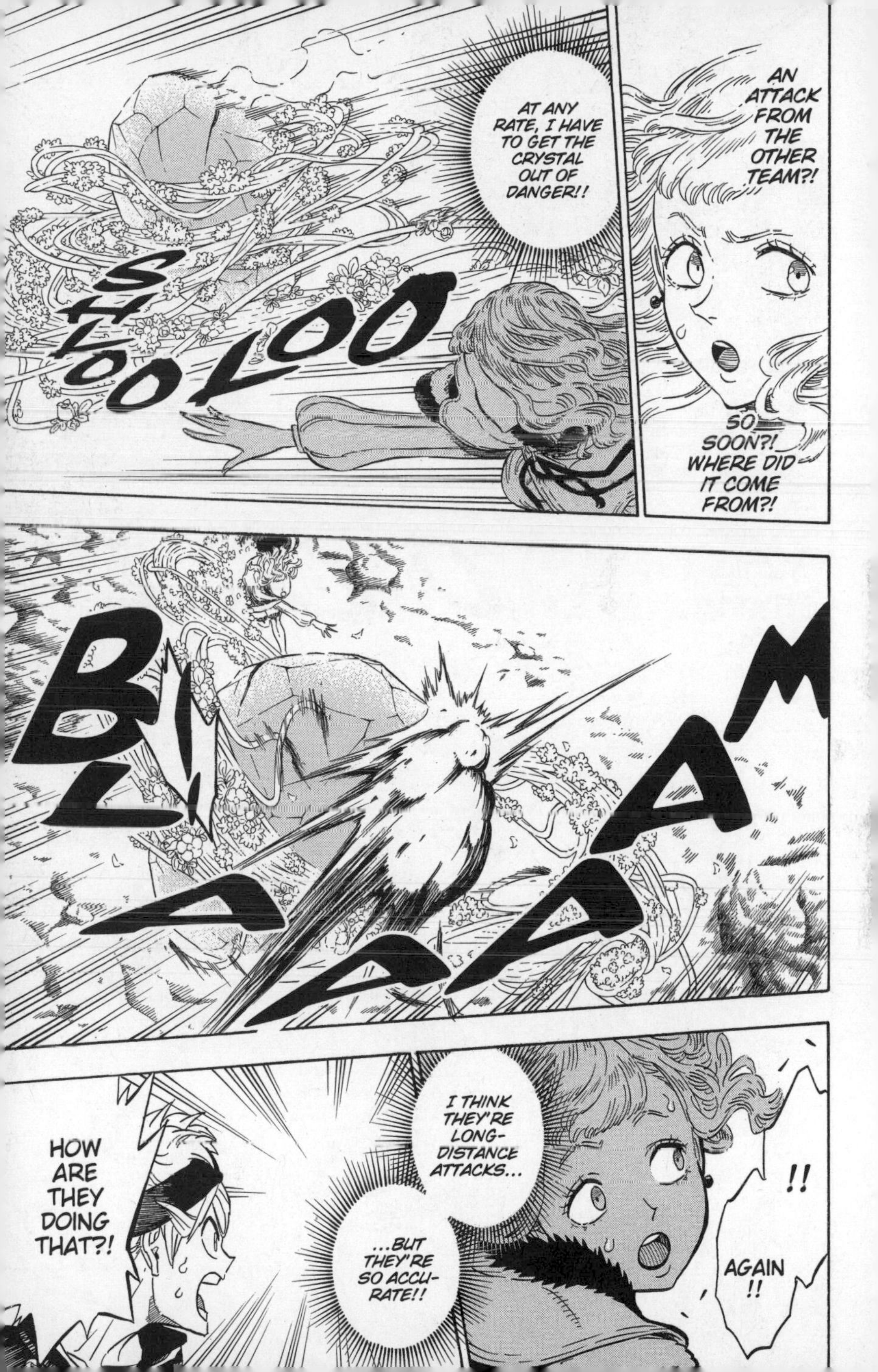
AN ATTACK FROM THE OTHER TEAM?!
SO SOON?! WHERE DID IT COME FROM?!
AT ANY RATE, I HAVE TO GET THE CRYSTAL OUT OF DANGER!!
SHLOOLOO
BLAAAM
!!
AGAIN!!
I THINK THEY'RE LONG-DISTANCE ATTACKS...
...BUT THEY'RE SO ACCURATE!!
HOW ARE THEY DOING THAT?!

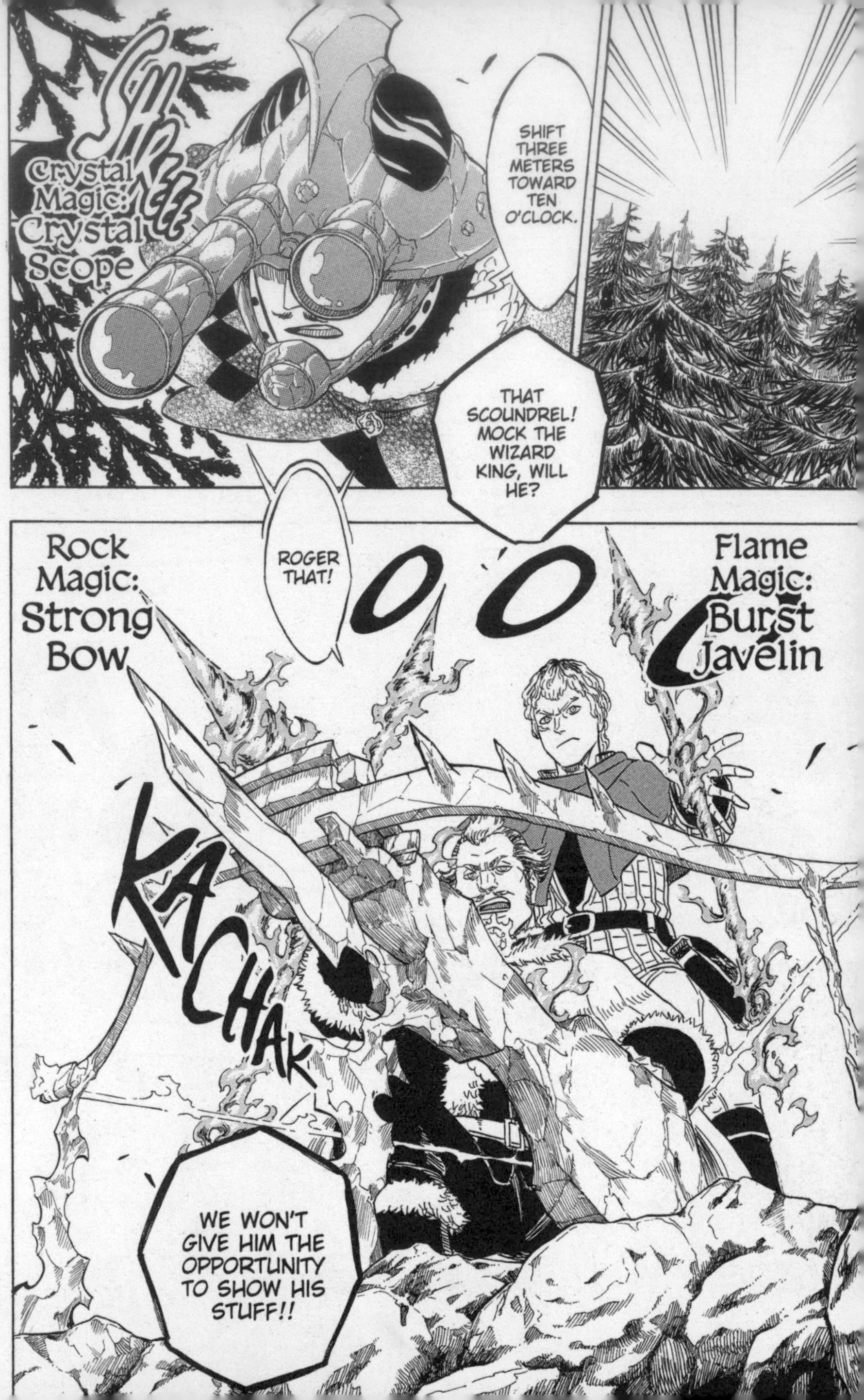
THAT SCOUNDREL! MOCK THE WIZARD KING, WILL HE?
SHHH
Crystal Magic: Crystal Scope
SHIFT THREE METERS TOWARD TEN O'CLOCK.
ROGER THAT!
OOO
Flame Magic: Burst Javelin
Rock Magic: Strong Bow
KACHAK
WE WON'T GIVE HIM THE OPPORTUNITY TO SHOW HIS STUFF!!

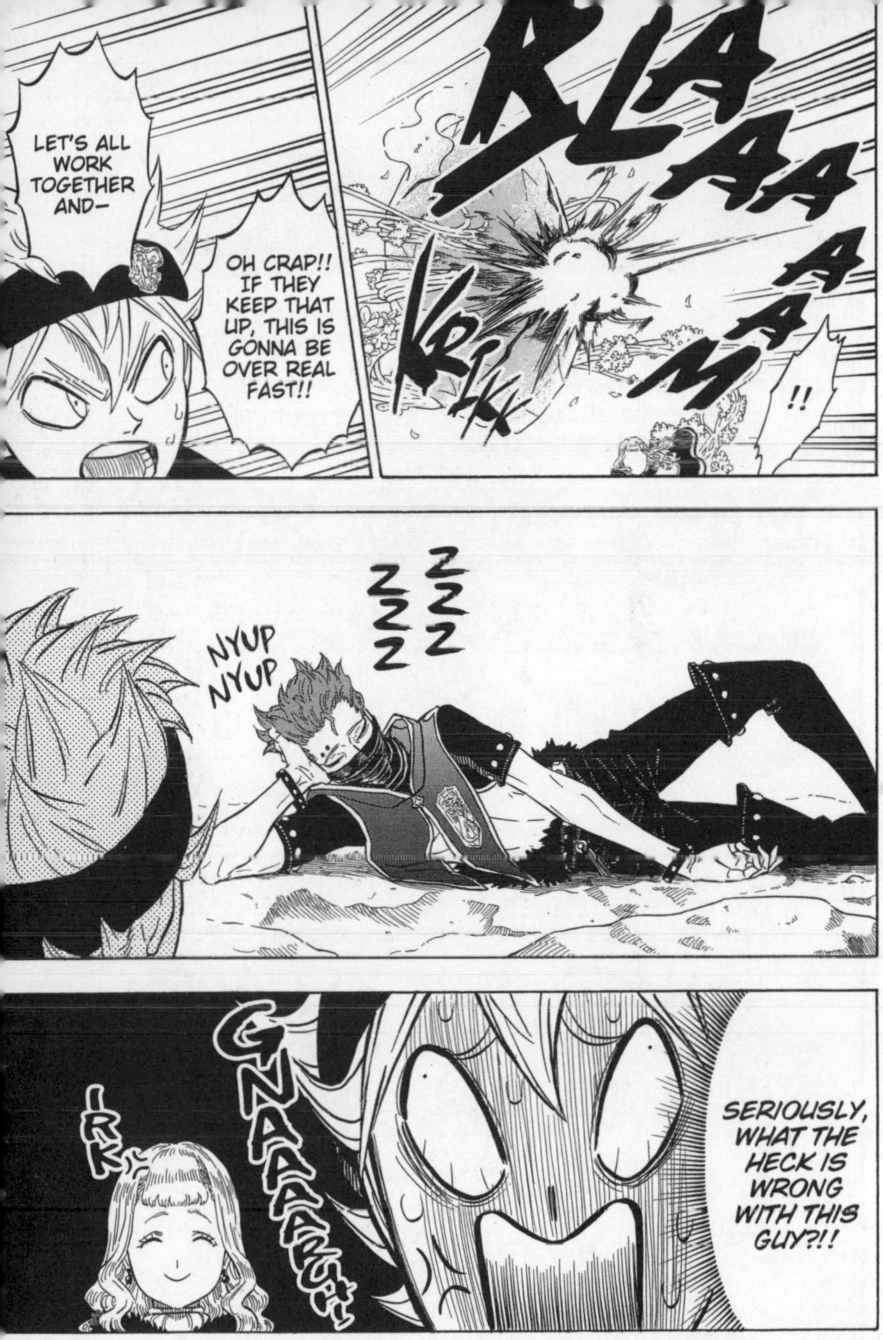
RLAAAAAM
KRIKKK
!!
LET'S ALL WORK TOGETHER AND–
OH CRAP!! IF THEY KEEP THAT UP, THIS IS GONNA BE OVER REAL FAST!!
ZZZ ZZZ
NYUP NYUP
SERIOUSLY, WHAT THE HECK IS WRONG WITH THIS GUY?!!
IRK

The Assorted Questions Brigade No. 2

Q: I'd like to see the captains ranked in order of intelligence. (Would Like to Stay Anonymous)

A: Presenting the captains, ranked in order of intelligence. (In addition to the current captains, I included Fuegoleon and Gueldre.)

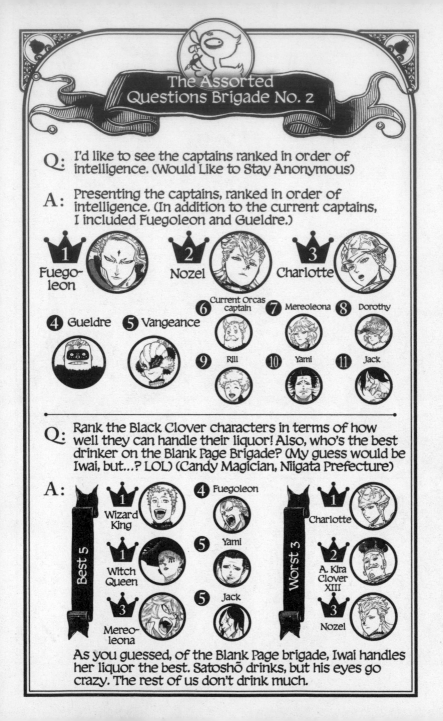

1 Fuegoleon
2 Nozel
3 Charlotte
4 Gueldre
5 Vangeance
6 Current Orcas captain
7 Mereoleona
8 Dorothy
9 Rill
10 Yami
11 Jack

Q: Rank the Black Clover characters in terms of how well they can handle their liquor! Also, who's the best drinker on the Blank Page Brigade? (My guess would be Iwai, but...? LOL) (Candy Magician, Niigata Prefecture)

A:

Best 5
1 Wizard King
1 Witch Queen
3 Mereoleona
4 Fuegoleon
5 Yami
5 Jack

Worst 3
1 Charlotte
2 A. Kira Clover XIII
3 Nozel

As you guessed, of the Blank Page brigade, Iwai handles her liquor the best. Satoshō drinks, but his eyes go crazy. The rest of us don't drink much.

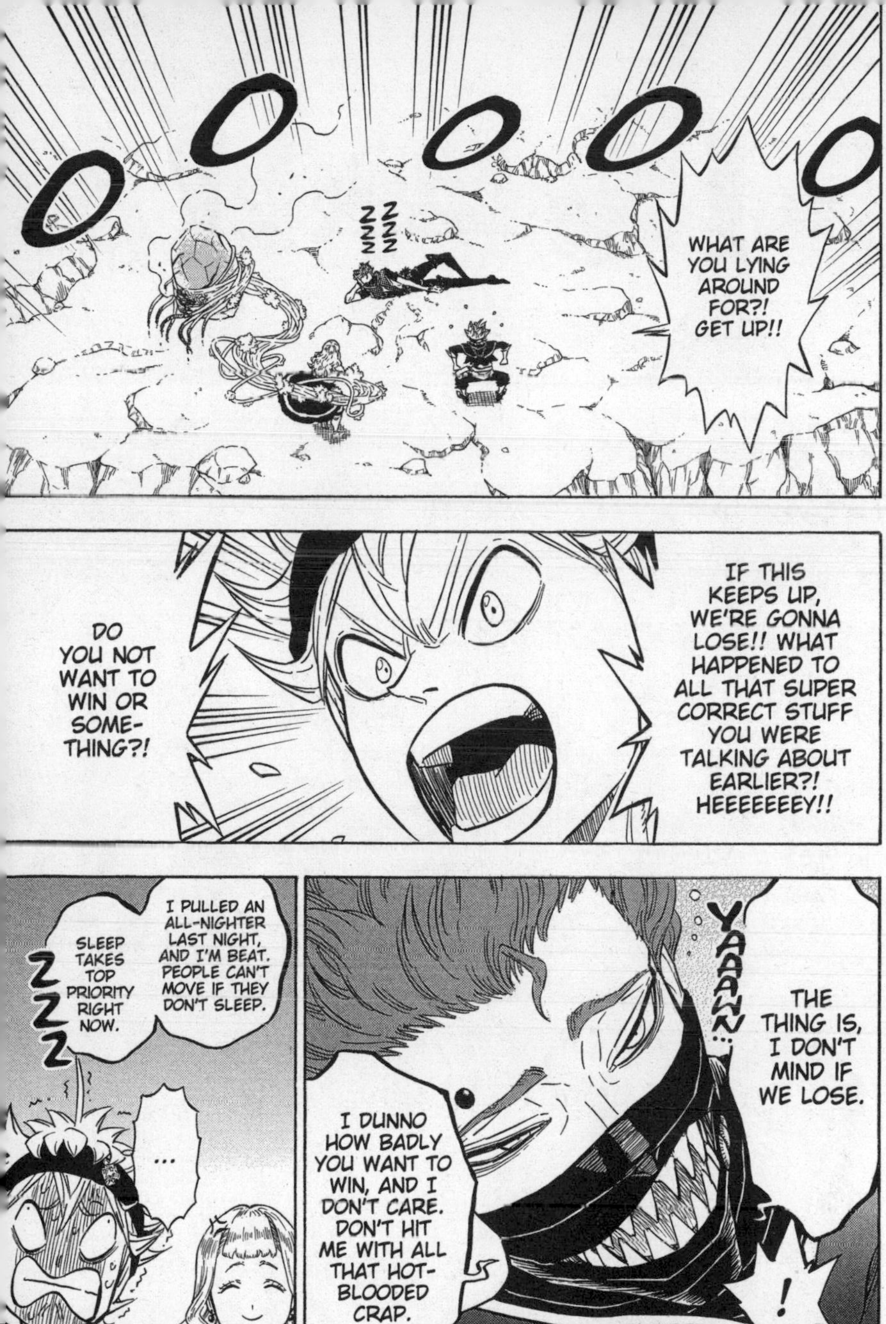
OOOOOO
WHAT ARE YOU LYING AROUND FOR?! GET UP!!
ZZZ
IF THIS KEEPS UP, WE'RE GONNA LOSE!! WHAT HAPPENED TO ALL THAT SUPER CORRECT STUFF YOU WERE TALKING ABOUT EARLIER?! HEEEEEEEY!!
DO YOU NOT WANT TO WIN OR SOME-THING?!
YAAAWN...
THE THING IS, I DON'T MIND IF WE LOSE.
I DUNNO HOW BADLY YOU WANT TO WIN, AND I DON'T CARE. DON'T HIT ME WITH ALL THAT HOT-BLOODED CRAP.
!
I PULLED AN ALL-NIGHTER LAST NIGHT, AND I'M BEAT. PEOPLE CAN'T MOVE IF THEY DON'T SLEEP.
SLEEP TAKES TOP PRIORITY RIGHT NOW.
ZZZ
...

Page 114: Flower of Resolution

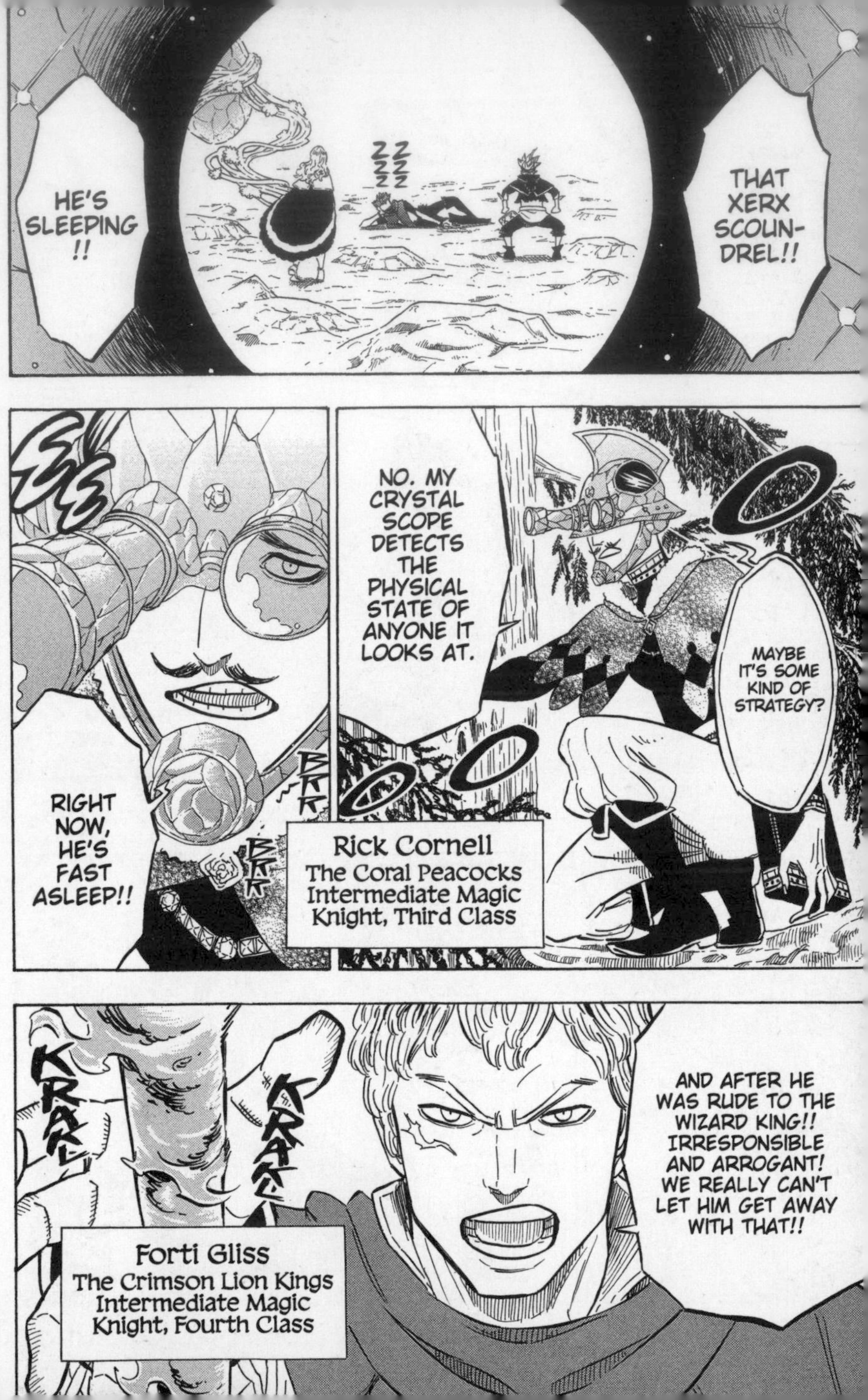
THAT XERX SCOUN-DREL!!
ZZZZZZ
HE'S SLEEPING!!
MAYBE IT'S SOME KIND OF STRATEGY?
NO. MY CRYSTAL SCOPE DETECTS THE PHYSICAL STATE OF ANYONE IT LOOKS AT.
Rick Cornell
The Coral Peacocks Intermediate Magic Knight, Third Class
BRR
BRR
RIGHT NOW, HE'S FAST ASLEEP!!
AND AFTER HE WAS RUDE TO THE WIZARD KING!! IRRESPONSIBLE AND ARROGANT! WE REALLY CAN'T LET HIM GET AWAY WITH THAT!!
KRAK
KRAK
Forti Gliss
The Crimson Lion Kings Intermediate Magic Knight, Fourth Class

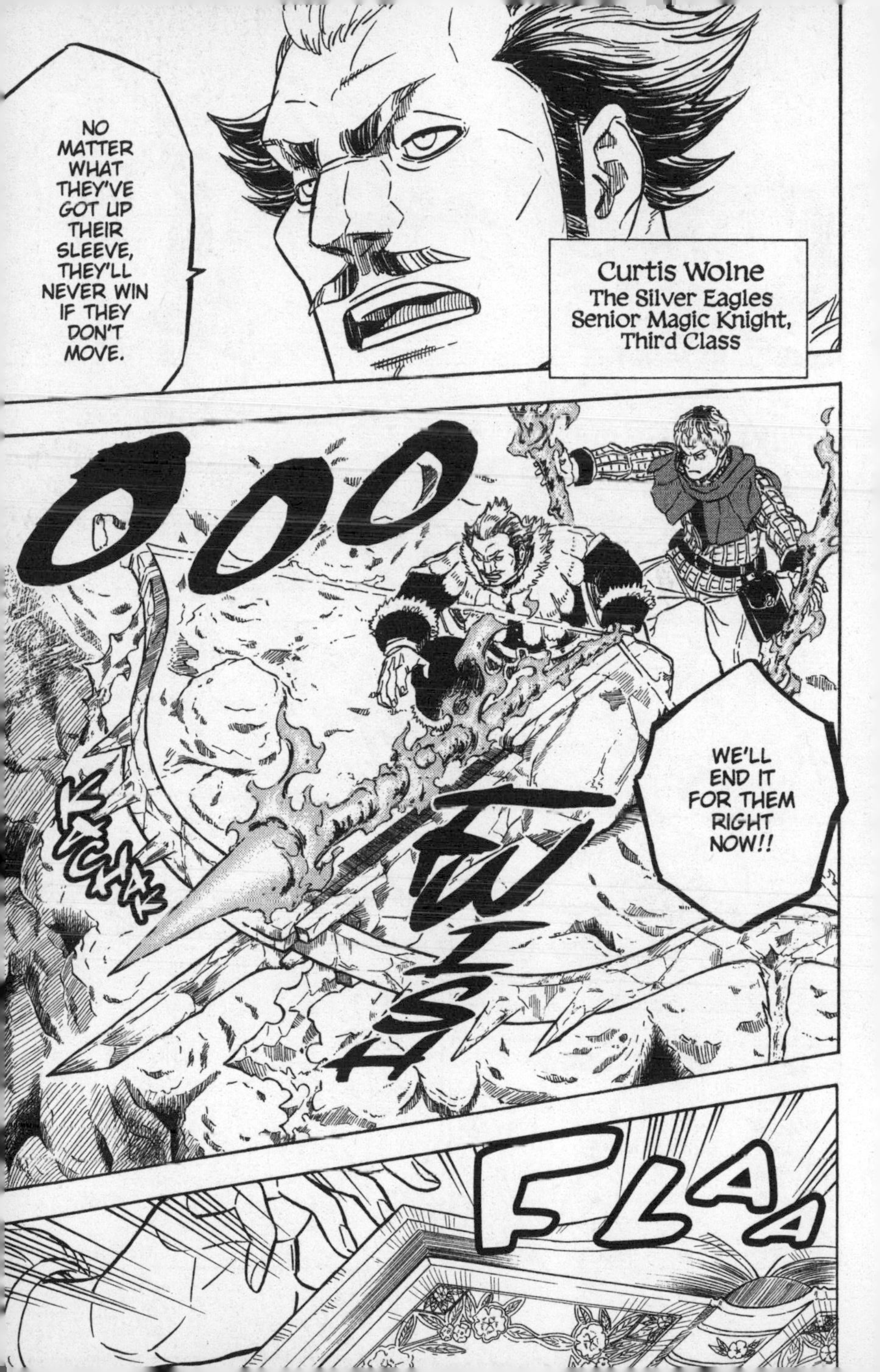
Curtis Wolne
The Silver Eagles Senior Magic Knight, Third Class
NO MATTER WHAT THEY'VE GOT UP THEIR SLEEVE, THEY'LL NEVER WIN IF THEY DON'T MOVE.
OOO
WE'LL END IT FOR THEM RIGHT NOW!!
TWISH
KATCHAK
FLAA

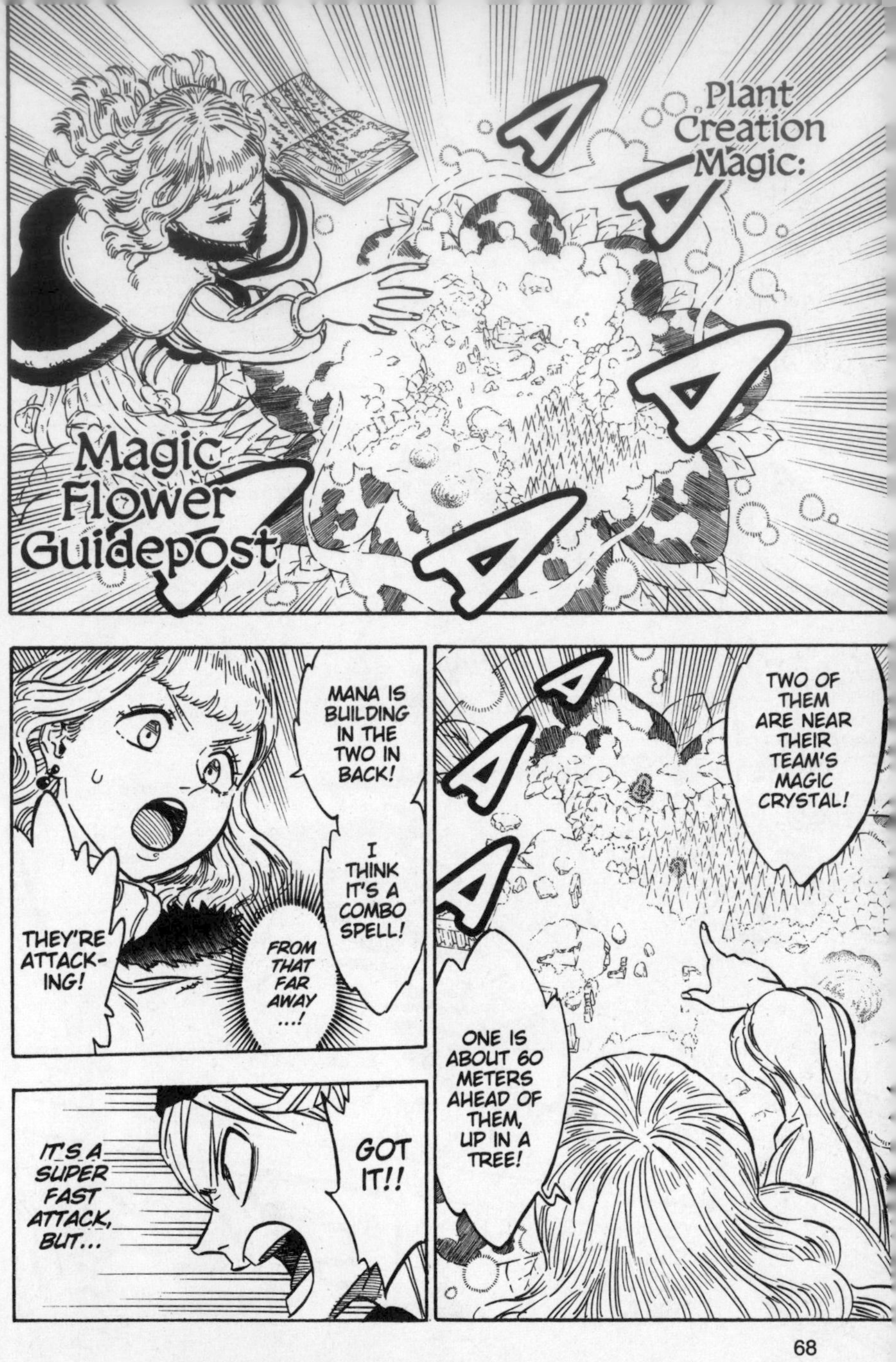
Plant Creation Magic:
AAAA
Magic Flower Guidepost
AAA
TWO OF THEM ARE NEAR THEIR TEAM'S MAGIC CRYSTAL!
ONE IS ABOUT 60 METERS AHEAD OF THEM, UP IN A TREE!
MANA IS BUILDING IN THE TWO IN BACK!
I THINK IT'S A COMBO SPELL!
FROM THAT FAR AWAY...!
THEY'RE ATTACKING!
GOT IT!!
IT'S A SUPER FAST ATTACK, BUT...

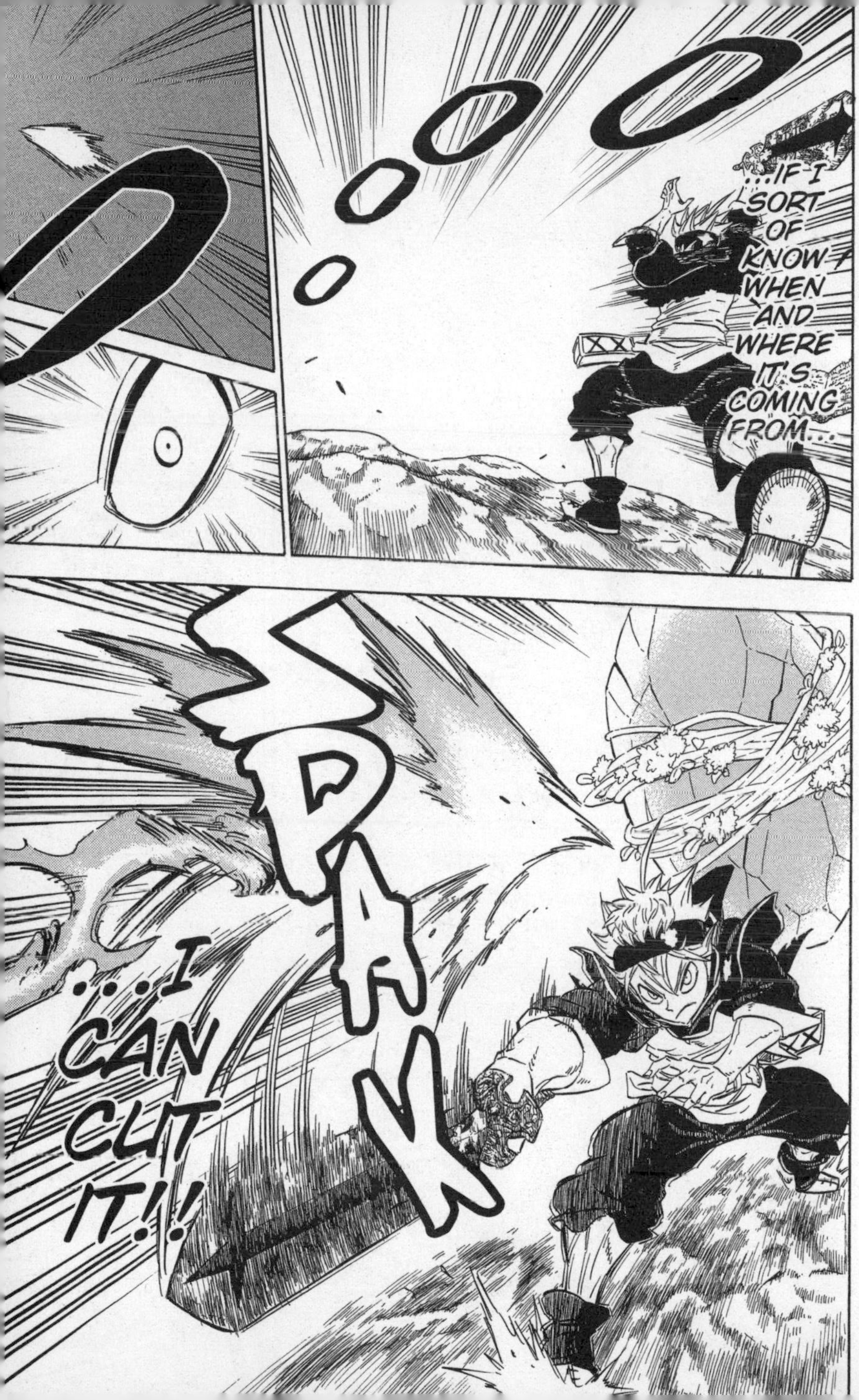
...IF I SORT OF KNOW WHEN AND WHERE IT'S COMING FROM...
SPAK
...I CAN CUT IT!!

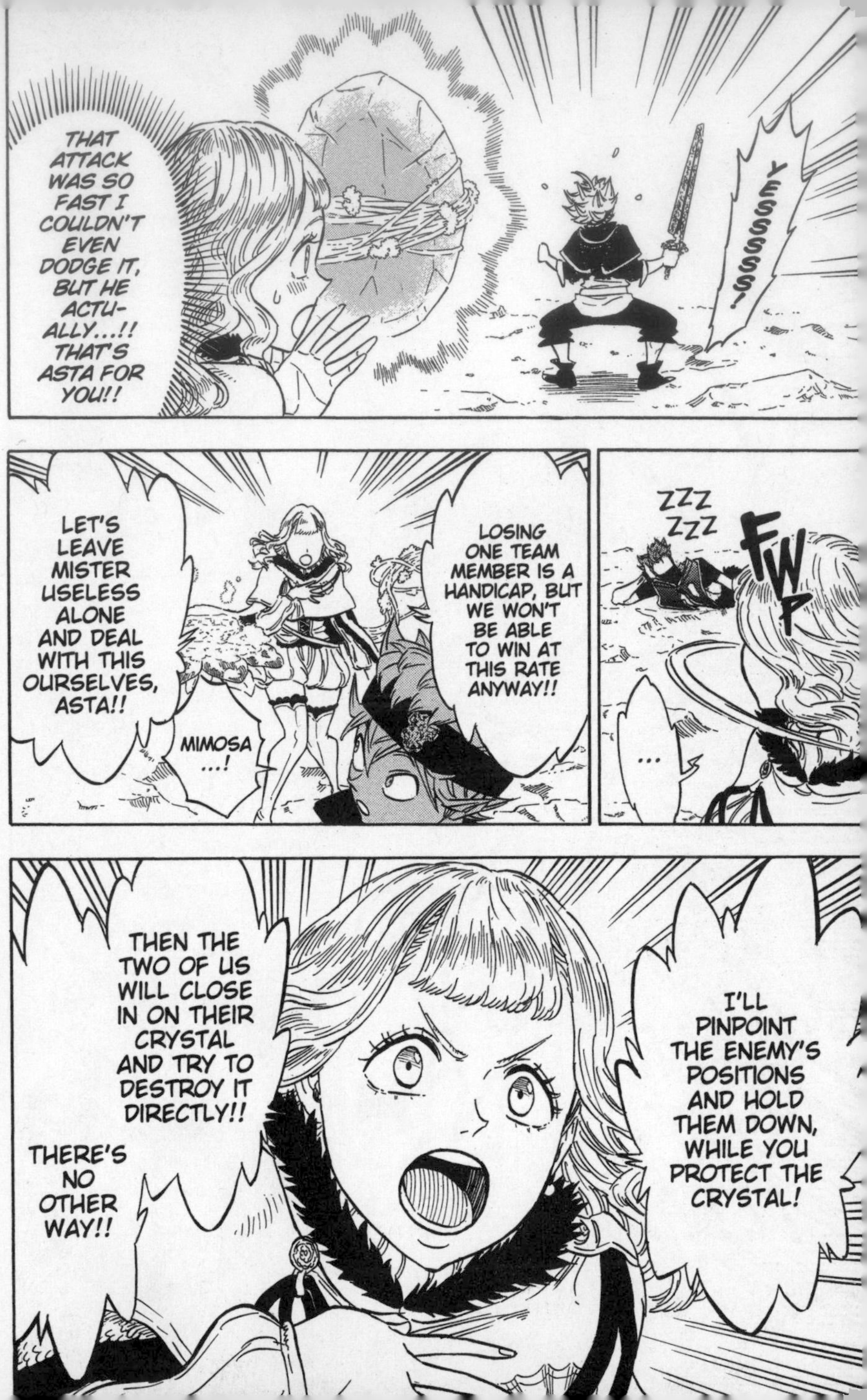
YESSSSS!
THAT ATTACK WAS SO FAST I COULDN'T EVEN DODGE IT, BUT HE ACTUALLY...!! THAT'S ASTA FOR YOU!!
ZZZ ZZZ
FWP
...
LOSING ONE TEAM MEMBER IS A HANDICAP, BUT WE WON'T BE ABLE TO WIN AT THIS RATE ANYWAY!!
LET'S LEAVE MISTER USELESS ALONE AND DEAL WITH THIS OURSELVES, ASTA!!
MIMOSA ...!
I'LL PINPOINT THE ENEMY'S POSITIONS AND HOLD THEM DOWN, WHILE YOU PROTECT THE CRYSTAL!
THEN THE TWO OF US WILL CLOSE IN ON THEIR CRYSTAL AND TRY TO DESTROY IT DIRECTLY!!
THERE'S NO OTHER WAY!!

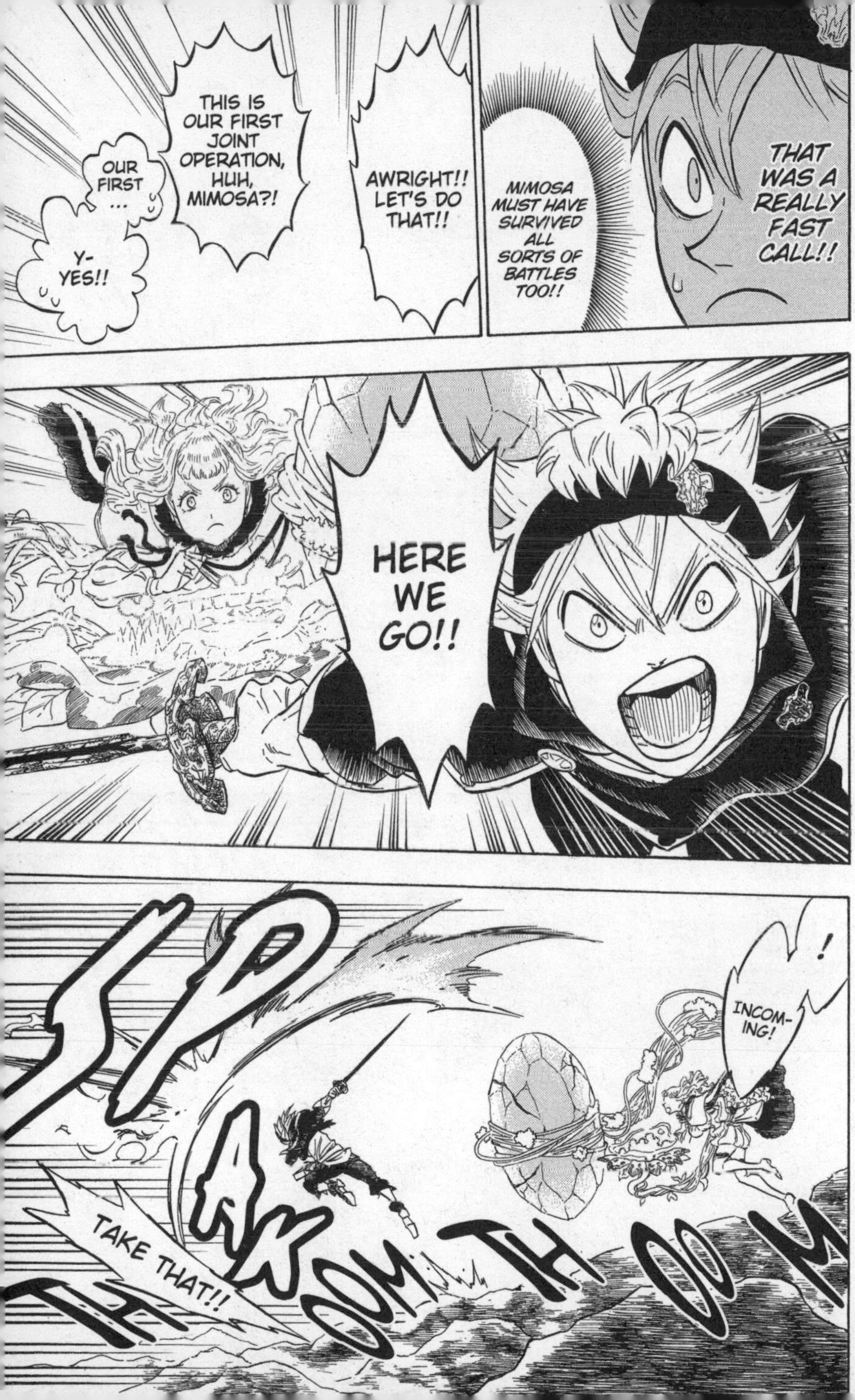

THAT WAS A REALLY FAST CALL!!
MIMOSA MUST HAVE SURVIVED ALL SORTS OF BATTLES TOO!!
AWRIGHT!! LET'S DO THAT!!
THIS IS OUR FIRST JOINT OPERATION, HUH, MIMOSA?!
OUR FIRST ...
Y- YES!!
HERE WE GO!!
!
INCOMING!
SHAK
THOOM THOOM
TAKE THAT!!

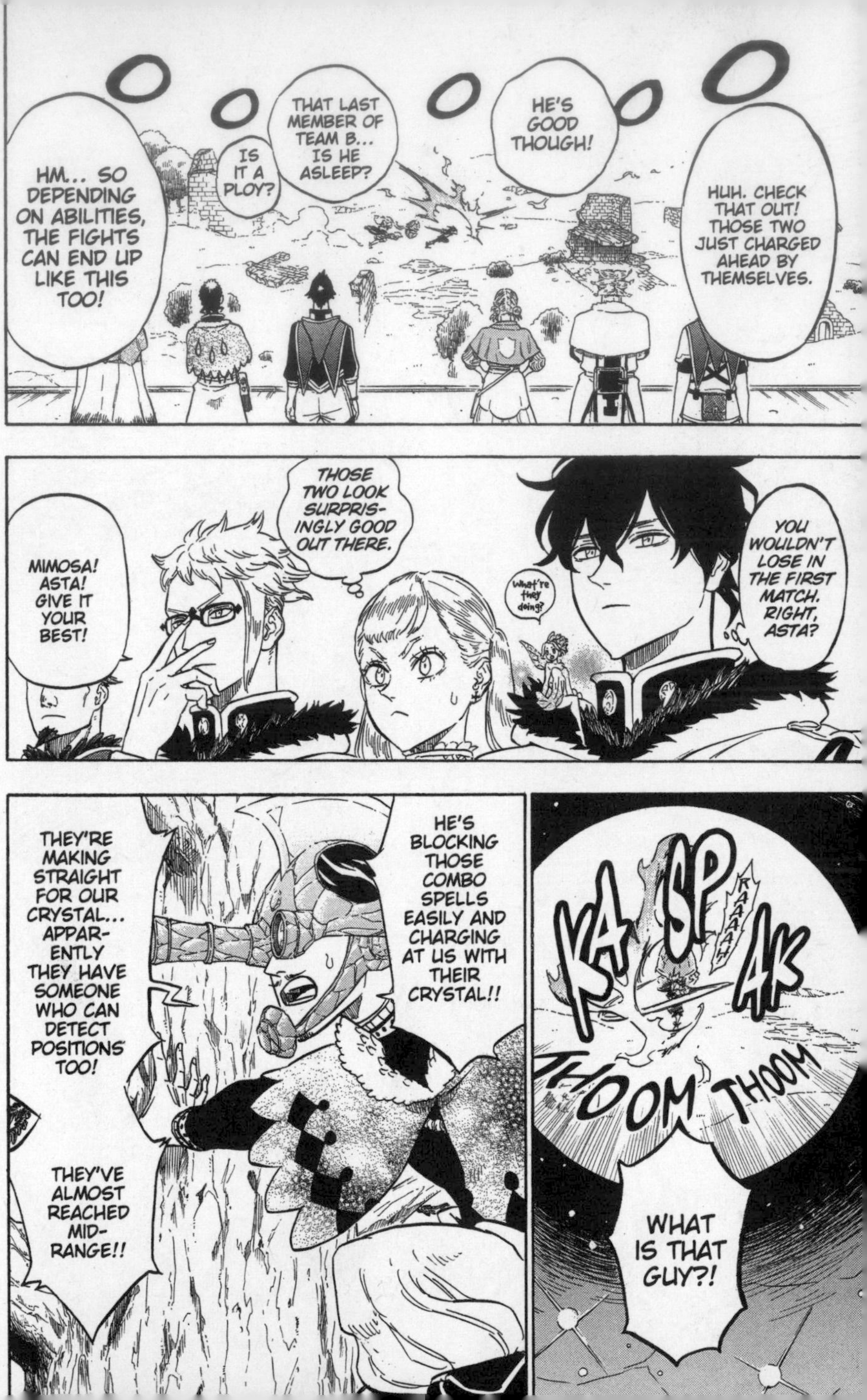
HUH. CHECK THAT OUT! THOSE TWO JUST CHARGED AHEAD BY THEMSELVES.
HE'S GOOD THOUGH!
THAT LAST MEMBER OF TEAM B... IS HE ASLEEP?
IS IT A PLOY?
HM... SO DEPENDING ON ABILITIES, THE FIGHTS CAN END UP LIKE THIS TOO!
YOU WOULDN'T LOSE IN THE FIRST MATCH. RIGHT, ASTA?
What're they doing?
THOSE TWO LOOK SURPRISINGLY GOOD OUT THERE.
MIMOSA! ASTA! GIVE IT YOUR BEST!
KA SPAK
RAAAAH
THOOM THOOM
WHAT IS THAT GUY?!
HE'S BLOCKING THOSE COMBO SPELLS EASILY AND CHARGING AT US WITH THEIR CRYSTAL!!
THEY'RE MAKING STRAIGHT FOR OUR CRYSTAL... APPARENTLY THEY HAVE SOMEONE WHO CAN DETECT POSITIONS TOO!
THEY'VE ALMOST REACHED MID-RANGE!!

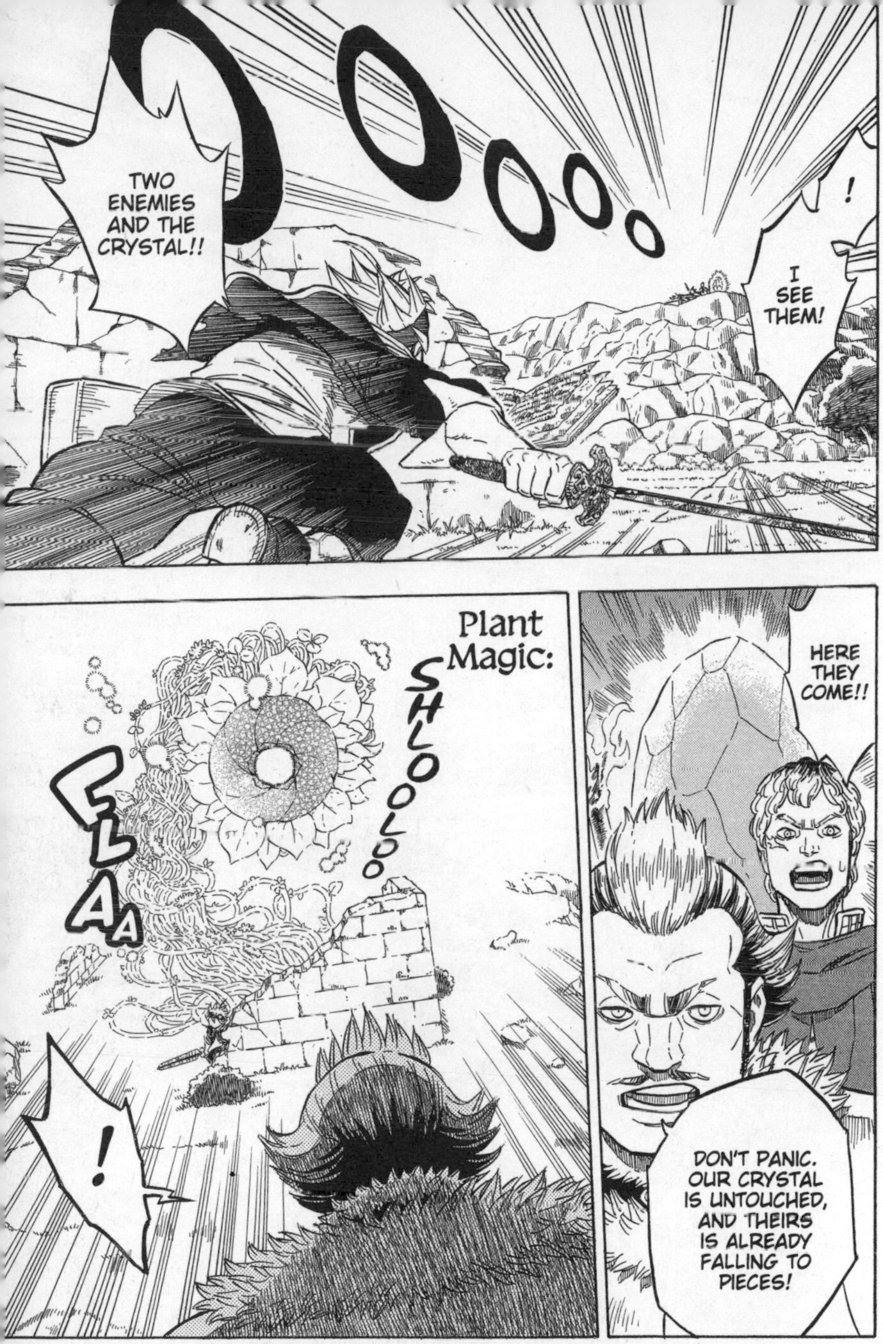
!
I SEE THEM!
TWO ENEMIES AND THE CRYSTAL!!
HERE THEY COME!!
DON'T PANIC. OUR CRYSTAL IS UNTOUCHED, AND THEIRS IS ALREADY FALLING TO PIECES!
Plant Magic:
SHLOOOLOO
FLAAA
!

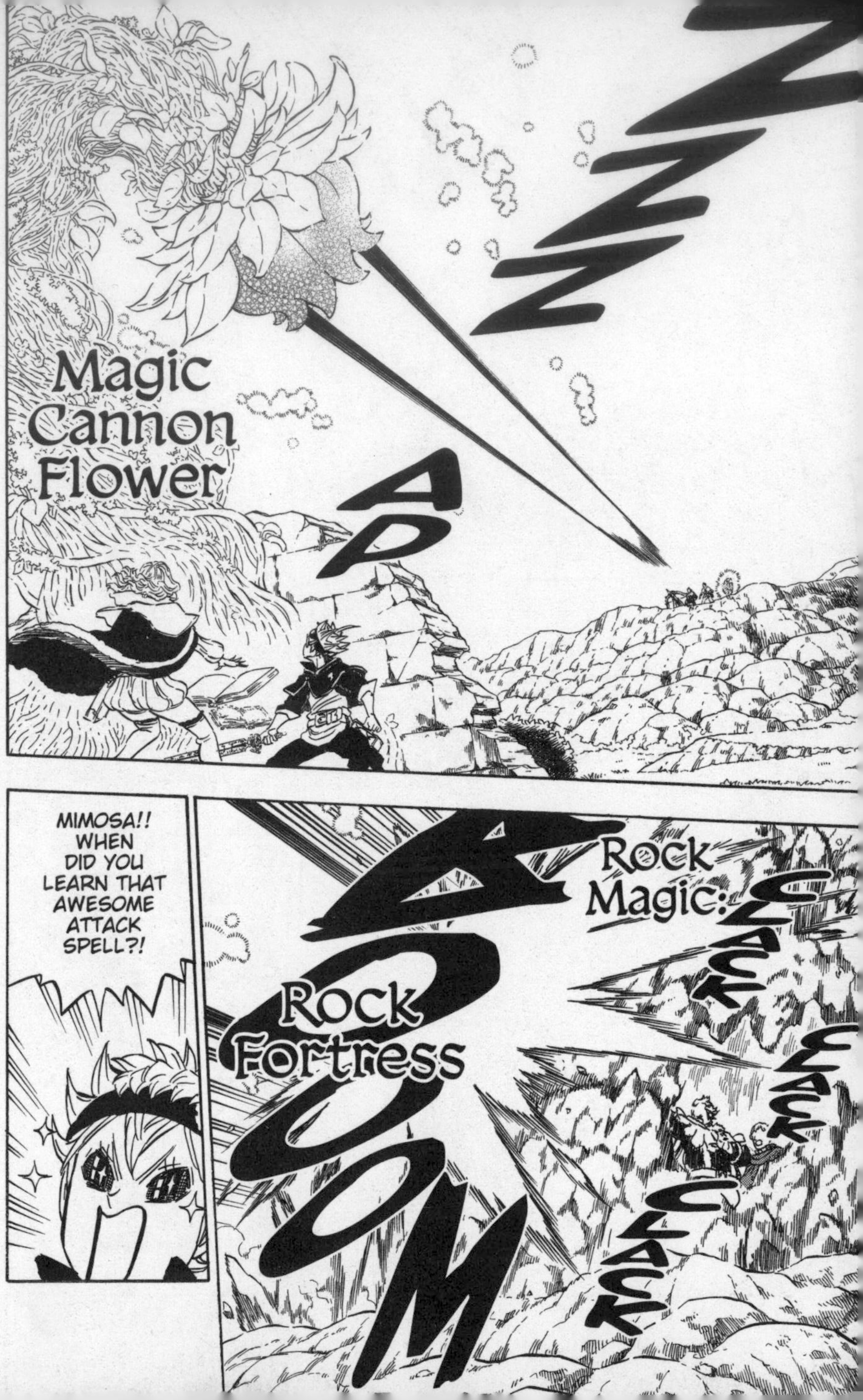
Magic Cannon Flower
Rock Magic:
Rock Fortress
CLACK
CLACK
CLACK
MIMOSA!! WHEN DID YOU LEARN THAT AWESOME ATTACK SPELL?!

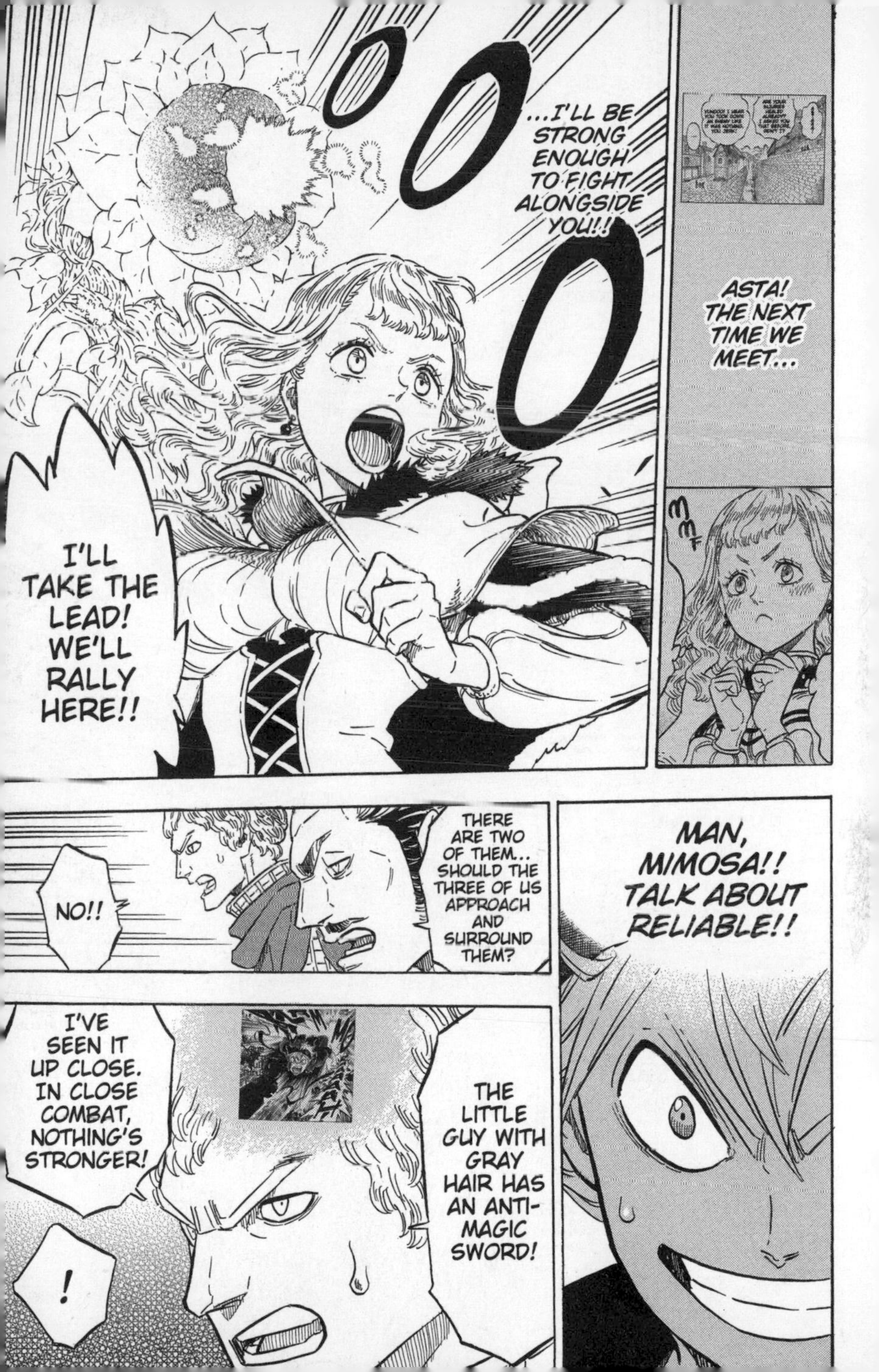
ASTA! THE NEXT TIME WE MEET...
MMF
...I'LL BE STRONG ENOUGH TO FIGHT ALONGSIDE YOU!!
I'LL TAKE THE LEAD! WE'LL RALLY HERE!!
MAN, MIMOSA!! TALK ABOUT RELIABLE!!
THERE ARE TWO OF THEM... SHOULD THE THREE OF US APPROACH AND SURROUND THEM?
NO!!
THE LITTLE GUY WITH GRAY HAIR HAS AN ANTI-MAGIC SWORD!
I'VE SEEN IT UP CLOSE. IN CLOSE COMBAT, NOTHING'S STRONGER!
!

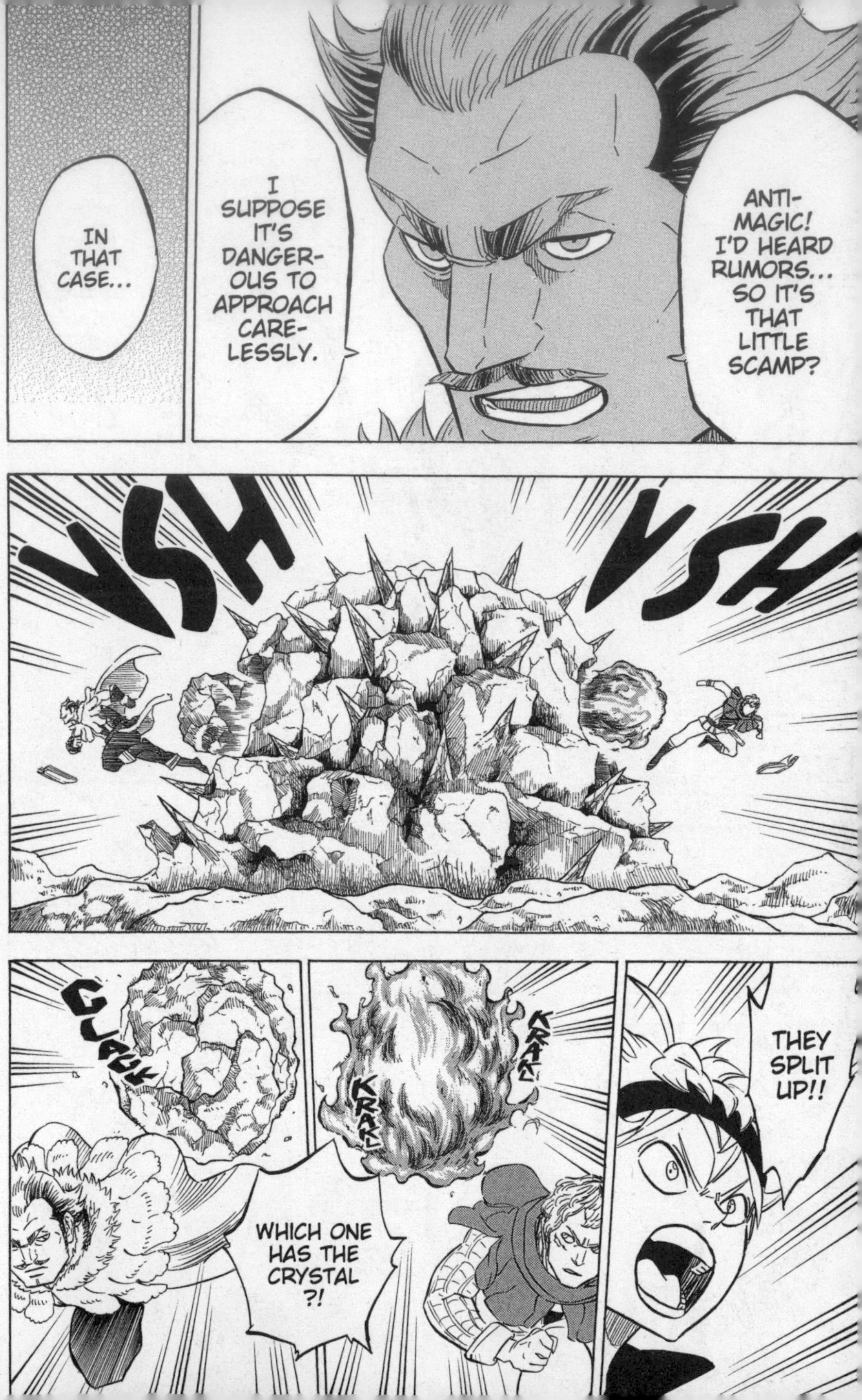
ANTI-MAGIC! I'D HEARD RUMORS... SO IT'S THAT LITTLE SCAMP?
I SUPPOSE IT'S DANGEROUS TO APPROACH CARELESSLY.
IN THAT CASE...
VSH
VSH
THEY SPLIT UP!!
KRAK
KRAK
WHICH ONE HAS THE CRYSTAL ?!
GLACK

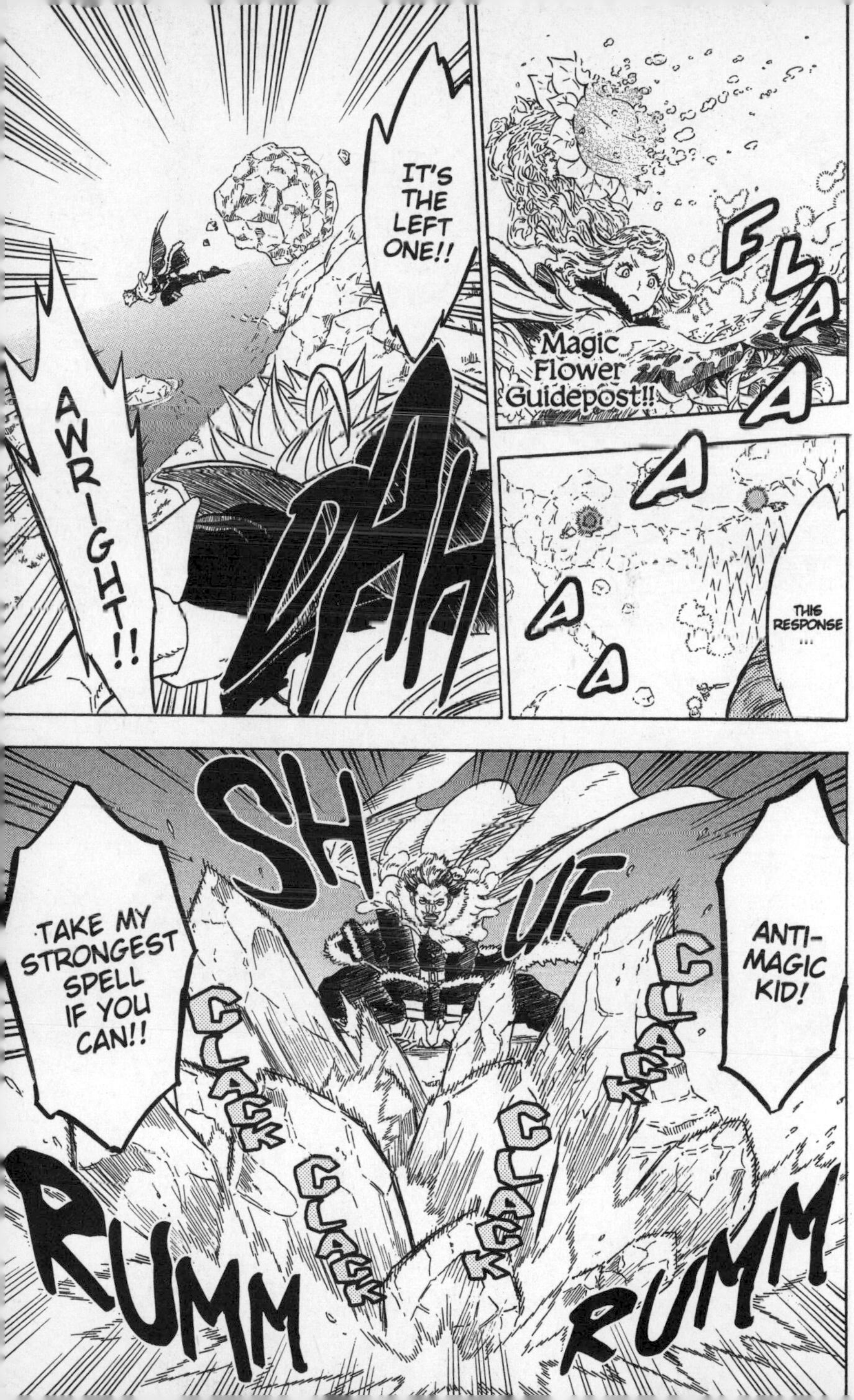

Magic Flower Guidepost!!
FLAAAAAA
THIS RESPONSE...
IT'S THE LEFT ONE!!
AWRIGHT!!
ANTI-MAGIC KID!
TAKE MY STRONGEST SPELL IF YOU CAN!!
SHUF
CLACK CLACK
CLACK CLACK
CLACK CLACK
RUMM
RUMM

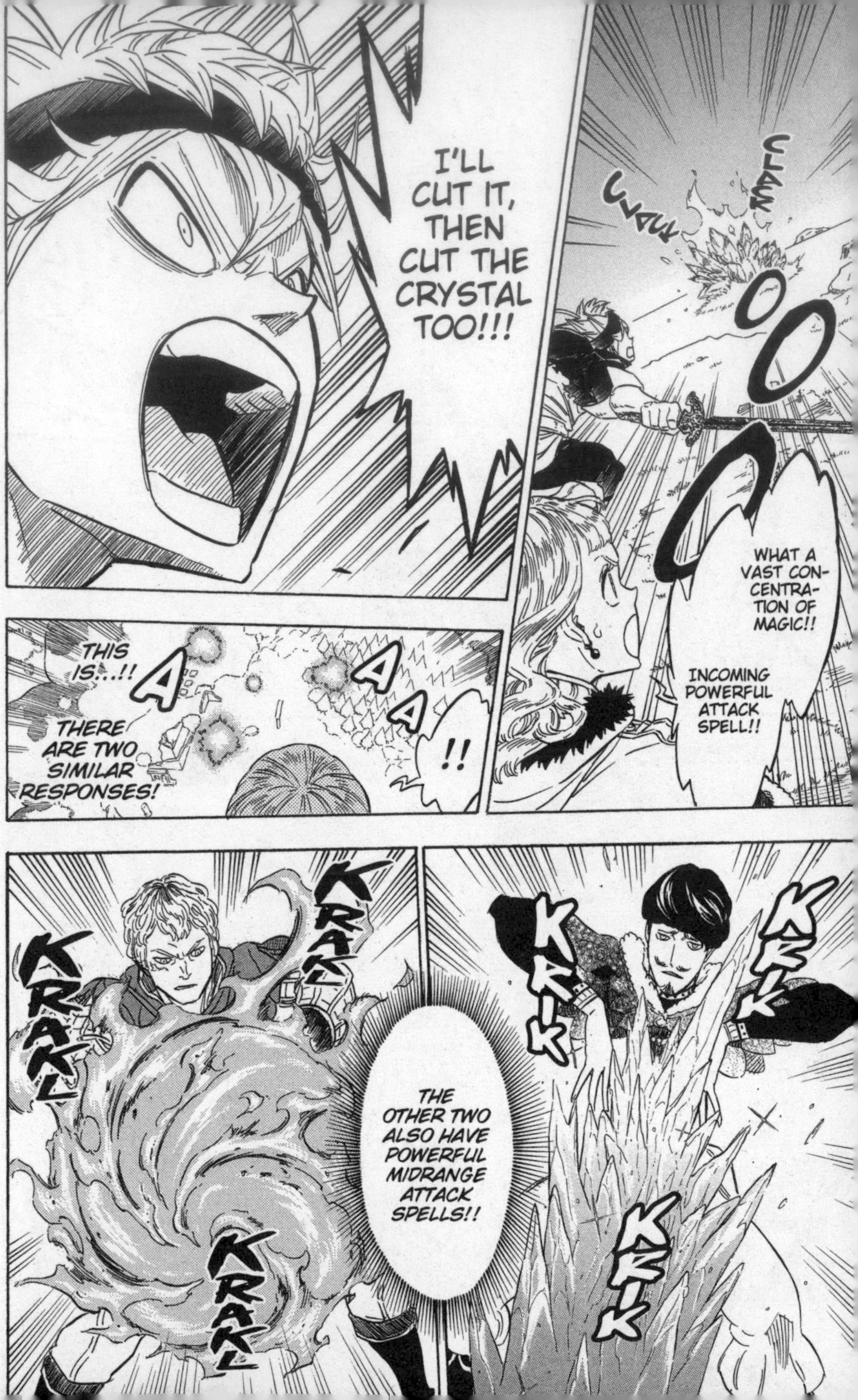
CLACK
WHAT A VAST CONCENTRATION OF MAGIC!!
INCOMING POWERFUL ATTACK SPELL!!
I'LL CUT IT, THEN CUT THE CRYSTAL TOO!!!
THIS IS...!!
THERE ARE TWO SIMILAR RESPONSES!
AAA
!!
KRIK KRIK
THE OTHER TWO ALSO HAVE POWERFUL MIDRANGE ATTACK SPELLS!!
KRIK
KRAKL KRAKL
KRAKL

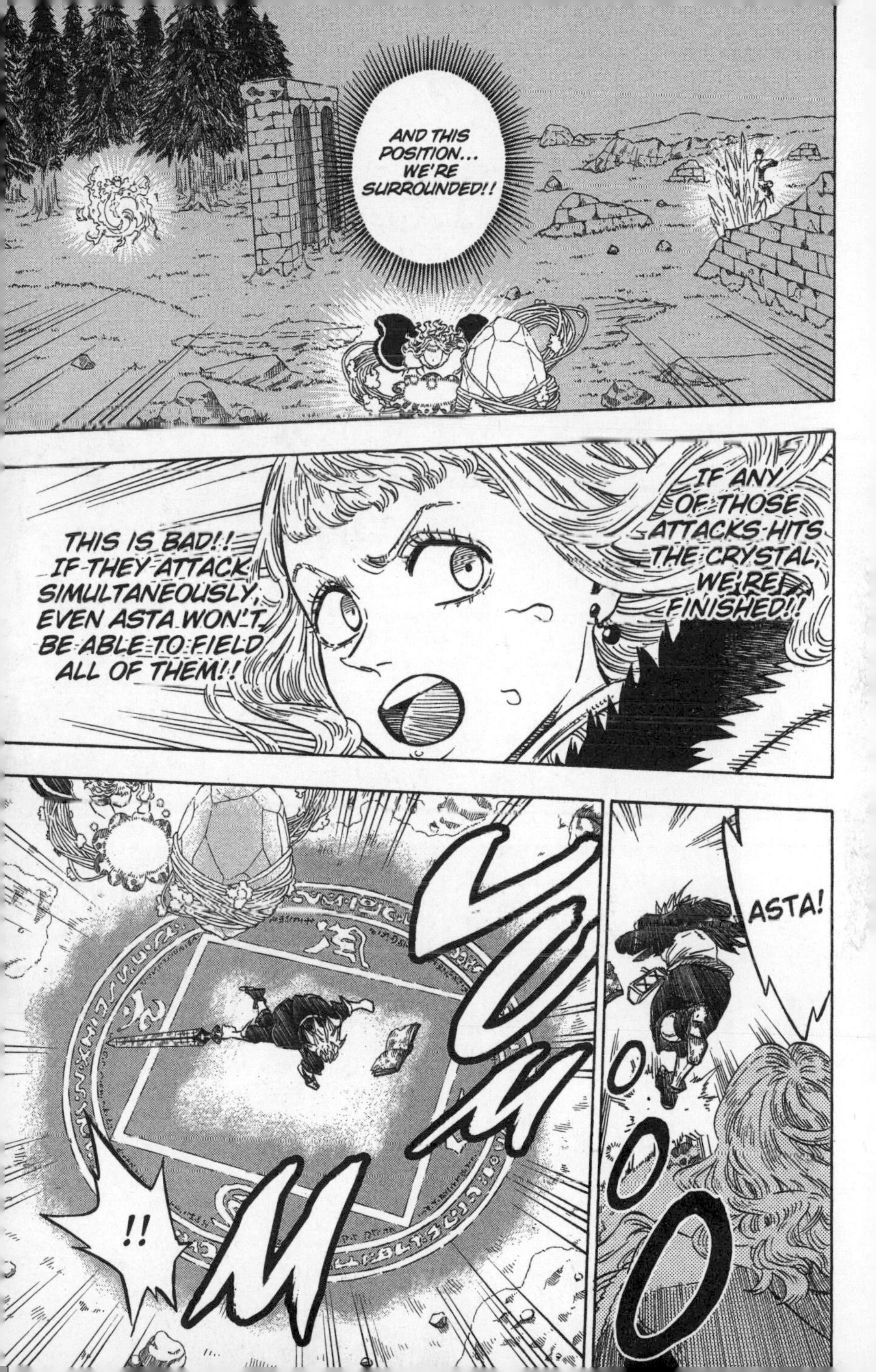
AND THIS POSITION... WE'RE SURROUNDED!!
IF ANY OF THOSE ATTACKS HITS THE CRYSTAL, WE'RE FINISHED!!
THIS IS BAD!! IF THEY ATTACK SIMULTANEOUSLY, EVEN ASTA WON'T BE ABLE TO FIELD ALL OF THEM!!
ASTA!
!!

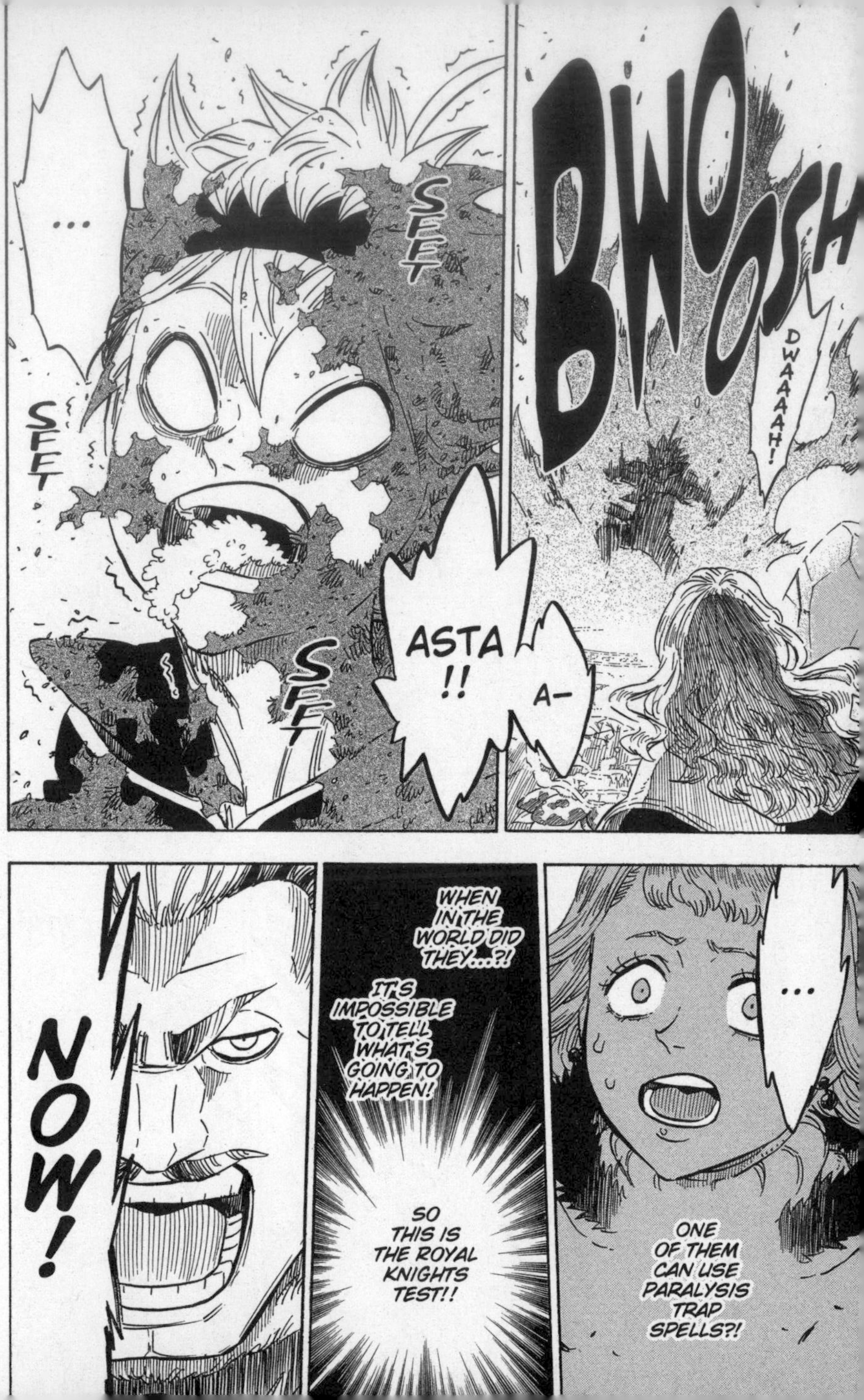
BWOOSH
DWAAAAAH!
A-
ASTA!!
...
SFFT
SFEET
SFFT
...
ONE OF THEM CAN USE PARALYSIS TRAP SPELLS?!
WHEN IN THE WORLD DID THEY...?!
IT'S IMPOSSIBLE TO TELL WHAT'S GOING TO HAPPEN!
SO THIS IS THE ROYAL KNIGHTS TEST!!
NOW!

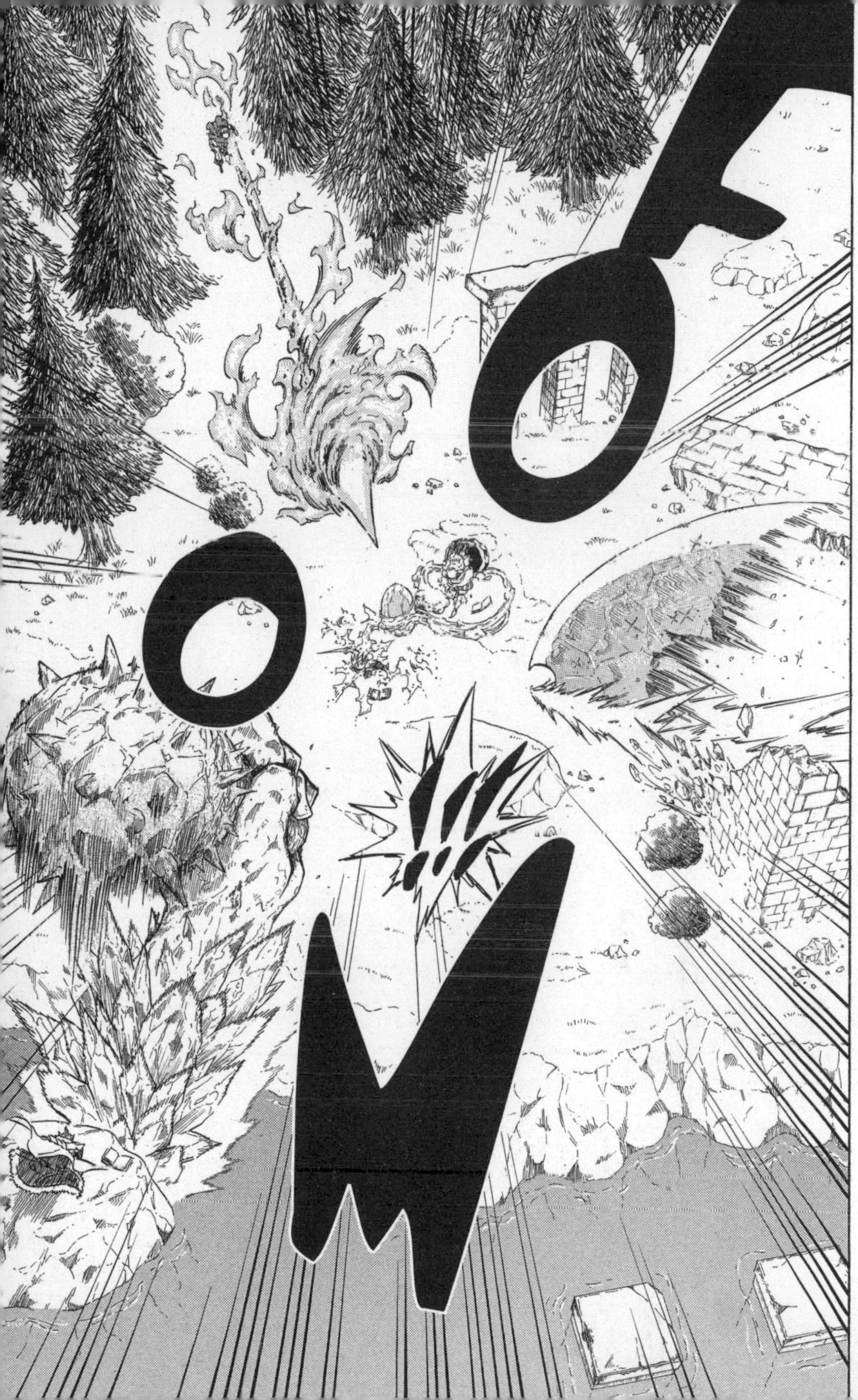

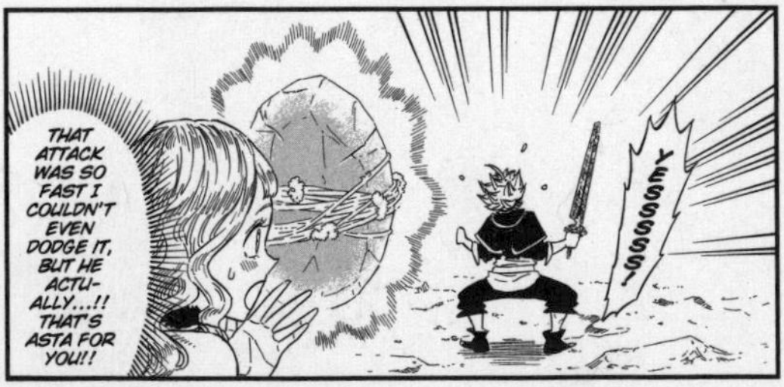
YESSSSSS!
THAT ATTACK WAS SO FAST I COULDN'T EVEN DODGE IT, BUT HE ACTUALLY...!! THAT'S ASTA FOR YOU!!

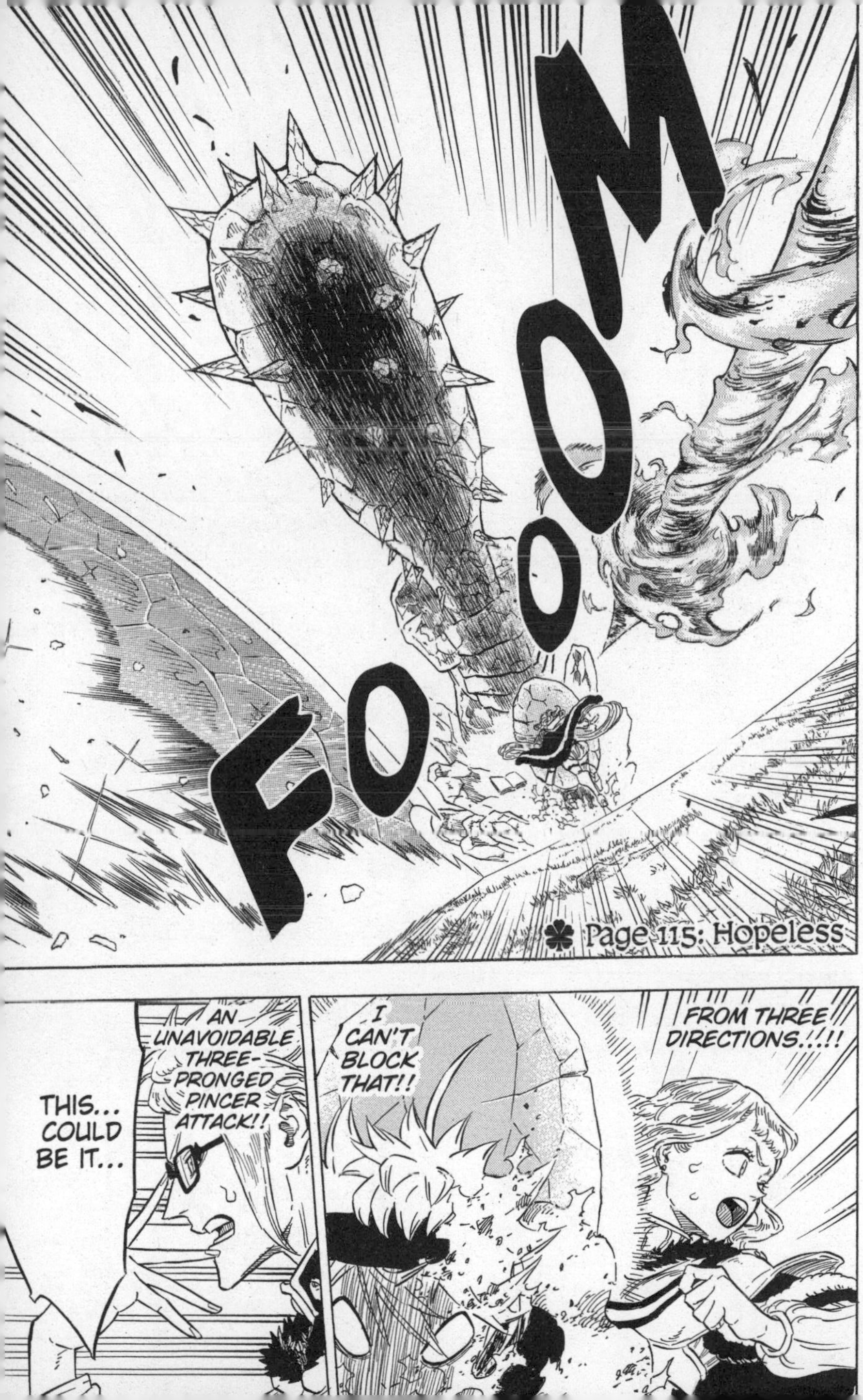
FOOOOM
Page 115: Hopeless
FROM THREE DIRECTIONS...!!
I CAN'T BLOCK THAT!!
AN UNAVOIDABLE THREE-PRONGED PINCER ATTACK!!
THIS... COULD BE IT...

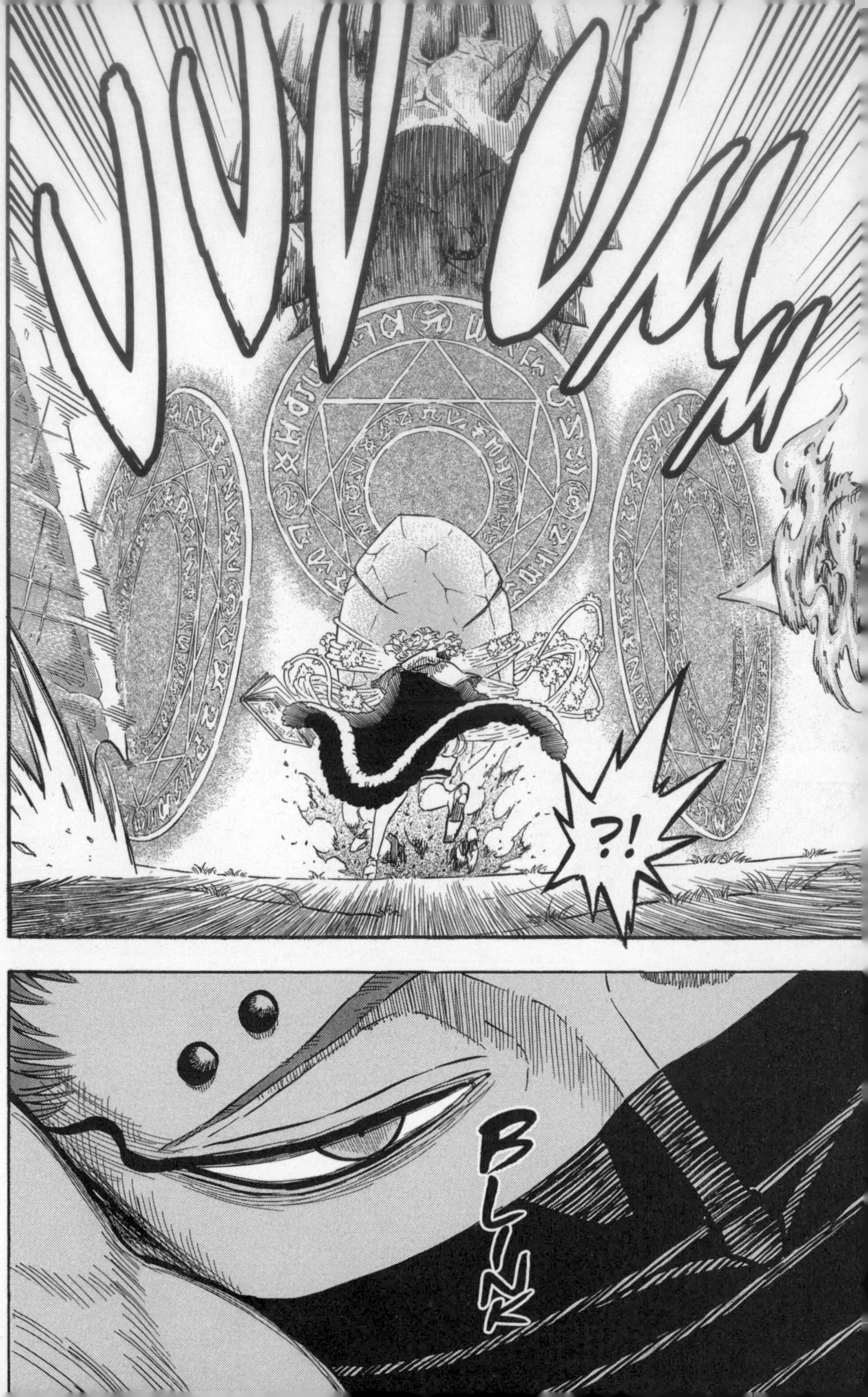
?!
BLINK

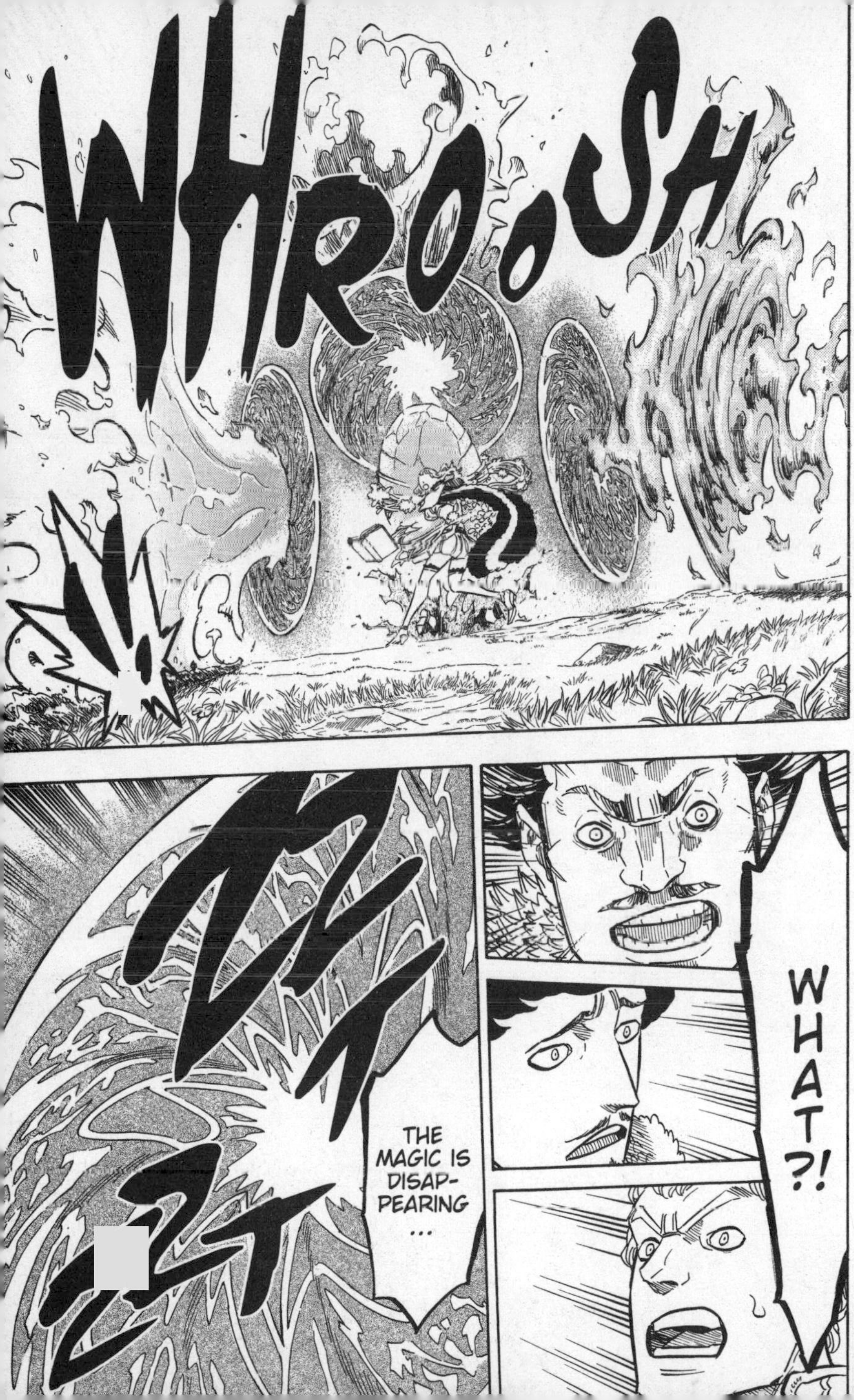
WHROOSH
WHAT?!
THE MAGIC IS DISAPPEARING...

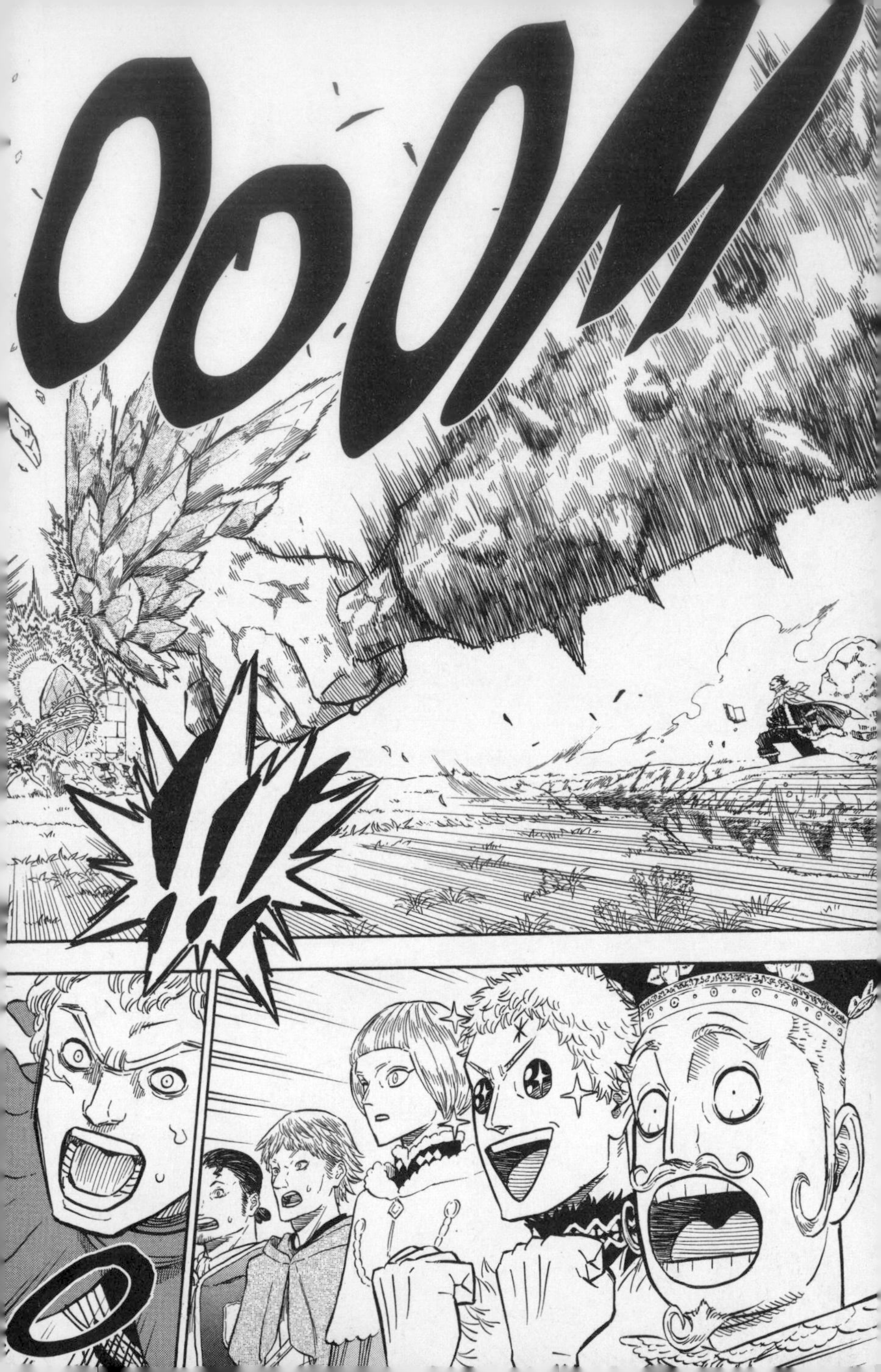
OOOM
!!

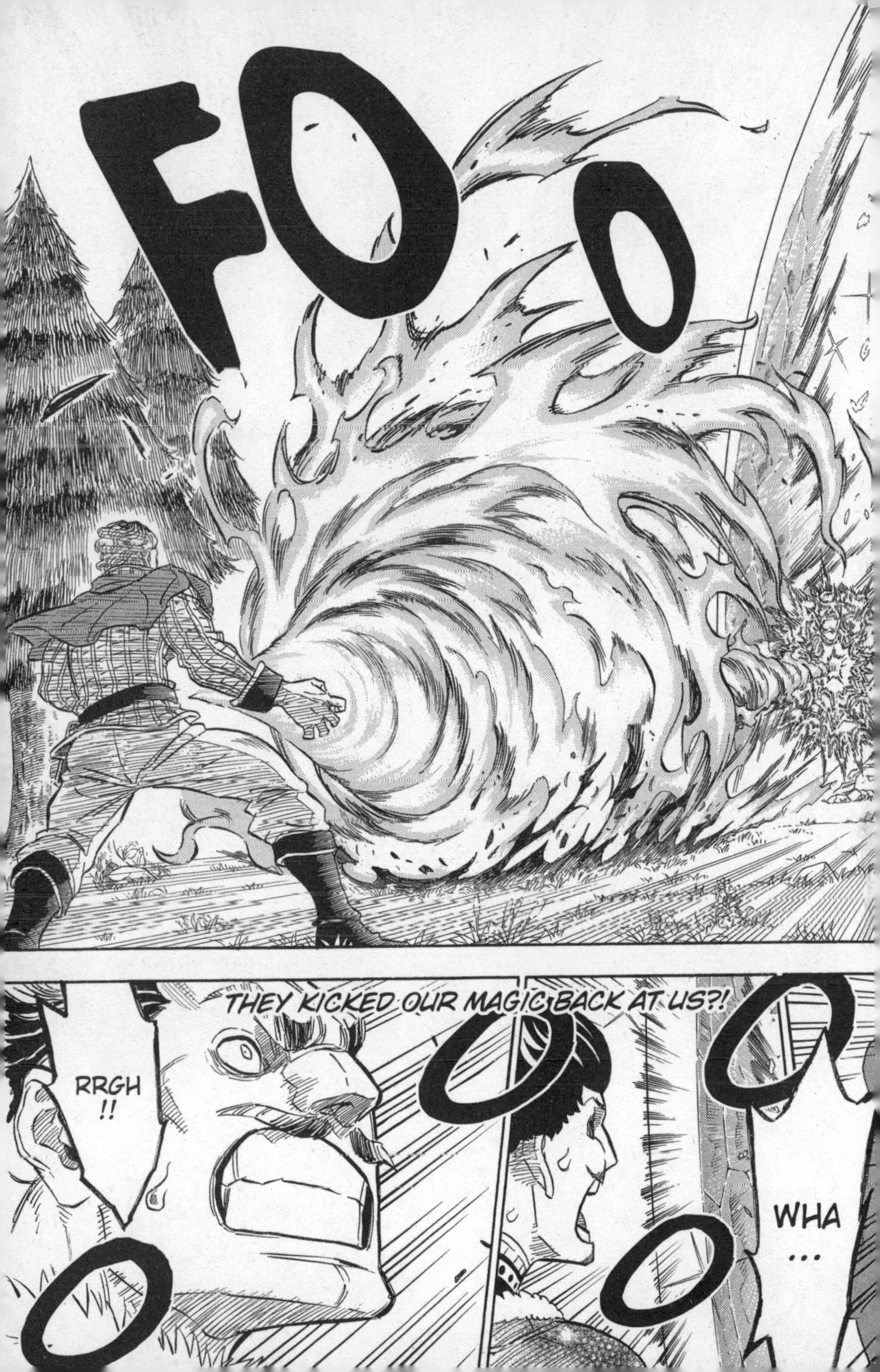
FOO
THEY KICKED OUR MAGIC BACK AT US?!
WHA...
RRGH!!

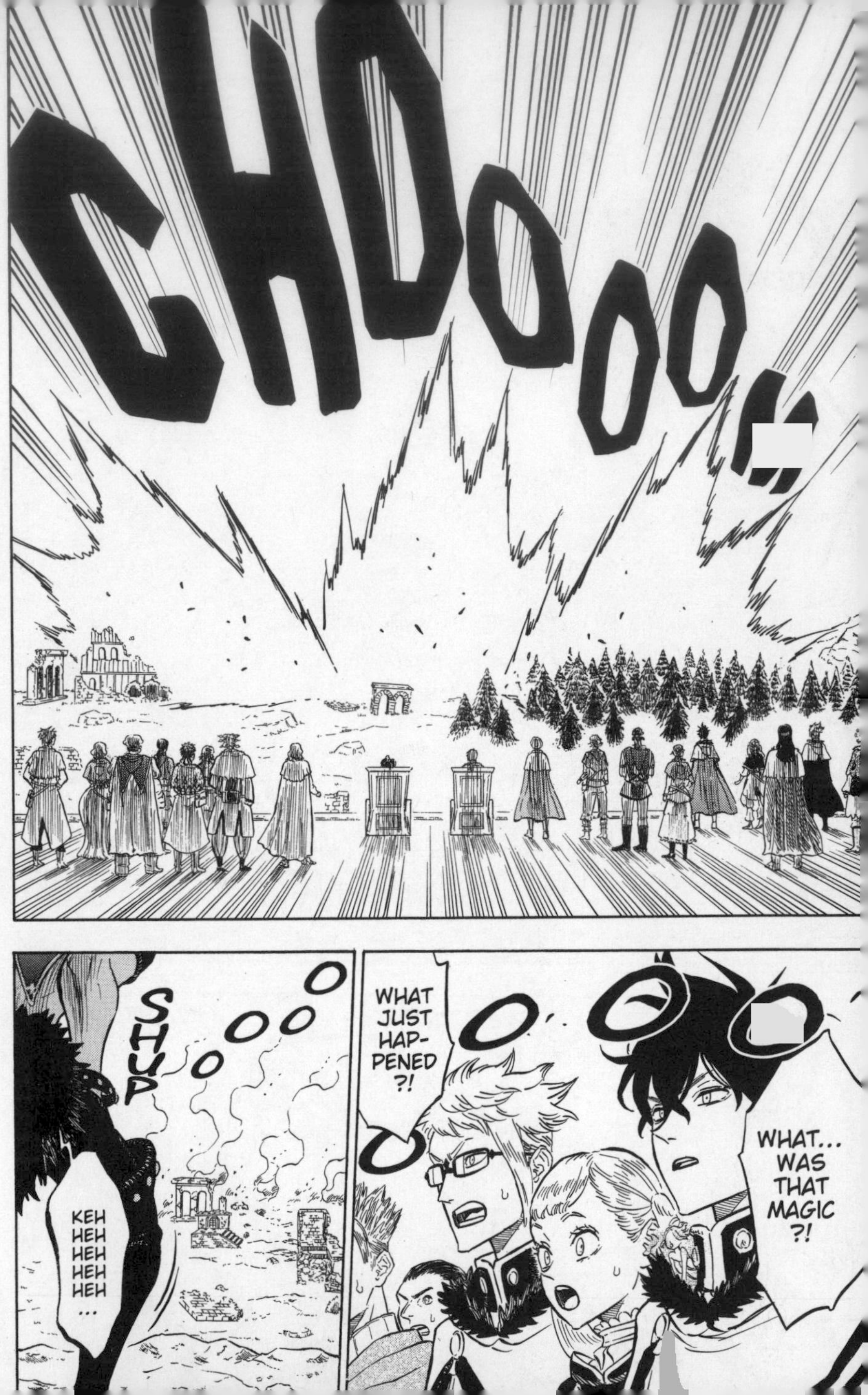
CHOOOO
WHAT... WAS THAT MAGIC?!
WHAT JUST HAPPENED?!
SHUP
KEH HEH HEH HEH HEH...

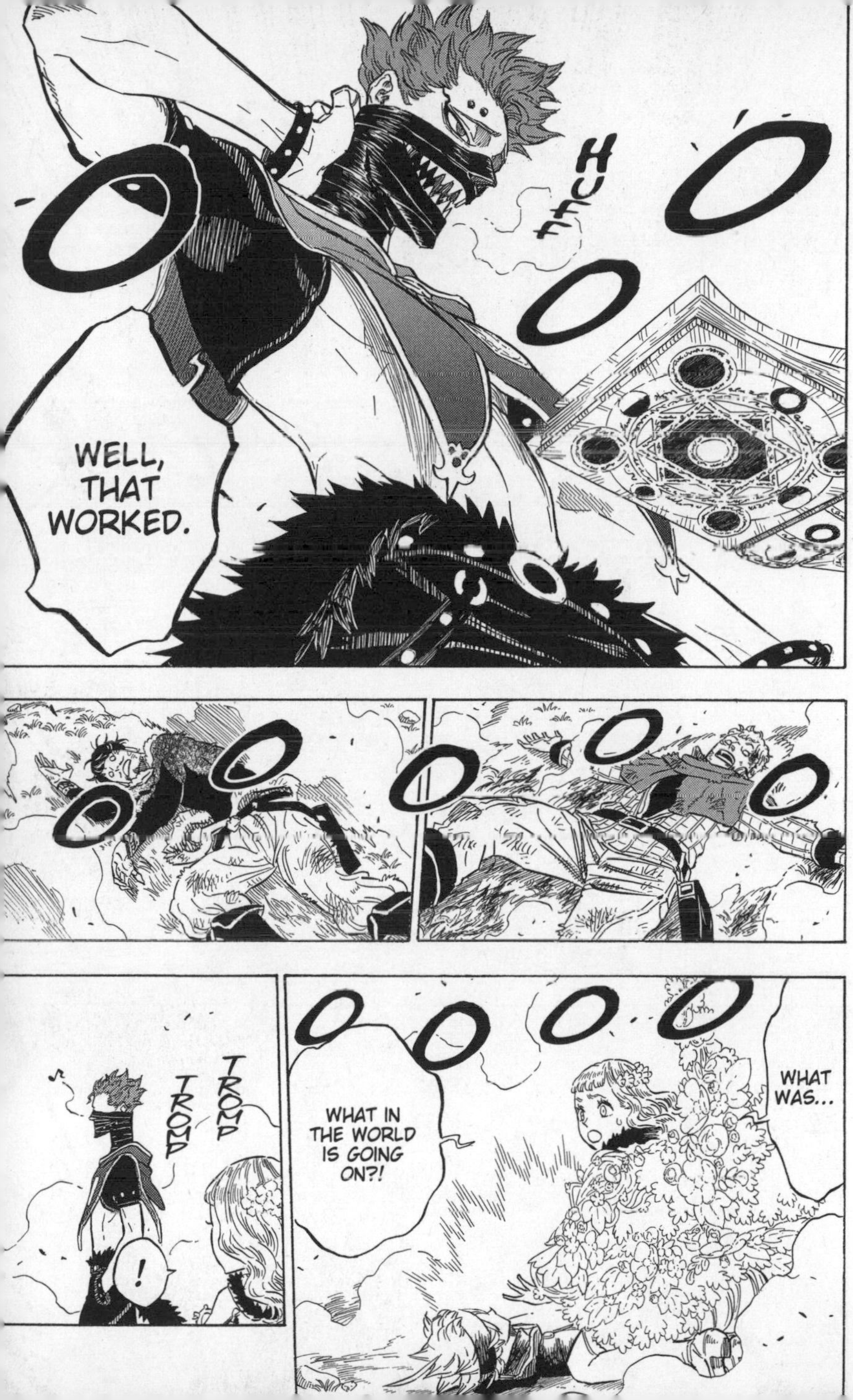
HUFF
WELL, THAT WORKED.
WHAT WAS...
WHAT IN THE WORLD IS GOING ON?!
TROMP TROMP
!

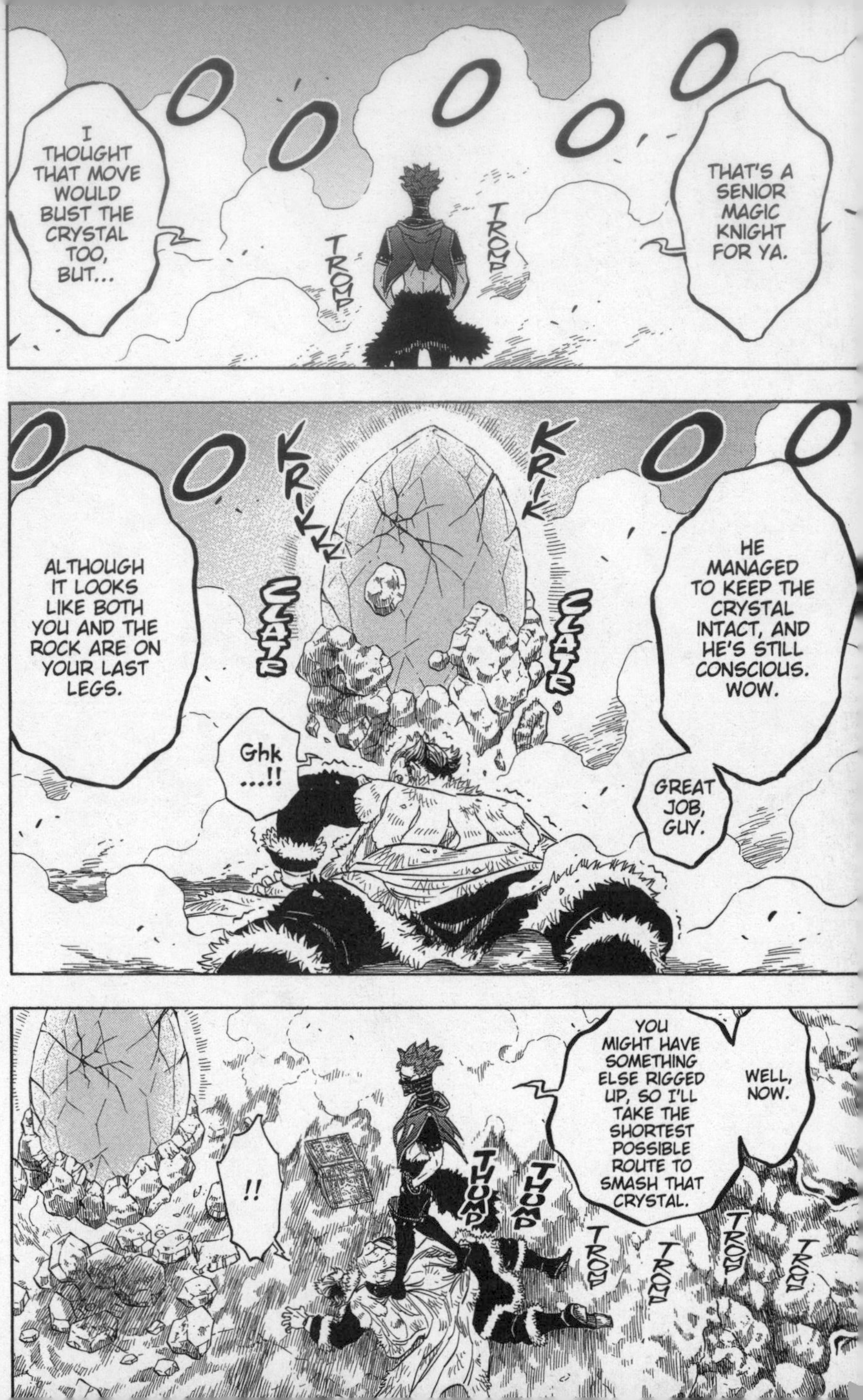
OOOOOOO
THAT'S A SENIOR MAGIC KNIGHT FOR YA.
TROMP
TROMP
I THOUGHT THAT MOVE WOULD BUST THE CRYSTAL TOO, BUT...
HE MANAGED TO KEEP THE CRYSTAL INTACT, AND HE'S STILL CONSCIOUS. WOW.
KRIK
KRIKKK
GREAT JOB, GUY.
Ghk ...!!
ALTHOUGH IT LOOKS LIKE BOTH YOU AND THE ROCK ARE ON YOUR LAST LEGS.
WELL, NOW.
YOU MIGHT HAVE SOMETHING ELSE RIGGED UP, SO I'LL TAKE THE SHORTEST POSSIBLE ROUTE TO SMASH THAT CRYSTAL.
TROMP
TROMP
TROMP
TROMP
THUMP
THUMP
!!

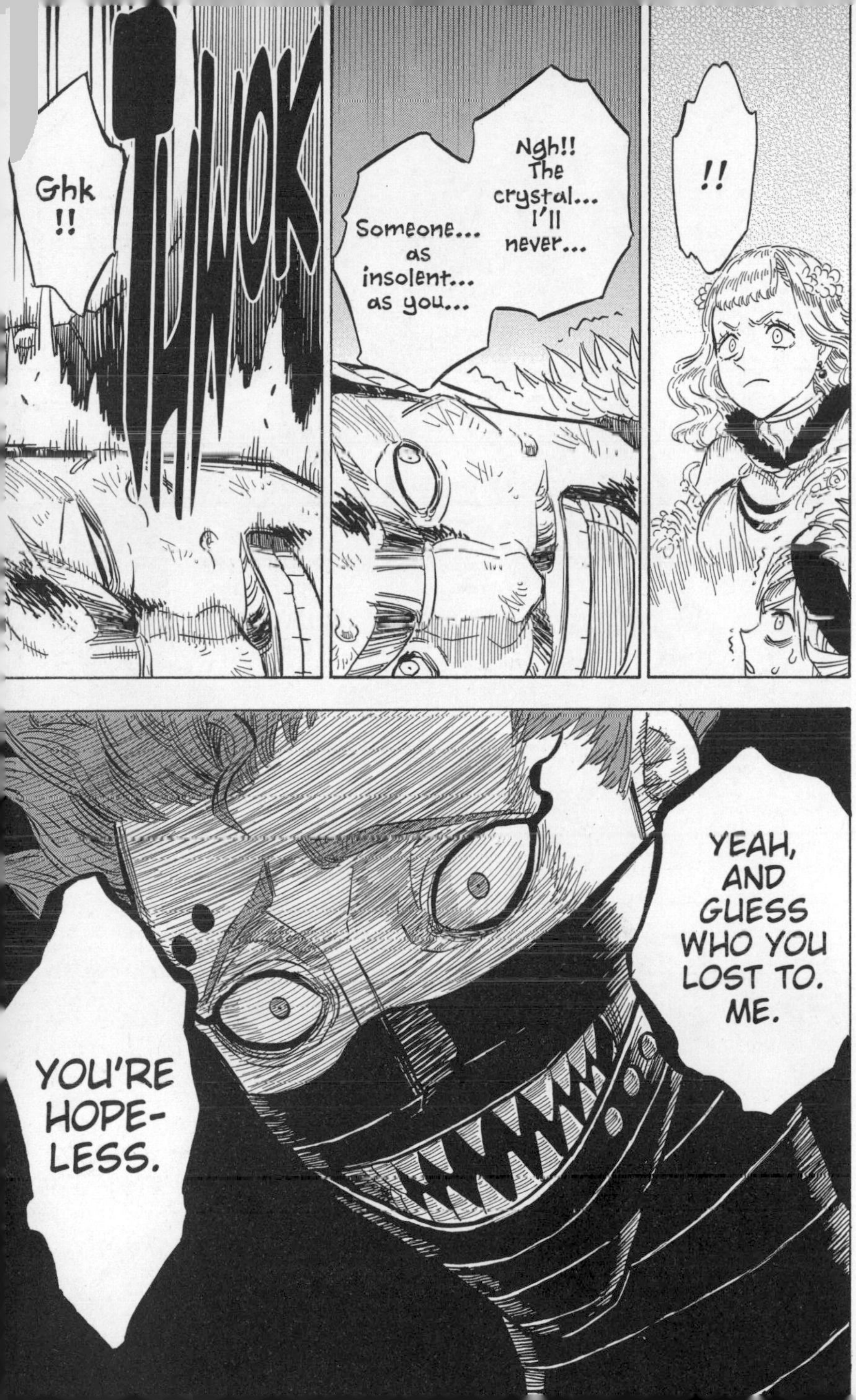
!!
Ngh!! The crystal... I'll never...
Someone... as insolent... as you...
THWOCK
Ghk !!
YEAH, AND GUESS WHO YOU LOST TO. ME.
YOU'RE HOPE-LESS.

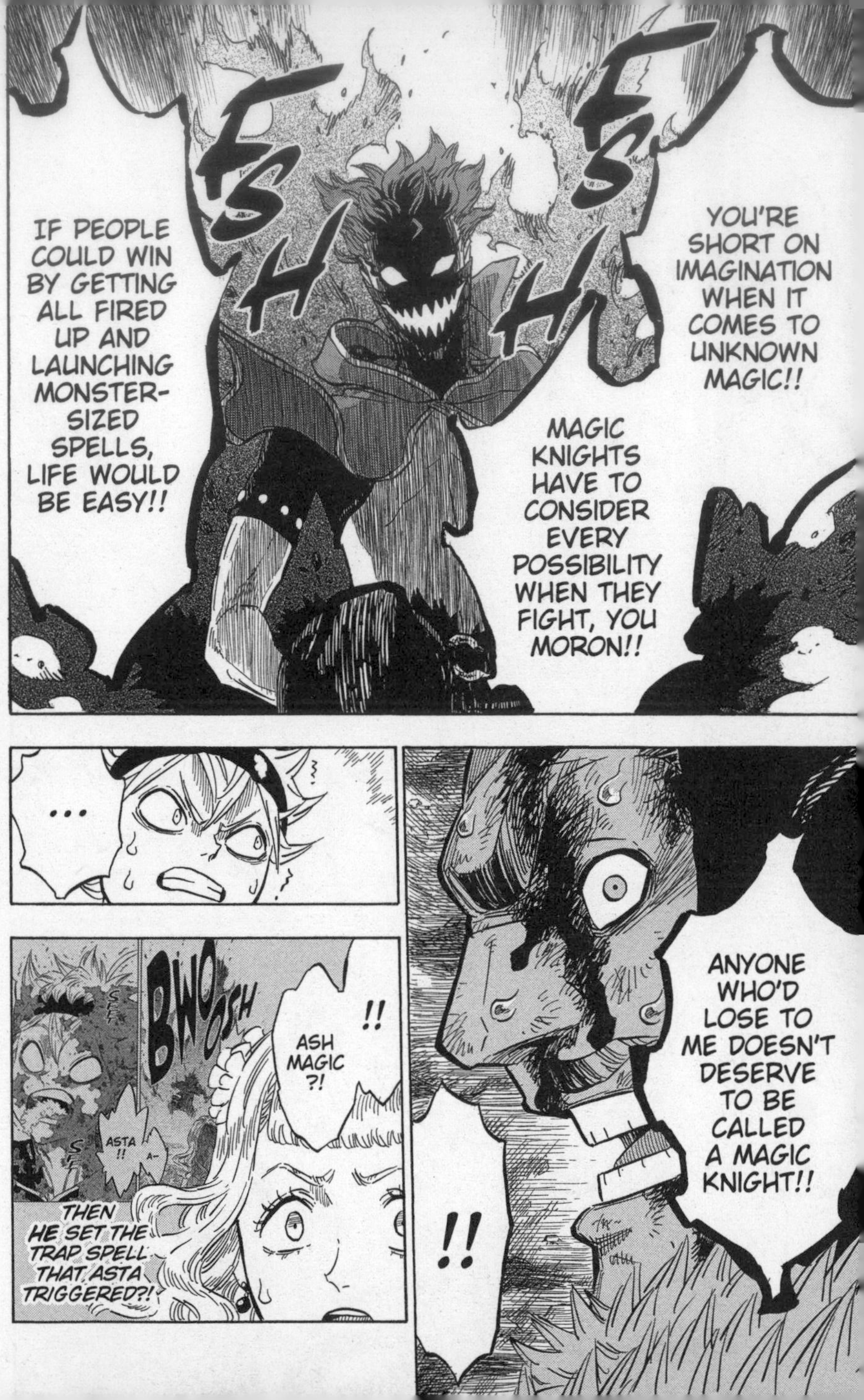
FSHH
YOU'RE SHORT ON IMAGINATION WHEN IT COMES TO UNKNOWN MAGIC!!
FSHH
IF PEOPLE COULD WIN BY GETTING ALL FIRED UP AND LAUNCHING MONSTER-SIZED SPELLS, LIFE WOULD BE EASY!!
MAGIC KNIGHTS HAVE TO CONSIDER EVERY POSSIBILITY WHEN THEY FIGHT, YOU MORON!!
ANYONE WHO'D LOSE TO ME DOESN'T DESERVE TO BE CALLED A MAGIC KNIGHT!!
!!
...
BWOOSH
!!
ASH MAGIC?!
ASTA!!
A-
THEN HE SET THE TRAP SPELL THAT ASTA TRIGGERED?!

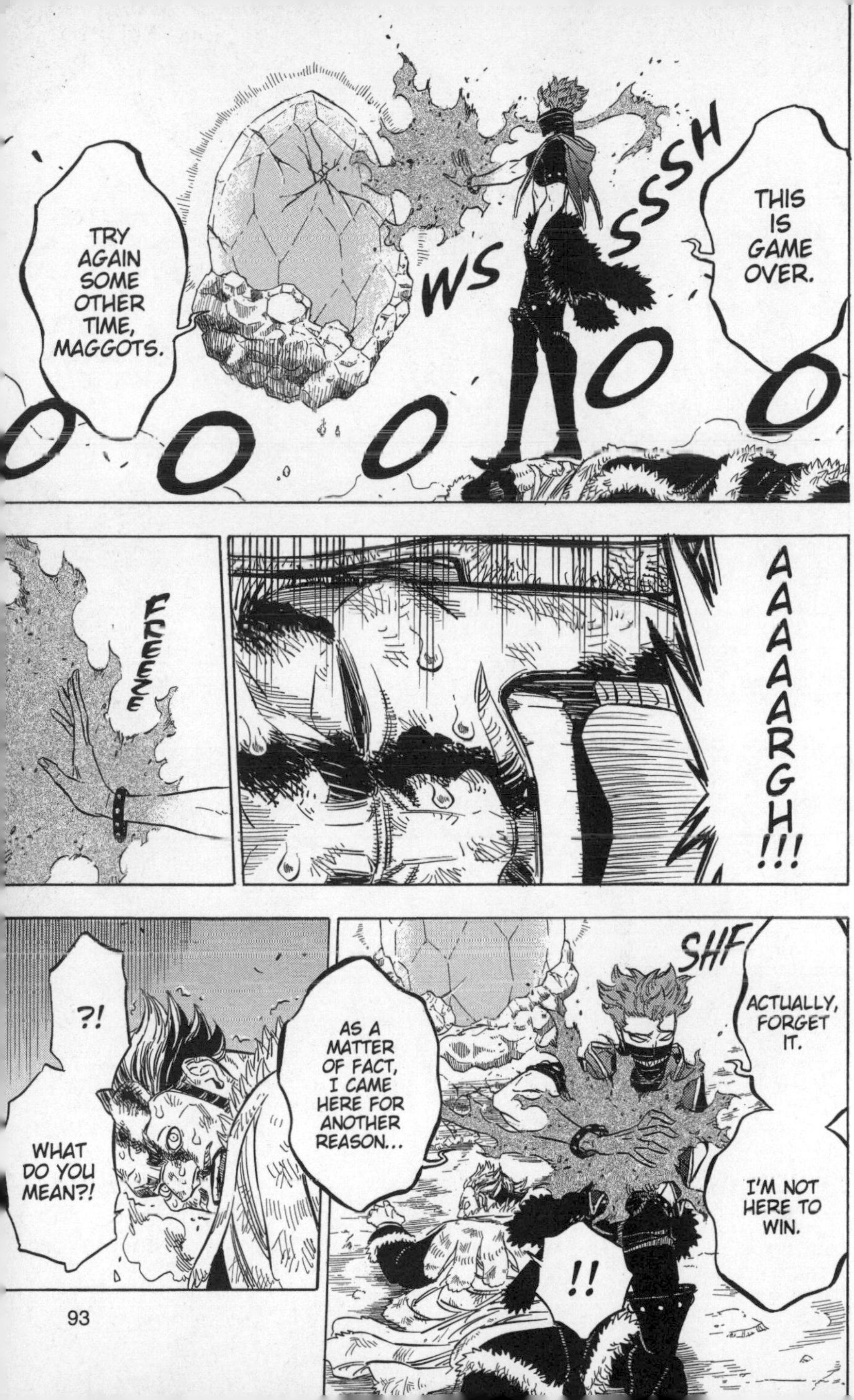
THIS IS GAME OVER.
WSSSSH
OOOOO
TRY AGAIN SOME OTHER TIME, MAGGOTS.
AAAAARGH!!!
FREEZE
SHF
ACTUALLY, FORGET IT.
I'M NOT HERE TO WIN.
AS A MATTER OF FACT, I CAME HERE FOR ANOTHER REASON...
!!
?!
WHAT DO YOU MEAN?!

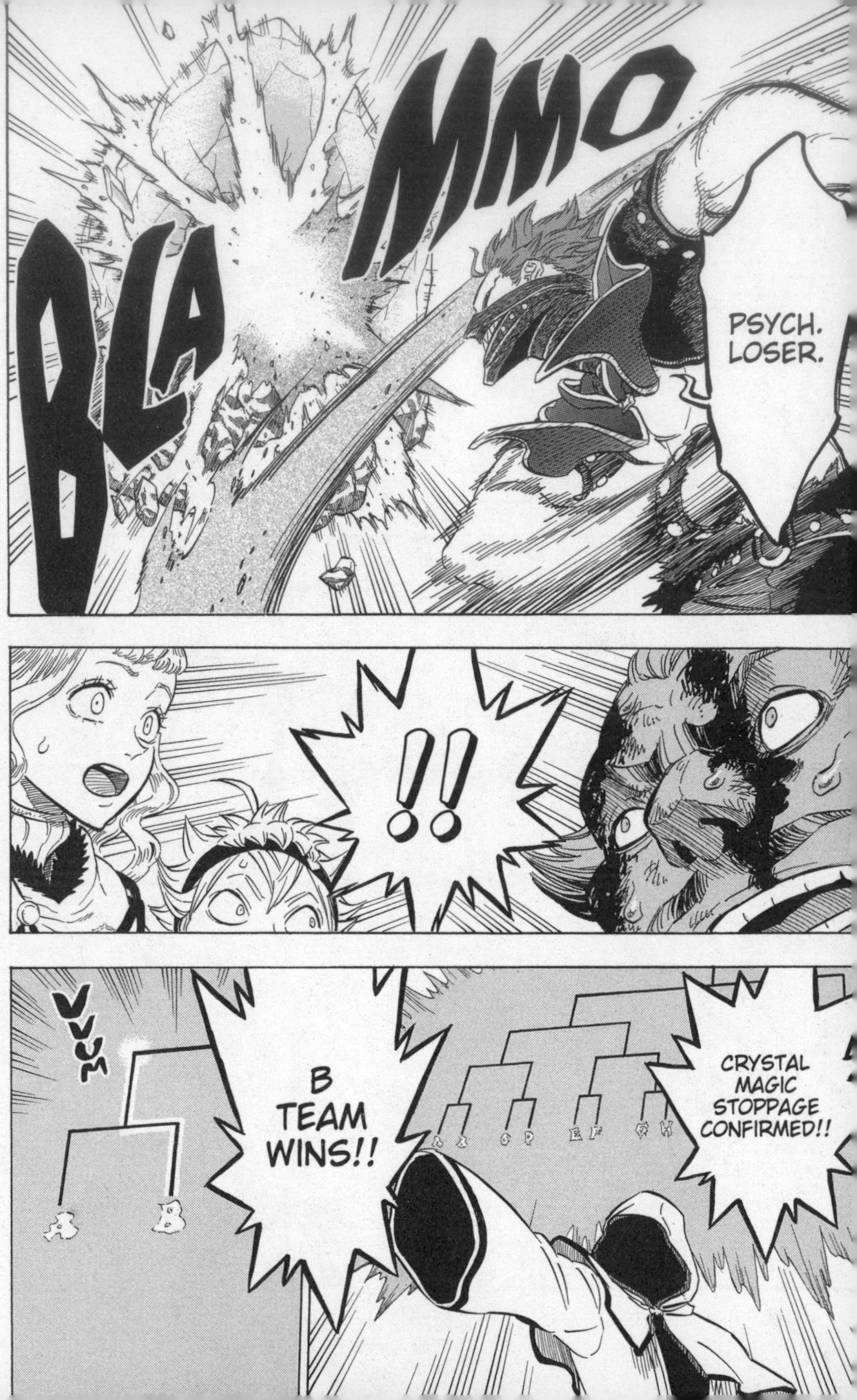
PSYCH. LOSER.
BLAMMO
!!
CRYSTAL MAGIC STOPPAGE CONFIRMED!!
B TEAM WINS!!
VVUM

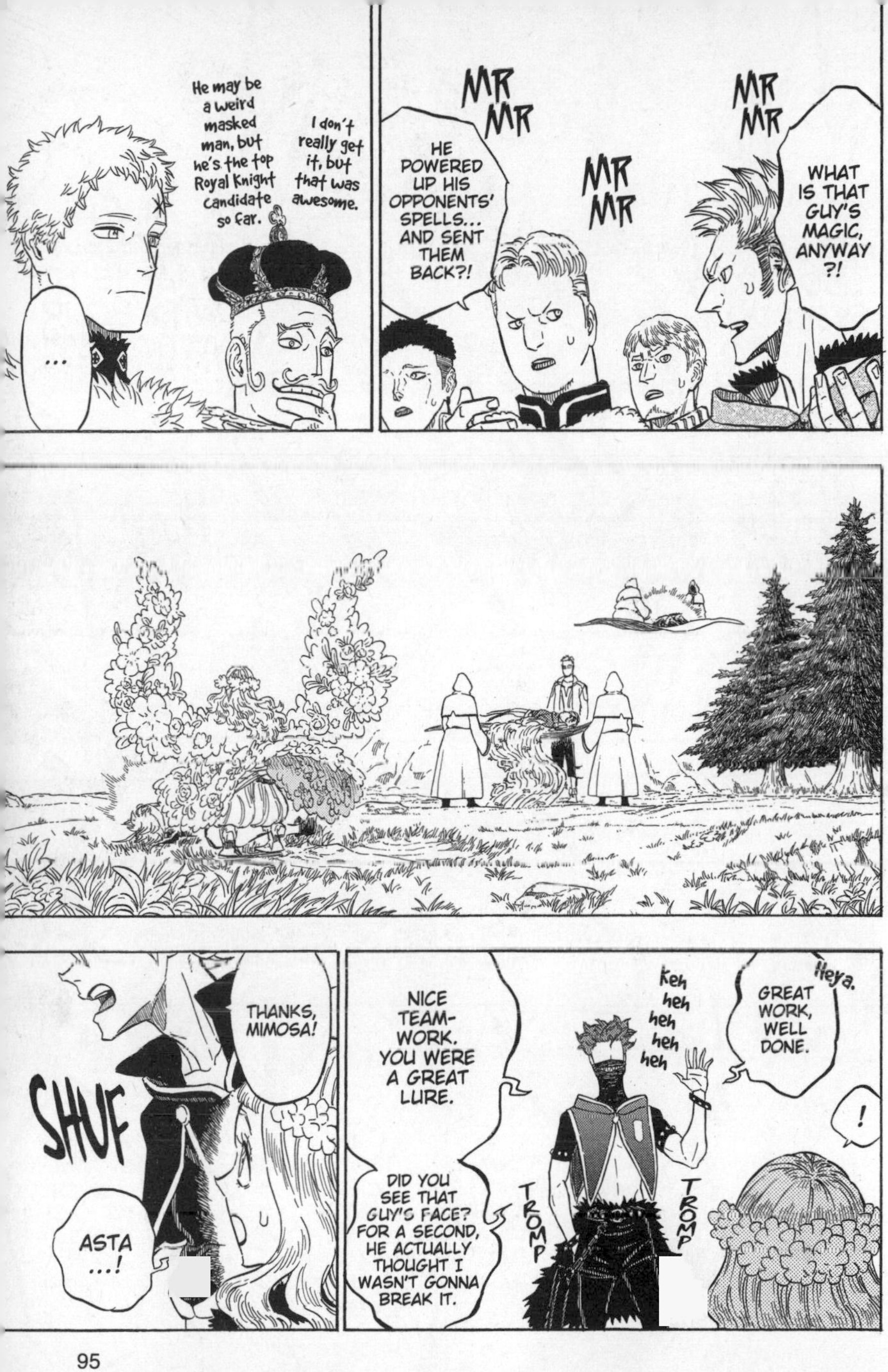
MR MR
WHAT IS THAT GUY'S MAGIC, ANYWAY?!
MR MR
MR MR
HE POWERED UP HIS OPPONENTS' SPELLS... AND SENT THEM BACK?!
I don't really get it, but that was awesome.
He may be a weird masked man, but he's the top Royal Knight candidate so far.
...
Heya.
GREAT WORK, WELL DONE.
!
Keh heh heh heh heh
NICE TEAM-WORK. YOU WERE A GREAT LURE.
TROMP
TROMP
DID YOU SEE THAT GUY'S FACE? FOR A SECOND, HE ACTUALLY THOUGHT I WASN'T GONNA BREAK IT.
THANKS, MIMOSA!
SHUF
ASTA...!

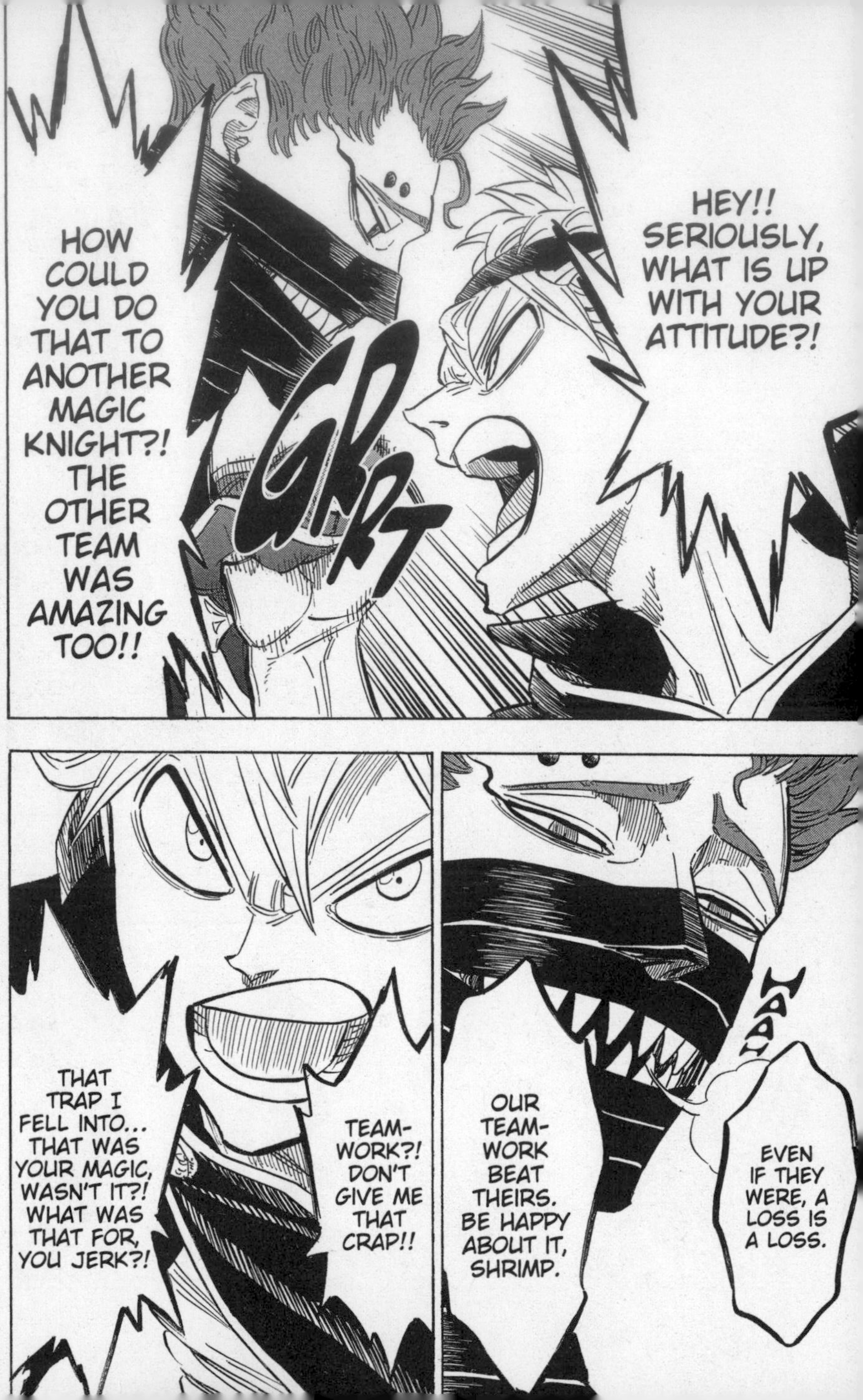
HEY!! SERIOUSLY, WHAT IS UP WITH YOUR ATTITUDE?!
GRRT
HOW COULD YOU DO THAT TO ANOTHER MAGIC KNIGHT?! THE OTHER TEAM WAS AMAZING TOO!!
HAAH
EVEN IF THEY WERE, A LOSS IS A LOSS.
OUR TEAM-WORK BEAT THEIRS. BE HAPPY ABOUT IT, SHRIMP.
TEAM-WORK?! DON'T GIVE ME THAT CRAP!!
THAT TRAP I FELL INTO... THAT WAS YOUR MAGIC, WASN'T IT?! WHAT WAS THAT FOR, YOU JERK?!

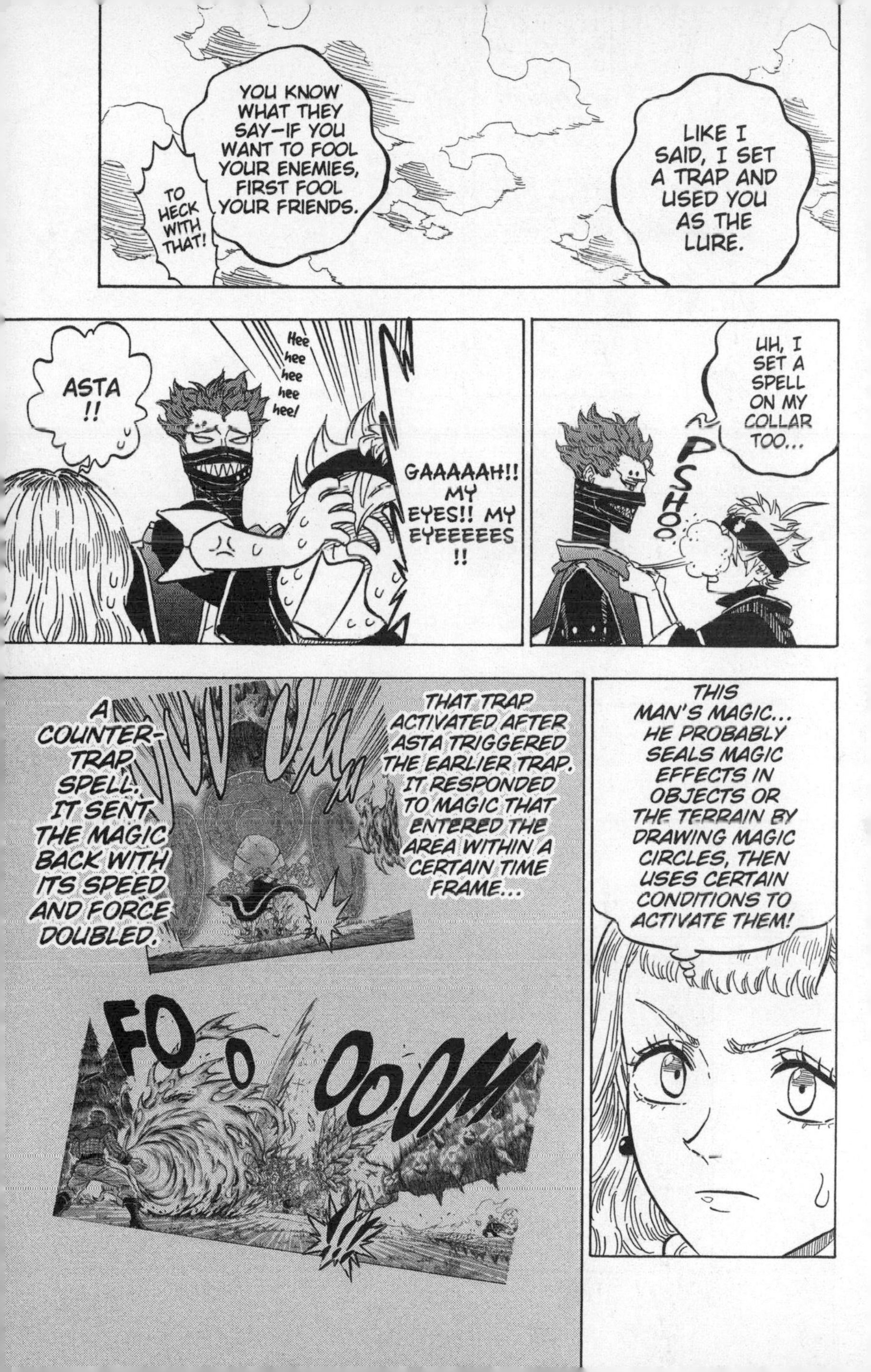
LIKE I SAID, I SET A TRAP AND USED YOU AS THE LURE.
YOU KNOW WHAT THEY SAY—IF YOU WANT TO FOOL YOUR ENEMIES, FIRST FOOL YOUR FRIENDS.
TO HECK WITH THAT!
UH, I SET A SPELL ON MY COLLAR TOO...
PSHOO
Hee hee hee hee hee!
GAAAAAH!! MY EYES!! MY EYEEEEES!!
ASTA!!
THIS MAN'S MAGIC... HE PROBABLY SEALS MAGIC EFFECTS IN OBJECTS OR THE TERRAIN BY DRAWING MAGIC CIRCLES, THEN USES CERTAIN CONDITIONS TO ACTIVATE THEM!
THAT TRAP ACTIVATED AFTER ASTA TRIGGERED THE EARLIER TRAP. IT RESPONDED TO MAGIC THAT ENTERED THE AREA WITHIN A CERTAIN TIME FRAME...
A COUNTER-TRAP SPELL. IT SENT THE MAGIC BACK WITH ITS SPEED AND FORCE DOUBLED.
FO O OOOM

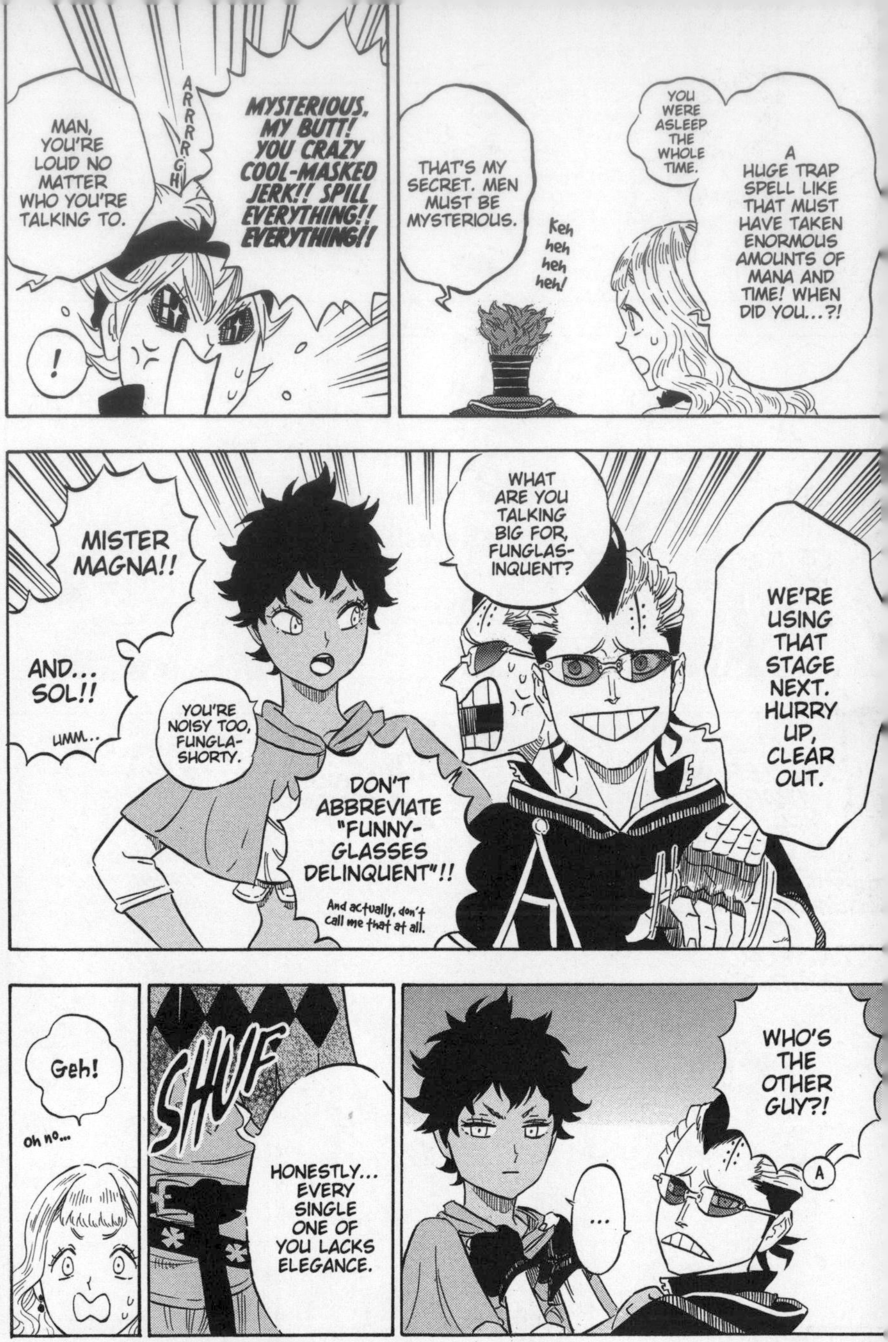
A HUGE TRAP SPELL LIKE THAT MUST HAVE TAKEN ENORMOUS AMOUNTS OF MANA AND TIME! WHEN DID YOU...?!
YOU WERE ASLEEP THE WHOLE TIME.
Keh heh heh heh!
THAT'S MY SECRET. MEN MUST BE MYSTERIOUS.
MYSTERIOUS, MY BUTT! YOU CRAZY COOL-MASKED JERK!! SPILL EVERYTHING!! EVERYTHING!!
ARRRRGH
MAN, YOU'RE LOUD NO MATTER WHO YOU'RE TALKING TO.
!
WE'RE USING THAT STAGE NEXT. HURRY UP, CLEAR OUT.
WHAT ARE YOU TALKING BIG FOR, FUNGLAS-INQUENT?
MISTER MAGNA!!
AND... SOL!!
UMM...
DON'T ABBREVIATE "FUNNY-GLASSES DELINQUENT"!!
And actually, don't call me that at all.
YOU'RE NOISY TOO, FUNGLA-SHORTY.
WHO'S THE OTHER GUY?!
A
...
SHUF
HONESTLY... EVERY SINGLE ONE OF YOU LACKS ELEGANCE.
Geh!
oh no...

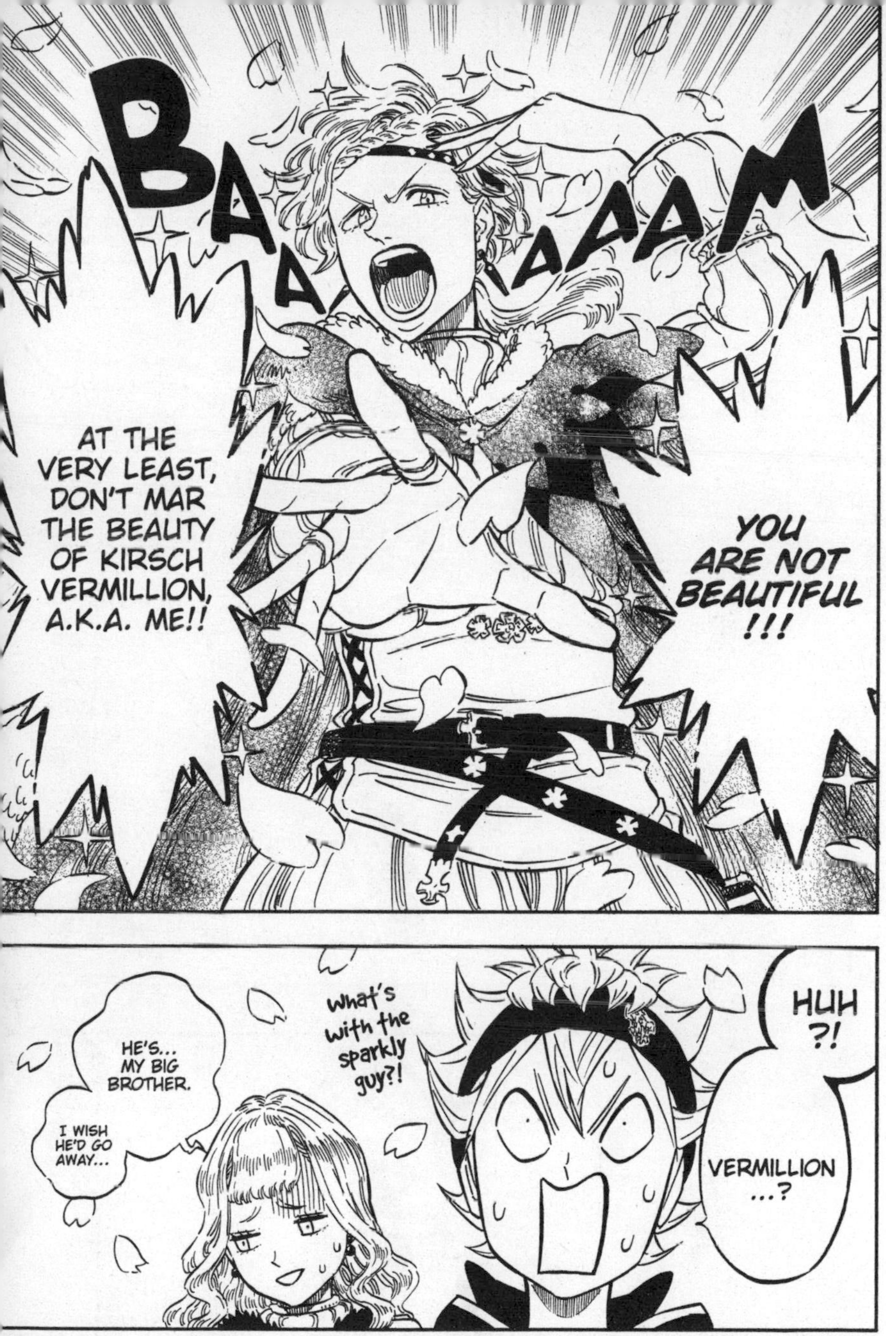
BAAAAAAM
YOU ARE NOT BEAUTIFUL!!!
AT THE VERY LEAST, DON'T MAR THE BEAUTY OF KIRSCH VERMILLION, A.K.A. ME!!
HUH?!
VERMILLION...?
what's with the sparkly guy?!
HE'S... MY BIG BROTHER.
I WISH HE'D GO AWAY...

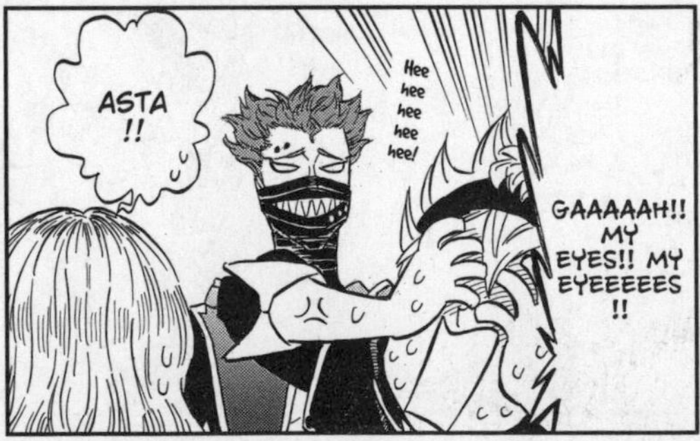
GAAAAAH!! MY EYES!! MY EYEEEEES !!
Hee hee hee hee hee!
ASTA !!

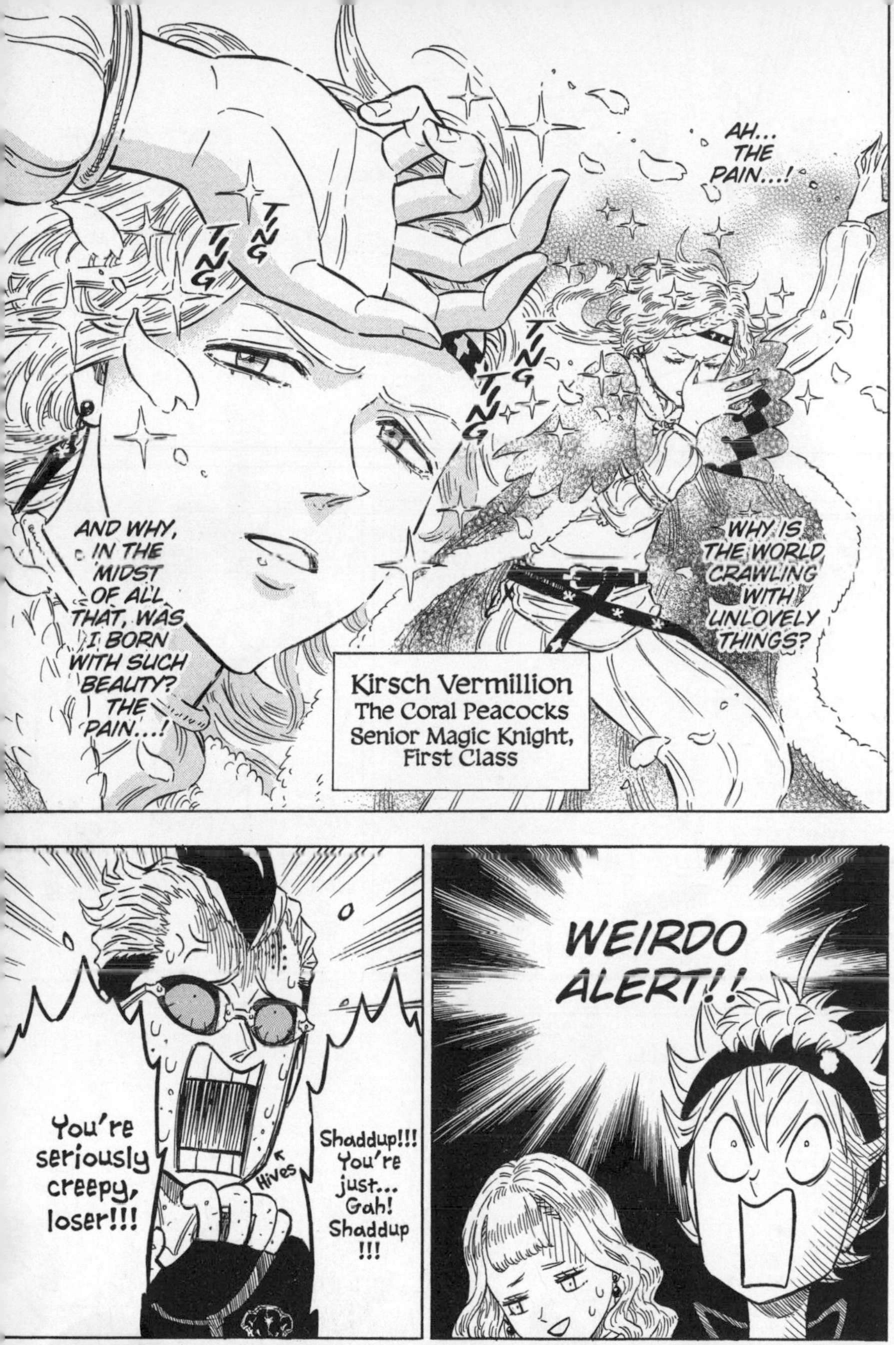
AH... THE PAIN...!
TING TING
TING TING
WHY IS THE WORLD CRAWLING WITH UNLOVELY THINGS?
AND WHY, IN THE MIDST OF ALL THAT, WAS I BORN WITH SUCH BEAUTY? THE PAIN...!
Kirsch Vermillion
The Coral Peacocks
Senior Magic Knight, First Class
WEIRDO ALERT!!
Shaddup!!! You're just... Gah! Shaddup!!!
Hives
You're seriously creepy, loser!!!

Page 116: The Vice Captain of the Coral Peacocks

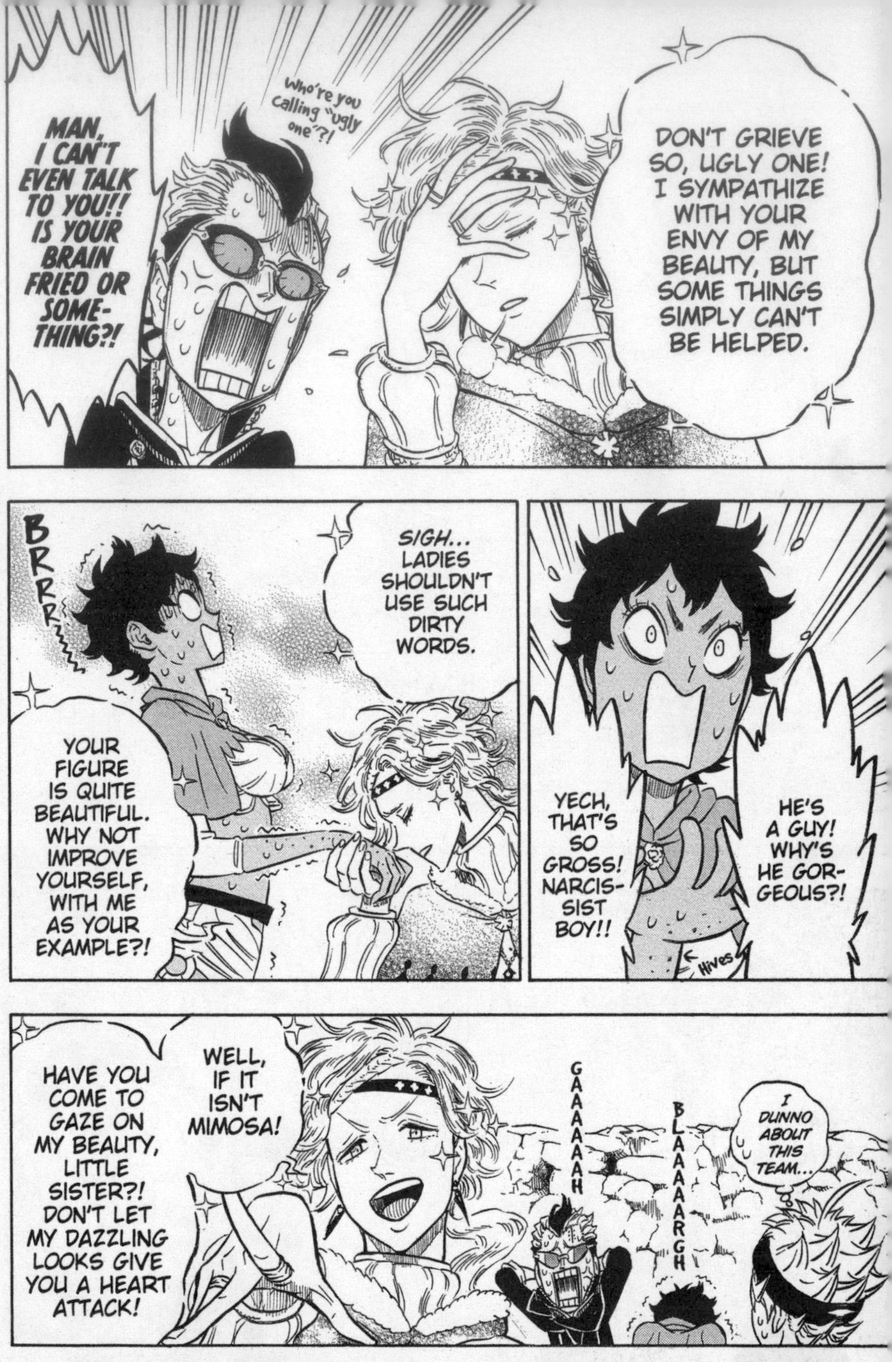
DON'T GRIEVE SO, UGLY ONE! I SYMPATHIZE WITH YOUR ENVY OF MY BEAUTY, BUT SOME THINGS SIMPLY CAN'T BE HELPED.
Who're you calling "ugly one"?!
MAN, I CAN'T EVEN TALK TO YOU!! IS YOUR BRAIN FRIED OR SOME-THING?!
HE'S A GUY! WHY'S HE GOR-GEOUS?!
YECH, THAT'S SO GROSS! NARCIS-SIST BOY!!
Hives
SIGH... LADIES SHOULDN'T USE SUCH DIRTY WORDS.
BRRR
YOUR FIGURE IS QUITE BEAUTIFUL. WHY NOT IMPROVE YOURSELF, WITH ME AS YOUR EXAMPLE?!
I DUNNO ABOUT THIS TEAM...
BLAAAAARGH
GAAAAAAH
WELL, IF IT ISN'T MIMOSA!
HAVE YOU COME TO GAZE ON MY BEAUTY, LITTLE SISTER?! DON'T LET MY DAZZLING LOOKS GIVE YOU A HEART ATTACK!

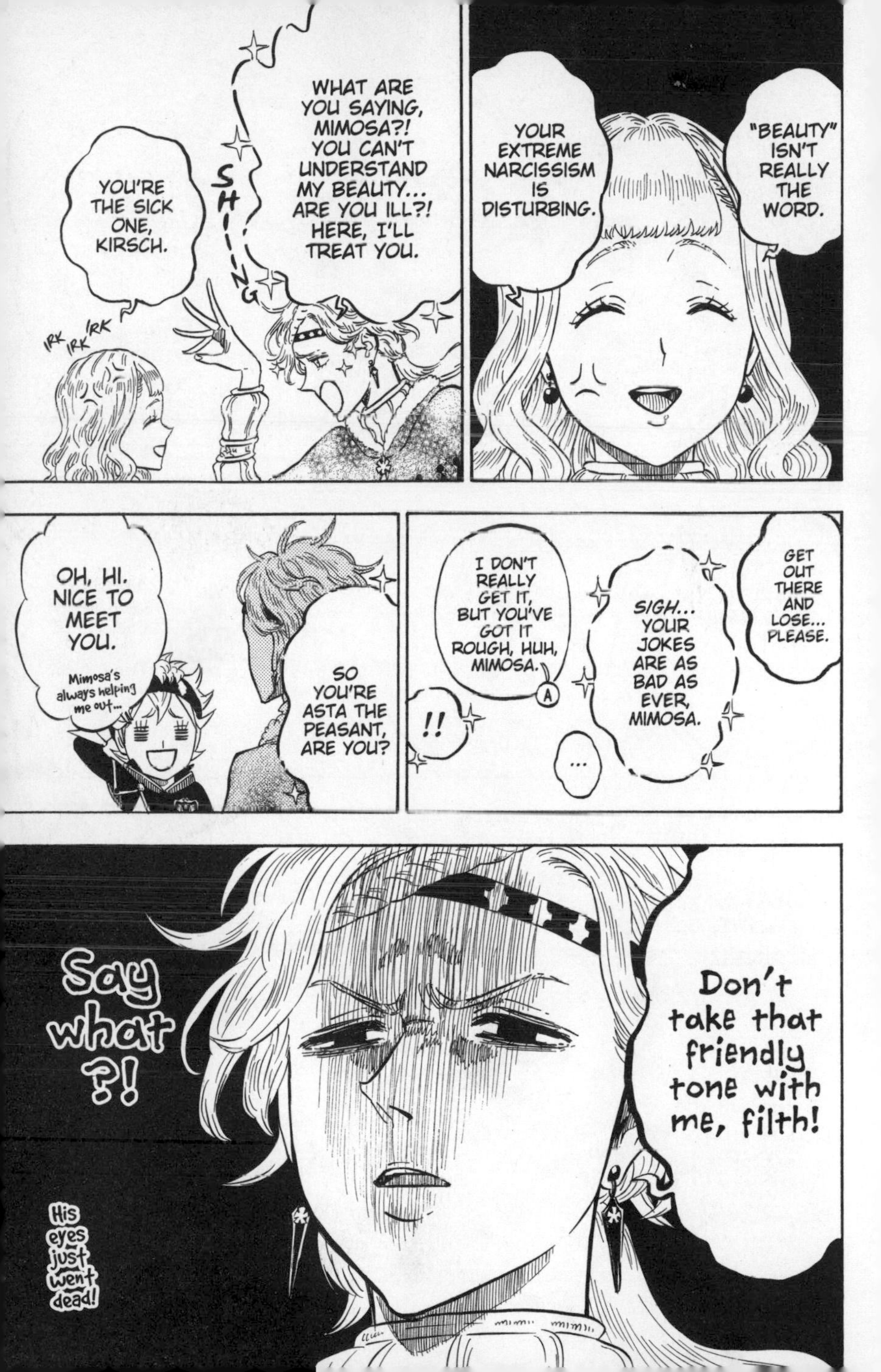
"BEAUTY" ISN'T REALLY THE WORD.
YOUR EXTREME NARCISSISM IS DISTURBING.
WHAT ARE YOU SAYING, MIMOSA?! YOU CAN'T UNDERSTAND MY BEAUTY... ARE YOU ILL?! HERE, I'LL TREAT YOU.
SHIIING
YOU'RE THE SICK ONE, KIRSCH.
IRK IRK IRK
GET OUT THERE AND LOSE... PLEASE.
SIGH... YOUR JOKES ARE AS BAD AS EVER, MIMOSA.
I DON'T REALLY GET IT, BUT YOU'VE GOT IT ROUGH, HUH, MIMOSA.
A
!!
...
SO YOU'RE ASTA THE PEASANT, ARE YOU?
OH, HI. NICE TO MEET YOU.
Mimosa's always helping me out...
Don't take that friendly tone with me, filth!
Say what?!
His eyes just went dead!

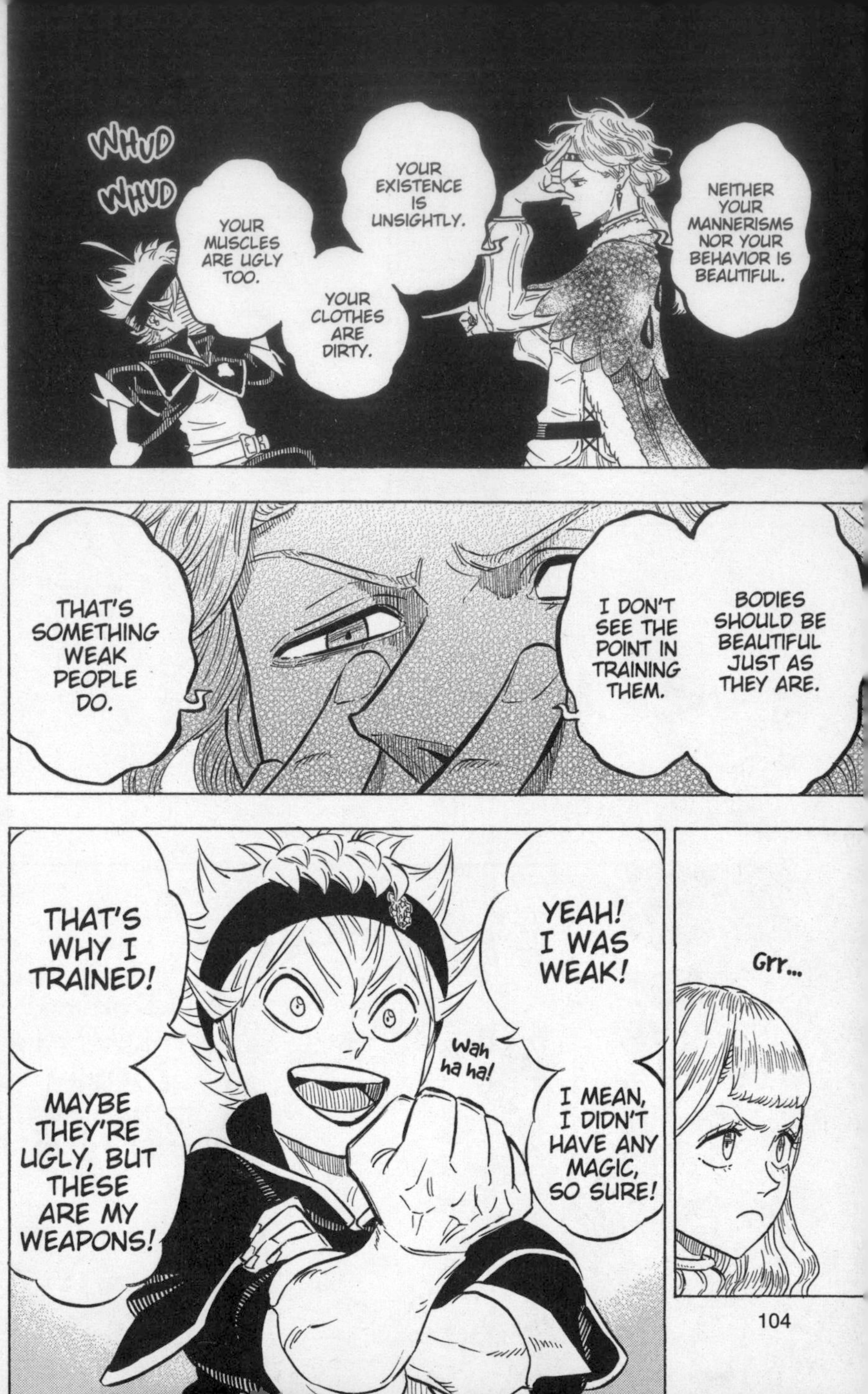
NEITHER YOUR MANNERISMS NOR YOUR BEHAVIOR IS BEAUTIFUL.
YOUR EXISTENCE IS UNSIGHTLY.
YOUR CLOTHES ARE DIRTY.
YOUR MUSCLES ARE UGLY TOO.
WHUD
WHUD
BODIES SHOULD BE BEAUTIFUL JUST AS THEY ARE.
I DON'T SEE THE POINT IN TRAINING THEM.
THAT'S SOMETHING WEAK PEOPLE DO.
Grr...
YEAH! I WAS WEAK!
I MEAN, I DIDN'T HAVE ANY MAGIC, SO SURE!
Wah ha ha!
THAT'S WHY I TRAINED!
MAYBE THEY'RE UGLY, BUT THESE ARE MY WEAPONS!

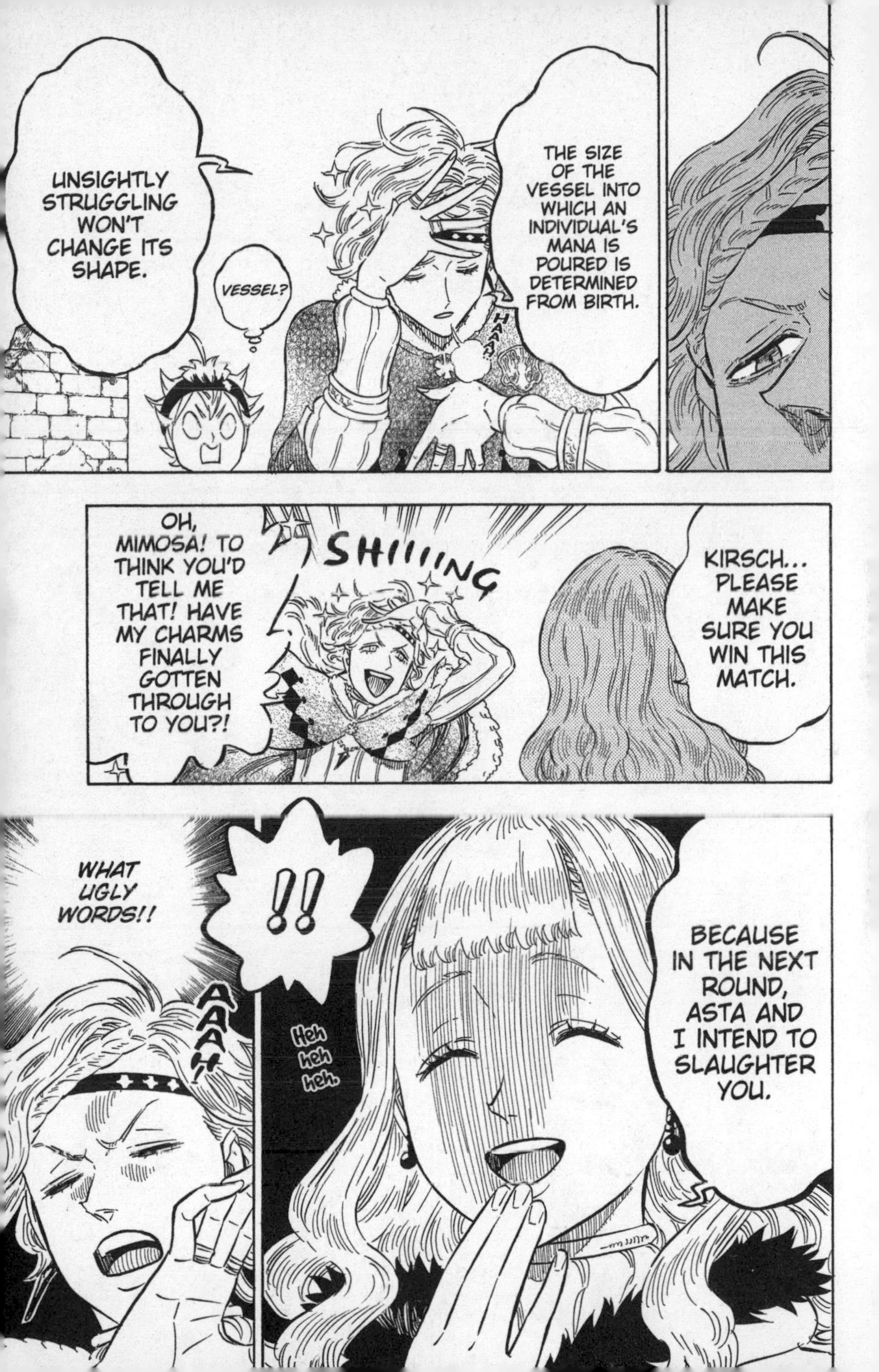
THE SIZE OF THE VESSEL INTO WHICH AN INDIVIDUAL'S MANA IS POURED IS DETERMINED FROM BIRTH.
HAAA
UNSIGHTLY STRUGGLING WON'T CHANGE ITS SHAPE.
VESSEL?
KIRSCH... PLEASE MAKE SURE YOU WIN THIS MATCH.
SHIIIING
OH, MIMOSA! TO THINK YOU'D TELL ME THAT! HAVE MY CHARMS FINALLY GOTTEN THROUGH TO YOU?!
BECAUSE IN THE NEXT ROUND, ASTA AND I INTEND TO SLAUGHTER YOU.
Heh heh heh.
!!
AAAH!
WHAT UGLY WORDS!!

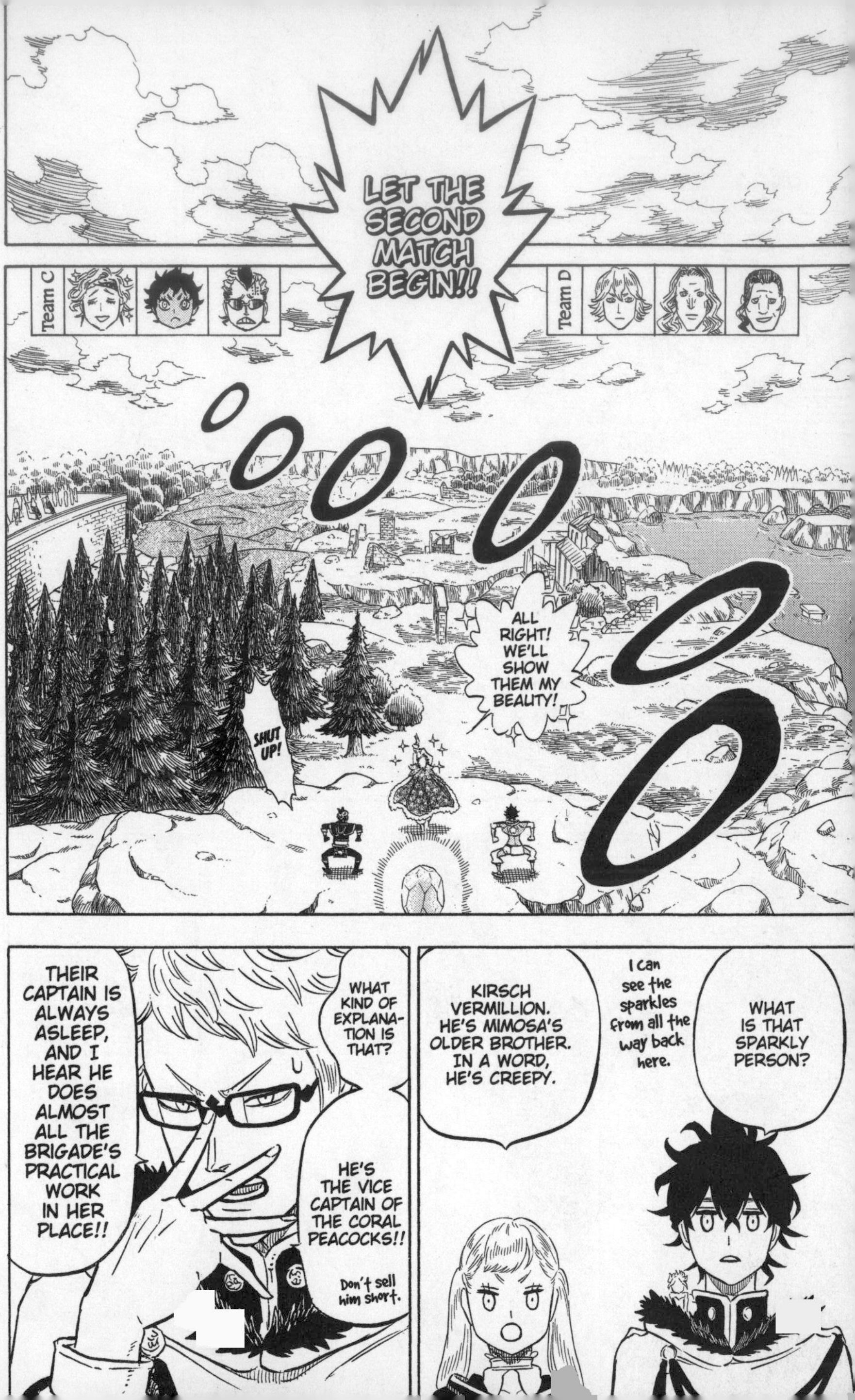
LET THE SECOND MATCH BEGIN!!
Team D
Team C
ALL RIGHT! WE'LL SHOW THEM MY BEAUTY!
SHUT UP!
WHAT IS THAT SPARKLY PERSON?
I can see the sparkles from all the way back here.
KIRSCH VERMILLION. HE'S MIMOSA'S OLDER BROTHER. IN A WORD, HE'S CREEPY.
WHAT KIND OF EXPLANATION IS THAT?
HE'S THE VICE CAPTAIN OF THE CORAL PEACOCKS!!
THEIR CAPTAIN IS ALWAYS ASLEEP, AND I HEAR HE DOES ALMOST ALL THE BRIGADE'S PRACTICAL WORK IN HER PLACE!!
Don't sell him short.

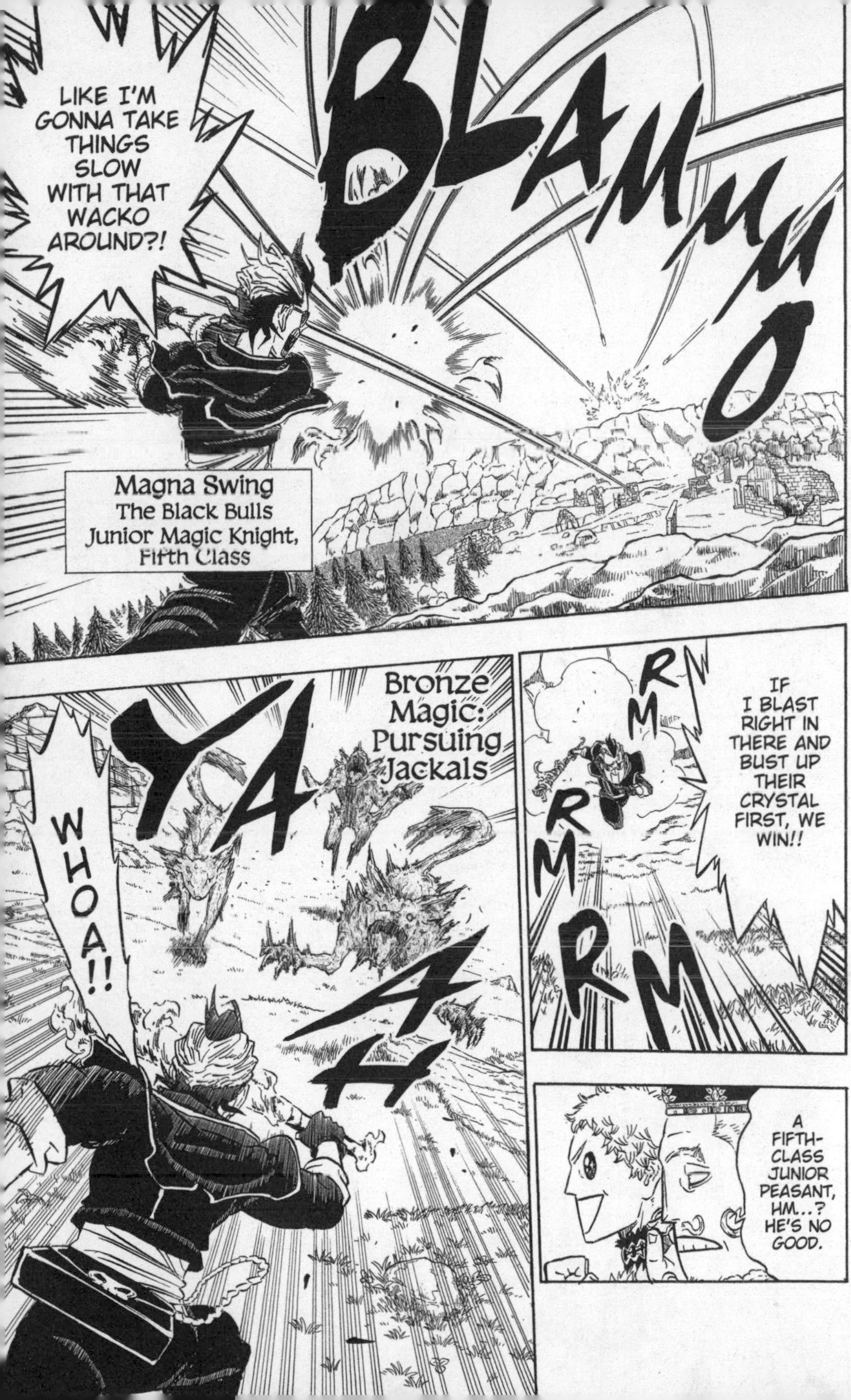

BLAMMMO
LIKE I'M GONNA TAKE THINGS SLOW WITH THAT WACKO AROUND?!
Magna Swing
The Black Bulls
Junior Magic Knight, Fifth Class
RMRMRM
IF I BLAST RIGHT IN THERE AND BUST UP THEIR CRYSTAL FIRST, WE WIN!!
A FIFTH-CLASS JUNIOR PEASANT, HM...? HE'S NO GOOD.
Bronze Magic: Pursuing Jackals
YAAAH
WHOA!!

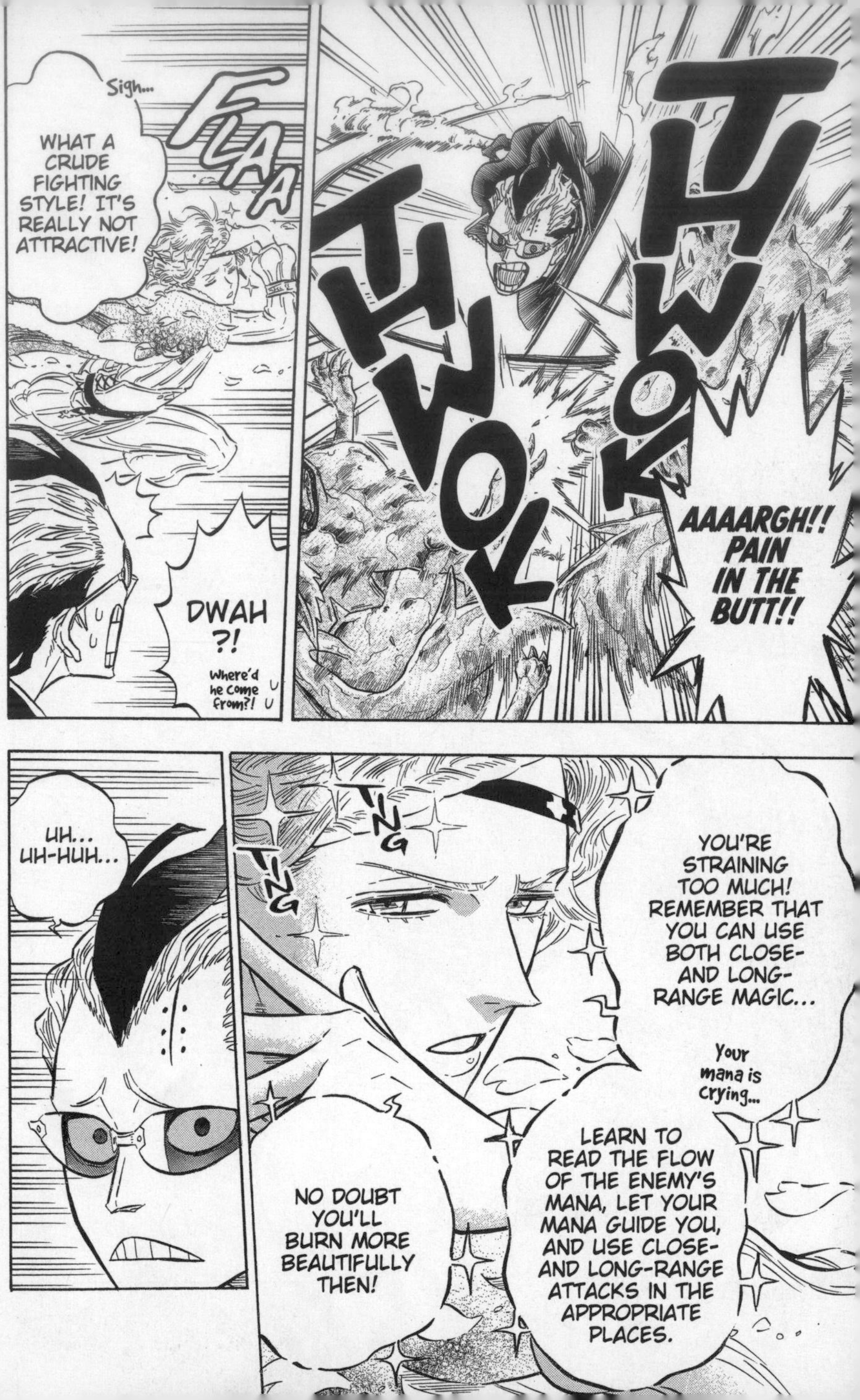
THWOK
THWOK
AAAARGH!! PAIN IN THE BUTT!!
Sigh...
WHAT A CRUDE FIGHTING STYLE! IT'S REALLY NOT ATTRACTIVE!
FLAAA
DWAH ?!
Where'd he come from?!
TING
TING
YOU'RE STRAINING TOO MUCH! REMEMBER THAT YOU CAN USE BOTH CLOSE- AND LONG-RANGE MAGIC...
Your mana is crying...
LEARN TO READ THE FLOW OF THE ENEMY'S MANA, LET YOUR MANA GUIDE YOU, AND USE CLOSE- AND LONG-RANGE ATTACKS IN THE APPROPRIATE PLACES.
NO DOUBT YOU'LL BURN MORE BEAUTIFULLY THEN!
UH... UH-HUH...

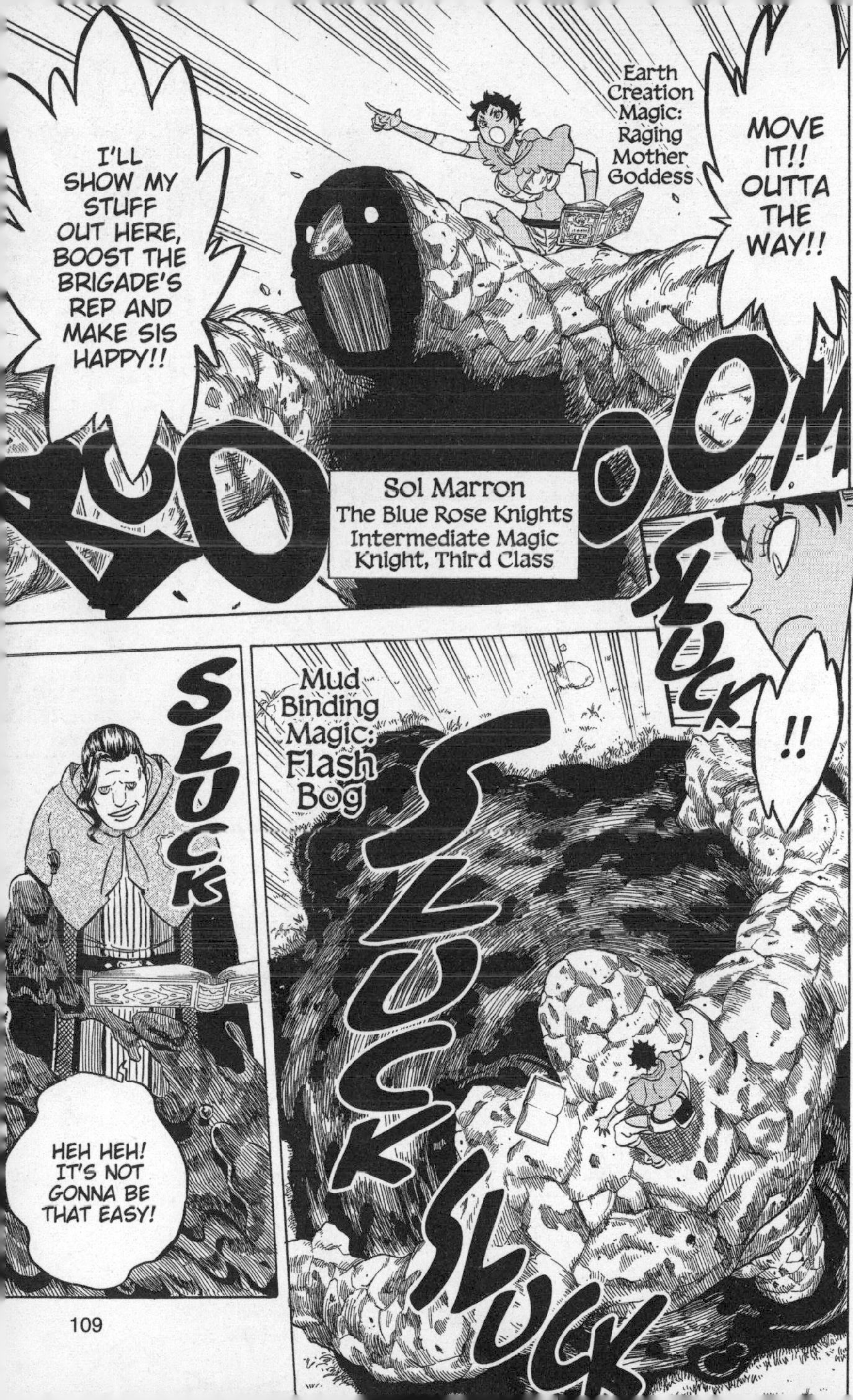
MOVE IT!! OUTTA THE WAY!!
Earth Creation Magic: Raging Mother Goddess
I'LL SHOW MY STUFF OUT HERE, BOOST THE BRIGADE'S REP AND MAKE SIS HAPPY!!
Sol Marron
The Blue Rose Knights
Intermediate Magic Knight, Third Class
SLUCK
!!
Mud Binding Magic: Flash Bog
SLUCK
HEH HEH! IT'S NOT GONNA BE THAT EASY!

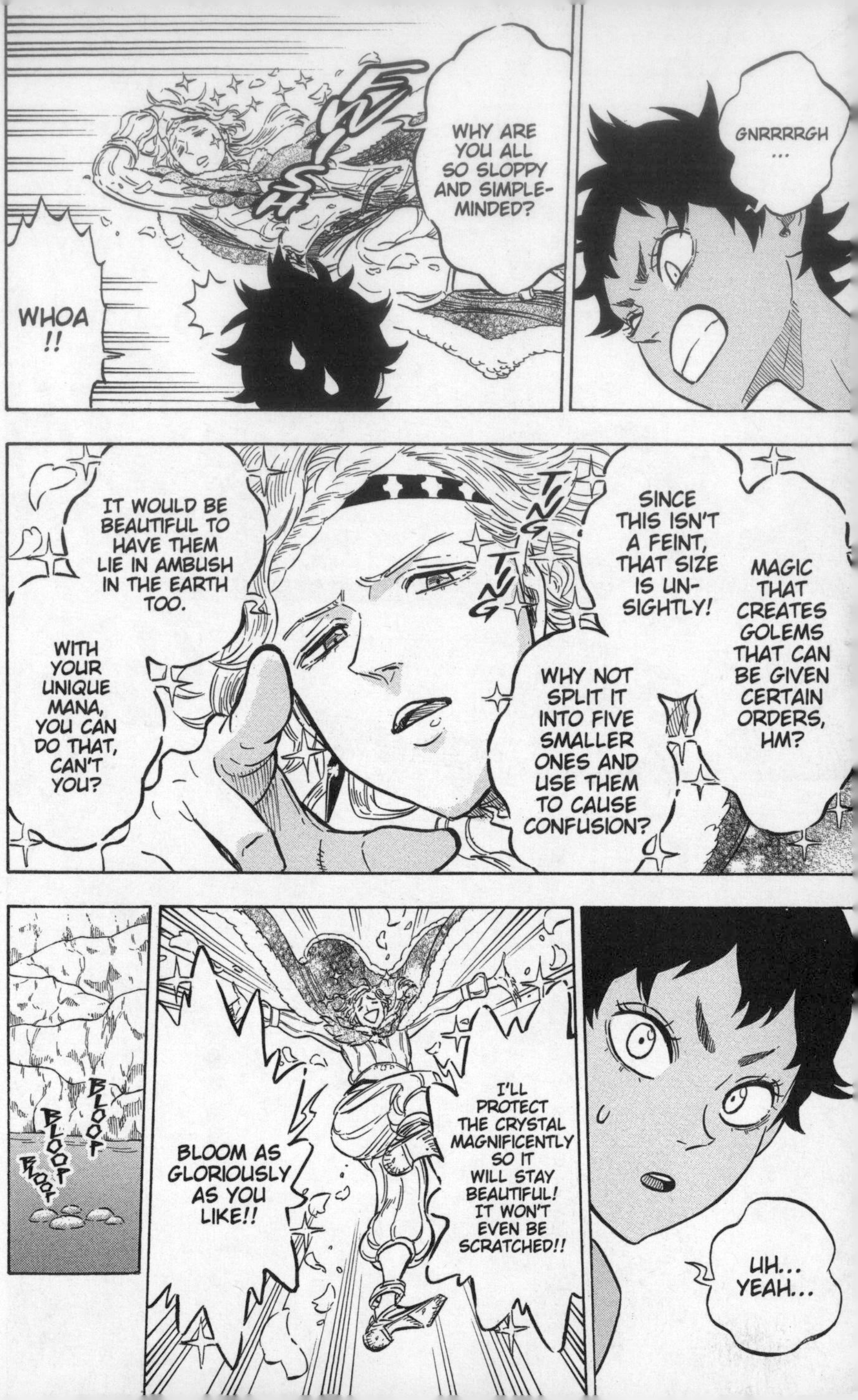
GNRRRRGH ...
WHY ARE YOU ALL SO SLOPPY AND SIMPLE-MINDED?
SWISH
WHOA !!
MAGIC THAT CREATES GOLEMS THAT CAN BE GIVEN CERTAIN ORDERS, HM?
SINCE THIS ISN'T A FEINT, THAT SIZE IS UN-SIGHTLY!
WHY NOT SPLIT IT INTO FIVE SMALLER ONES AND USE THEM TO CAUSE CONFUSION?
TING TING
IT WOULD BE BEAUTIFUL TO HAVE THEM LIE IN AMBUSH IN THE EARTH TOO.
WITH YOUR UNIQUE MANA, YOU CAN DO THAT, CAN'T YOU?
UH... YEAH...
I'LL PROTECT THE CRYSTAL MAGNIFICENTLY SO IT WILL STAY BEAUTIFUL! IT WON'T EVEN BE SCRATCHED!!
BLOOM AS GLORIOUSLY AS YOU LIKE!!
BLOOP
BLOOP
BLOOP

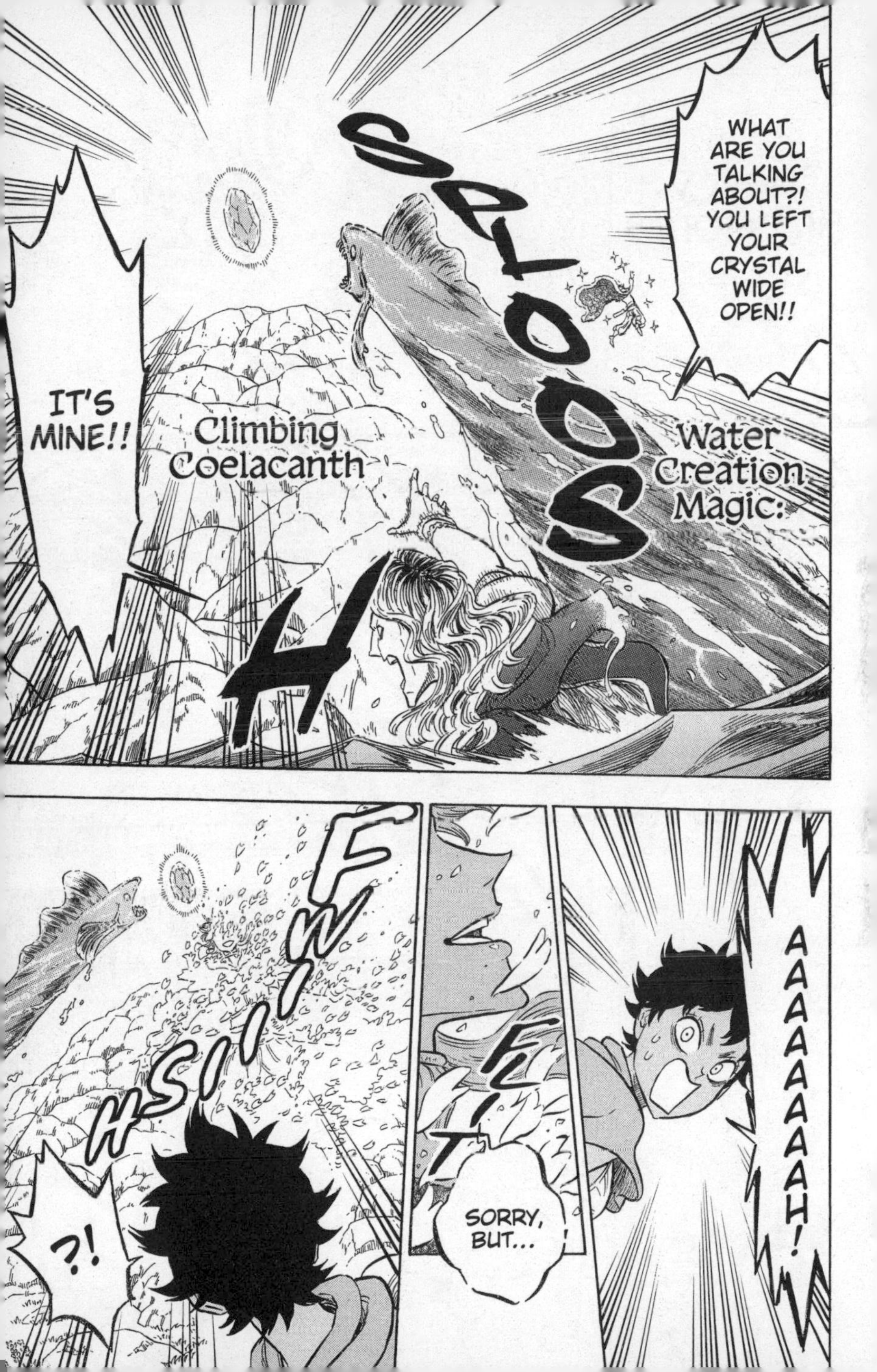
WHAT ARE YOU TALKING ABOUT?! YOU LEFT YOUR CRYSTAL WIDE OPEN!!
Water Creation Magic:
SPLOOSH
Climbing Coelacanth
IT'S MINE!!
AAAAAAAAAH!
SORRY, BUT...
FLIT
FWIISH
?!

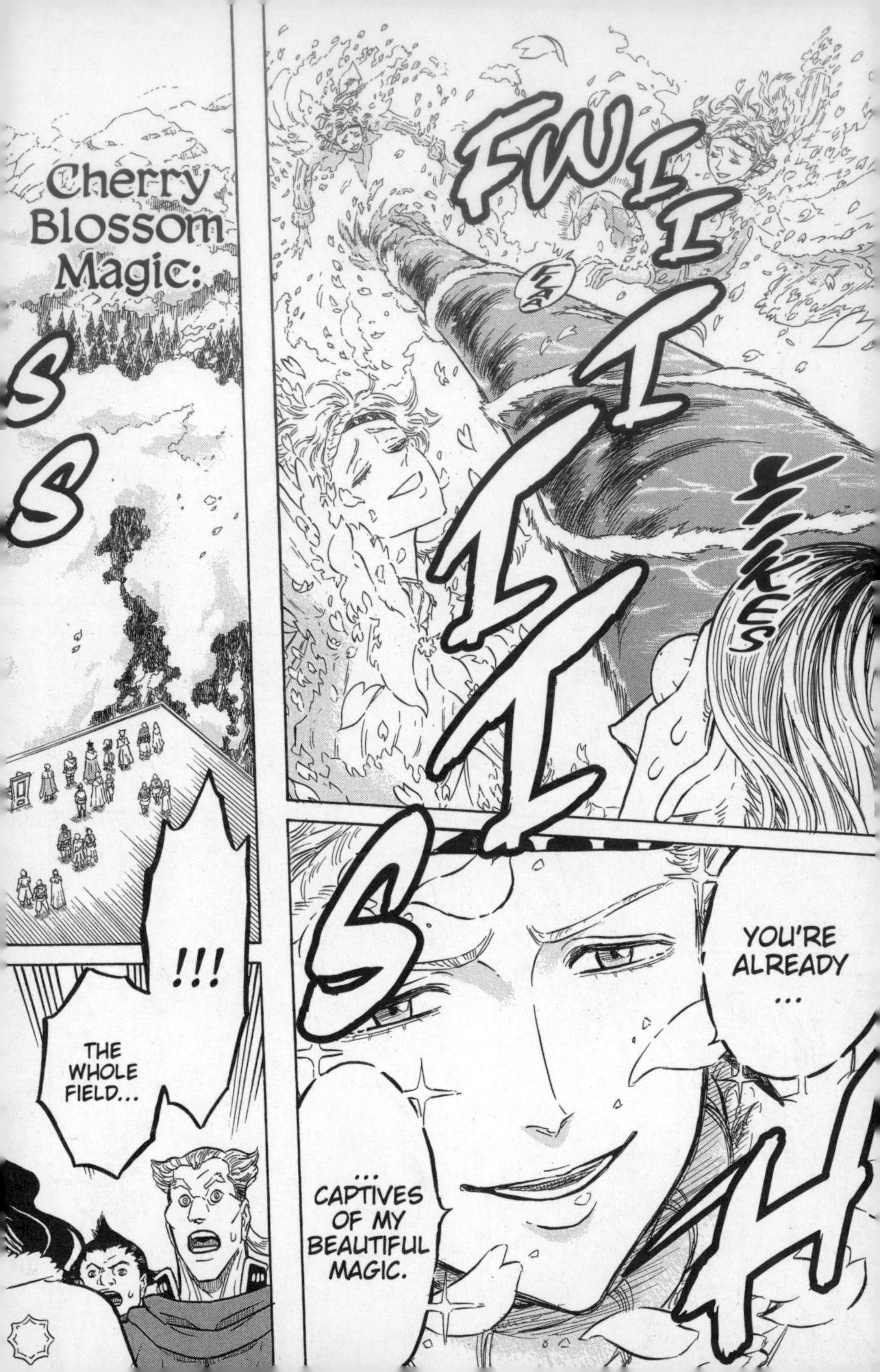
FWIIIIIISH
YIKES
YOU'RE ALREADY ...
... CAPTIVES OF MY BEAUTIFUL MAGIC.
Cherry Blossom Magic:
SS
!!!
THE WHOLE FIELD...

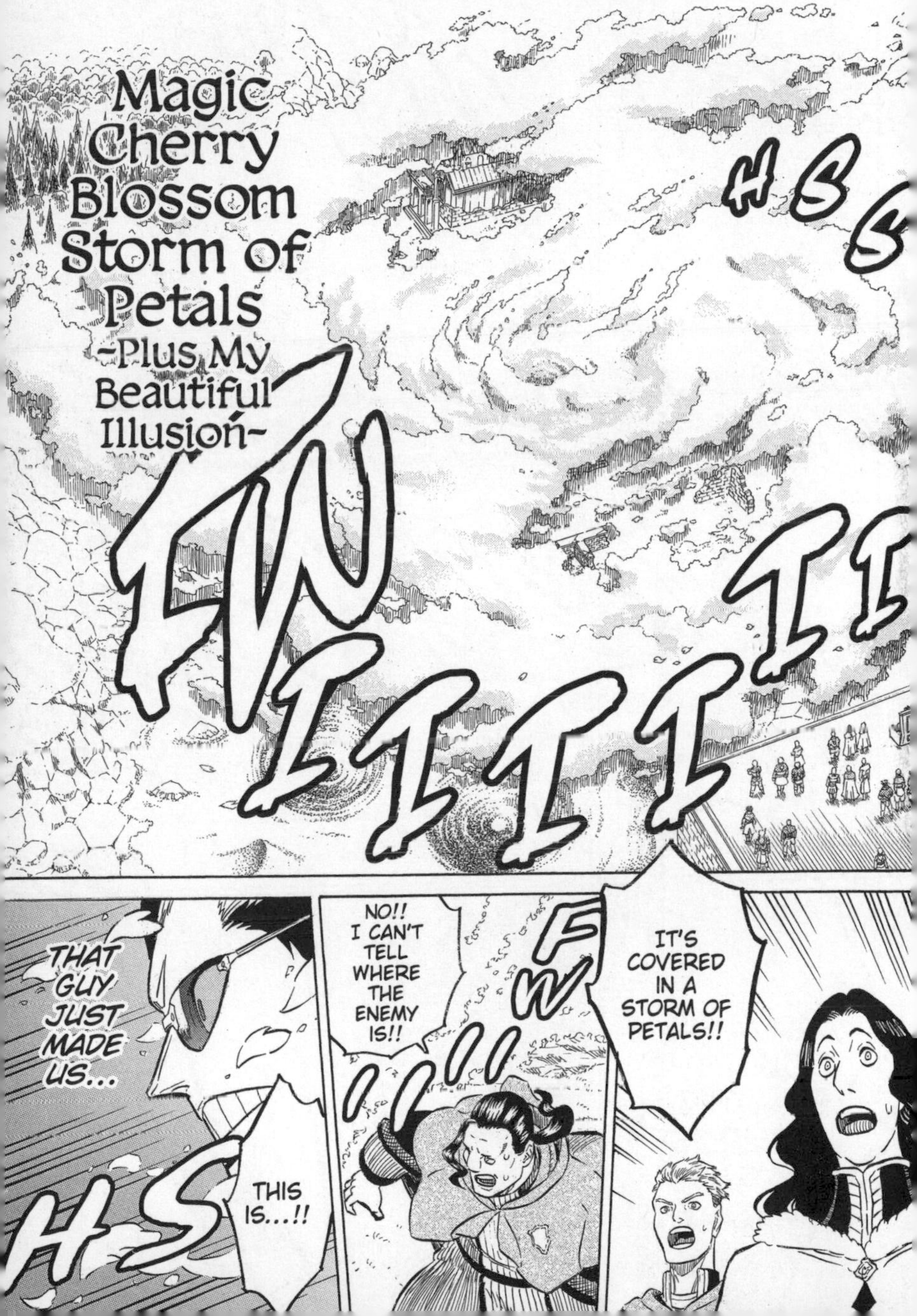
HSS
Magic Cherry Blossom Storm of Petals -Plus My Beautiful Illusion-
FWIIIIII
IT'S COVERED IN A STORM OF PETALS!!
FW
NO!! I CAN'T TELL WHERE THE ENEMY IS!!
THAT GUY JUST MADE US...
THIS IS...!!
HS

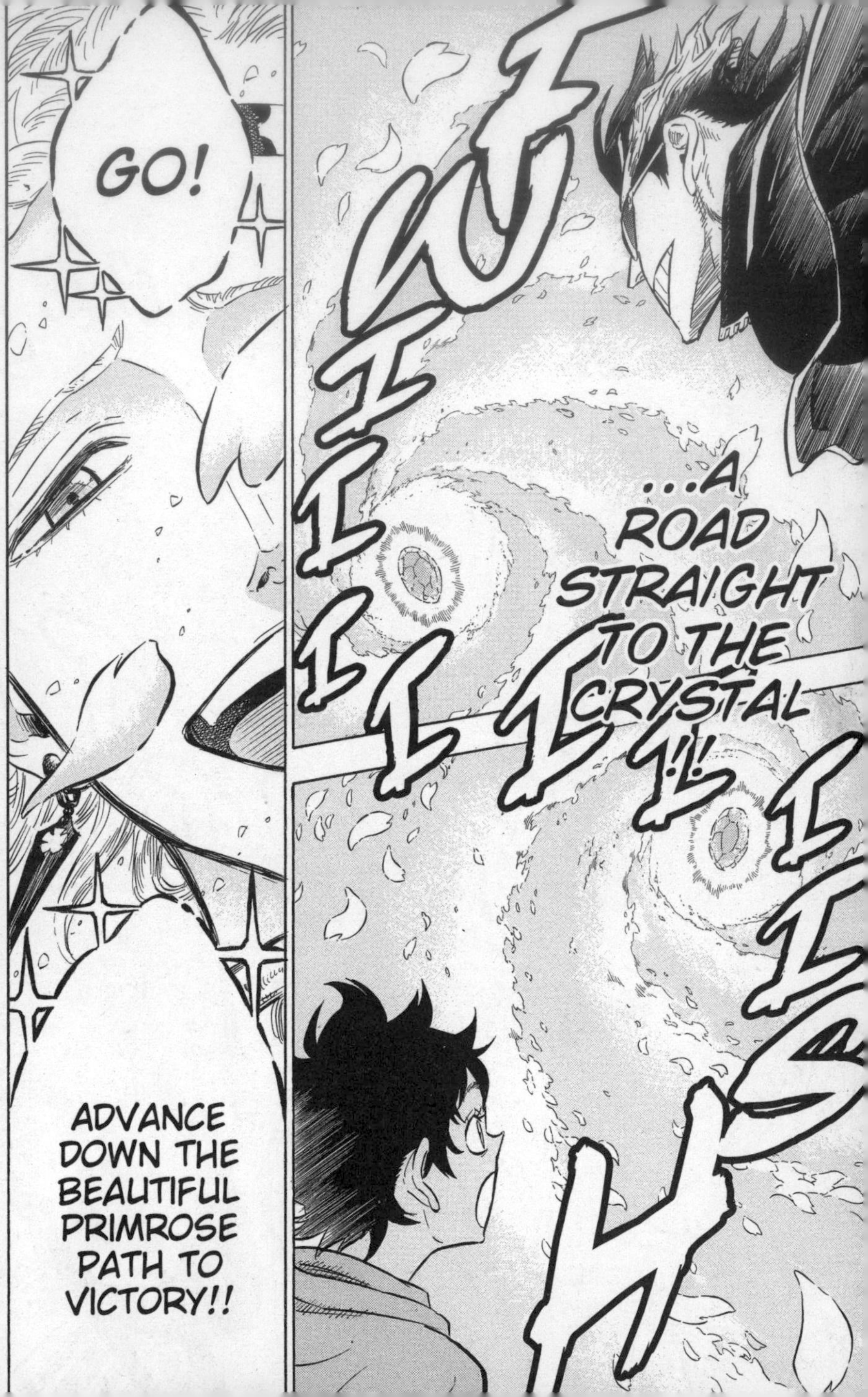
...A ROAD STRAIGHT TO THE CRYSTAL!!
GO!
ADVANCE DOWN THE BEAUTIFUL PRIMROSE PATH TO VICTORY!!

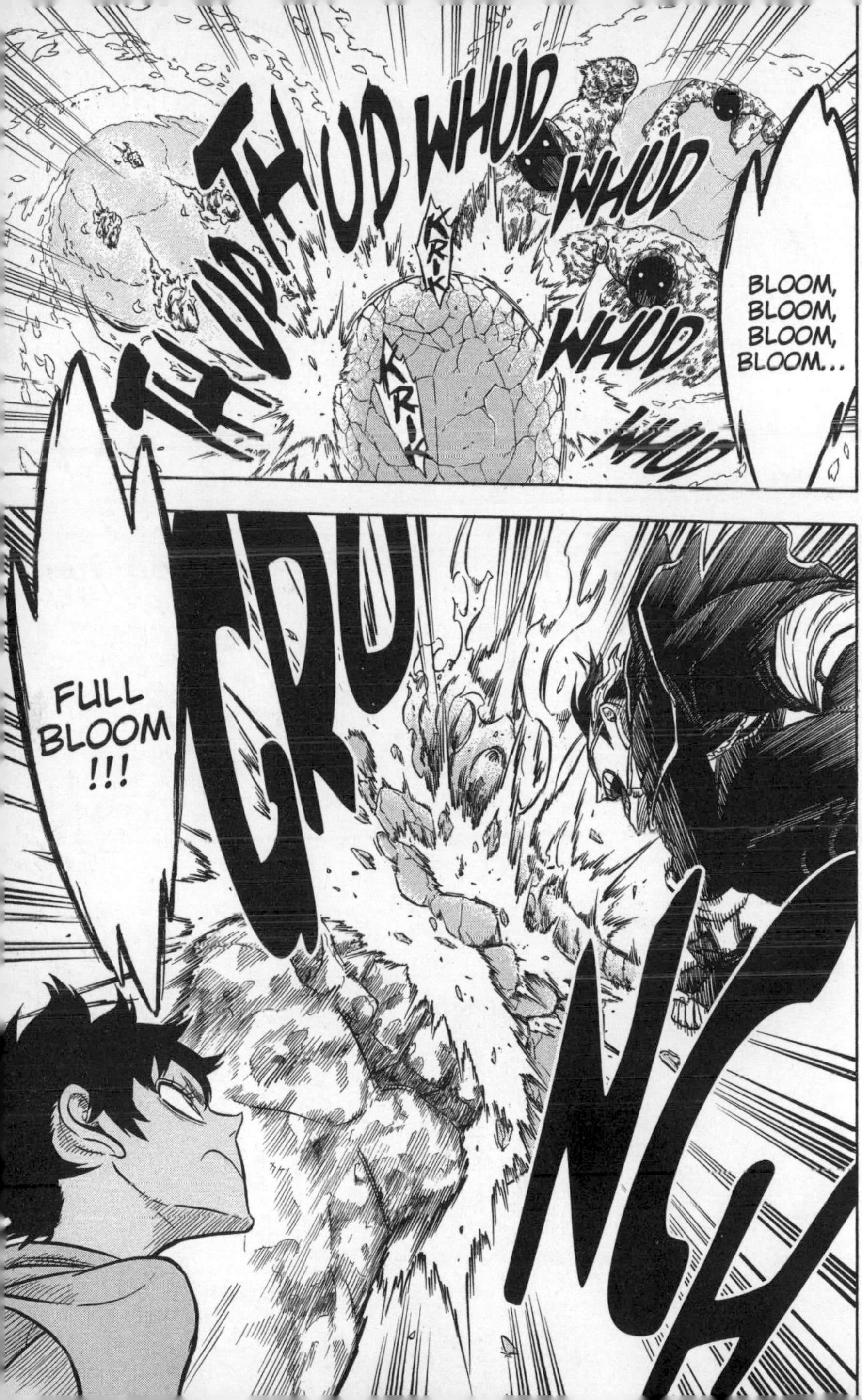
BLOOM, BLOOM, BLOOM, BLOOM...
WHUD
WHUD
WHUD
WHUD
KRIK
KRIK
THUD
THUD
FULL BLOOM !!!
CRUNCH

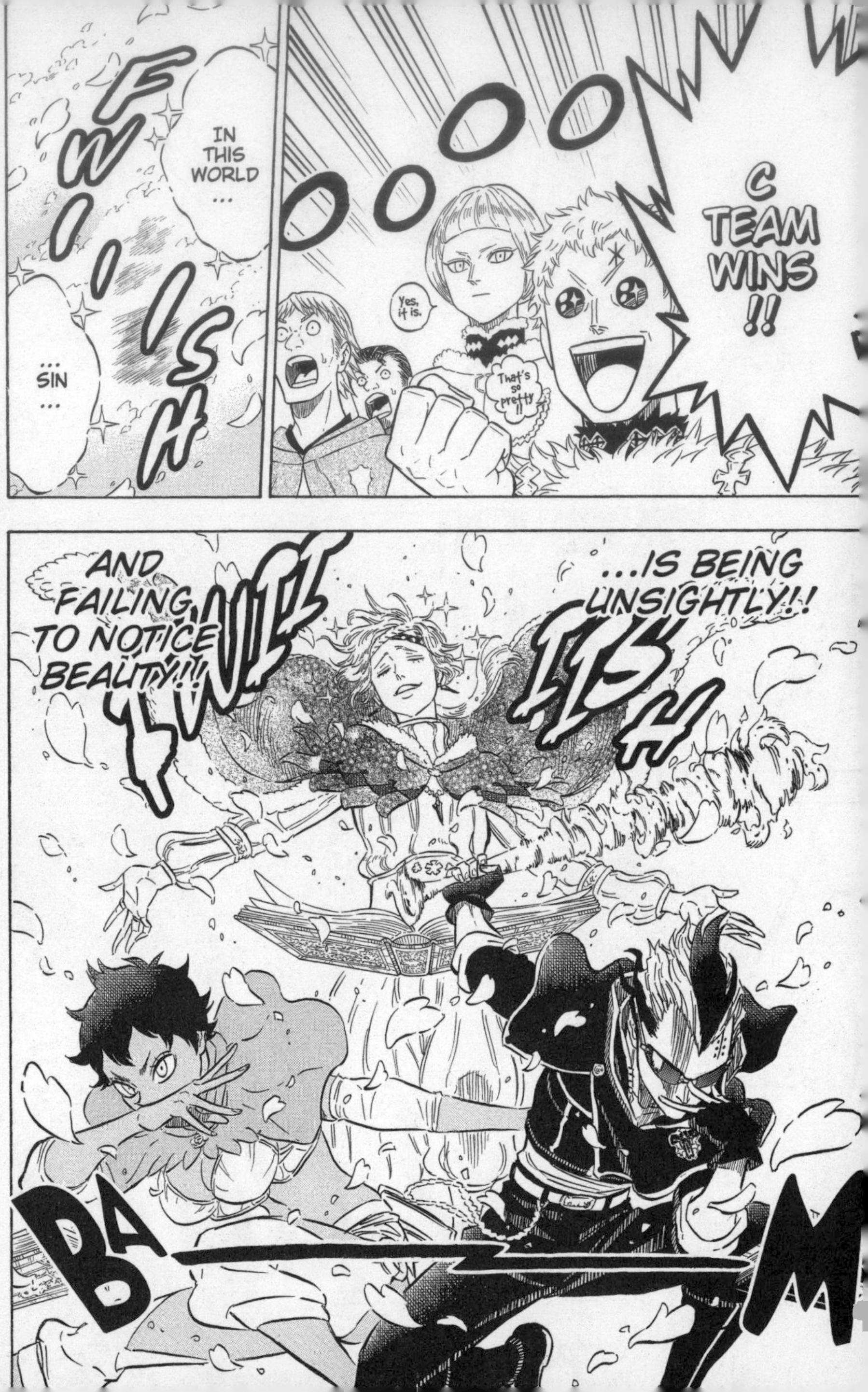
OOOOOOW
C TEAM WINS!!
Yes, it is.
That's so pretty!!
FWIIISH
IN THIS WORLD...
...SIN...
AND FAILING TO NOTICE BEAUTY!!
...IS BEING UNSIGHTLY!!
BAM

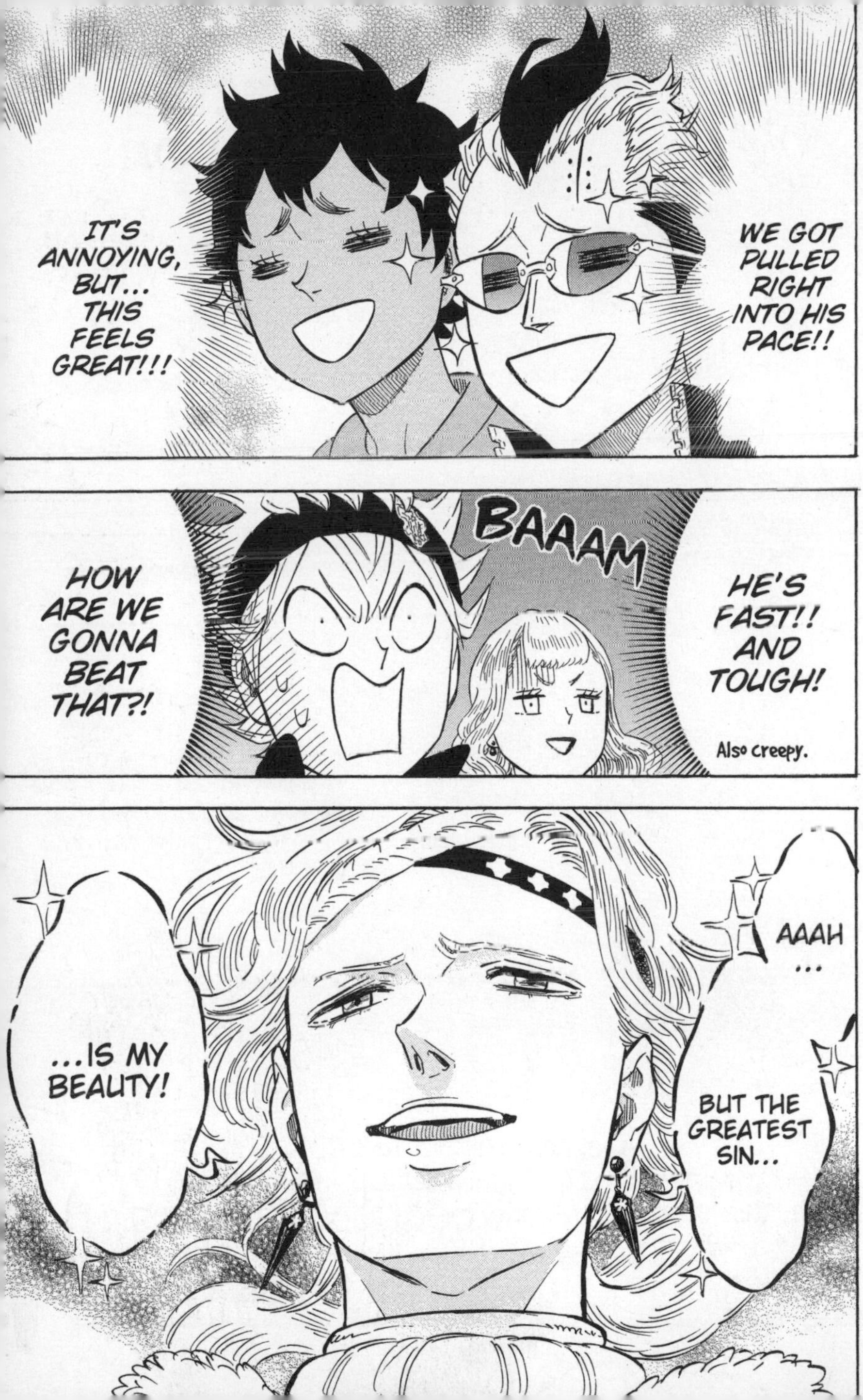
WE GOT PULLED RIGHT INTO HIS PACE!!
IT'S ANNOYING, BUT... THIS FEELS GREAT!!!
HE'S FAST!! AND TOUGH!
Also creepy.
BAAAM
HOW ARE WE GONNA BEAT THAT?!
AAAH...
BUT THE GREATEST SIN...
...IS MY BEAUTY!

Kirsch Vermillion

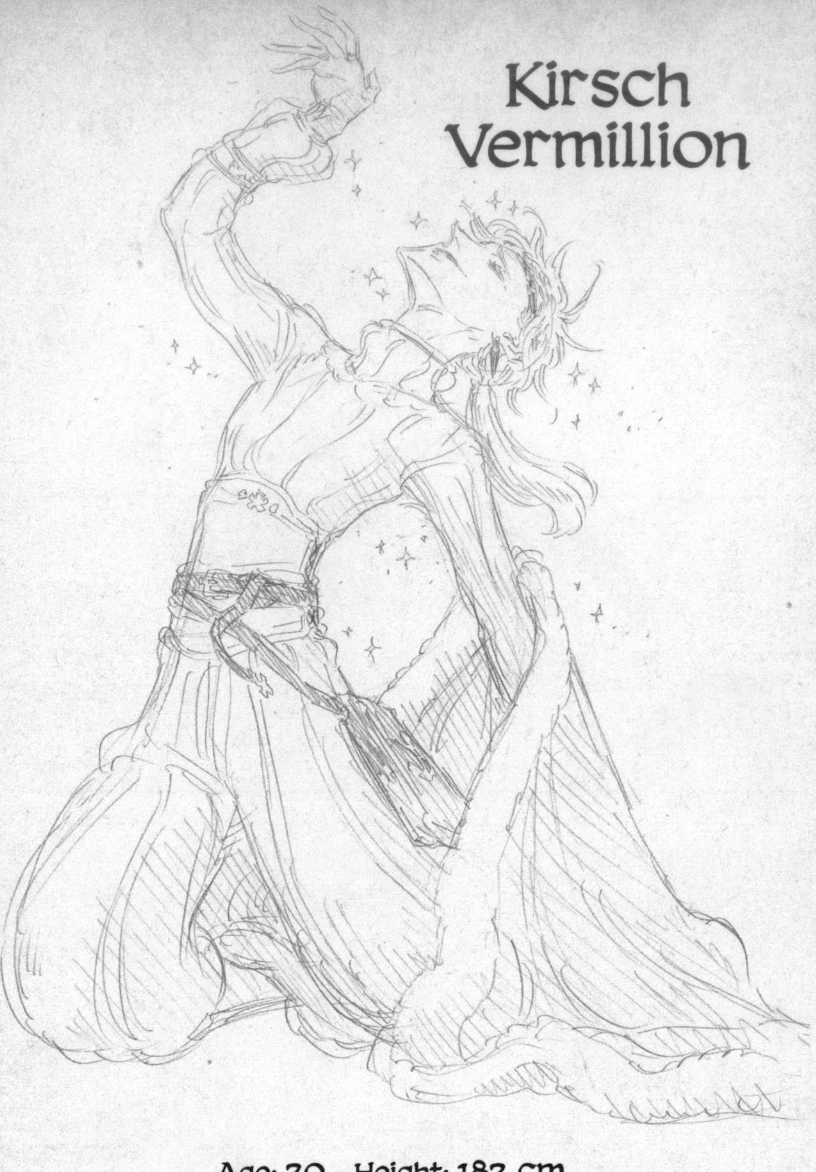

Age: 20 Height: 182 cm
Birthday: April 24 Sign: Taurus Blood Type: O
Likes: Vegetable terrine, beautiful things

Character Profile

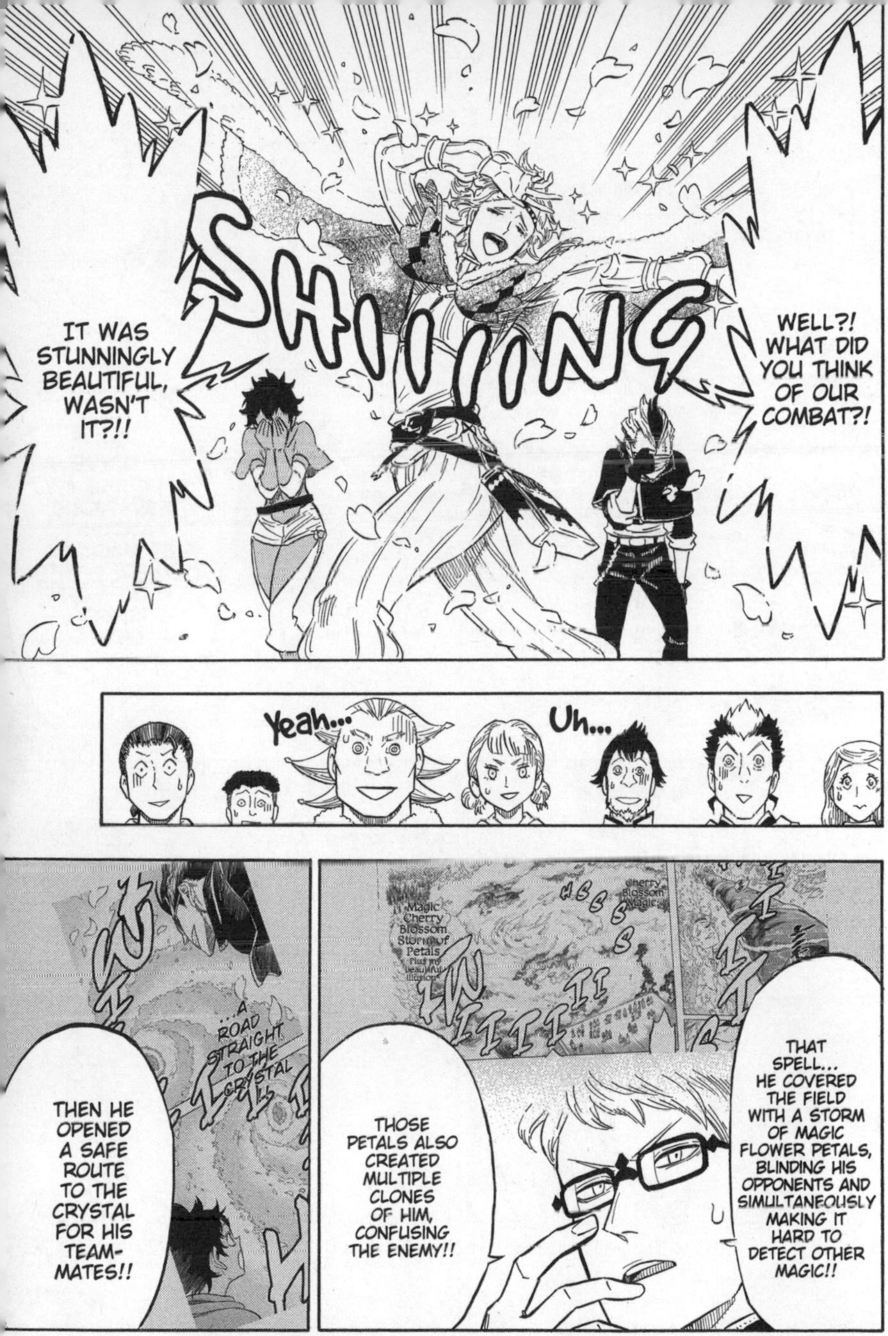
WELL?! WHAT DID YOU THINK OF OUR COMBAT?!
SHIIIING
IT WAS STUNNINGLY BEAUTIFUL, WASN'T IT?!!
Uh...
Yeah...
Cherry Blossom Magic
HSSSS
Magic Cherry Blossom Storm of Petals
Plus my beautiful illusion
THAT SPELL... HE COVERED THE FIELD WITH A STORM OF MAGIC FLOWER PETALS, BLINDING HIS OPPONENTS AND SIMULTANEOUSLY MAKING IT HARD TO DETECT OTHER MAGIC!!
THOSE PETALS ALSO CREATED MULTIPLE CLONES OF HIM, CONFUSING THE ENEMY!!
...A ROAD STRAIGHT TO THE CRYSTAL
THEN HE OPENED A SAFE ROUTE TO THE CRYSTAL FOR HIS TEAM-MATES!!

Page 117: The Two Spatial Magic Users

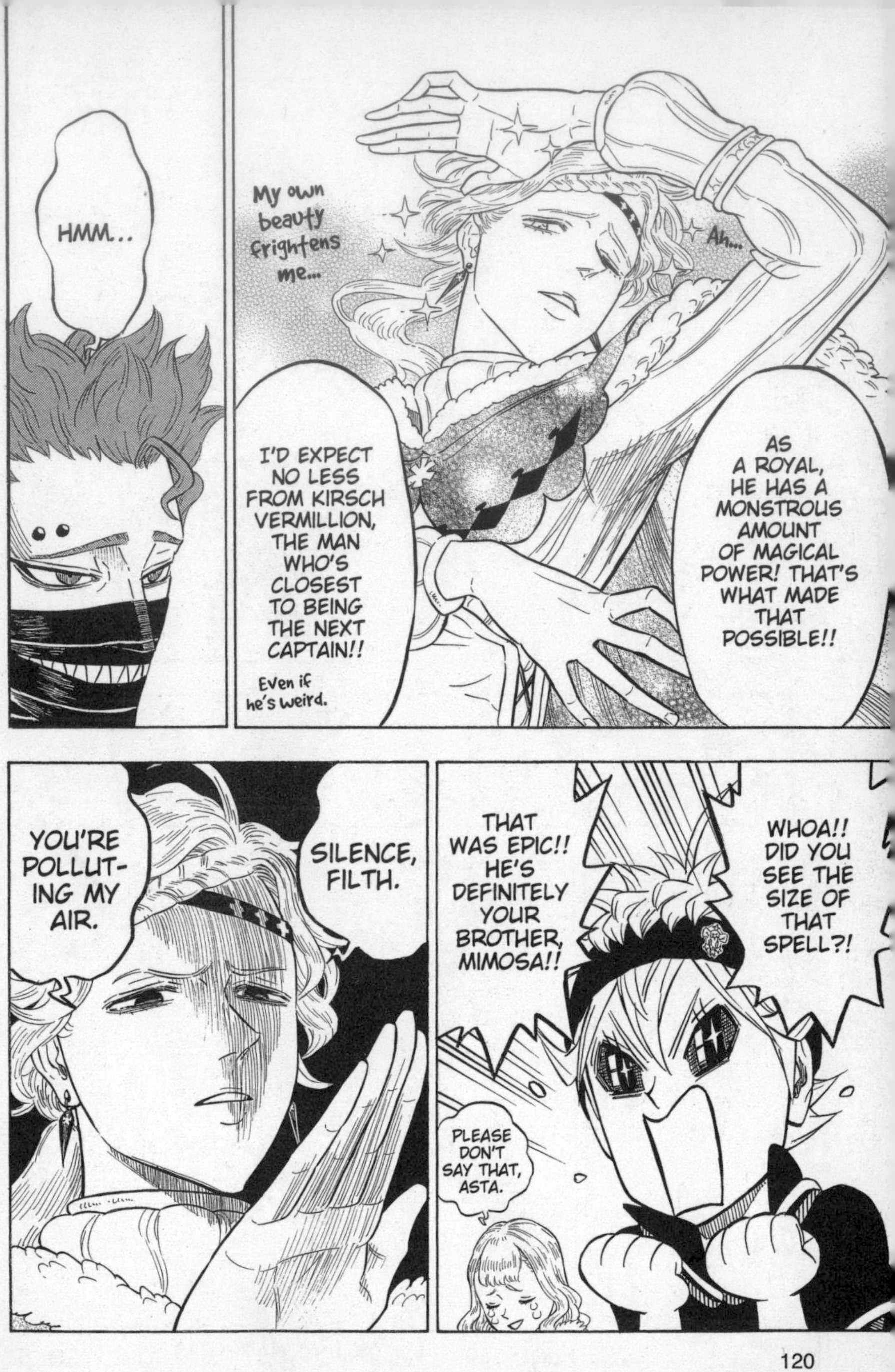
Ah...
My own beauty frightens me...
AS A ROYAL, HE HAS A MONSTROUS AMOUNT OF MAGICAL POWER! THAT'S WHAT MADE THAT POSSIBLE!!
I'D EXPECT NO LESS FROM KIRSCH VERMILLION, THE MAN WHO'S CLOSEST TO BEING THE NEXT CAPTAIN!!
Even if he's weird.
HMM...
WHOA!! DID YOU SEE THE SIZE OF THAT SPELL?!
THAT WAS EPIC!! HE'S DEFINITELY YOUR BROTHER, MIMOSA!!
PLEASE DON'T SAY THAT, ASTA.
SILENCE, FILTH.
YOU'RE POLLUT-ING MY AIR.

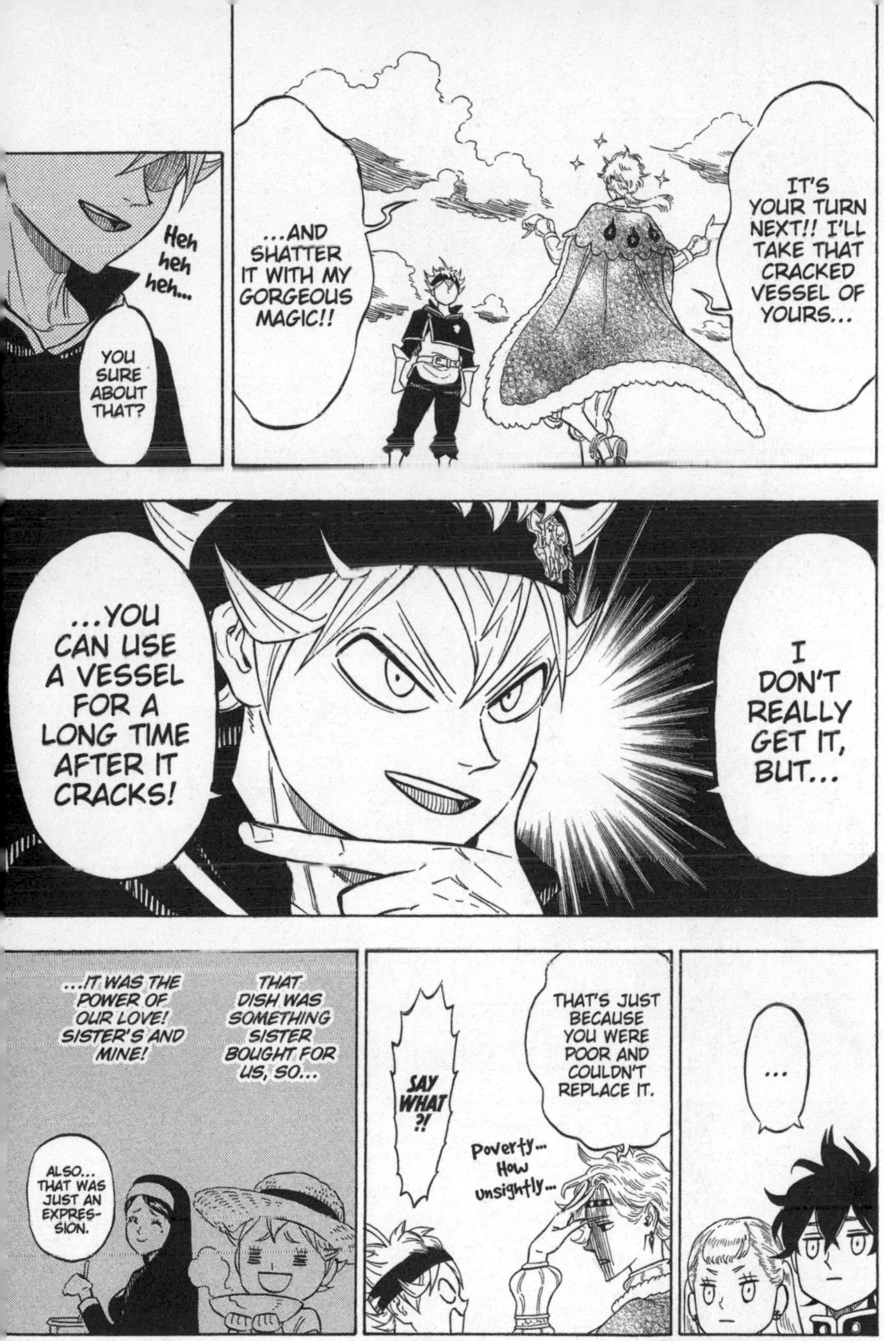
IT'S YOUR TURN NEXT!! I'LL TAKE THAT CRACKED VESSEL OF YOURS...
...AND SHATTER IT WITH MY GORGEOUS MAGIC!!
Heh heh heh...
YOU SURE ABOUT THAT?
I DON'T REALLY GET IT, BUT...
...YOU CAN USE A VESSEL FOR A LONG TIME AFTER IT CRACKS!
...
THAT'S JUST BECAUSE YOU WERE POOR AND COULDN'T REPLACE IT.
SAY WHAT?!
Poverty... How unsightly...
THAT DISH WAS SOMETHING SISTER BOUGHT FOR US, SO...
...IT WAS THE POWER OF OUR LOVE! SISTER'S AND MINE!
ALSO... THAT WAS JUST AN EXPRESSION.

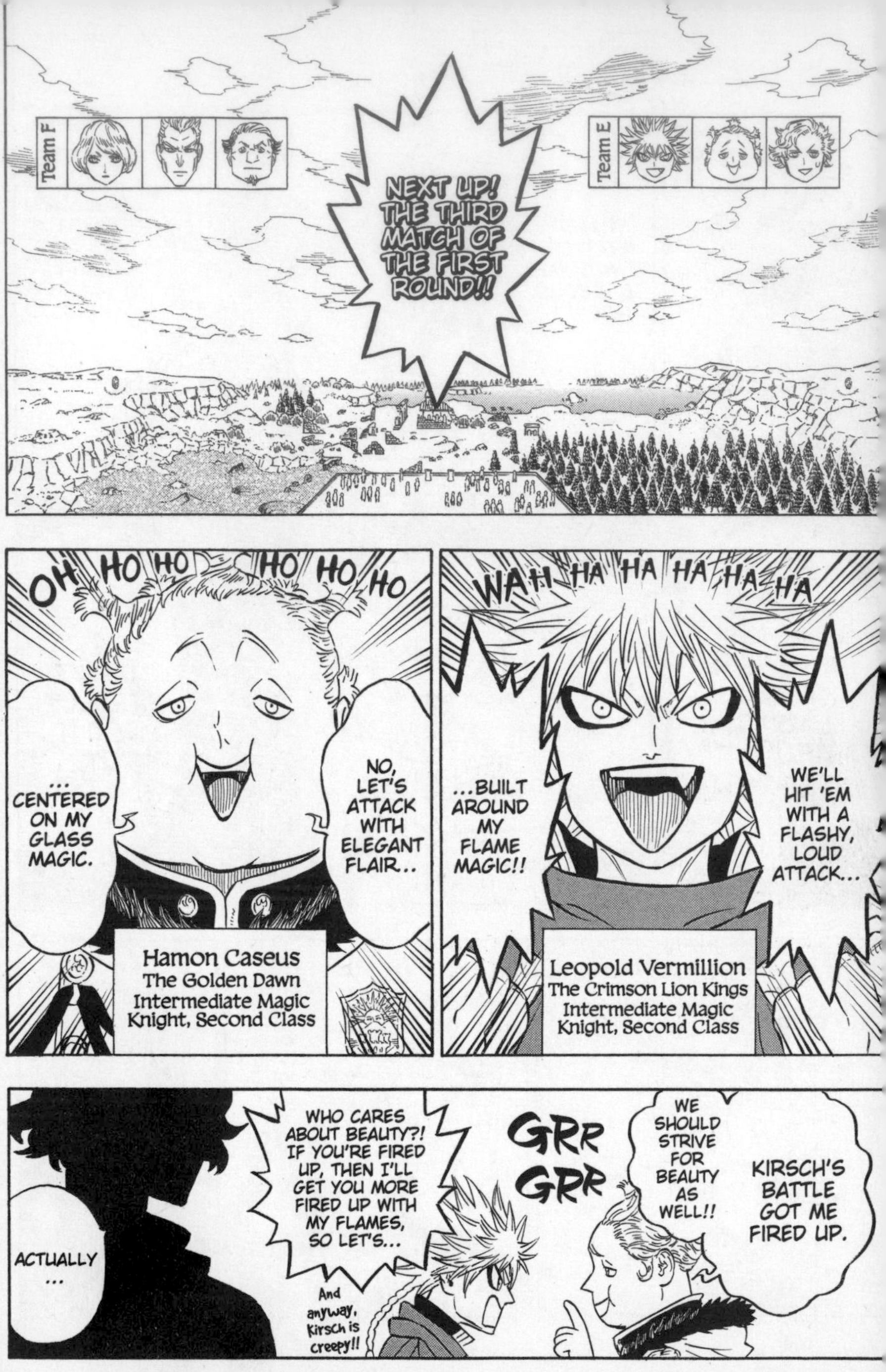
Team E
NEXT UP! THE THIRD MATCH OF THE FIRST ROUND!!
Team F
WAH HA HA HA HA HA
WE'LL HIT 'EM WITH A FLASHY, LOUD ATTACK...
...BUILT AROUND MY FLAME MAGIC!!
Leopold Vermillion The Crimson Lion Kings Intermediate Magic Knight, Second Class
OH HO HO HO HO HO
NO, LET'S ATTACK WITH ELEGANT FLAIR...
...CENTERED ON MY GLASS MAGIC.
Hamon Caseus The Golden Dawn Intermediate Magic Knight, Second Class
KIRSCH'S BATTLE GOT ME FIRED UP.
WE SHOULD STRIVE FOR BEAUTY AS WELL!!
GRR GRR
WHO CARES ABOUT BEAUTY?! IF YOU'RE FIRED UP, THEN I'LL GET YOU MORE FIRED UP WITH MY FLAMES, SO LET'S...
And anyway, Kirsch is creepy!!
ACTUALLY...

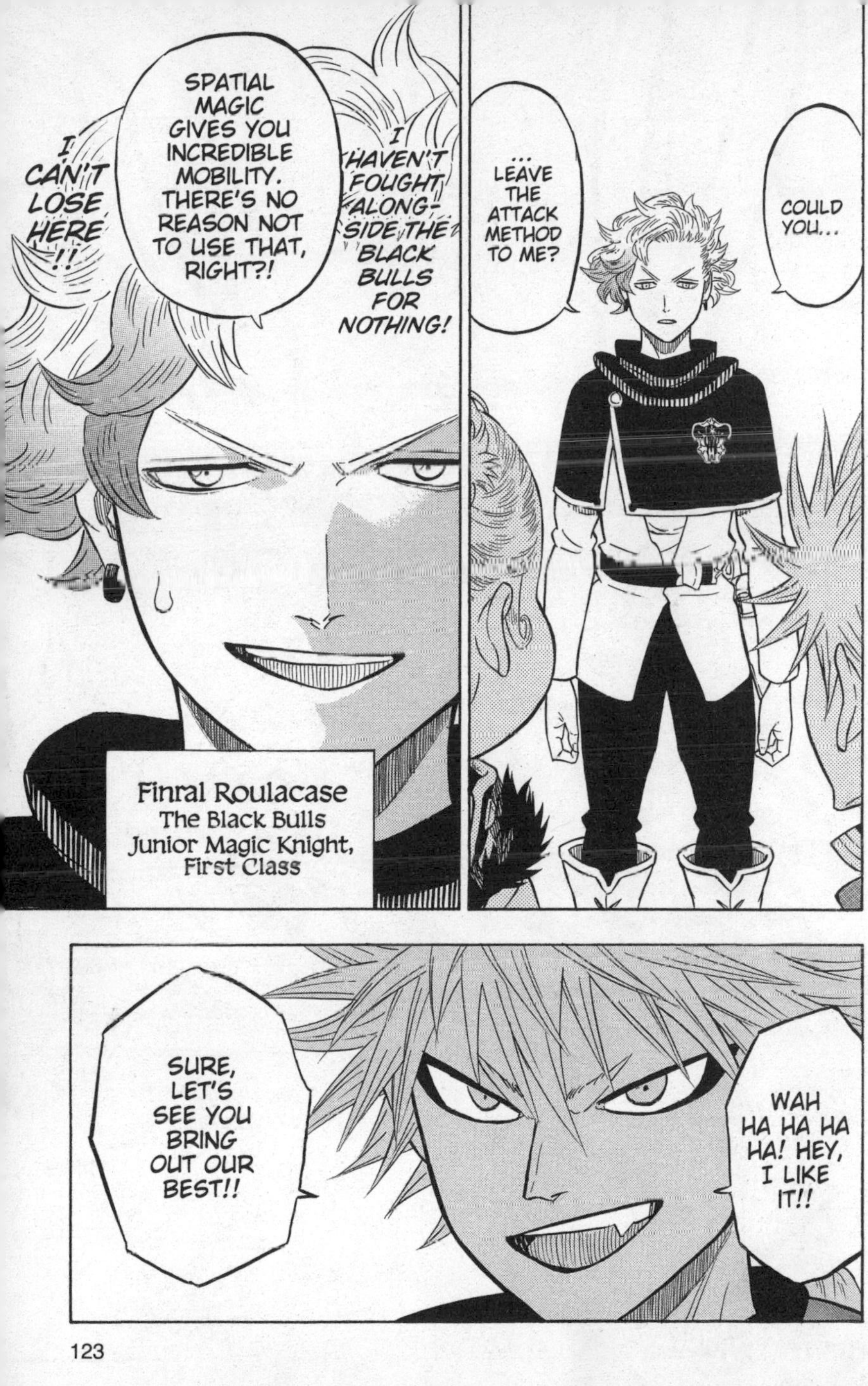
COULD YOU...
...LEAVE THE ATTACK METHOD TO ME?
I HAVEN'T FOUGHT ALONGSIDE THE BLACK BULLS FOR NOTHING!
SPATIAL MAGIC GIVES YOU INCREDIBLE MOBILITY. THERE'S NO REASON NOT TO USE THAT, RIGHT?!
I CAN'T LOSE HERE!!
Finral Roulacase
The Black Bulls
Junior Magic Knight, First Class
WAH HA HA HA HA! HEY, I LIKE IT!!
SURE, LET'S SEE YOU BRING OUT OUR BEST!!

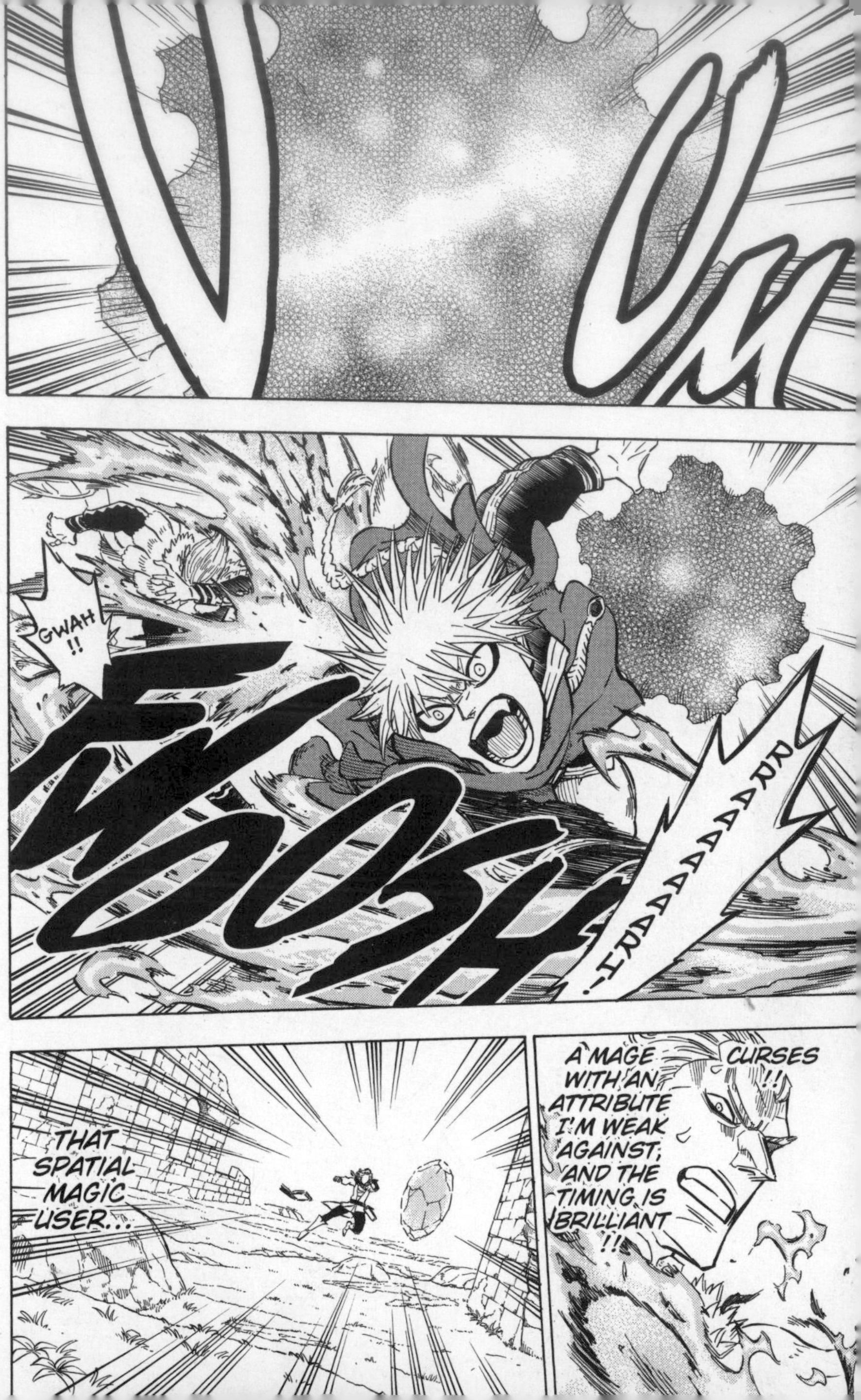
RRAAAAAAAAAAH!!
WOOSH
GWAH !!
CURSES !!
A MAGE WITH AN ATTRIBUTE I'M WEAK AGAINST, AND THE TIMING IS BRILLIANT !!
THAT SPATIAL MAGIC USER...

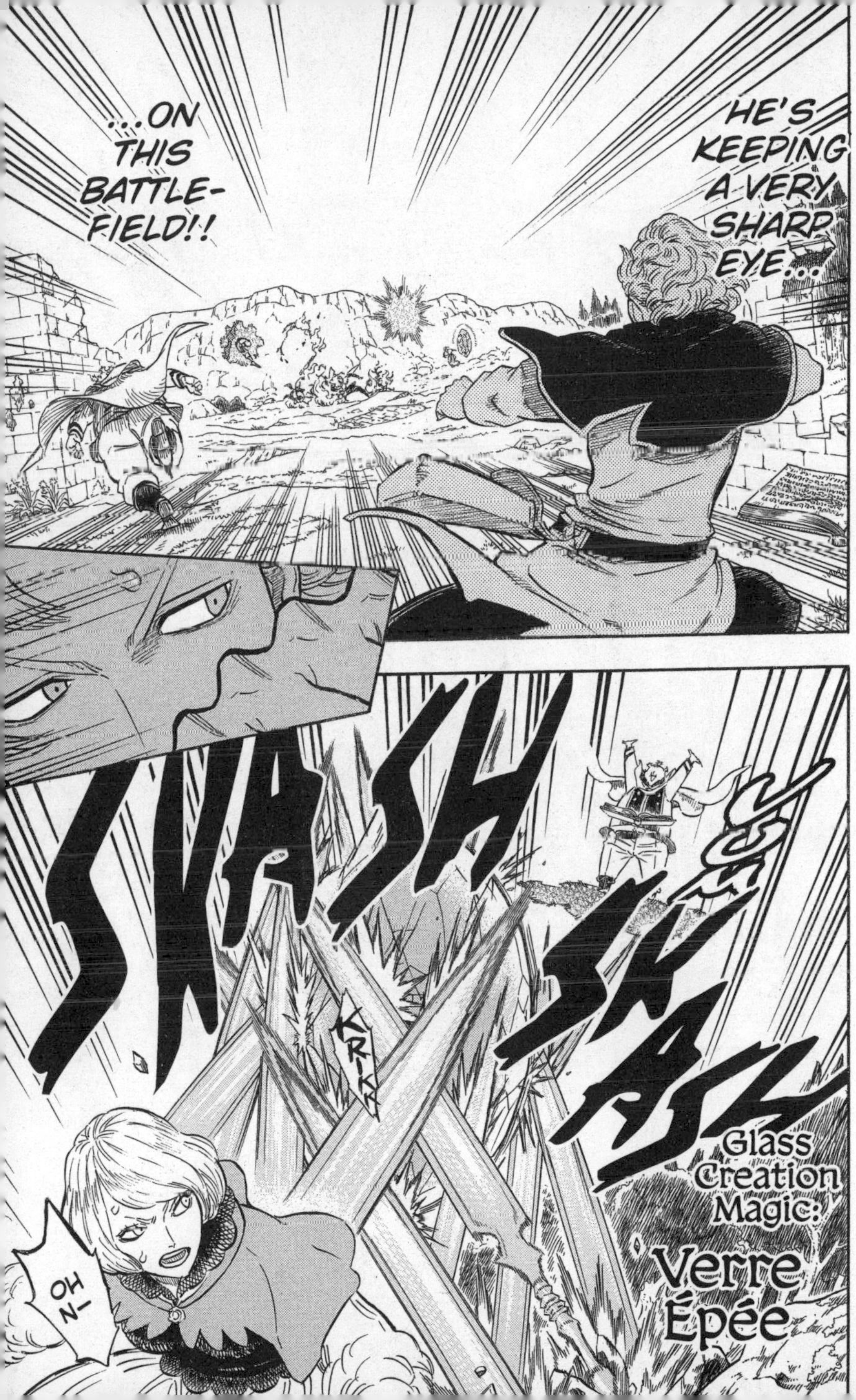
HE'S KEEPING A VERY SHARP EYE...
...ON THIS BATTLE-FIELD!!
SWASH
Glass Creation Magic: Verre Épée
KRIKK
OH N-

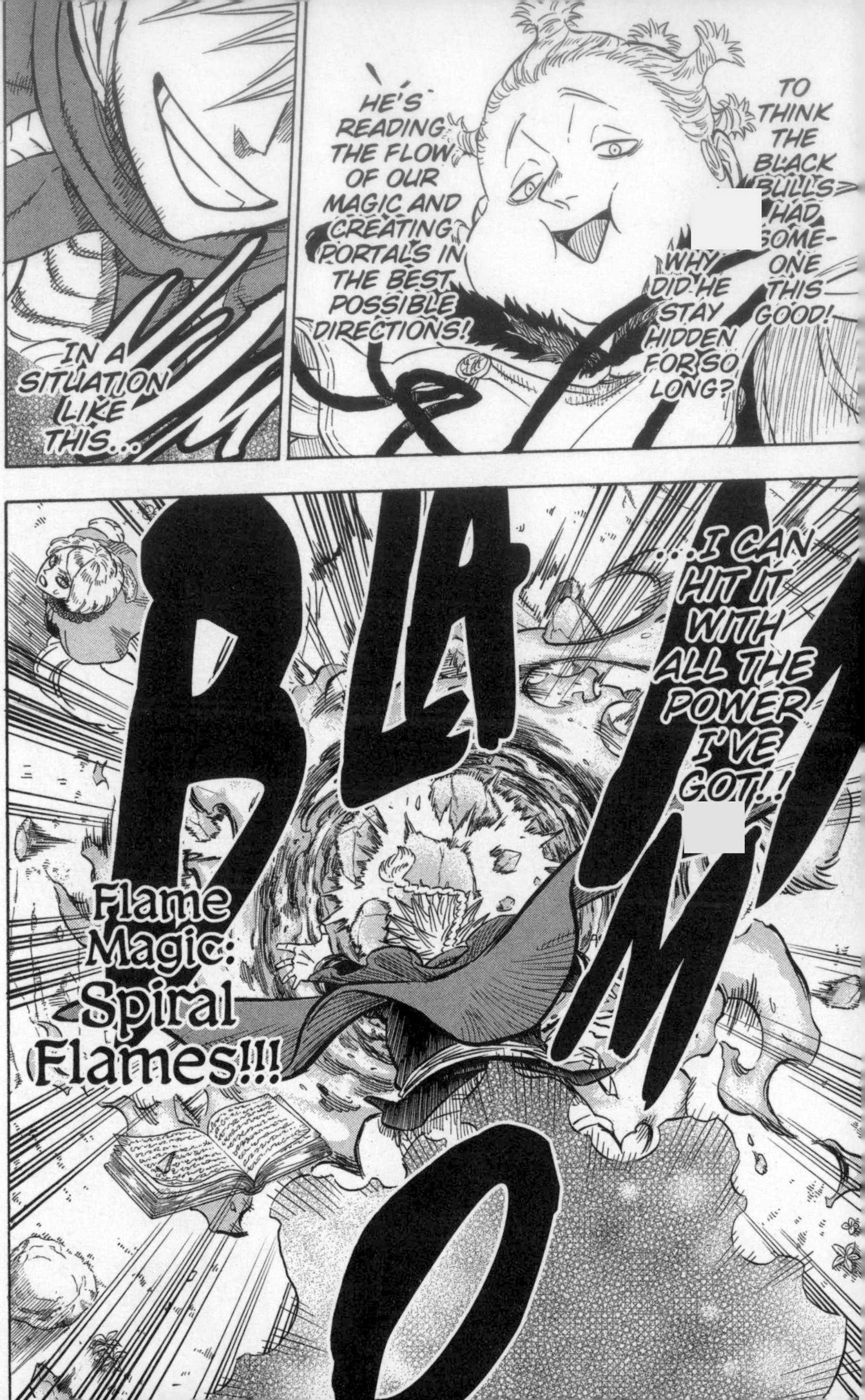
TO THINK THE BLACK BULLS HAD SOMEONE THIS GOOD!
WHY DID HE STAY HIDDEN FOR SO LONG?
HE'S READING THE FLOW OF OUR MAGIC AND CREATING PORTALS IN THE BEST POSSIBLE DIRECTIONS!
IN A SITUATION LIKE THIS...
...I CAN HIT IT WITH ALL THE POWER I'VE GOT!!
BLAM
Flame Magic: Spiral Flames!!!

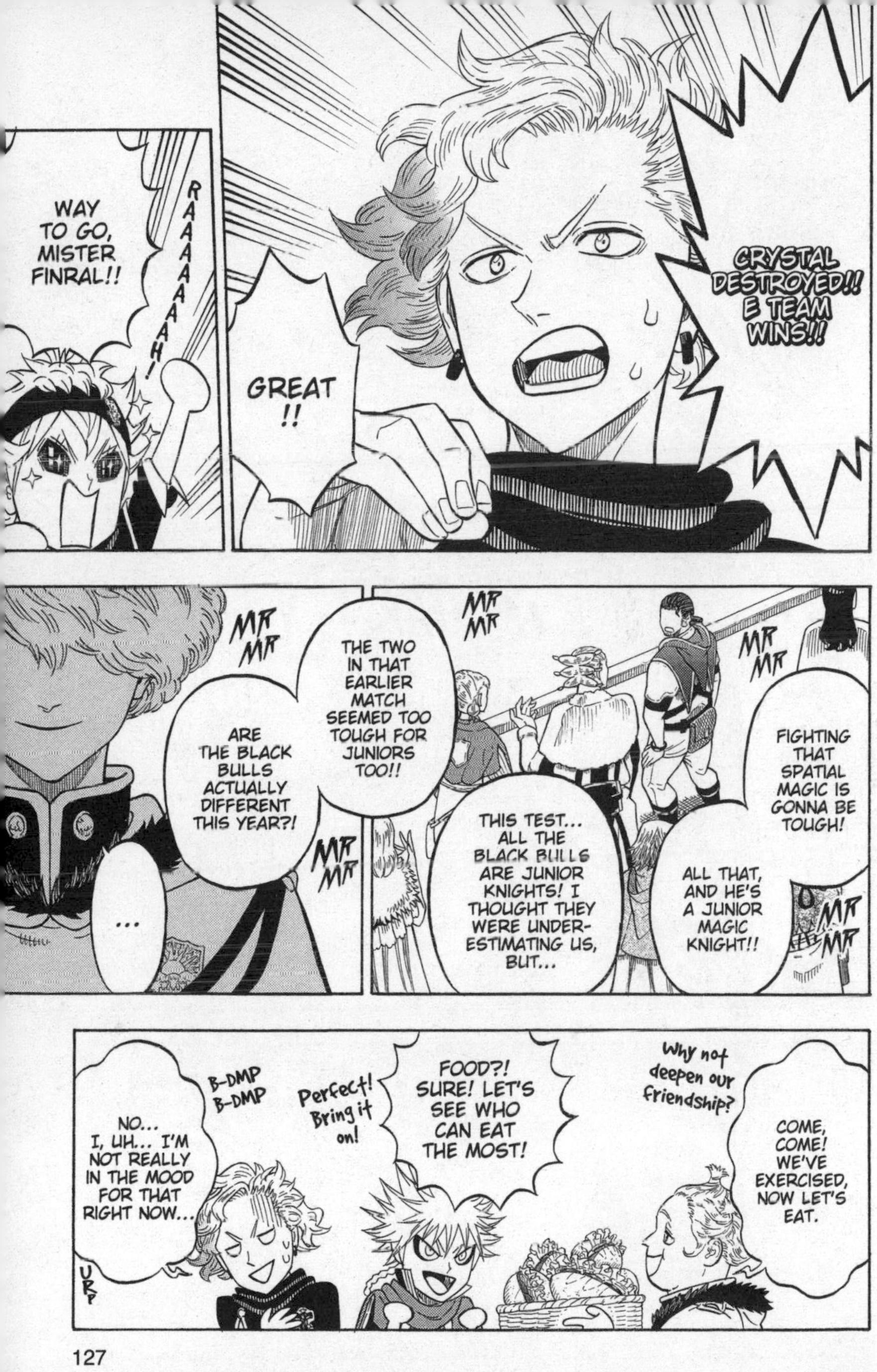

CRYSTAL DESTROYED!! E TEAM WINS!!
GREAT!!
RAAAAAAAH!
WAY TO GO, MISTER FINRAL!!
MR MR
MR MR
FIGHTING THAT SPATIAL MAGIC IS GONNA BE TOUGH!
ALL THAT, AND HE'S A JUNIOR MAGIC KNIGHT!!
MR MR
THIS TEST... ALL THE BLACK BULLS ARE JUNIOR KNIGHTS! I THOUGHT THEY WERE UNDER-ESTIMATING US, BUT...
MR MR
THE TWO IN THAT EARLIER MATCH SEEMED TOO TOUGH FOR JUNIORS TOO!!
MR MR
ARE THE BLACK BULLS ACTUALLY DIFFERENT THIS YEAR?!
...
COME, COME! WE'VE EXERCISED, NOW LET'S EAT.
Why not deepen our friendship?
FOOD?! SURE! LET'S SEE WHO CAN EAT THE MOST!
Perfect! Bring it on!
B-DMP B-DMP
NO... I, UH... I'M NOT REALLY IN THE MOOD FOR THAT RIGHT NOW...
URP

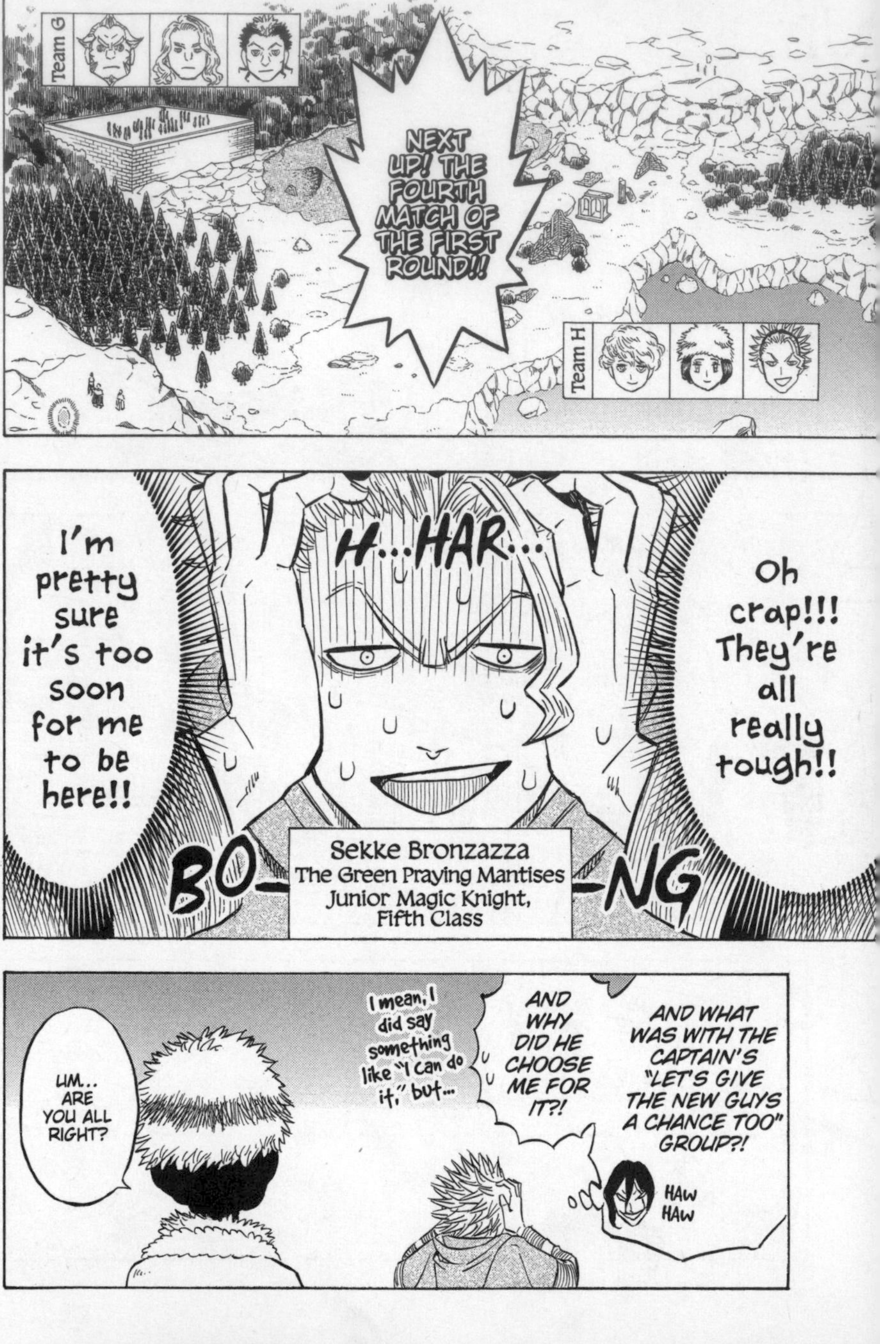
Team G
NEXT UP! THE FOURTH MATCH OF THE FIRST ROUND!!
Team H
Oh crap!!! They're all really tough!!
H...HAR...
I'm pretty sure it's too soon for me to be here!!
Sekke Bronzazza
The Green Praying Mantises
Junior Magic Knight, Fifth Class
BO—
—NG
AND WHAT WAS WITH THE CAPTAIN'S "LET'S GIVE THE NEW GUYS A CHANCE TOO" GROUP?!
HAW HAW
AND WHY DID HE CHOOSE ME FOR IT?!
I mean, I did say something like "I can do it," but...
UM... ARE YOU ALL RIGHT?

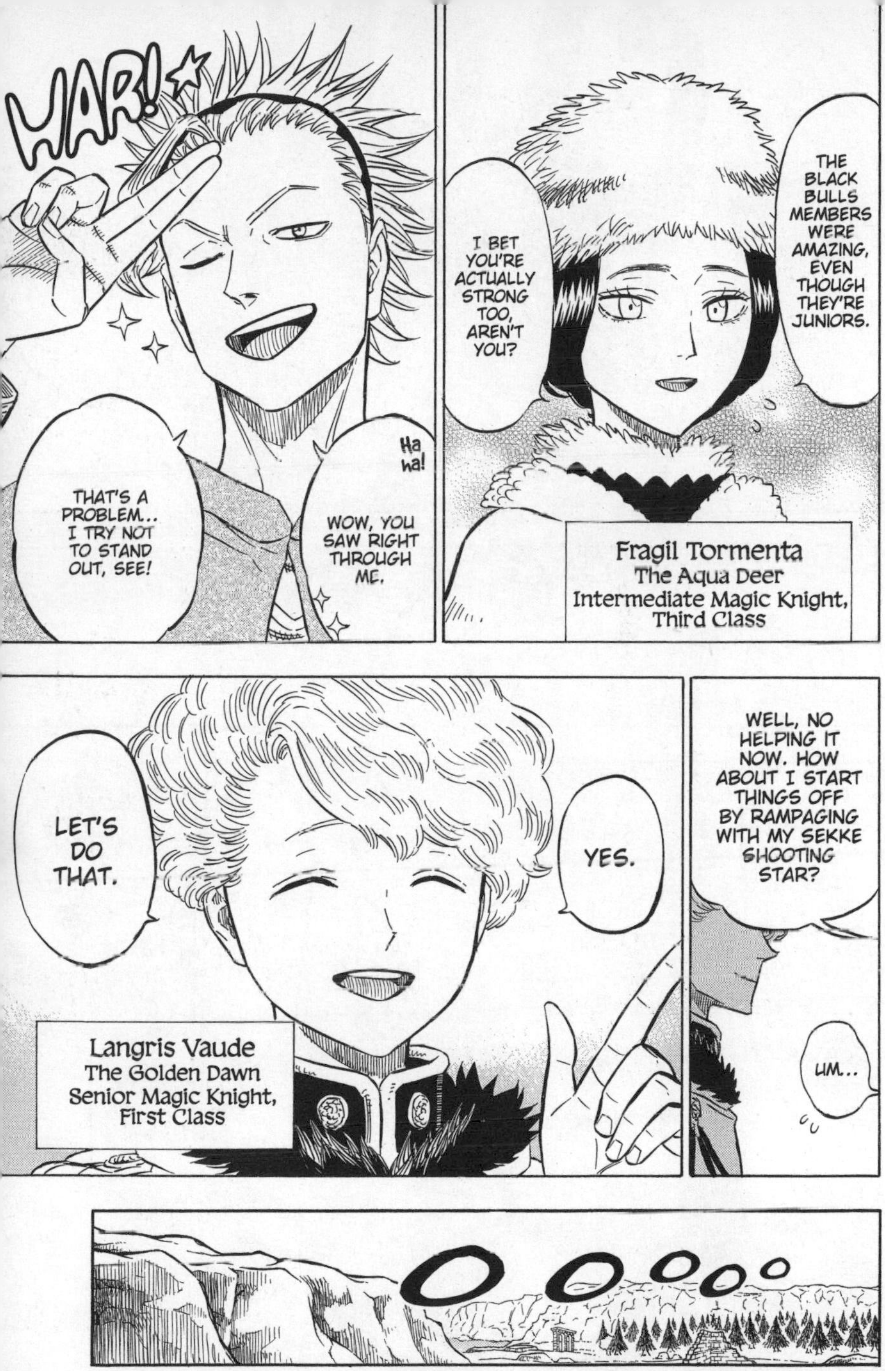
THE BLACK BULLS MEMBERS WERE AMAZING, EVEN THOUGH THEY'RE JUNIORS.
I BET YOU'RE ACTUALLY STRONG TOO, AREN'T YOU?
Fragil Tormenta
The Aqua Deer
Intermediate Magic Knight, Third Class
HAR!☆
Ha ha!
WOW, YOU SAW RIGHT THROUGH ME.
THAT'S A PROBLEM.. I TRY NOT TO STAND OUT, SEE!
WELL, NO HELPING IT NOW. HOW ABOUT I START THINGS OFF BY RAMPAGING WITH MY SEKKE SHOOTING STAR?
UM..
YES.
LET'S DO THAT.
Langris Vaude
The Golden Dawn
Senior Magic Knight, First Class

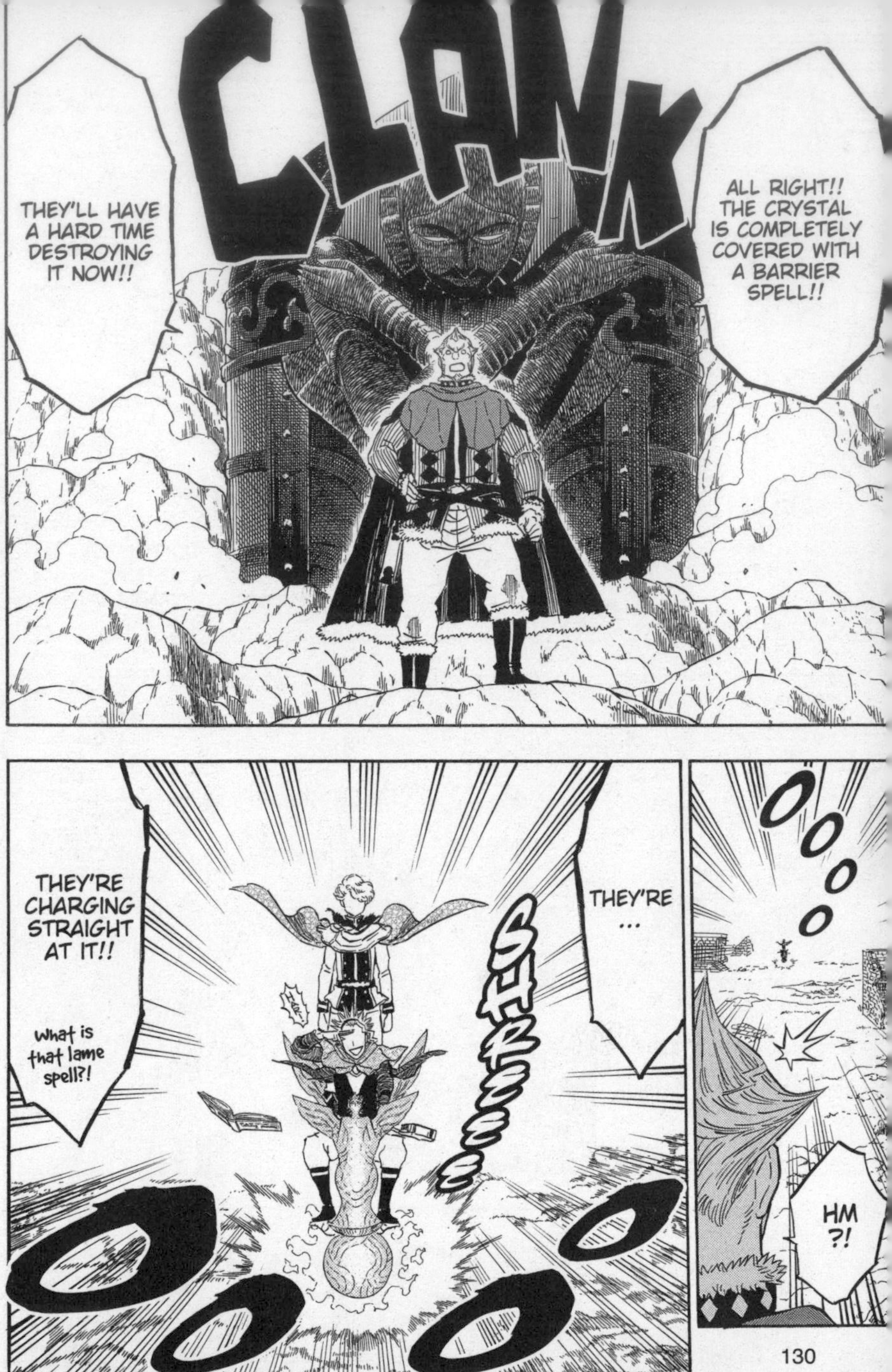
ALL RIGHT!! THE CRYSTAL IS COMPLETELY COVERED WITH A BARRIER SPELL!!
CLANK
THEY'LL HAVE A HARD TIME DESTROYING IT NOW!!
OOOOO
HM?!
THEY'RE ...
SHREEEEEE
THEY'RE CHARGING STRAIGHT AT IT!!
what is that lame spell?!
OOOOO

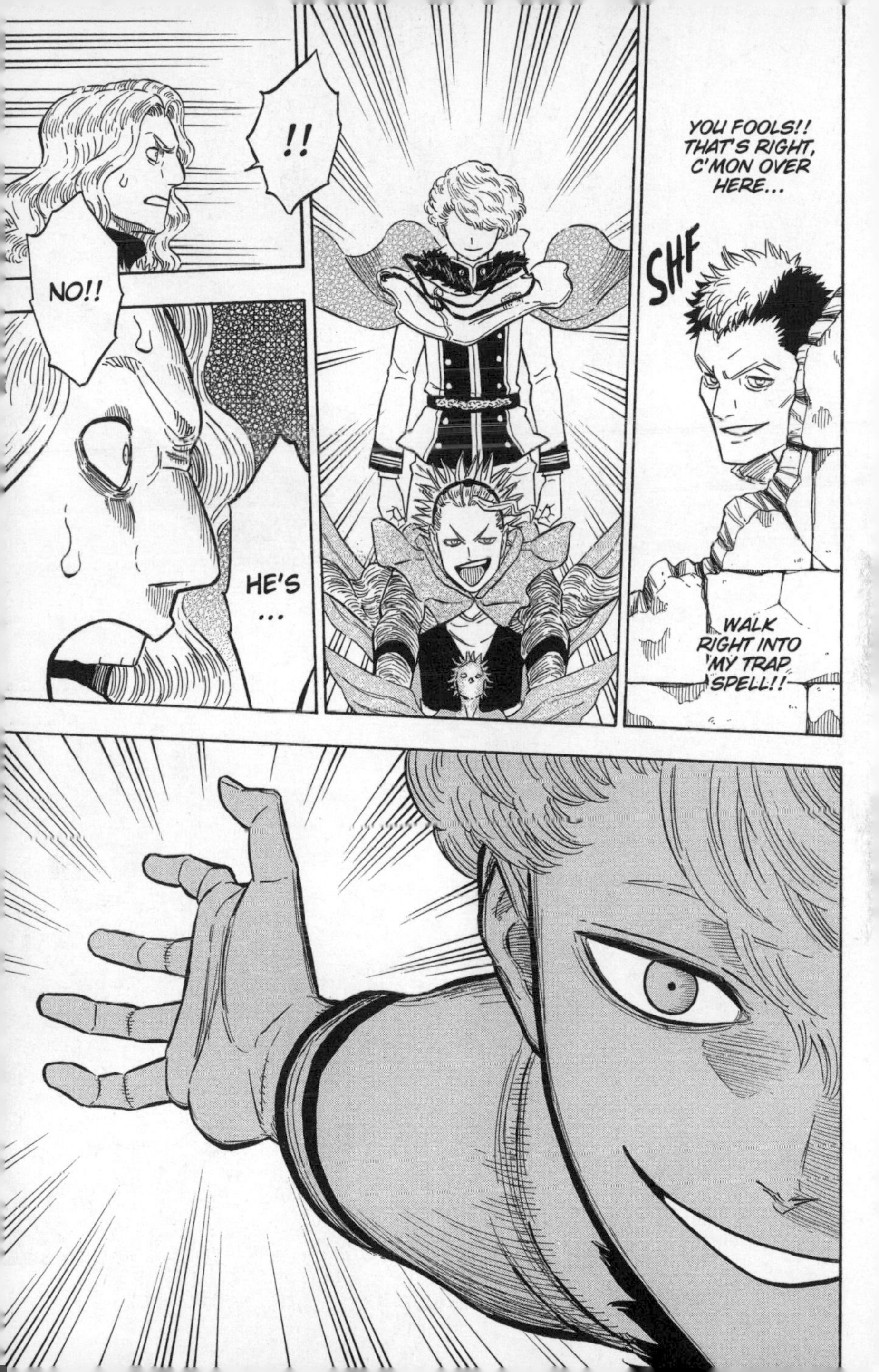
YOU FOOLS!! THAT'S RIGHT, C'MON OVER HERE...
SHF
WALK RIGHT INTO MY TRAP SPELL!!
!!
NO!!
HE'S ...

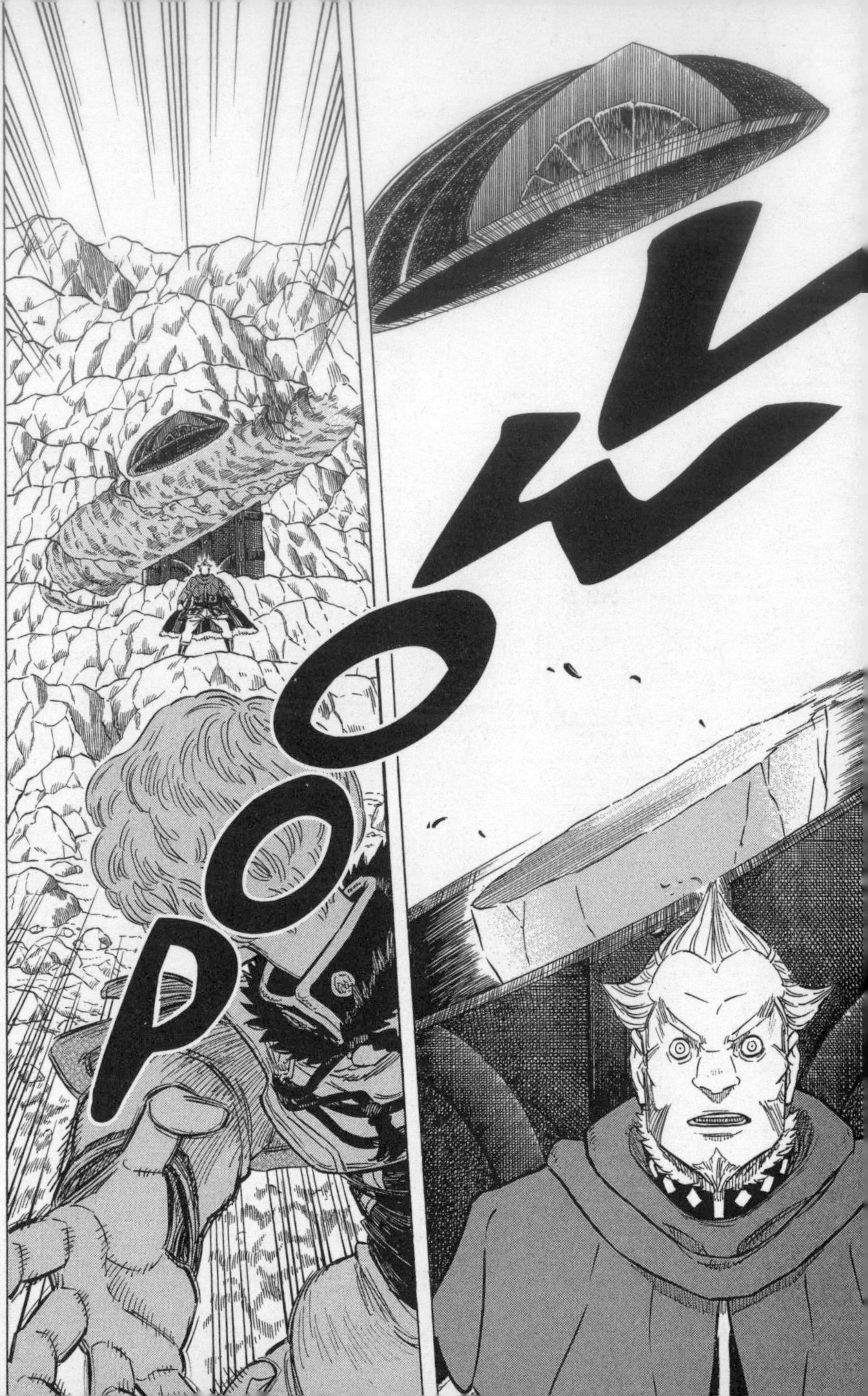
POOOW

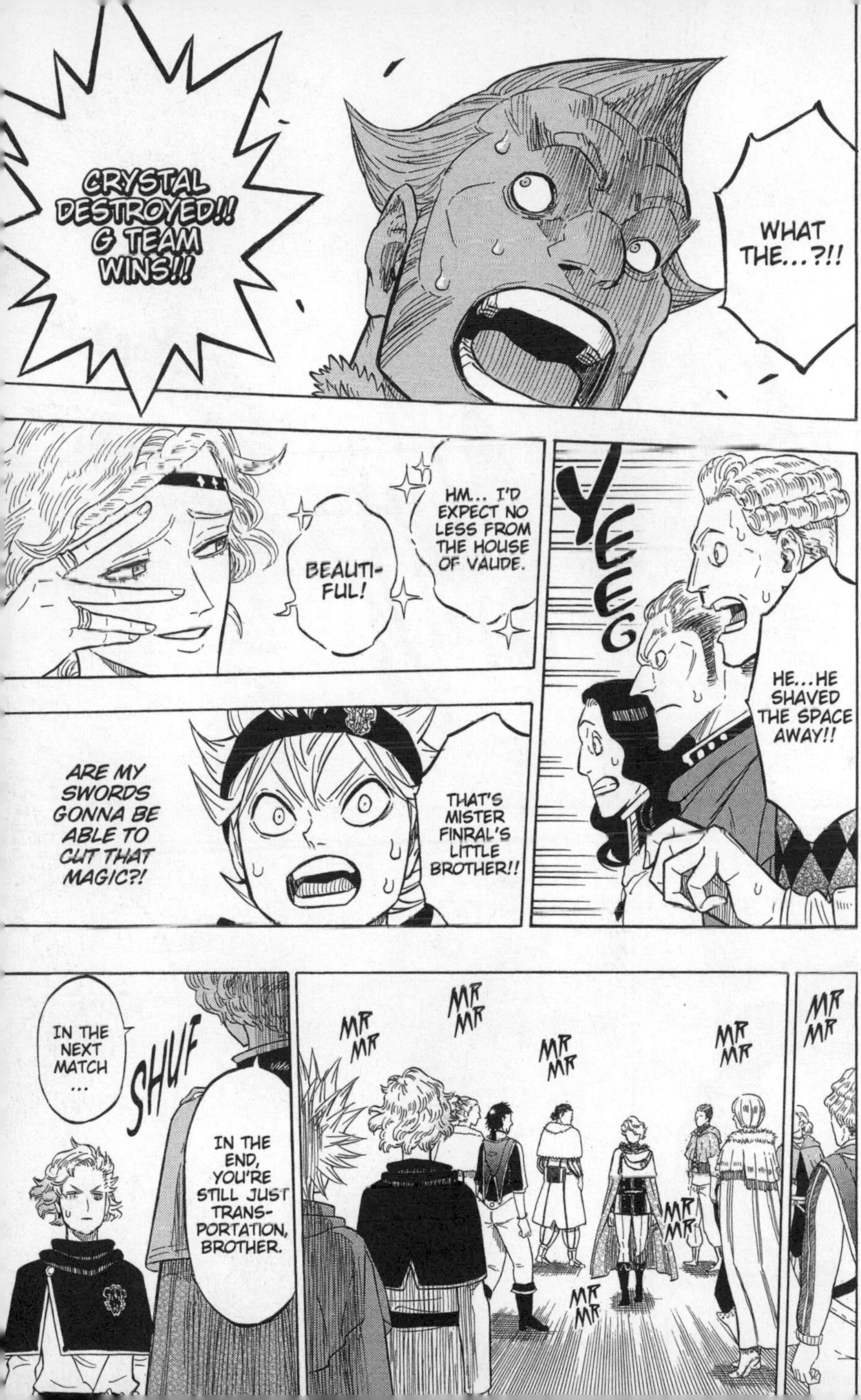
WHAT THE...?!!
CRYSTAL DESTROYED!! G TEAM WINS!!
YEEG
HE...HE SHAVED THE SPACE AWAY!!
HM... I'D EXPECT NO LESS FROM THE HOUSE OF VAUDE.
BEAUTI-FUL!
THAT'S MISTER FINRAL'S LITTLE BROTHER!!
ARE MY SWORDS GONNA BE ABLE TO CUT THAT MAGIC?!
MR MR
MR MR
MR MR
MR MR
MR MR
MR MR
MR MR
IN THE NEXT MATCH ...
SHUF
IN THE END, YOU'RE STILL JUST TRANS-PORTATION, BROTHER.

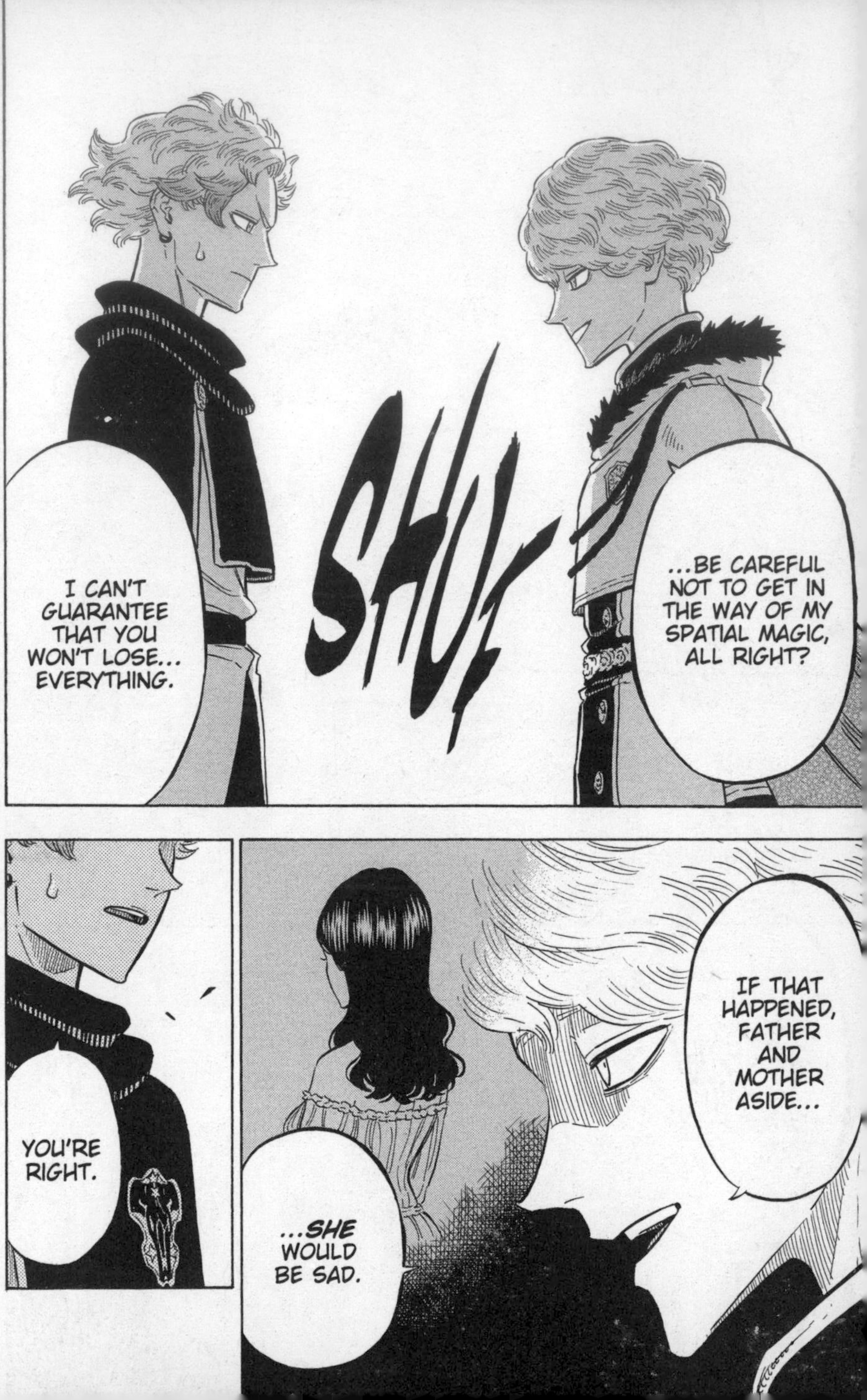
...BE CAREFUL NOT TO GET IN THE WAY OF MY SPATIAL MAGIC, ALL RIGHT?
SHU
I CAN'T GUARANTEE THAT YOU WON'T LOSE... EVERYTHING.
IF THAT HAPPENED, FATHER AND MOTHER ASIDE...
...SHE WOULD BE SAD.
YOU'RE RIGHT.

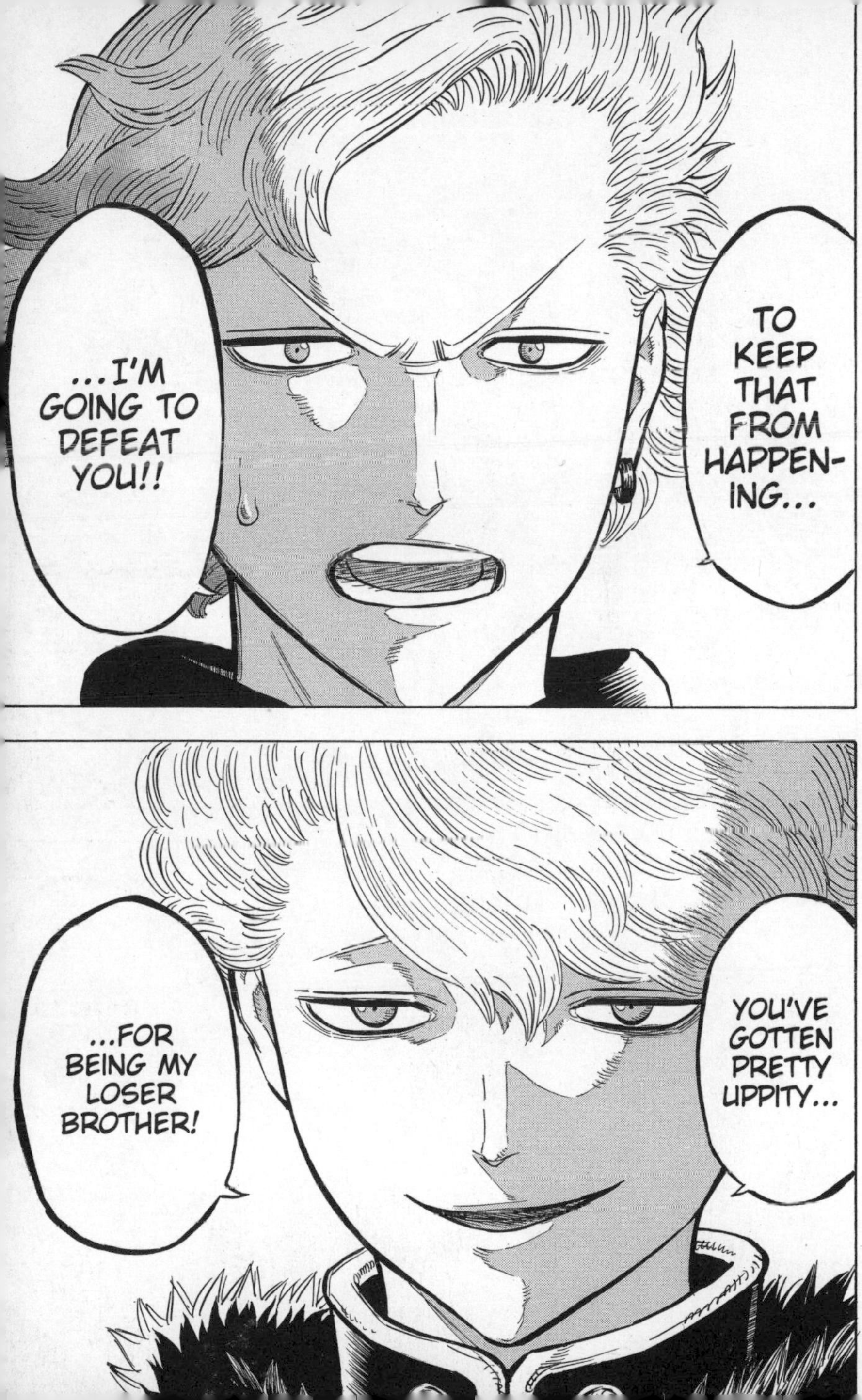
TO KEEP THAT FROM HAPPEN-ING...
...I'M GOING TO DEFEAT YOU!!
YOU'VE GOTTEN PRETTY UPPITY...
...FOR BEING MY LOSER BROTHER!

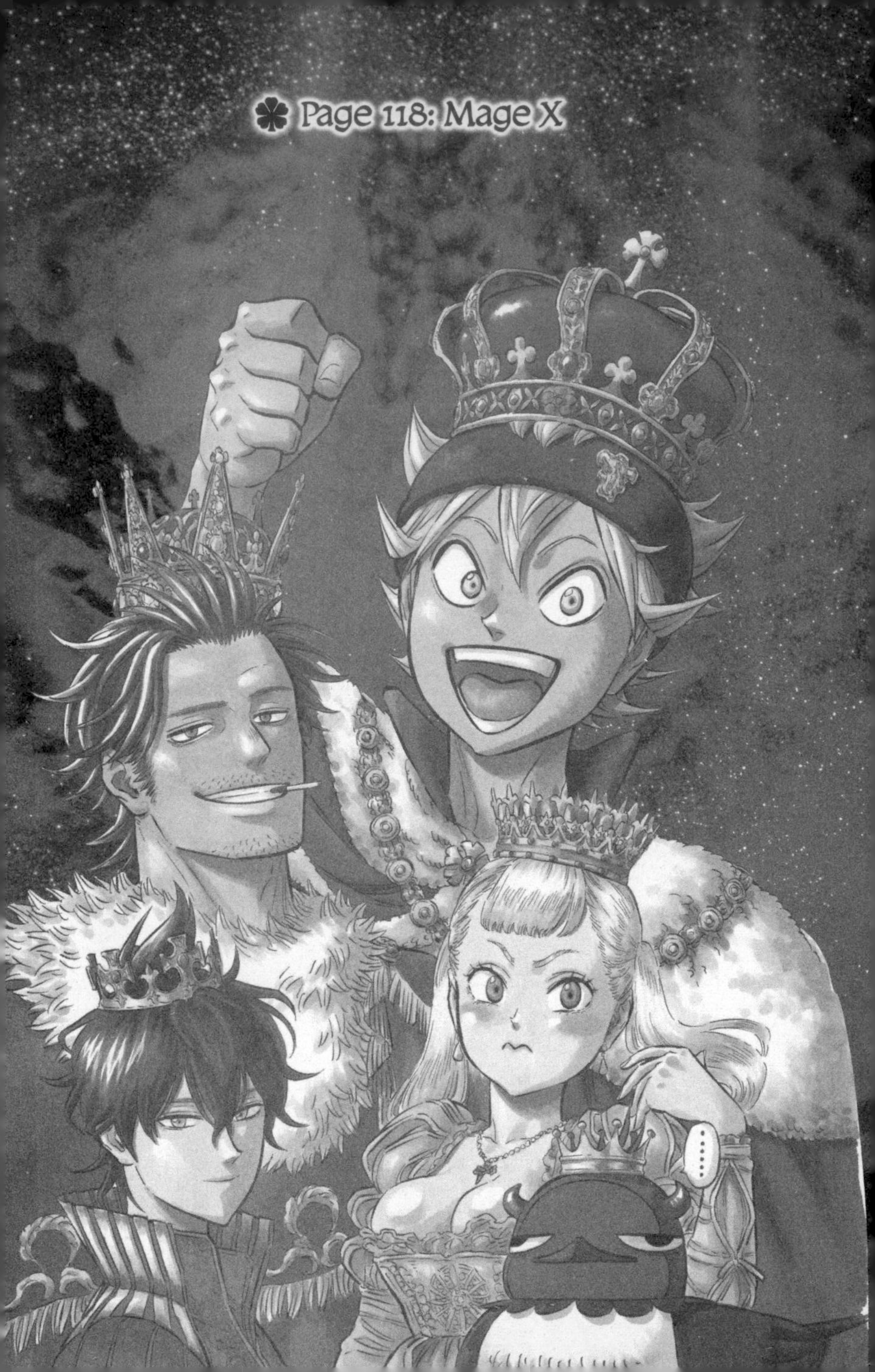
Page 118: Mage X
......

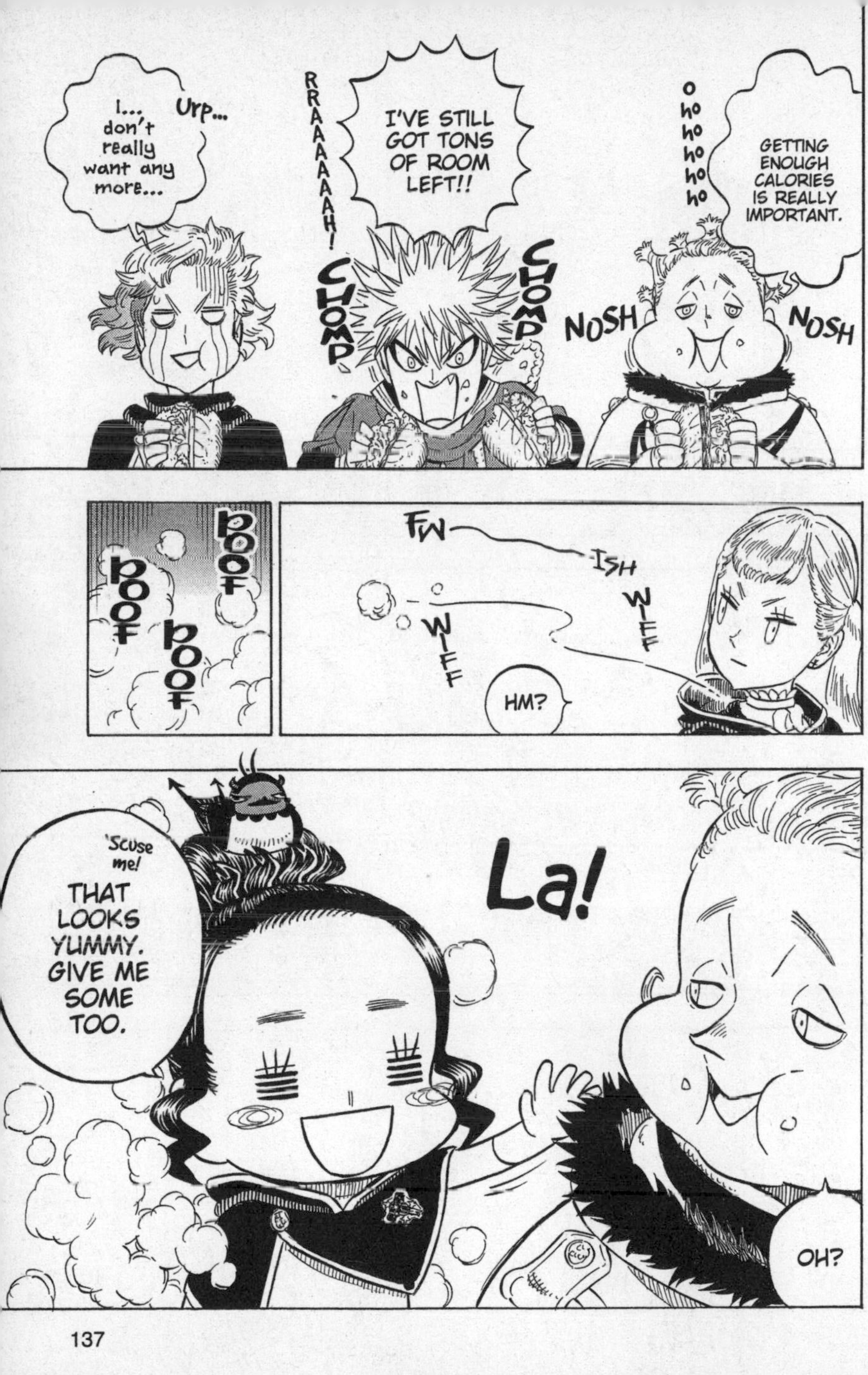
o ho ho ho ho ho
GETTING ENOUGH CALORIES IS REALLY IMPORTANT.
NOSH
NOSH
I'VE STILL GOT TONS OF ROOM LEFT!!
RRAAAAAAAH!
CHOMP
CHOMP
Urp...
I... don't really want any more...
FW-ISH
WIFF
WIFF
HM?
boof
boof
boof
OH?
La!
'Scuse me!
THAT LOOKS YUMMY. GIVE ME SOME TOO.

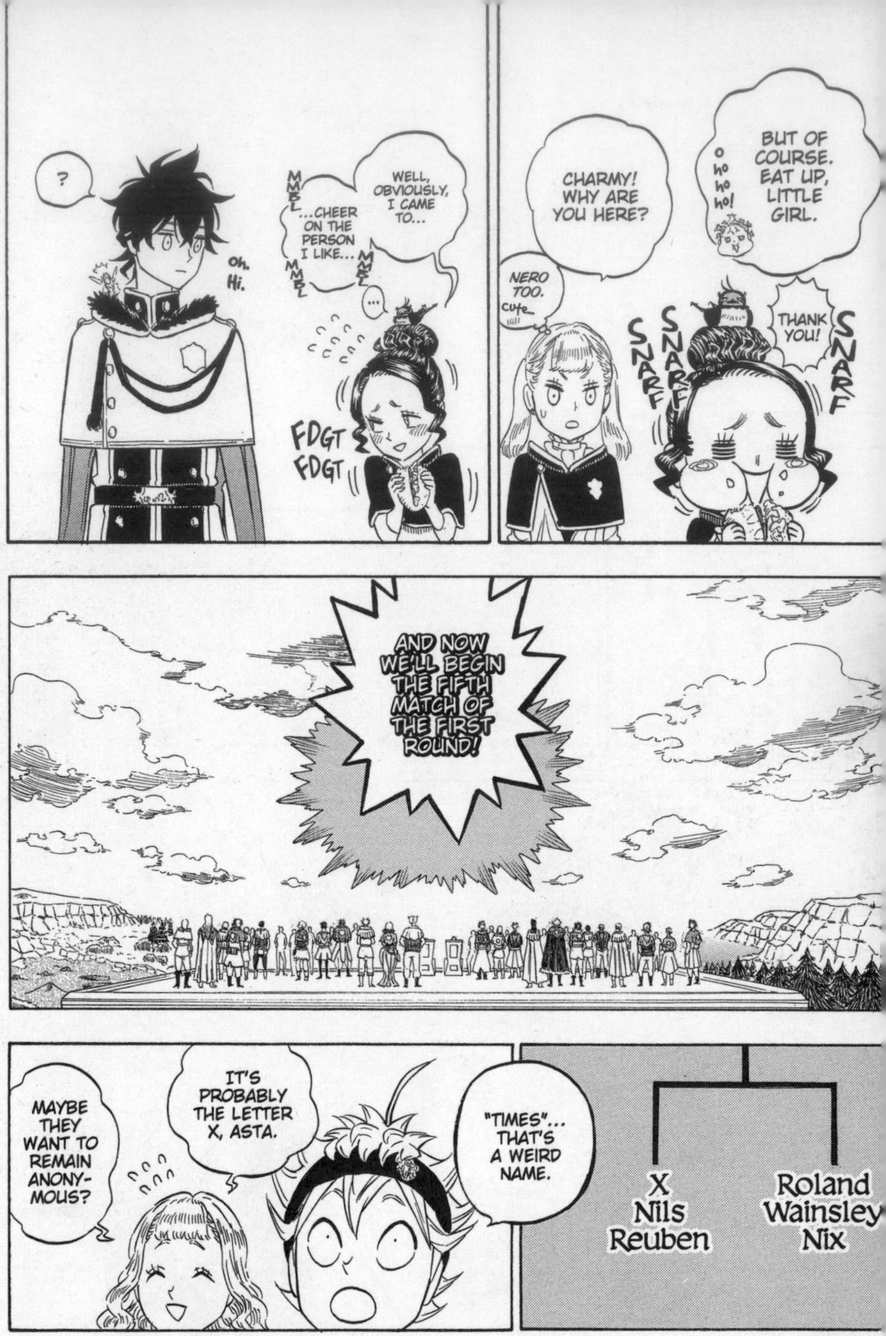
CHARMY! WHY ARE YOU HERE?
O ho ho ho!
BUT OF COURSE. EAT UP, LITTLE GIRL.
NERO TOO. cute...
THANK YOU!
SNARF SNARF SNARF
WELL, OBVIOUSLY, I CAME TO...
...CHEER ON THE PERSON I LIKE...
MMBL MMBL MMBL
...
FDGT FDGT
?
Oh. Hi.
AND NOW WE'LL BEGIN THE FIFTH MATCH OF THE FIRST ROUND!
X Nils Reuben
Roland Wainsley Nix
"TIMES"... THAT'S A WEIRD NAME.
IT'S PROBABLY THE LETTER X, ASTA.
MAYBE THEY WANT TO REMAIN ANONY-MOUS?

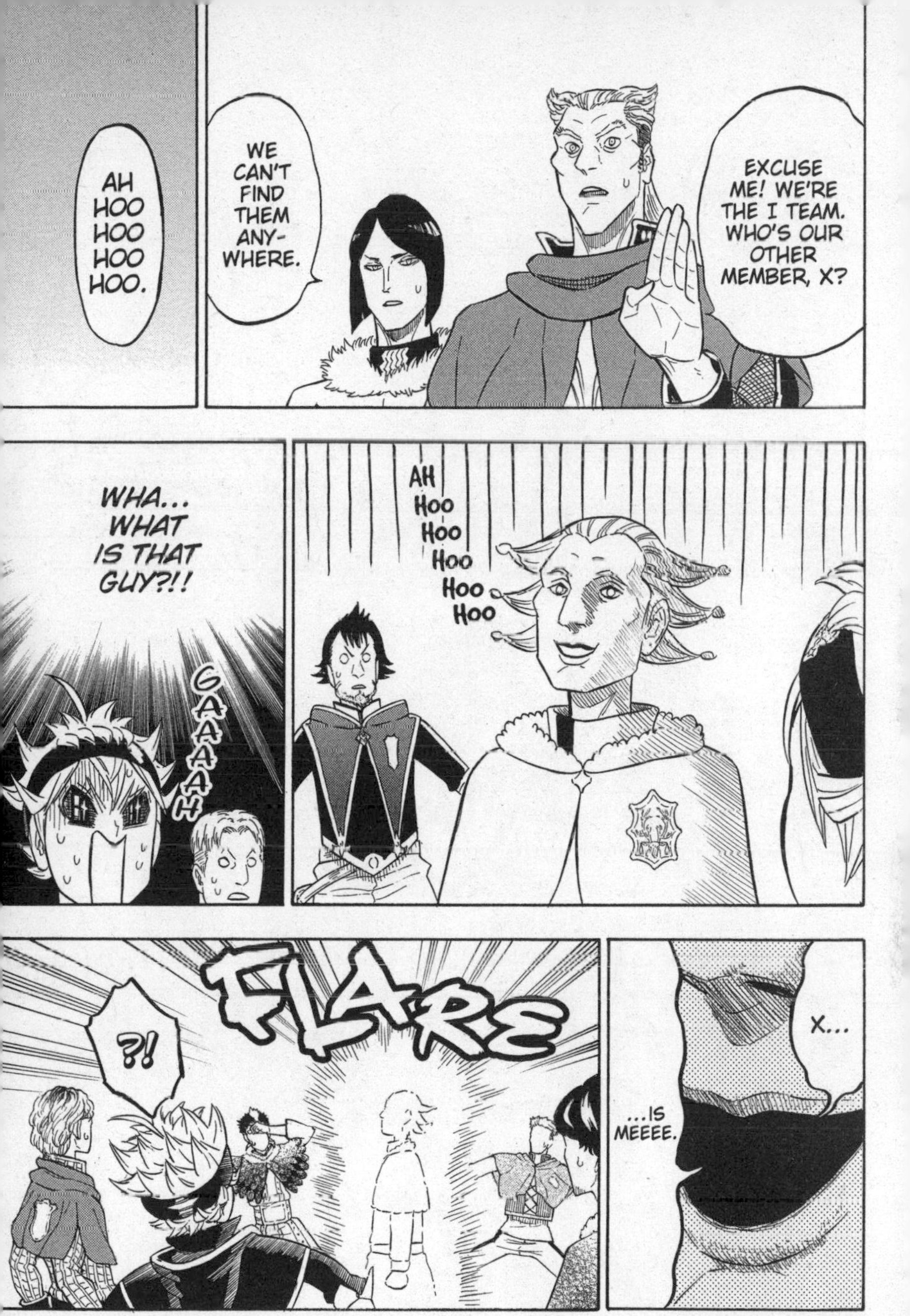
EXCUSE ME! WE'RE THE I TEAM. WHO'S OUR OTHER MEMBER, X?
WE CAN'T FIND THEM ANY-WHERE.
AH HOO HOO HOO HOO.
AH Hoo Hoo Hoo Hoo Hoo
WHA... WHAT IS THAT GUY?!!
GAAAAAH
X...
...IS MEEEE.
FLARE
?!

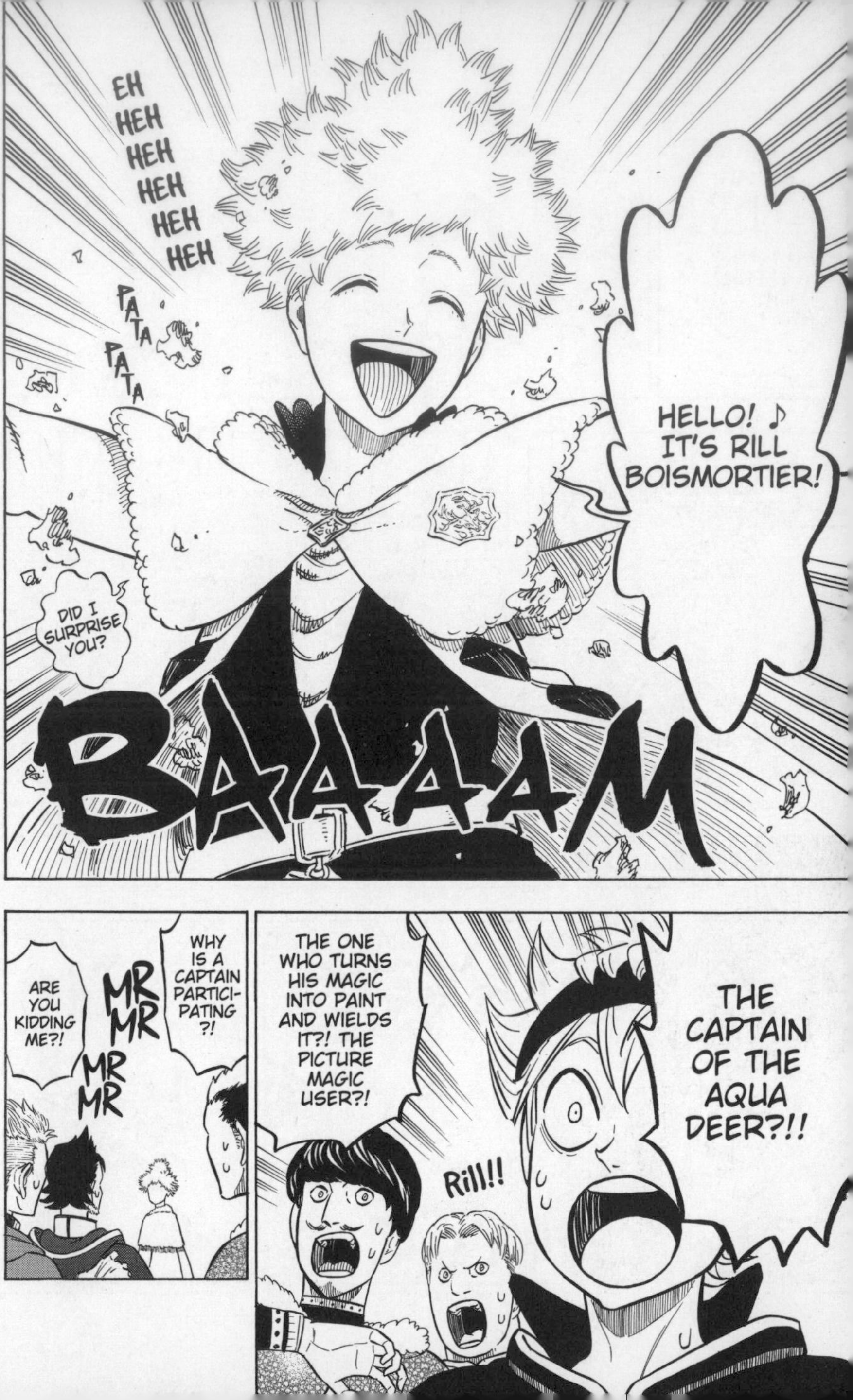
HELLO! ♪ IT'S RILL BOISMORTIER!
EH HEH HEH HEH HEH HEH
PATA PATA
DID I SURPRISE YOU?
BAAAAM
THE CAPTAIN OF THE AQUA DEER?!!
THE ONE WHO TURNS HIS MAGIC INTO PAINT AND WIELDS IT?! THE PICTURE MAGIC USER?!
Rill!!
WHY IS A CAPTAIN PARTICI-PATING?!
MR MR
ARE YOU KIDDING ME?!
MR MR

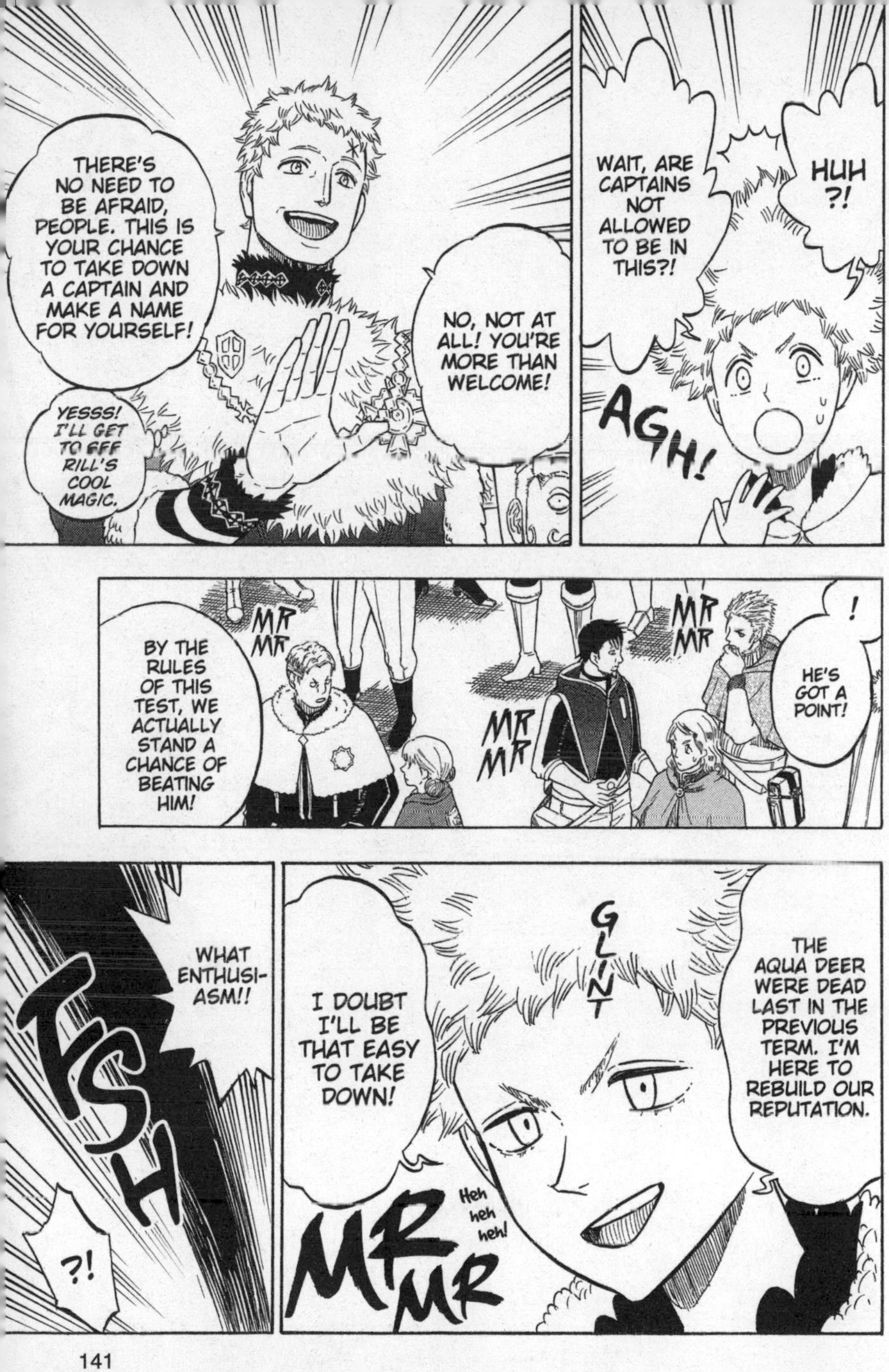
HUH ?!
WAIT, ARE CAPTAINS NOT ALLOWED TO BE IN THIS?!
AGH!
NO, NOT AT ALL! YOU'RE MORE THAN WELCOME!
THERE'S NO NEED TO BE AFRAID, PEOPLE. THIS IS YOUR CHANCE TO TAKE DOWN A CAPTAIN AND MAKE A NAME FOR YOURSELF!
YESSS! I'LL GET TO SEE RILL'S COOL MAGIC.
!
HE'S GOT A POINT!
MR MR
MR MR
MR MR
BY THE RULES OF THIS TEST, WE ACTUALLY STAND A CHANCE OF BEATING HIM!
THE AQUA DEER WERE DEAD LAST IN THE PREVIOUS TERM. I'M HERE TO REBUILD OUR REPUTATION.
GLINT
I DOUBT I'LL BE THAT EASY TO TAKE DOWN!
Heh heh heh!
MR MR
WHAT ENTHUSI-ASM!!
TSSH
?!

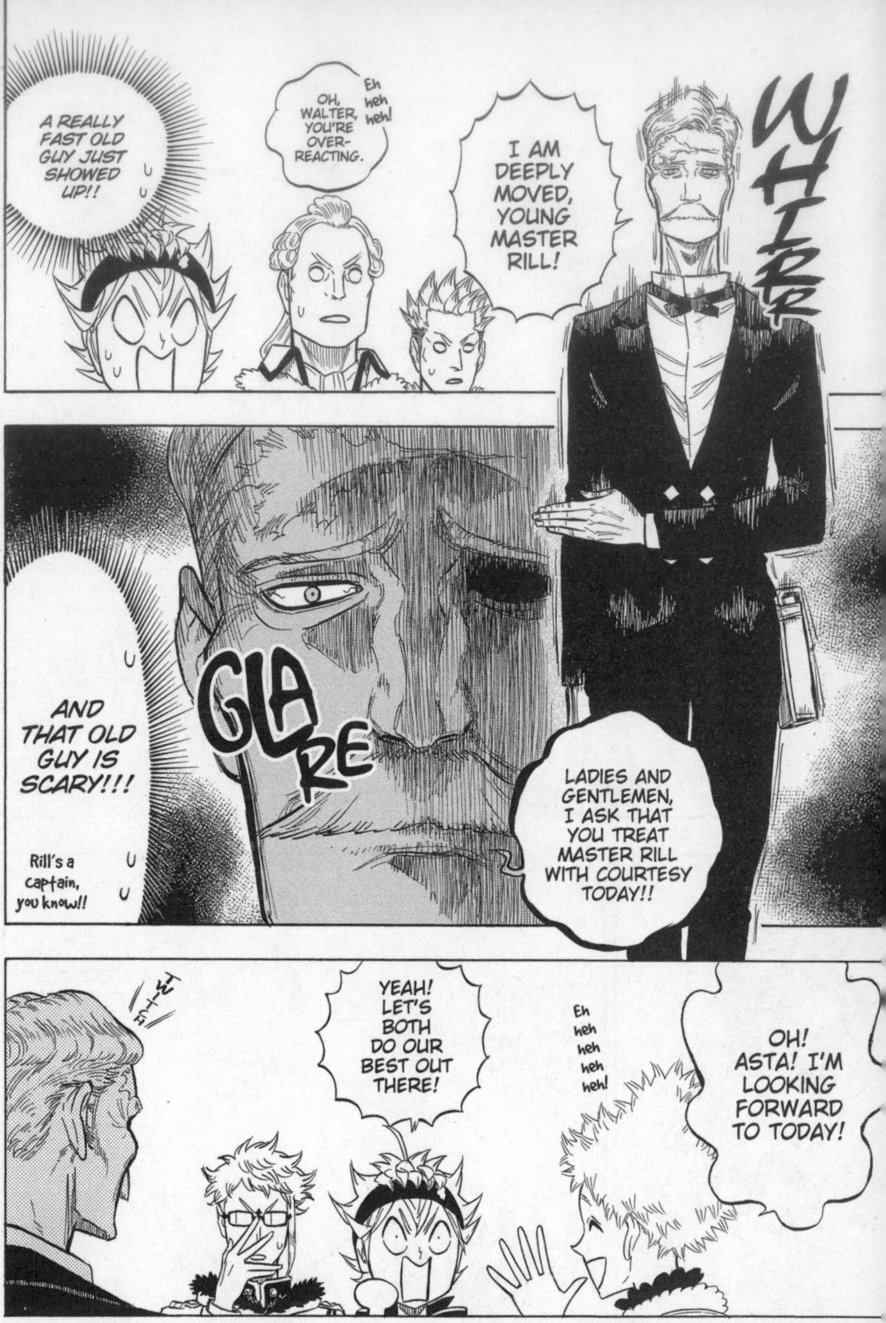
WHIRR
I AM DEEPLY MOVED, YOUNG MASTER RILL!
Eh heh heh!
OH, WALTER, YOU'RE OVER-REACTING.
A REALLY FAST OLD GUY JUST SHOWED UP!!
LADIES AND GENTLEMEN, I ASK THAT YOU TREAT MASTER RILL WITH COURTESY TODAY!!
GLARE
AND THAT OLD GUY IS SCARY!!!
Rill's a captain, you know!!
OH! ASTA! I'M LOOKING FORWARD TO TODAY!
Eh heh heh heh heh!
YEAH! LET'S BOTH DO OUR BEST OUT THERE!
TWITCH

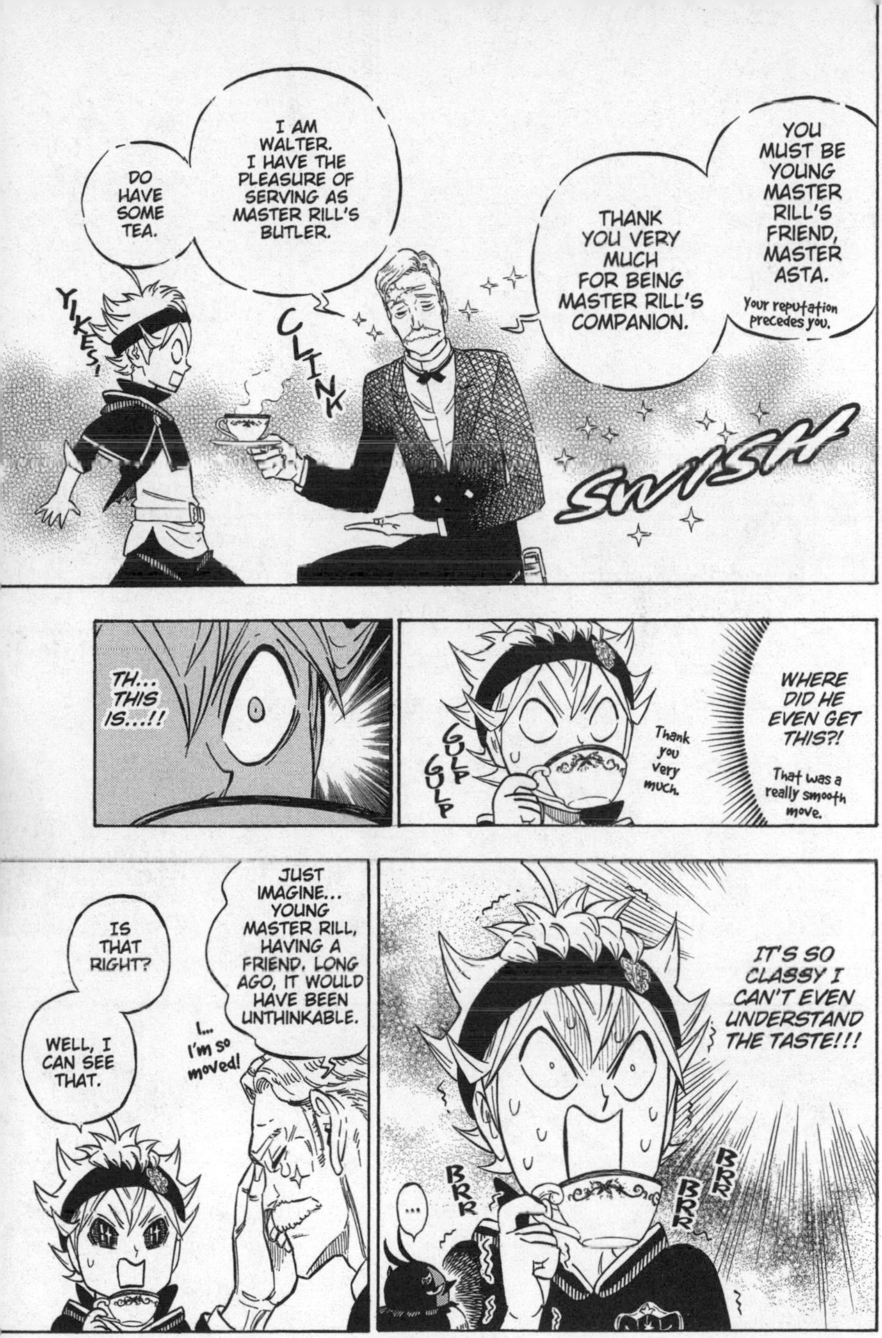
YOU MUST BE YOUNG MASTER RILL'S FRIEND, MASTER ASTA.
Your reputation precedes you.
THANK YOU VERY MUCH FOR BEING MASTER RILL'S COMPANION.
SWISH
I AM WALTER. I HAVE THE PLEASURE OF SERVING AS MASTER RILL'S BUTLER.
CLINK
DO HAVE SOME TEA.
YIKES!
WHERE DID HE EVEN GET THIS?!
That was a really smooth move.
Thank you very much.
GULP
GULP
TH... THIS IS...!!
IT'S SO CLASSY I CAN'T EVEN UNDERSTAND THE TASTE!!!
BRR
BRR
BRR
BRR
...
JUST IMAGINE... YOUNG MASTER RILL, HAVING A FRIEND. LONG AGO, IT WOULD HAVE BEEN UNTHINKABLE.
I... I'm so moved!
IS THAT RIGHT?
WELL, I CAN SEE THAT.

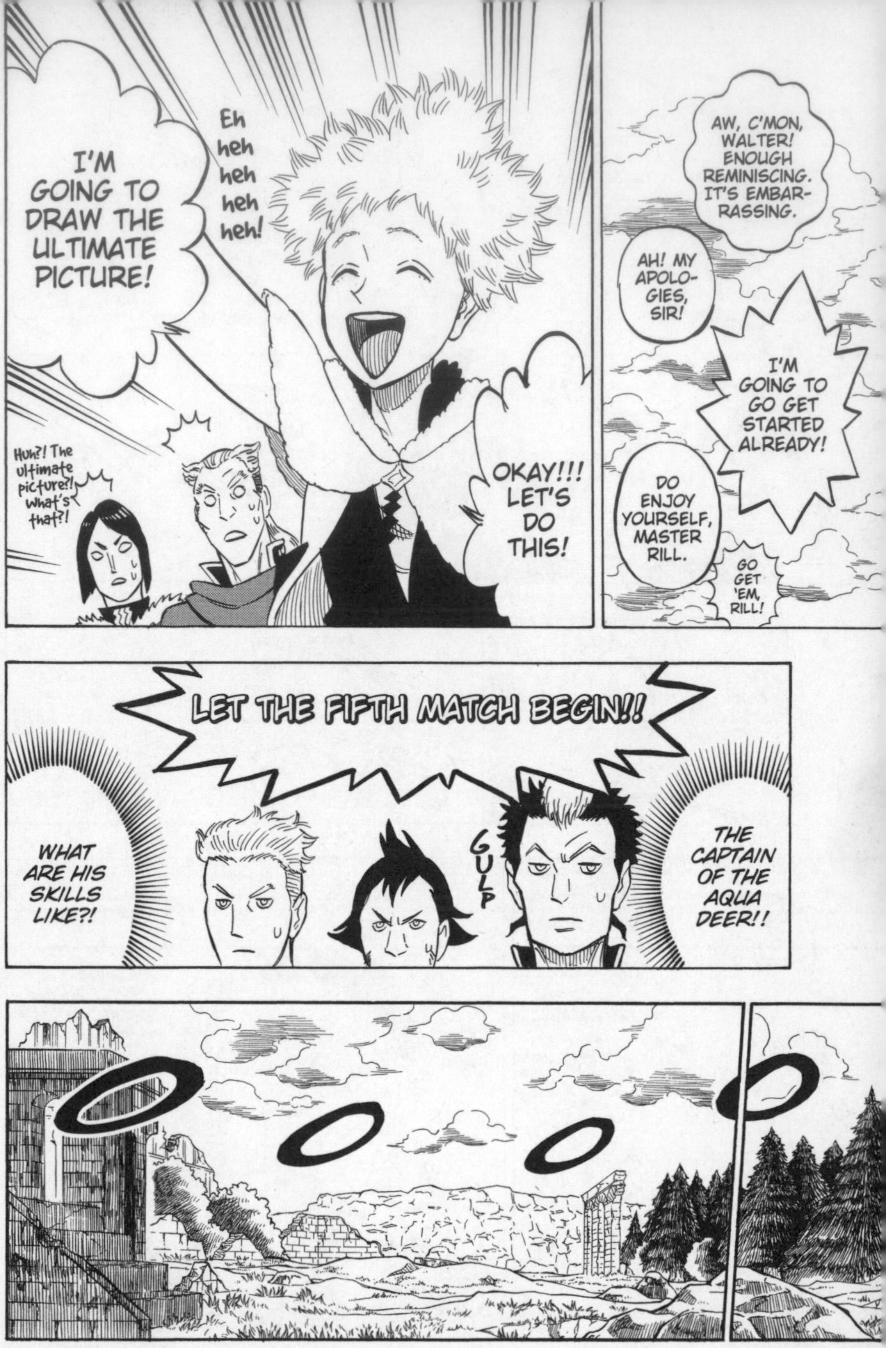
AW, C'MON, WALTER! ENOUGH REMINISCING. IT'S EMBARRASSING.
AH! MY APOLOGIES, SIR!
I'M GOING TO GO GET STARTED ALREADY!
DO ENJOY YOURSELF, MASTER RILL.
GO GET 'EM, RILL!
OKAY!!! LET'S DO THIS!
Eh heh heh heh heh!
I'M GOING TO DRAW THE ULTIMATE PICTURE!
Huh?! The ultimate picture?! What's that?!
LET THE FIFTH MATCH BEGIN!!
THE CAPTAIN OF THE AQUA DEER!!
GULP
WHAT ARE HIS SKILLS LIKE?!

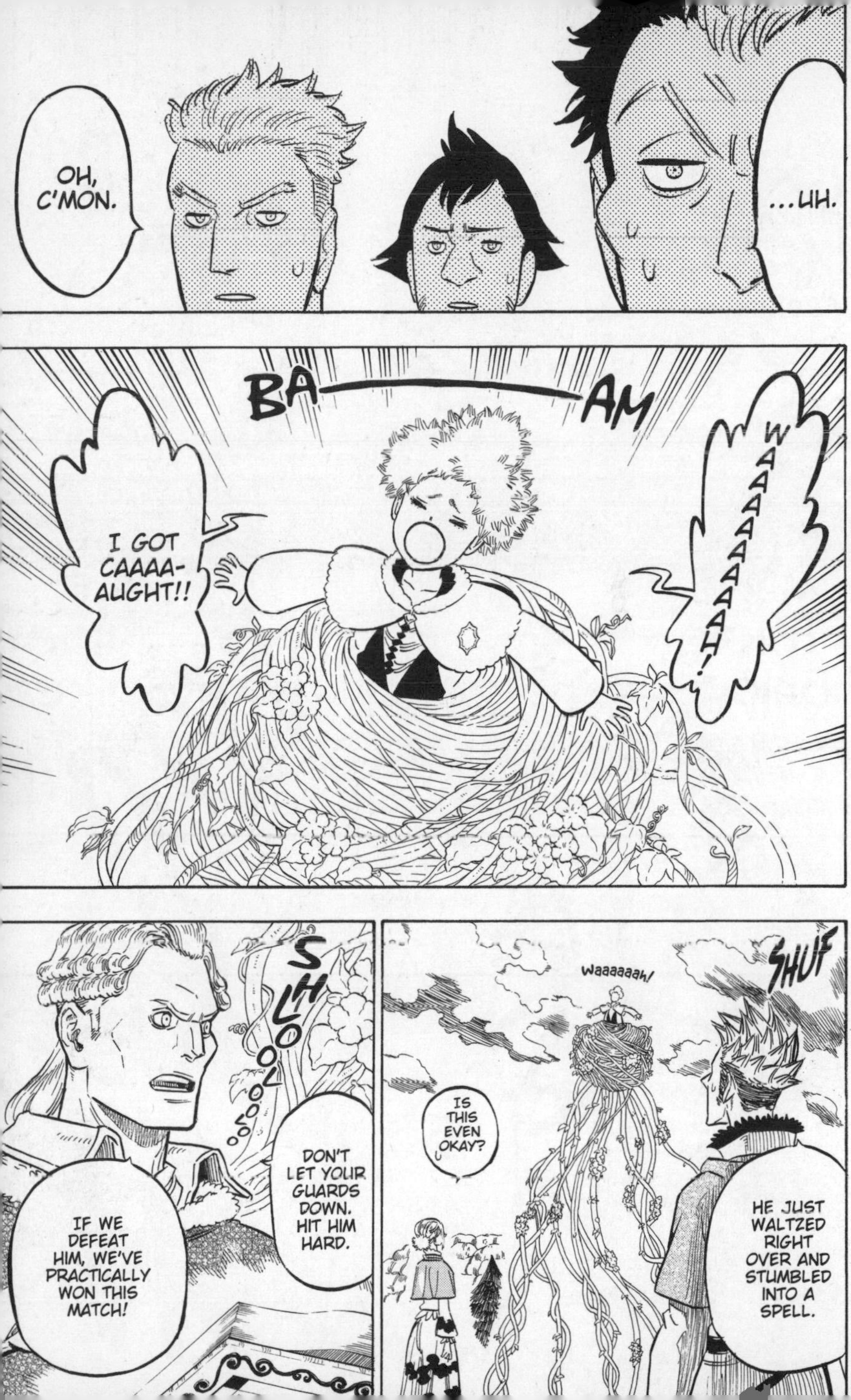
...UH.
OH, C'MON.
BA——AM
WAAAAAAAAAAH!
I GOT CAAAA-AUGHT!!
SHUF
Waaaaaah!
HE JUST WALTZED RIGHT OVER AND STUMBLED INTO A SPELL.
IS THIS EVEN OKAY?
SHLOOOOOOO
DON'T LET YOUR GUARDS DOWN. HIT HIM HARD.
IF WE DEFEAT HIM, WE'VE PRACTICALLY WON THIS MATCH!

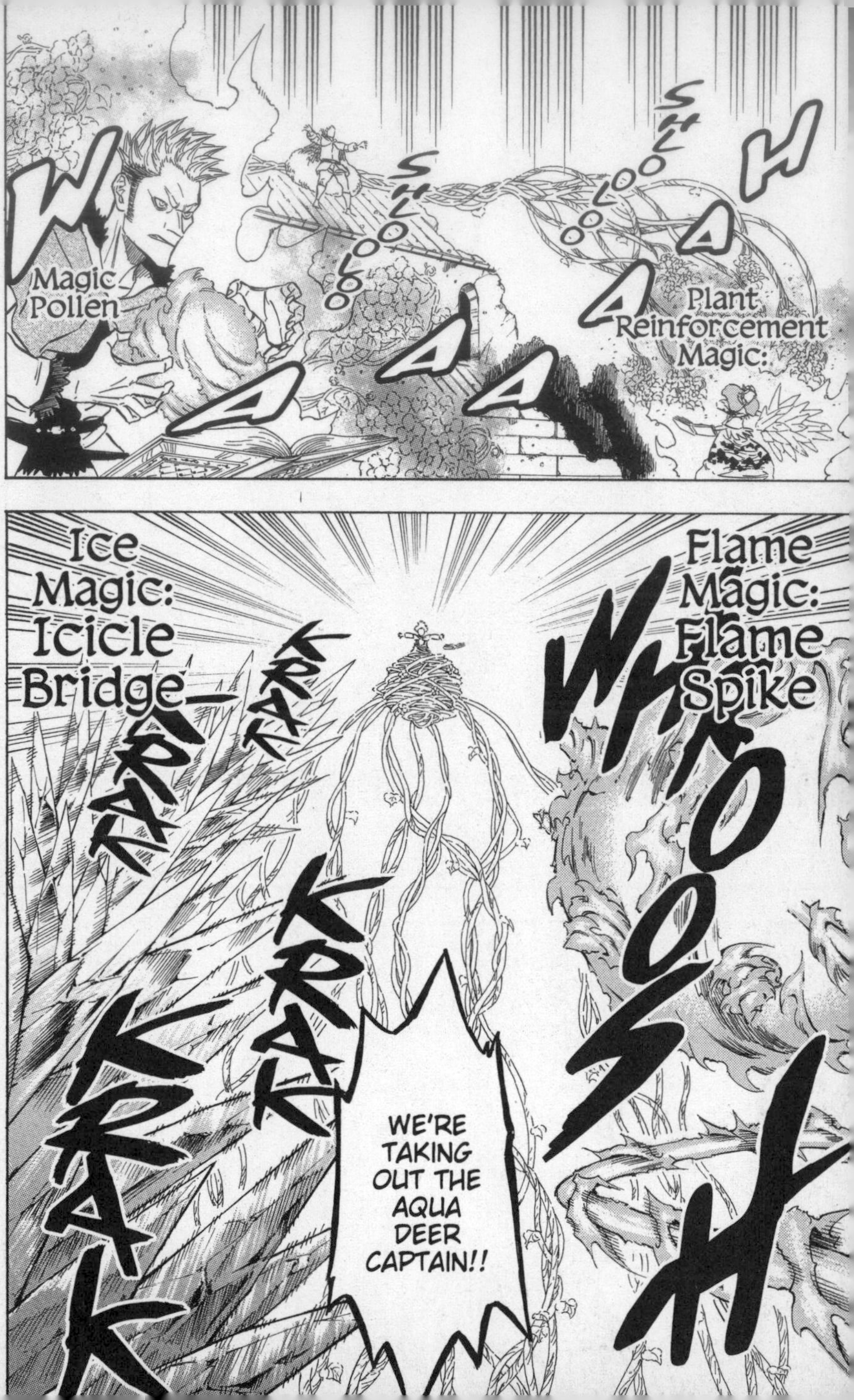
Plant Reinforcement Magic:
SHLOOLOO
SHLOOLOO
Magic Pollen
Flame Magic: Flame Spike
WHOOSH
WE'RE TAKING OUT THE AQUA DEER CAPTAIN!!
Ice Magic: Icicle Bridge—
KRAK
KRAK
KRAK
KRAK

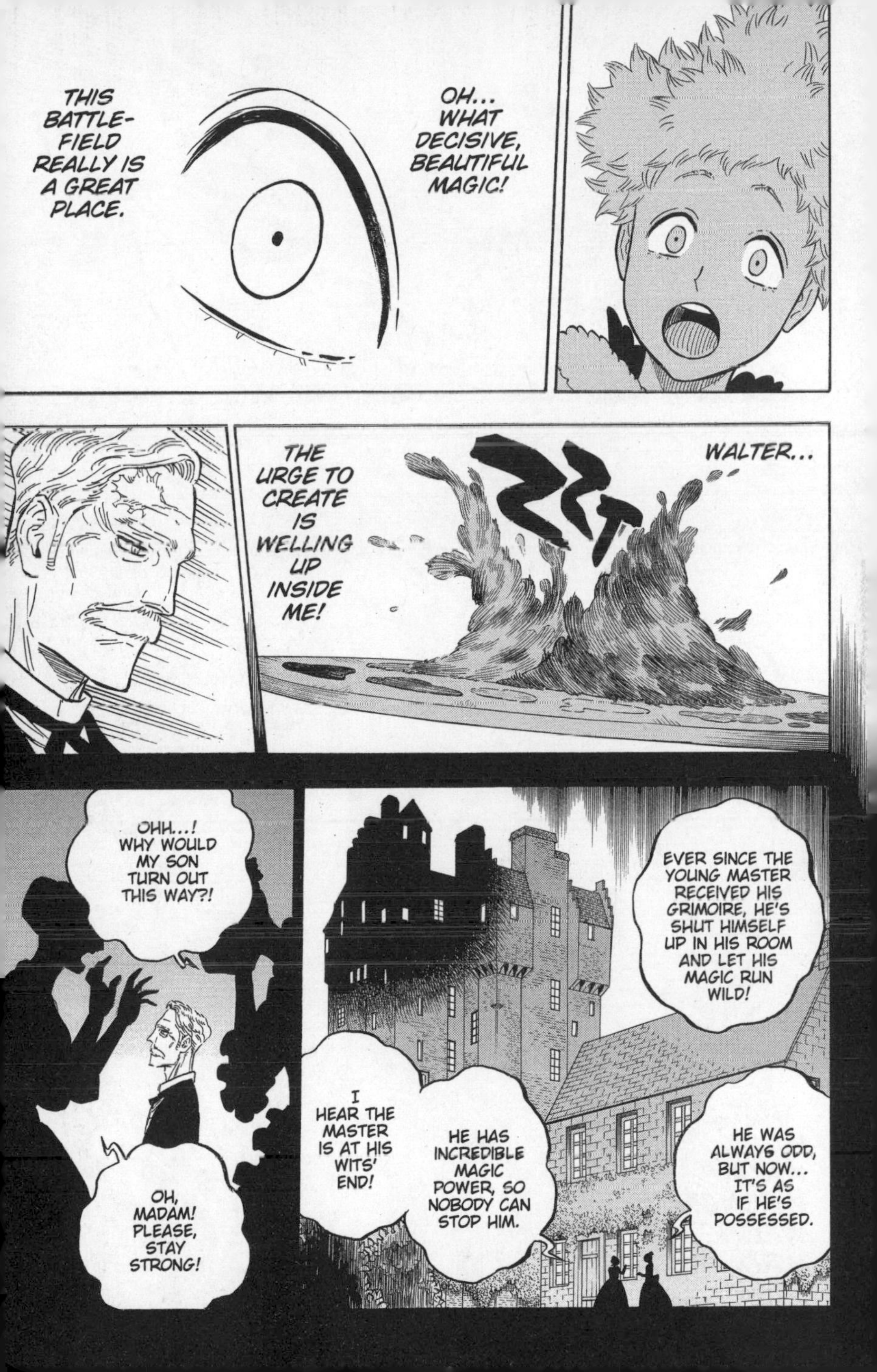
OH... WHAT DECISIVE, BEAUTIFUL MAGIC!
THIS BATTLE-FIELD REALLY IS A GREAT PLACE.
WALTER...
ZZT
THE URGE TO CREATE IS WELLING UP INSIDE ME!
EVER SINCE THE YOUNG MASTER RECEIVED HIS GRIMOIRE, HE'S SHUT HIMSELF UP IN HIS ROOM AND LET HIS MAGIC RUN WILD!
HE WAS ALWAYS ODD, BUT NOW... IT'S AS IF HE'S POSSESSED.
HE HAS INCREDIBLE MAGIC POWER, SO NOBODY CAN STOP HIM.
I HEAR THE MASTER IS AT HIS WITS' END!
OHH...! WHY WOULD MY SON TURN OUT THIS WAY?!
OH, MADAM! PLEASE, STAY STRONG!

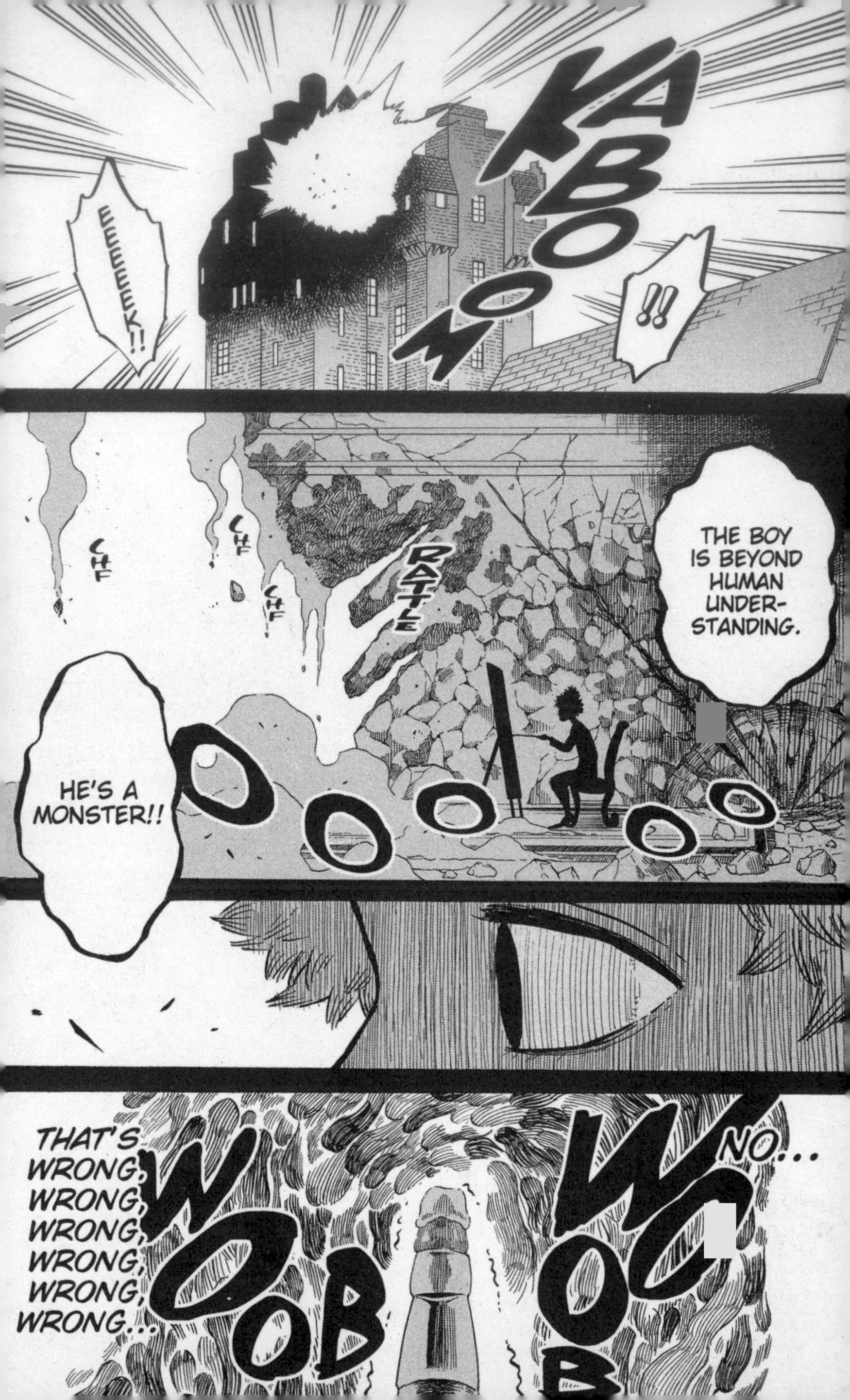
!!
KABOOM
EEEEEEK!!
THE BOY IS BEYOND HUMAN UNDER-STANDING.
RATTLE
CHF
CHF
CHF
OOOOOOO
HE'S A MONSTER!!
NO...
WOOB
THAT'S WRONG, WRONG, WRONG, WRONG, WRONG, WRONG...
WOOB

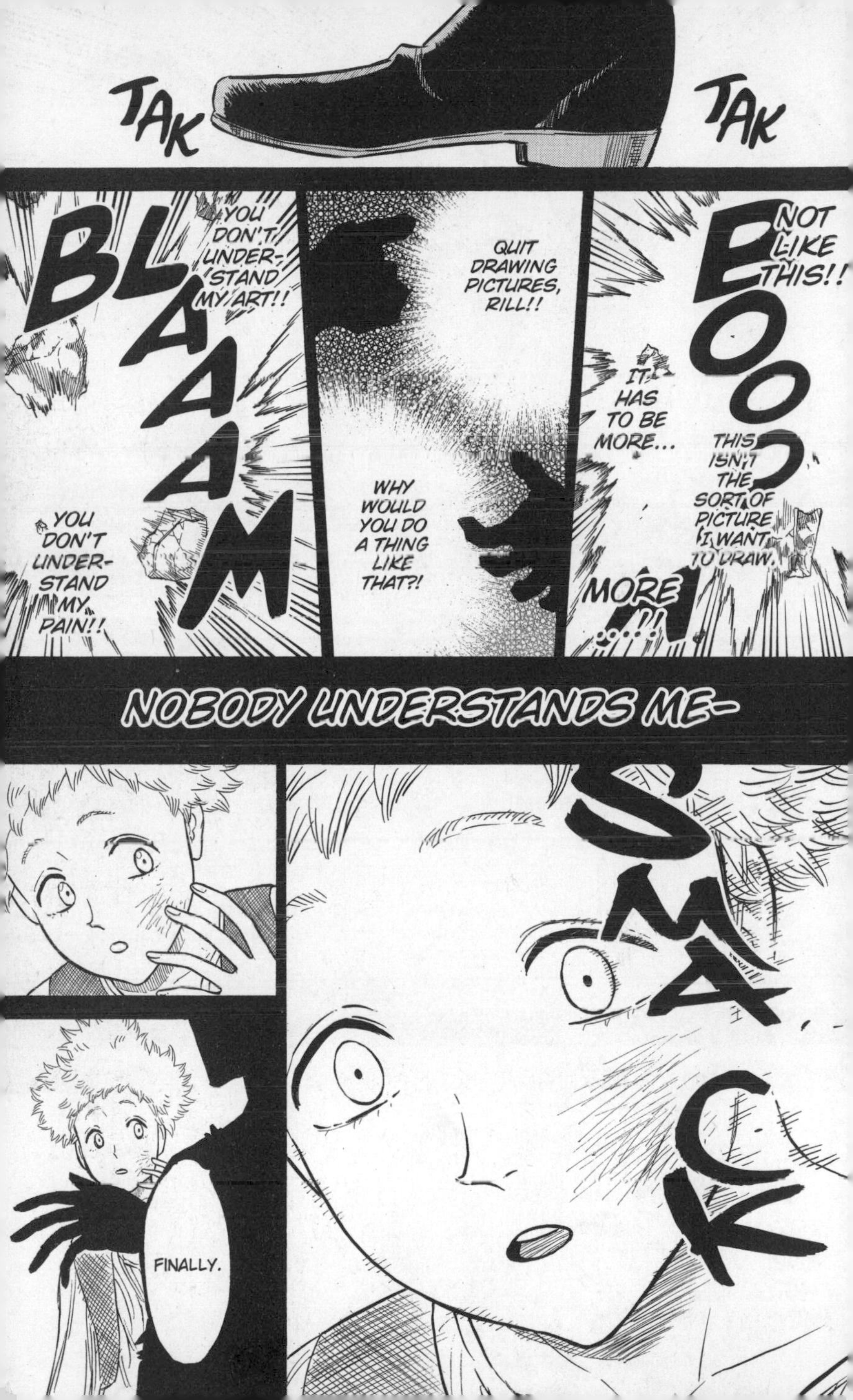
TAK
TAK
NOT LIKE THIS!!
BOOOOM
IT HAS TO BE MORE...
THIS ISN'T THE SORT OF PICTURE I WANT TO DRAW.
MORE...!!
QUIT DRAWING PICTURES, RILL!!
WHY WOULD YOU DO A THING LIKE THAT?!
BLAAAM
YOU DON'T UNDER-STAND MY ART!!
YOU DON'T UNDER-STAND MY PAIN!!
NOBODY UNDERSTANDS ME-
SMACK
FINALLY.

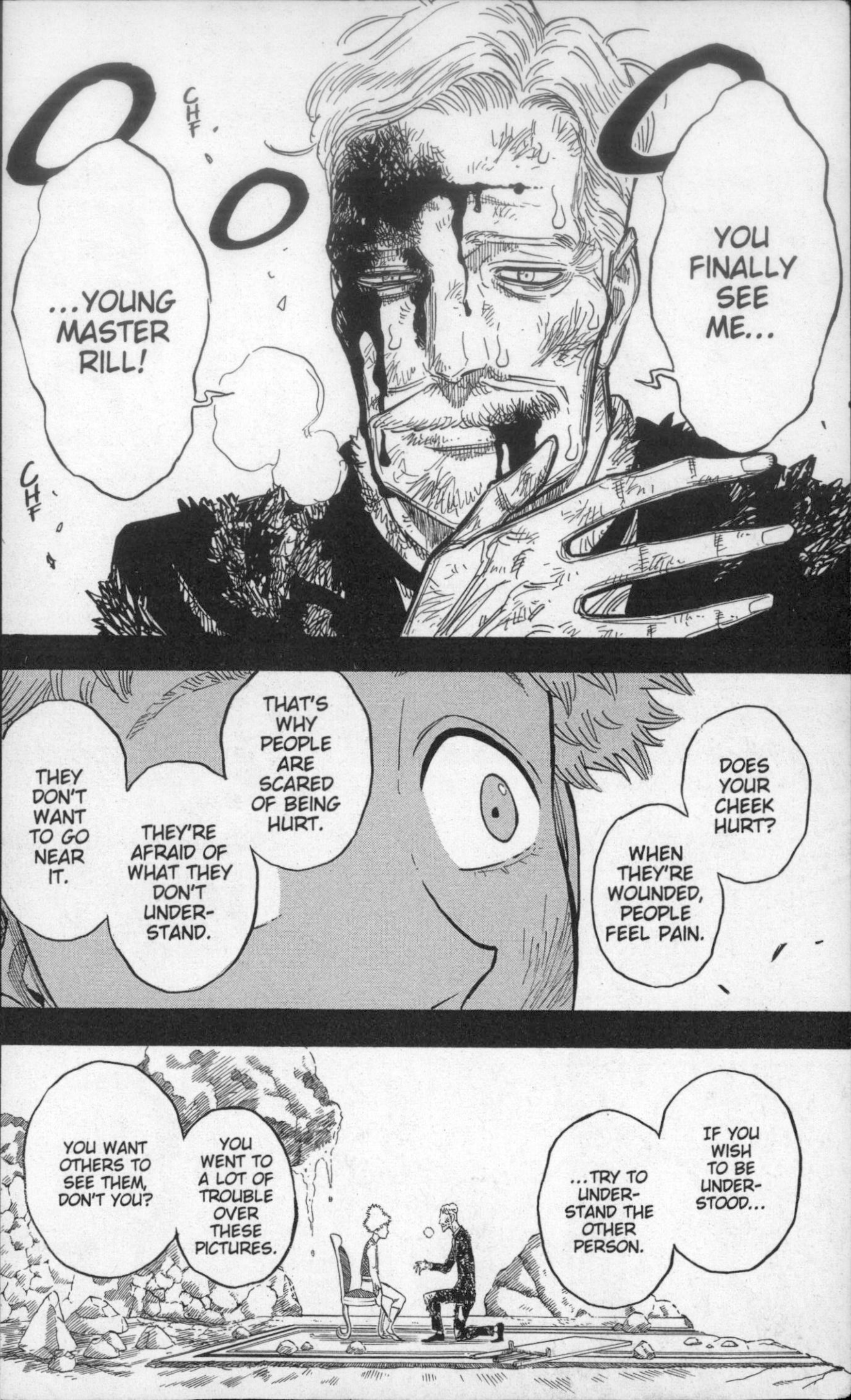

YOU FINALLY SEE ME...
CHF
...YOUNG MASTER RILL!
CHF
DOES YOUR CHEEK HURT?
WHEN THEY'RE WOUNDED, PEOPLE FEEL PAIN.
THAT'S WHY PEOPLE ARE SCARED OF BEING HURT.
THEY'RE AFRAID OF WHAT THEY DON'T UNDER-STAND.
THEY DON'T WANT TO GO NEAR IT.
IF YOU WISH TO BE UNDER-STOOD...
...TRY TO UNDER-STAND THE OTHER PERSON.
YOU WENT TO A LOT OF TROUBLE OVER THESE PICTURES.
YOU WANT OTHERS TO SEE THEM, DON'T YOU?

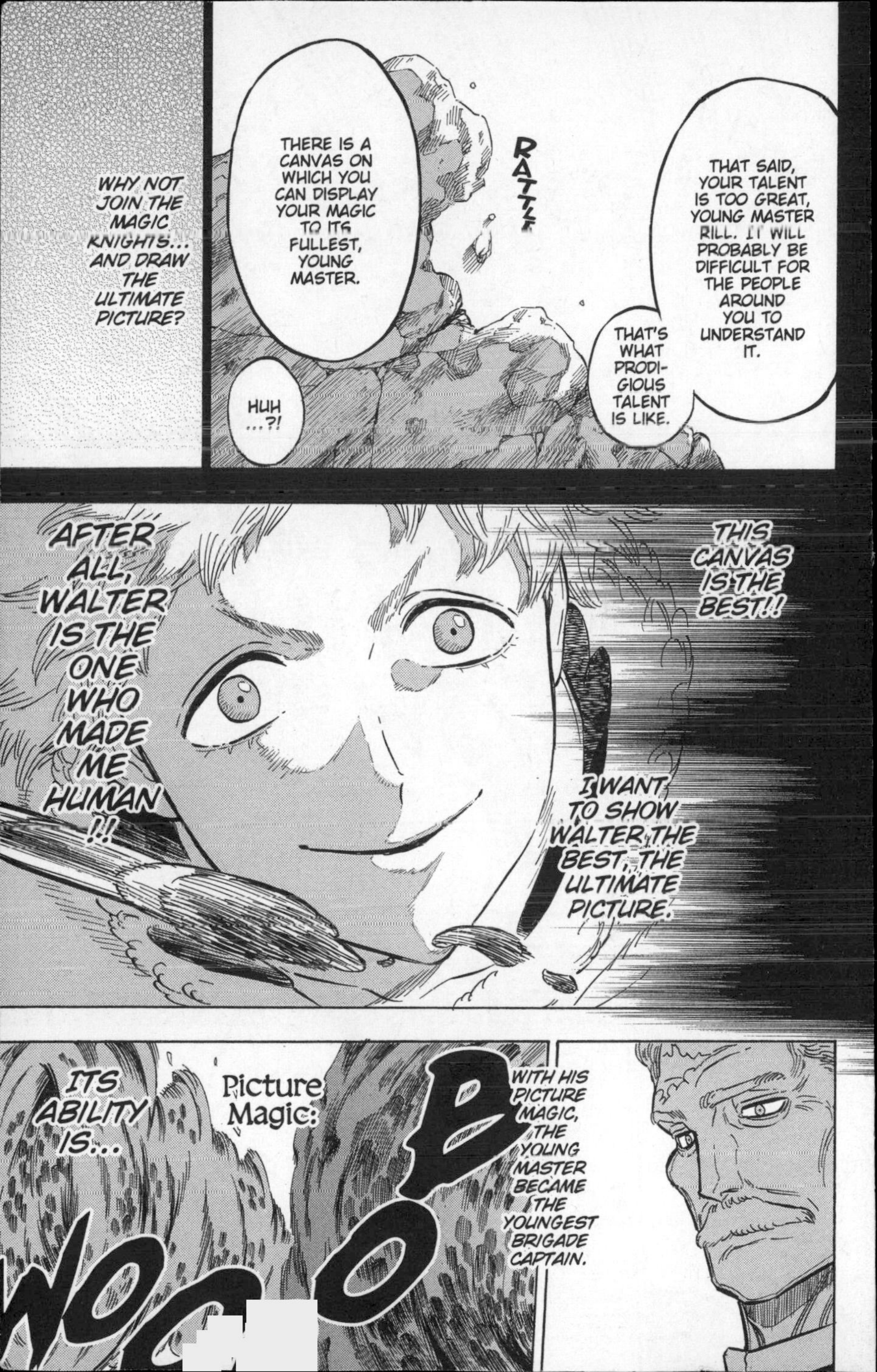
THAT SAID, YOUR TALENT IS TOO GREAT, YOUNG MASTER RILL. IT WILL PROBABLY BE DIFFICULT FOR THE PEOPLE AROUND YOU TO UNDERSTAND IT.
THAT'S WHAT PRODIGIOUS TALENT IS LIKE.
THERE IS A CANVAS ON WHICH YOU CAN DISPLAY YOUR MAGIC TO ITS FULLEST, YOUNG MASTER.
HUH...?!
WHY NOT JOIN THE MAGIC KNIGHTS... AND DRAW THE ULTIMATE PICTURE?
THIS CANVAS IS THE BEST!!
AFTER ALL, WALTER IS THE ONE WHO MADE ME HUMAN!!
I WANT TO SHOW WALTER THE BEST, THE ULTIMATE PICTURE.
WITH HIS PICTURE MAGIC, THE YOUNG MASTER BECAME THE YOUNGEST BRIGADE CAPTAIN.
Picture Magic:
ITS ABILITY IS...

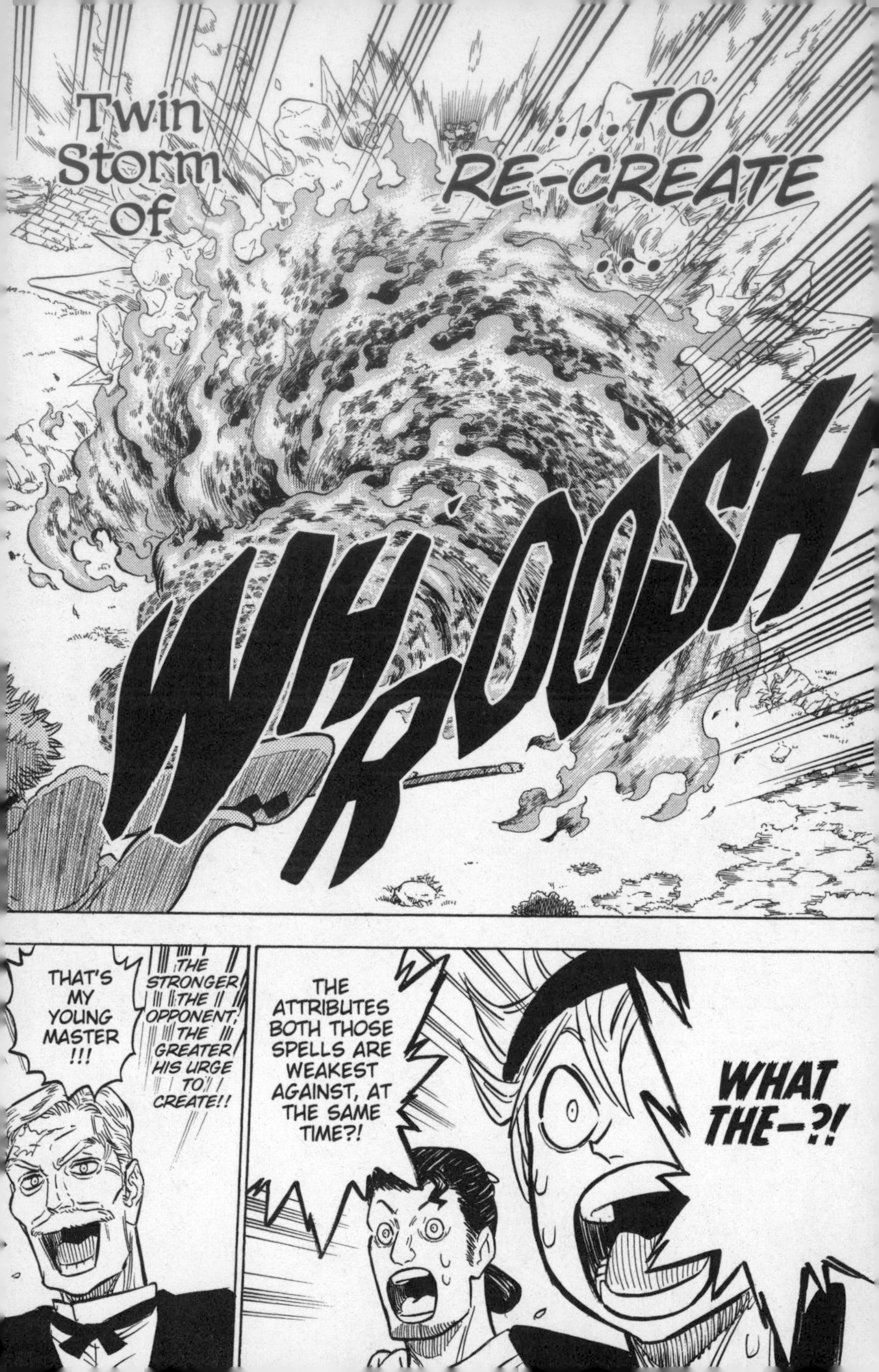
...TO RE-CREATE...
Twin Storm of
WHOOSH
WHAT THE-?!
THE ATTRIBUTES BOTH THOSE SPELLS ARE WEAKEST AGAINST, AT THE SAME TIME?!
THE STRONGER THE OPPONENT, THE GREATER HIS URGE TO CREATE!!
THAT'S MY YOUNG MASTER!!!

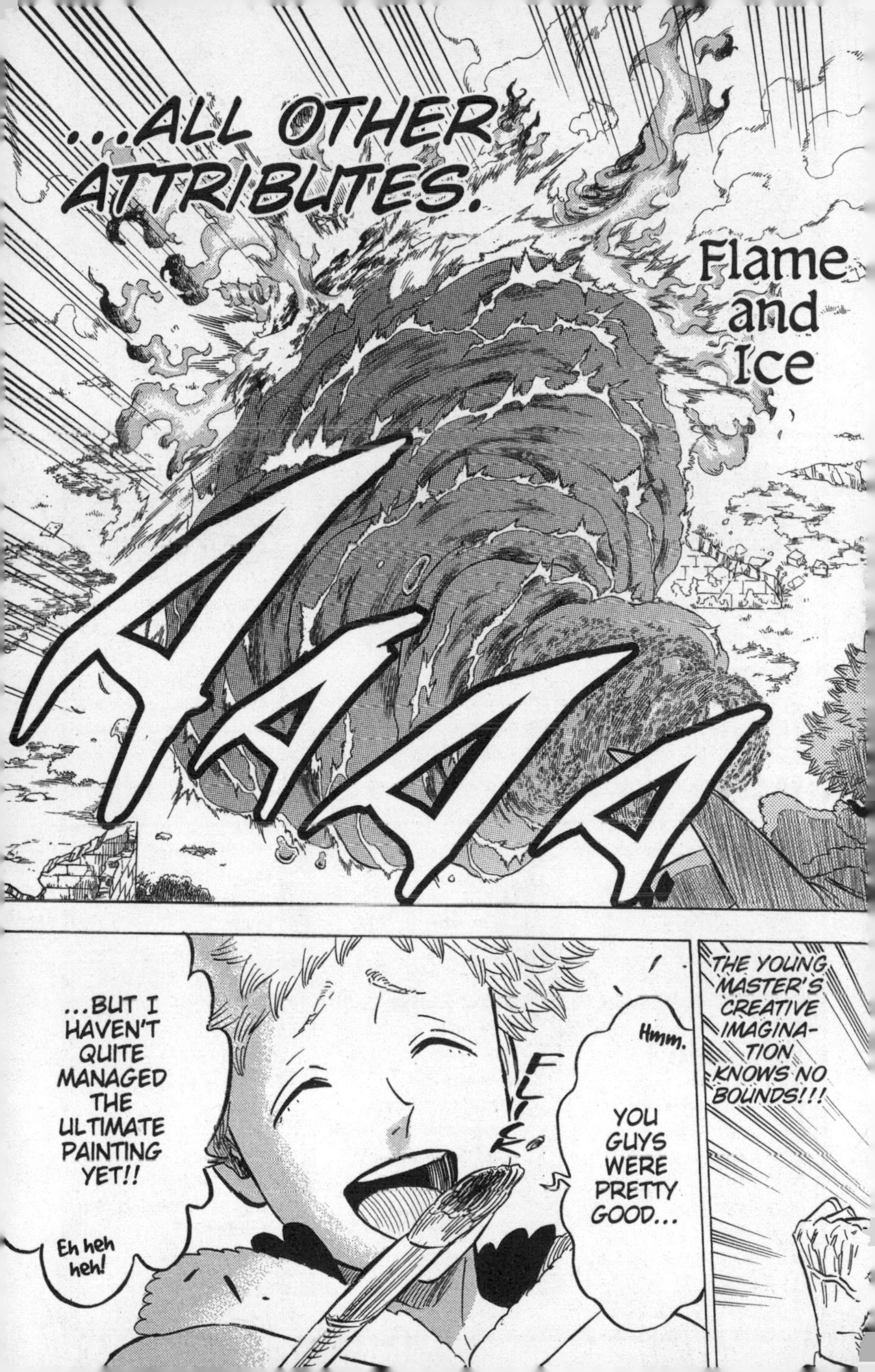
...ALL OTHER ATTRIBUTES.
Flame and Ice
THE YOUNG MASTER'S CREATIVE IMAGINATION KNOWS NO BOUNDS!!!
Hmm.
YOU GUYS WERE PRETTY GOOD...
FLICK
...BUT I HAVEN'T QUITE MANAGED THE ULTIMATE PAINTING YET!!
Eh heh heh!

The First Magic Knight General Election Results!

Presenting the results of the character popularity poll held in *Weekly Shonen Jump*!! Thanks for sending in so many votes!!

1 Asta 2,911 votes

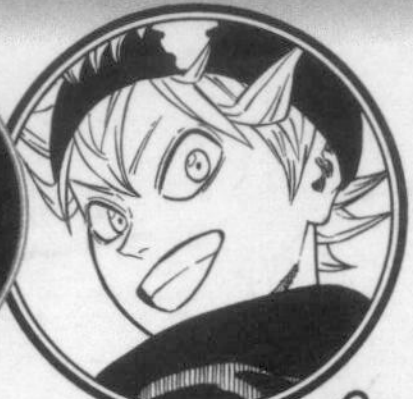

2 Yami Sukehiro 1,952 votes

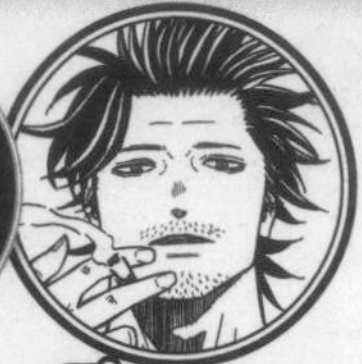

3 Noelle Silva 834 votes

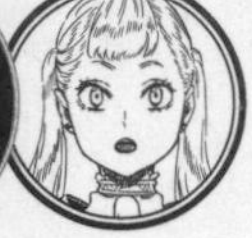

4 Yuno 827 votes

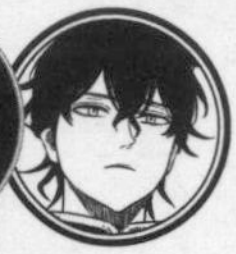

5 Nero 651 votes

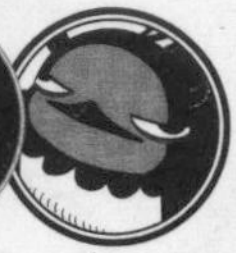

- 6 Charmy Pappitson 355 votes
- 7 Luck Voltia 302 votes
- 8 Vanessa Enoteca 257 votes
- 9 Fuegoleon Vermillion 251 votes
- 10 Charlotte Roselei 204 votes

- 11 Sister Lily 118 votes
- 12 Mimosa Vermillion 87 votes
- 13 Sally 83 votes
- 14 Kahono 79 votes
- 15 Finral Roulacase 60 votes
- 16 Mars 59 votes
- 17 Grey (real name unknown) 50 votes
- 18 Julius Novachrono 47 votes
- 19 Magna Swing 40 votes
- 20 Leopold Vermillion 38 votes
- 21 Gauche Adlai 37 votes
- 21 Fana (Fana the Hateful) 37 votes
- 22 Jack the Ripper 29 votes
- 23 Nozel Silva 28 votes
- 24 Mariella 25 votes

- 25 The Red Thread of Fate (Cat)
- 26 Klaus Lunettes
- 27 Ladros
- 28 Raia the Disloyal
- 29 Rebecca Scarlet
- 29 The Witch Queen
- 30 Revchi of Chain Magic
- 31 Lotus Whomalt
- 32 Gordon Agrippa
- 32 Solid Silva
- 33 William Vangeance
- 34 Langris Vaude
- 35 Dorothy Unsworth
- 36 Rill Boismortier
- 36 Sol Marron
- 37 Rades
- 38 Sister Theresa
- 39 Neige
- 40 Marx
- 41 Allen (Hungry Joker)
- 41 Fanzell Kruger
- 41 Alecdora Sandler
- 41 Bell (Sylph)
- 41 Golem
- 42 Gueldre Poizot
- 42 Licht (the Master)
- 42 Marie Adlai
- 42 Shiren Tium
- 42 Hamon Caseus
- 42 The First Wizard King
- 43 The Demon-Slayer Sword
- 43 Gifso (the high priest)
- 43 Kiato
- 43 William's Mask
- 43 Heath Grice
- 43 The Sheep Cook
- 44 Vetto the Despair
- 44 The Master of the Grimoire Tower
- 44 Sekke Bronzazza
- 44 Yūki Tabata
- 44 Valtos
- 44 Gio
- 44 Sticky Salamander
- 44 Nick
- 44 Amélie
- 45 Nashas (Hungry Joker)
- 45 Lagus
- 45 Salamander
- 46 Vivian Blanchard (Hungry Joker)
- 46 Heidi (Hungry Joker)
- 46 Nash, a kid at the church
- 46 Priest at the church where Asta grew up
- 46 Anti-birds
- 46 Catherine
- 46 Editor Katayama

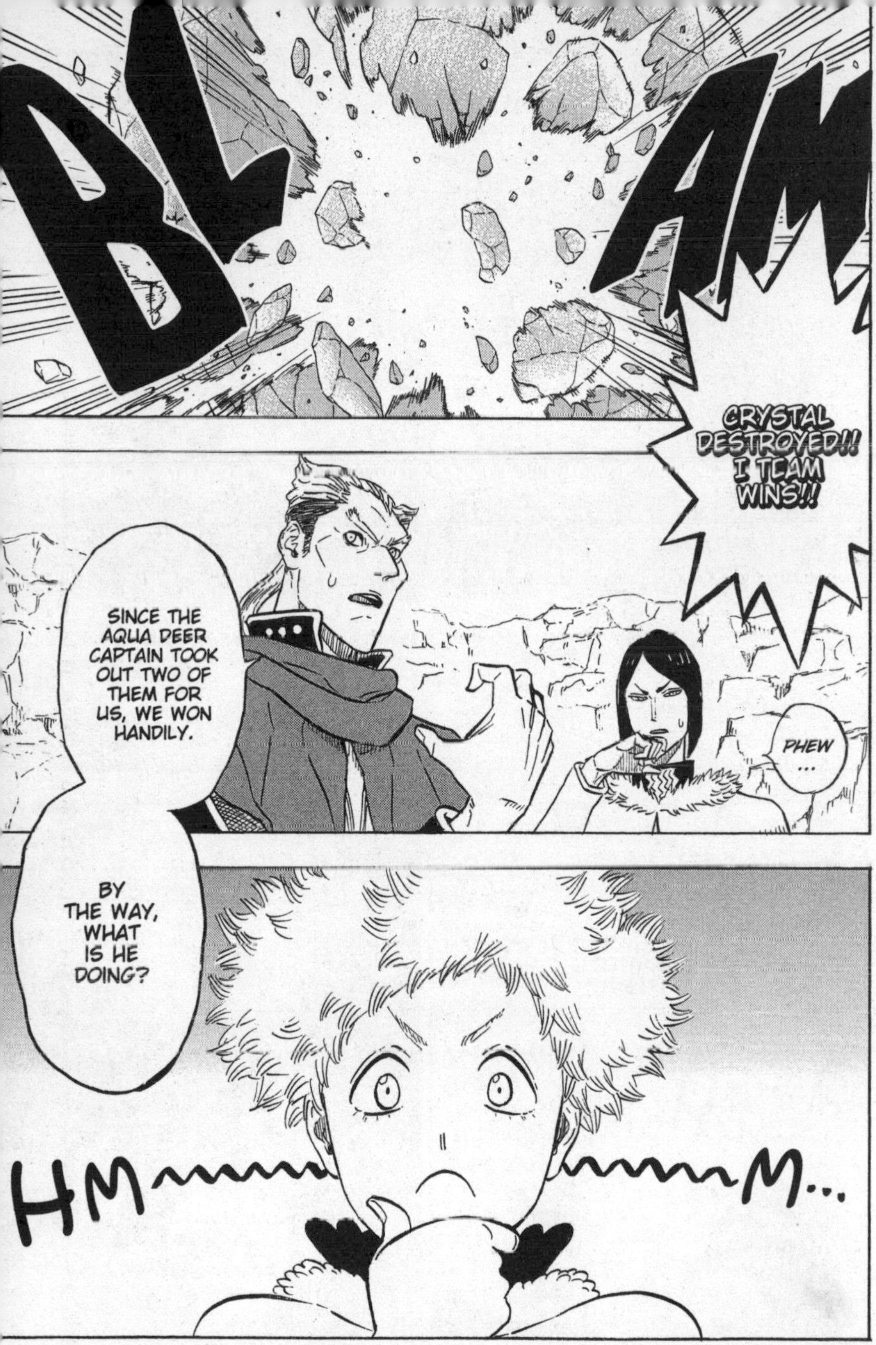
BLAM
CRYSTAL DESTROYED!! I TEAM WINS!!
PHEW...
SINCE THE AQUA DEER CAPTAIN TOOK OUT TWO OF THEM FOR US, WE WON HANDILY.
BY THE WAY, WHAT IS HE DOING?
HM~~~~~~~~~~M...

Page 119: More

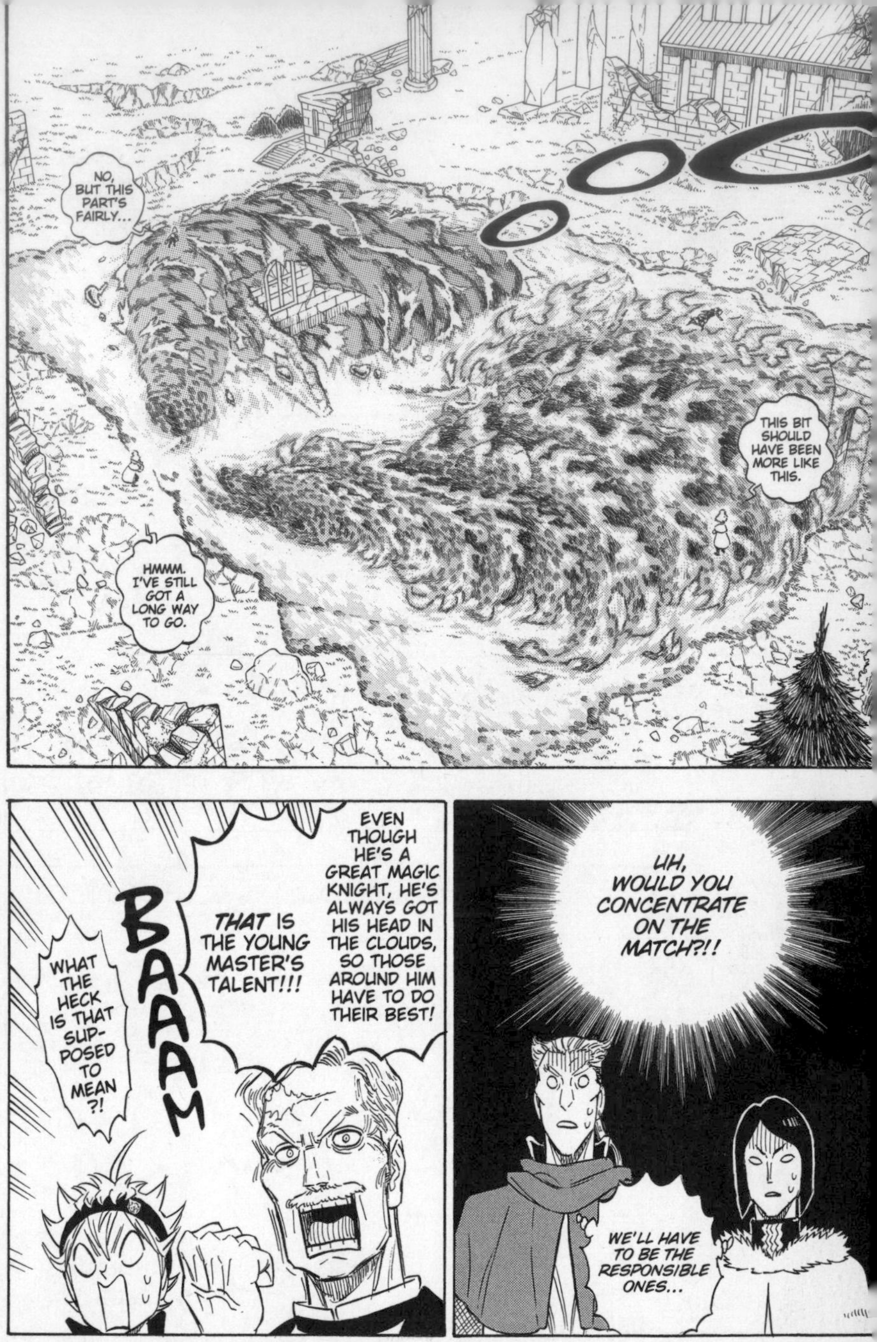
NO, BUT THIS PART'S FAIRLY...
THIS BIT SHOULD HAVE BEEN MORE LIKE THIS.
HMMM. I'VE STILL GOT A LONG WAY TO GO.
UH, WOULD YOU CONCENTRATE ON THE MATCH?!!
WE'LL HAVE TO BE THE RESPONSIBLE ONES...
EVEN THOUGH HE'S A GREAT MAGIC KNIGHT, HE'S ALWAYS GOT HIS HEAD IN THE CLOUDS, SO THOSE AROUND HIM HAVE TO DO THEIR BEST!
THAT IS THE YOUNG MASTER'S TALENT!!!
BAAAM
WHAT THE HECK IS THAT SUPPOSED TO MEAN?!

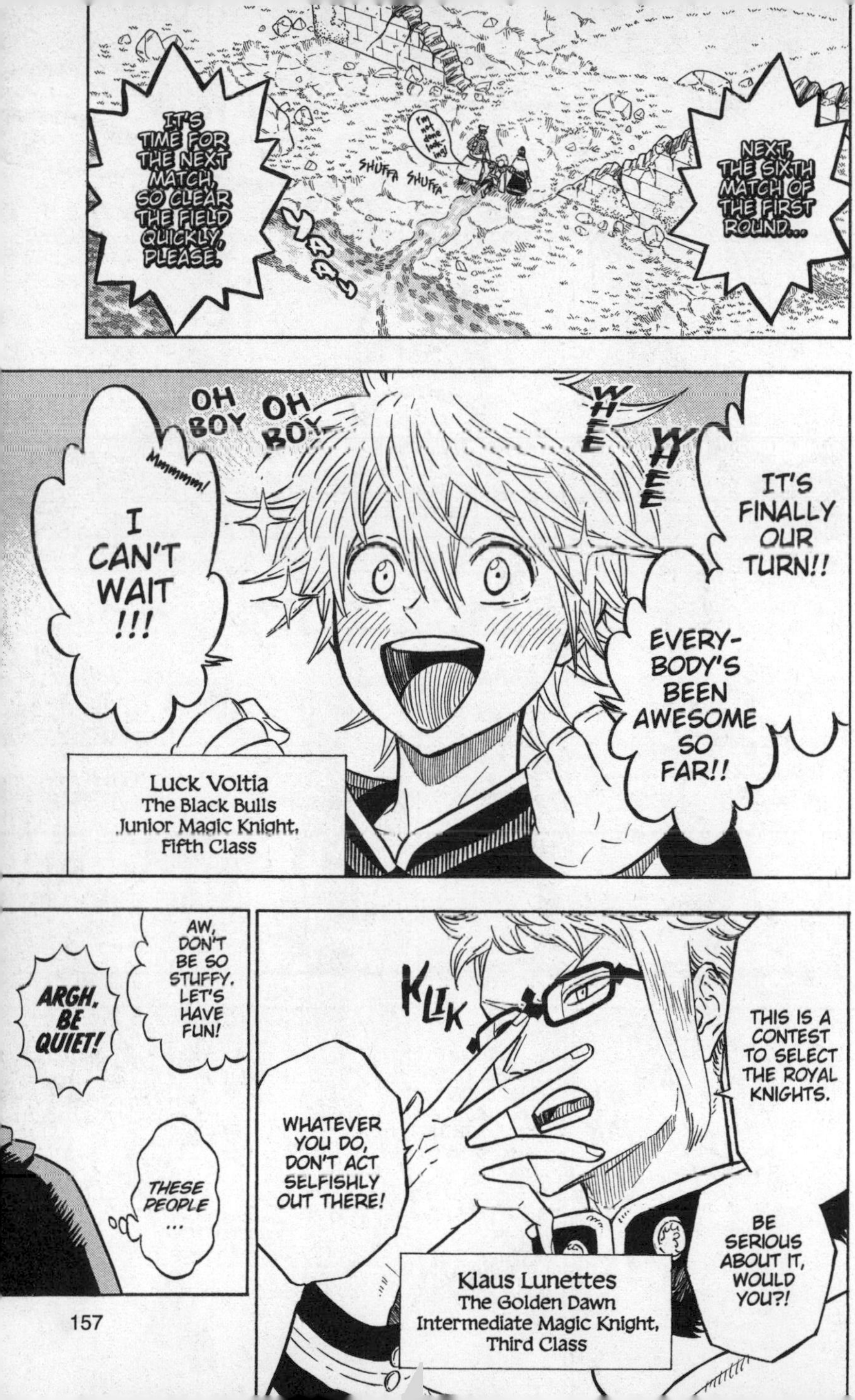
NEXT, THE SIXTH MATCH OF THE FIRST ROUND...
I'm not done looking!
SHUFFA SHUFFA
IT'S TIME FOR THE NEXT MATCH, SO CLEAR THE FIELD QUICKLY, PLEASE.
IT'S FINALLY OUR TURN!!
WHEE WHEE
EVERYBODY'S BEEN AWESOME SO FAR!!
OH BOY OH BOY
Mmmmmm!
I CAN'T WAIT!!!
Luck Voltia
The Black Bulls
Junior Magic Knight, Fifth Class
KLIK
THIS IS A CONTEST TO SELECT THE ROYAL KNIGHTS.
BE SERIOUS ABOUT IT, WOULD YOU?!
WHATEVER YOU DO, DON'T ACT SELFISHLY OUT THERE!
Klaus Lunettes
The Golden Dawn
Intermediate Magic Knight, Third Class
AW, DON'T BE SO STUFFY. LET'S HAVE FUN!
ARGH, BE QUIET!
THESE PEOPLE...

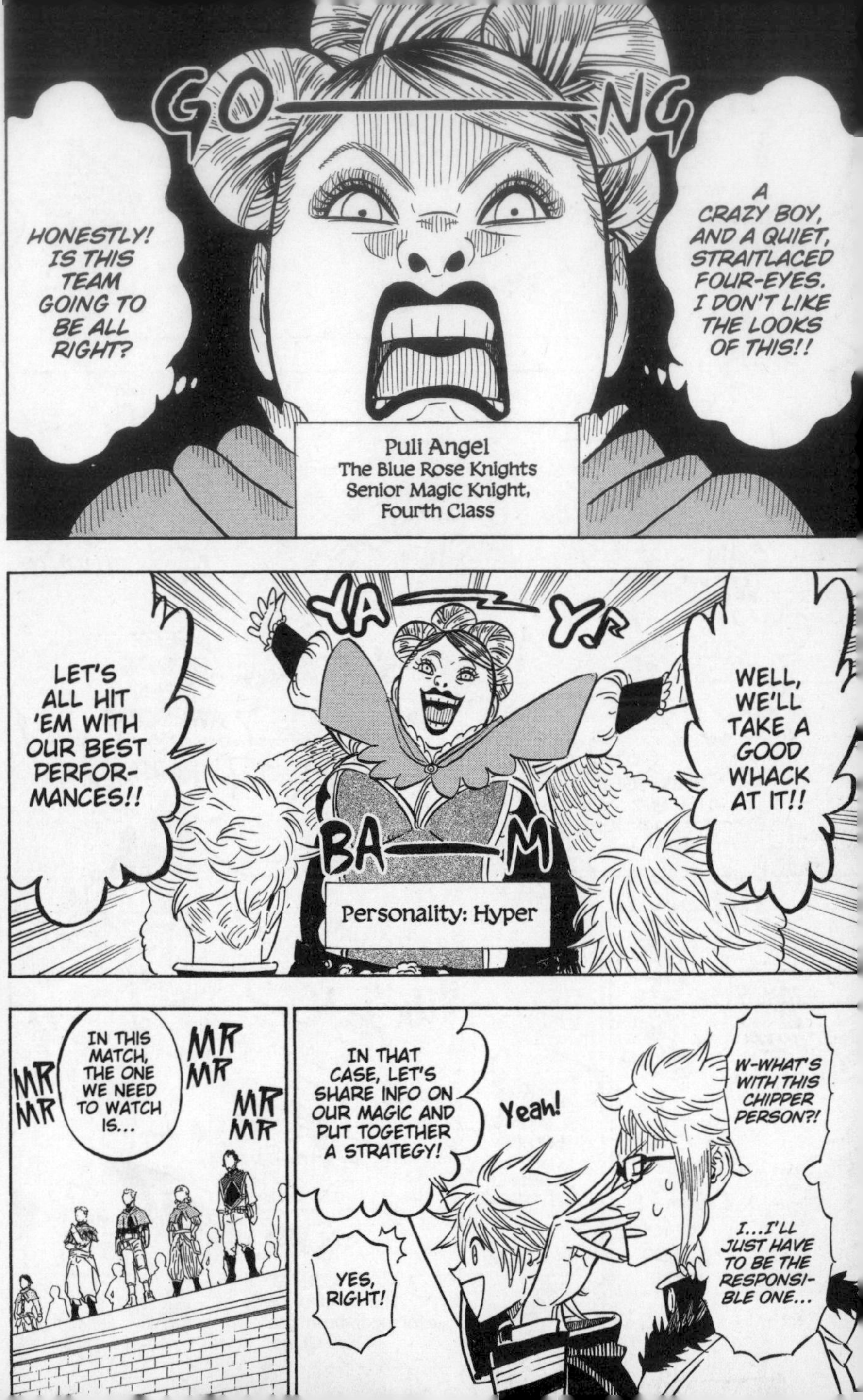
A CRAZY BOY, AND A QUIET, STRAITLACED FOUR-EYES. I DON'T LIKE THE LOOKS OF THIS!!
GO—NG
HONESTLY! IS THIS TEAM GOING TO BE ALL RIGHT?
Puli Angel The Blue Rose Knights Senior Magic Knight, Fourth Class
WELL, WE'LL TAKE A GOOD WHACK AT IT!!
YA—Y♪
LET'S ALL HIT 'EM WITH OUR BEST PERFORMANCES!!
BA—M
Personality: Hyper
W-WHAT'S WITH THIS CHIPPER PERSON?!
Yeah!
IN THAT CASE, LET'S SHARE INFO ON OUR MAGIC AND PUT TOGETHER A STRATEGY!
I...I'LL JUST HAVE TO BE THE RESPONSIBLE ONE...
YES, RIGHT!
MR MR
MR MR
IN THIS MATCH, THE ONE WE NEED TO WATCH IS...
MR MR

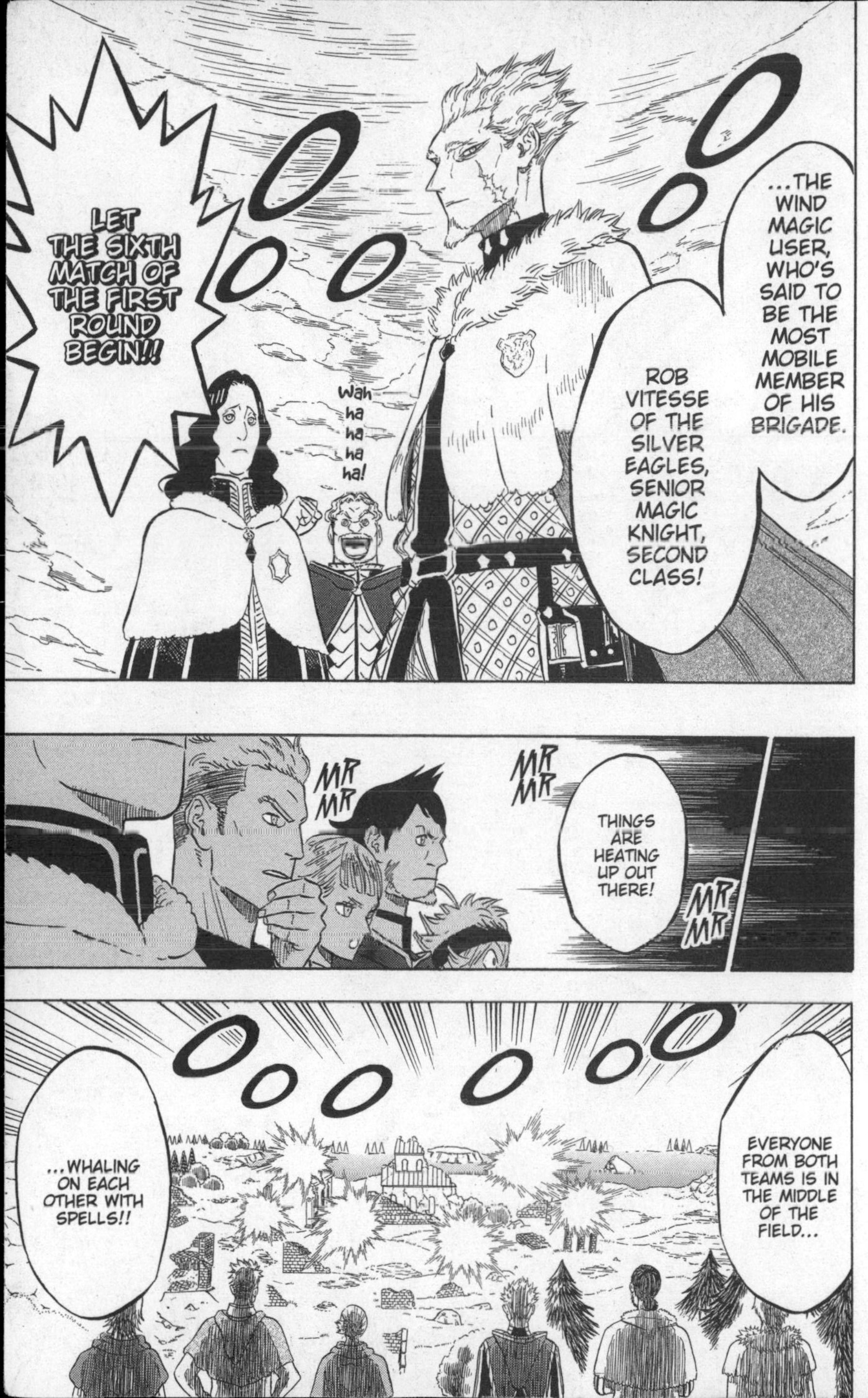
...THE WIND MAGIC USER, WHO'S SAID TO BE THE MOST MOBILE MEMBER OF HIS BRIGADE.
ROB VITESSE OF THE SILVER EAGLES, SENIOR MAGIC KNIGHT, SECOND CLASS!
LET THE SIXTH MATCH OF THE FIRST ROUND BEGIN!!
Wah ha ha ha ha!
MR MR
THINGS ARE HEATING UP OUT THERE!
MR MR
MR MR
EVERYONE FROM BOTH TEAMS IS IN THE MIDDLE OF THE FIELD...
...WHALING ON EACH OTHER WITH SPELLS!!

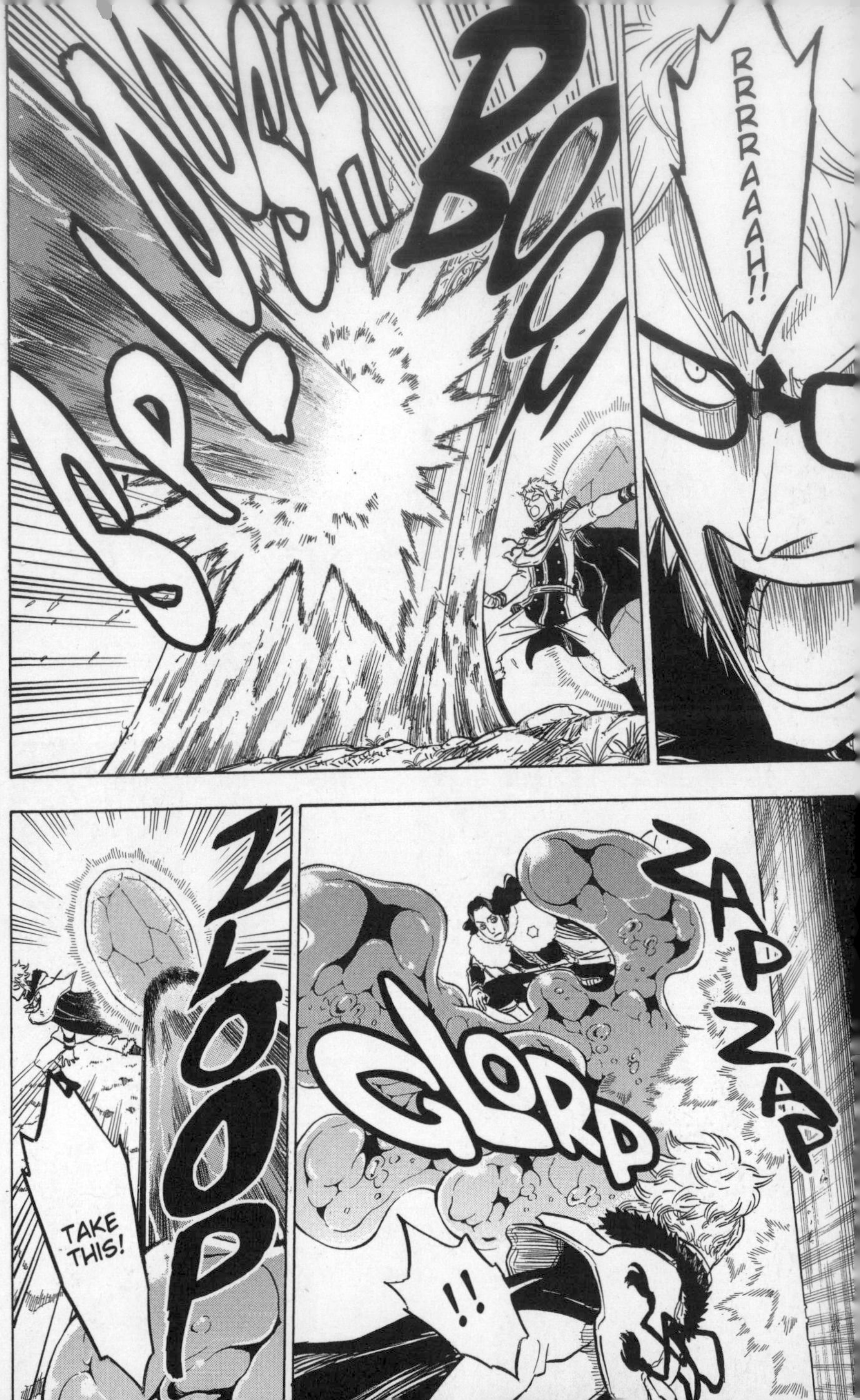
RRRRAAAH!!
BOOM
ZAP ZAP
GLORP
!!
TAKE THIS!

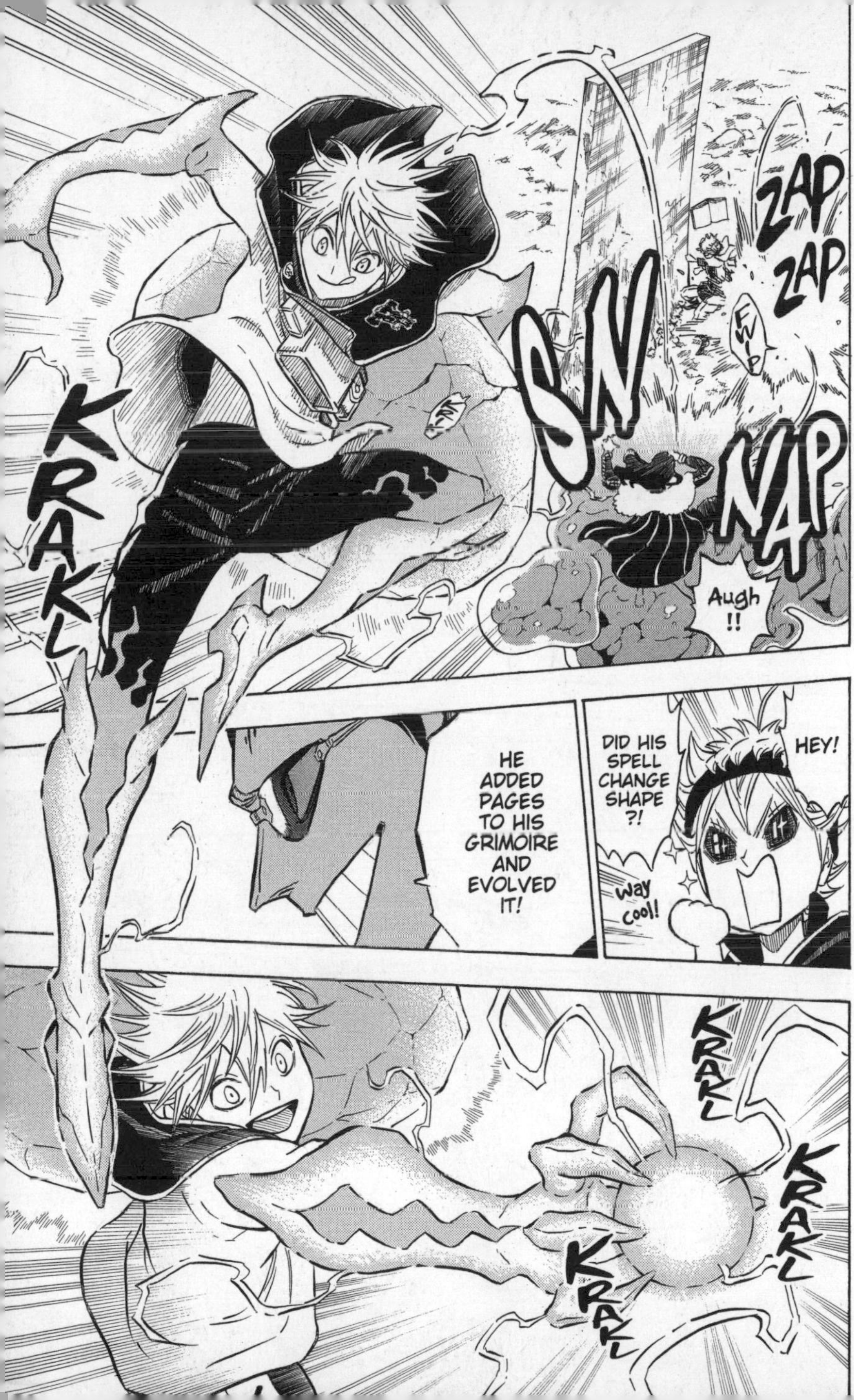
ZAP ZAP
FWIP
SNAP
Augh!!
KRAKL
HEY!
DID HIS SPELL CHANGE SHAPE?!
way cool!
HE ADDED PAGES TO HIS GRIMOIRE AND EVOLVED IT!
KRAKL
KRAKL
KRAKL

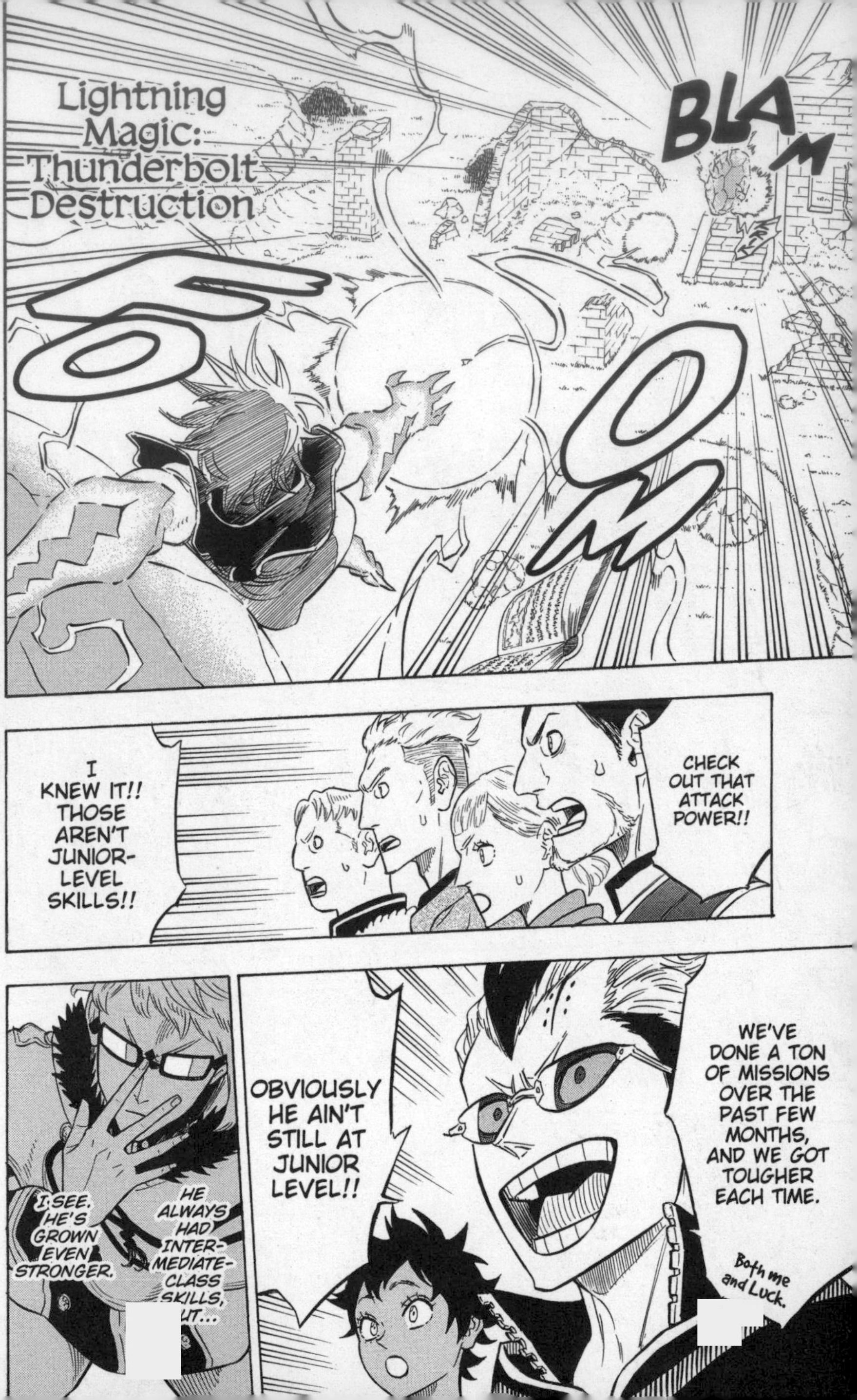
Lightning Magic: Thunderbolt Destruction
BLAM
FOOM
CHECK OUT THAT ATTACK POWER!!
I KNEW IT!! THOSE AREN'T JUNIOR-LEVEL SKILLS!!
WE'VE DONE A TON OF MISSIONS OVER THE PAST FEW MONTHS, AND WE GOT TOUGHER EACH TIME.
OBVIOUSLY HE AIN'T STILL AT JUNIOR LEVEL!!
Both me and Luck.
HE ALWAYS HAD INTERMEDIATE-CLASS SKILLS, UT...
I SEE. HE'S GROWN EVEN STRONGER.

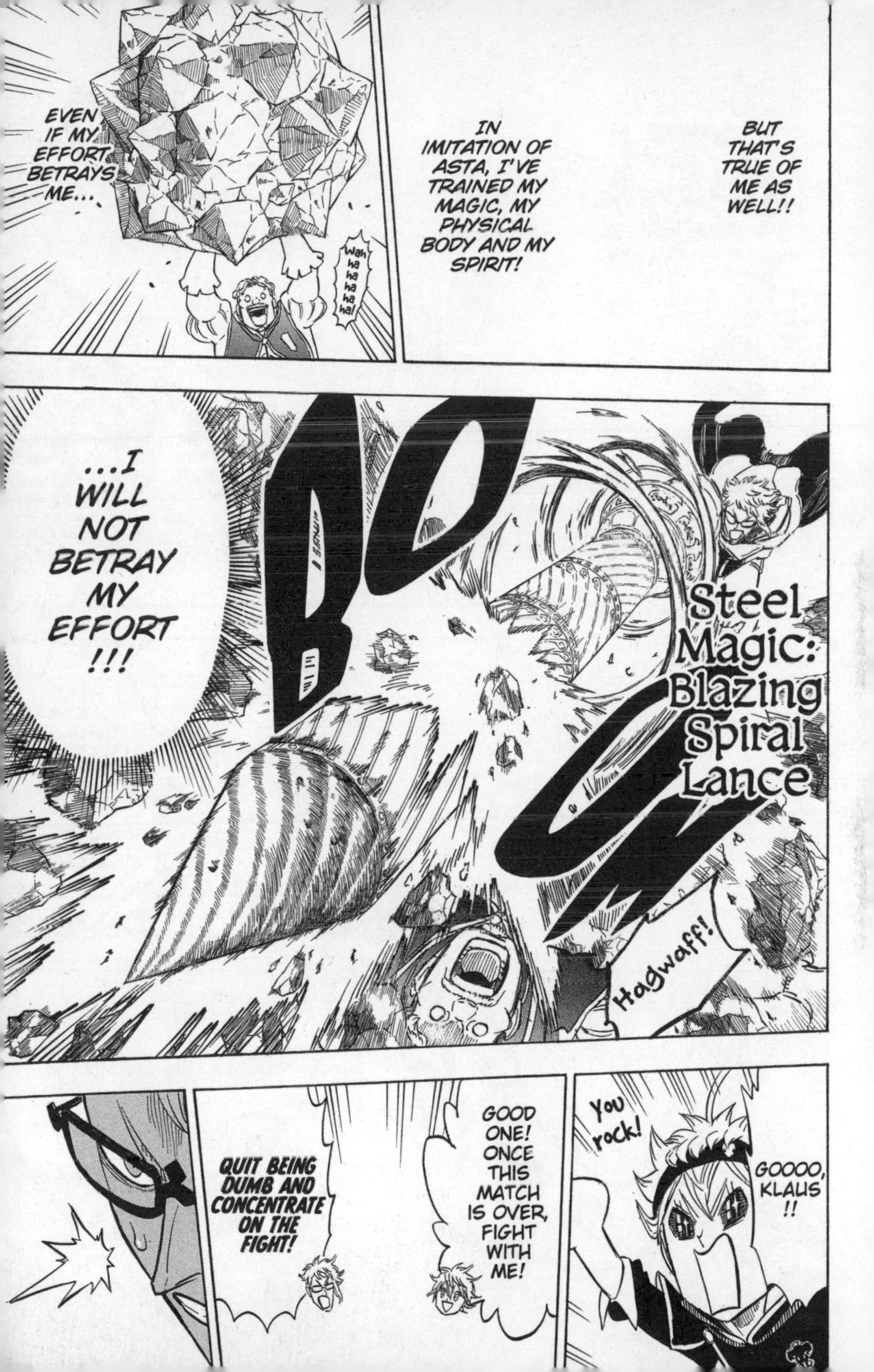
BUT THAT'S TRUE OF ME AS WELL!!
IN IMITATION OF ASTA, I'VE TRAINED MY MAGIC, MY PHYSICAL BODY AND MY SPIRIT!
EVEN IF MY EFFORT BETRAYS ME...
Wah ha ha ha ha ha!
Steel Magic: Blazing Spiral Lance
Hagwaff!
...I WILL NOT BETRAY MY EFFORT!!!
GOOOO, KLAUS!!
You rock!
GOOD ONE! ONCE THIS MATCH IS OVER, FIGHT WITH ME!
QUIT BEING DUMB AND CONCENTRATE ON THE FIGHT!

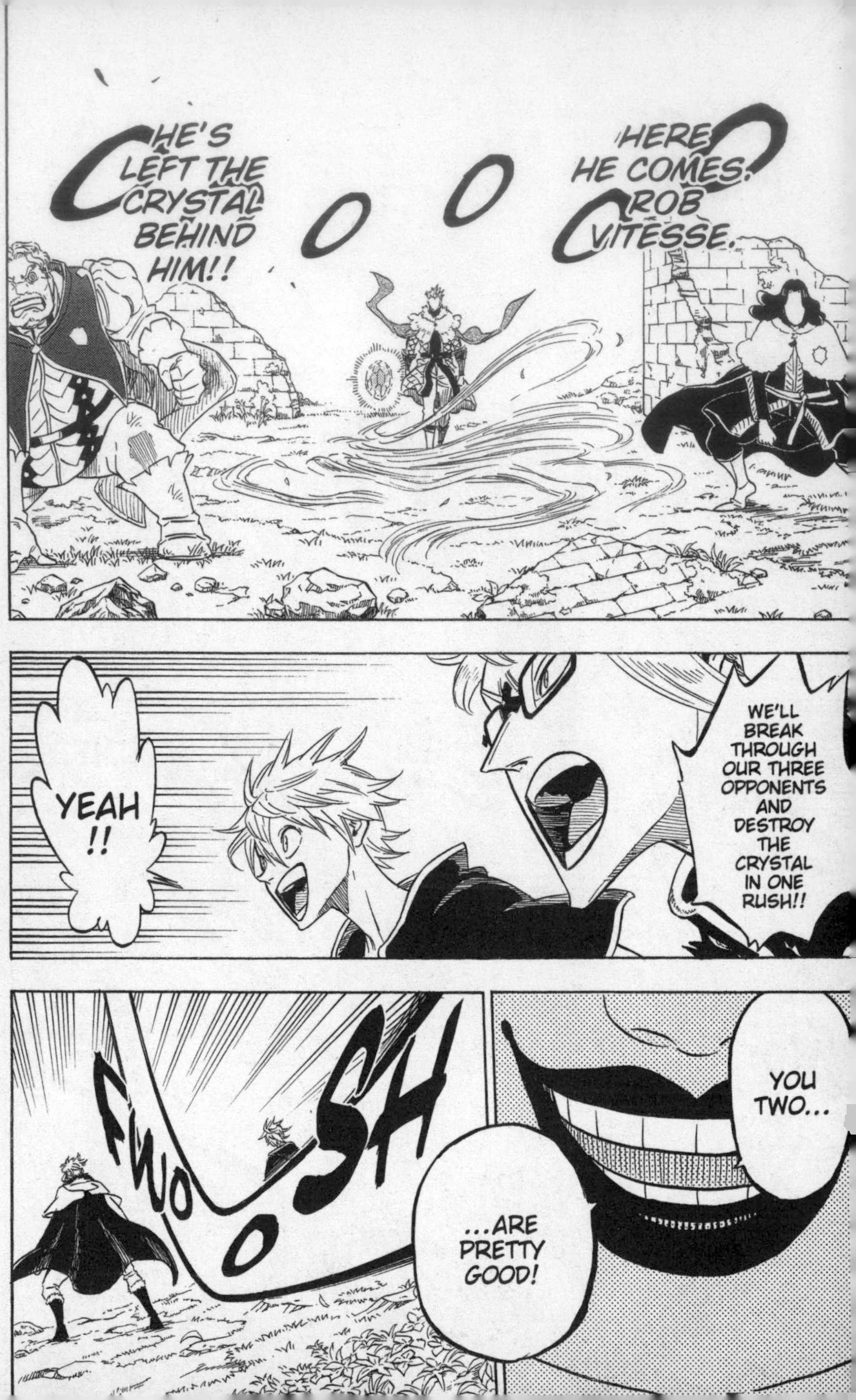
HERE HE COMES. ROB VITESSE.
HE'S LEFT THE CRYSTAL BEHIND HIM!!
WE'LL BREAK THROUGH OUR THREE OPPONENTS AND DESTROY THE CRYSTAL IN ONE RUSH!!
YEAH!!
YOU TWO...
...ARE PRETTY GOOD!
FWOOSH

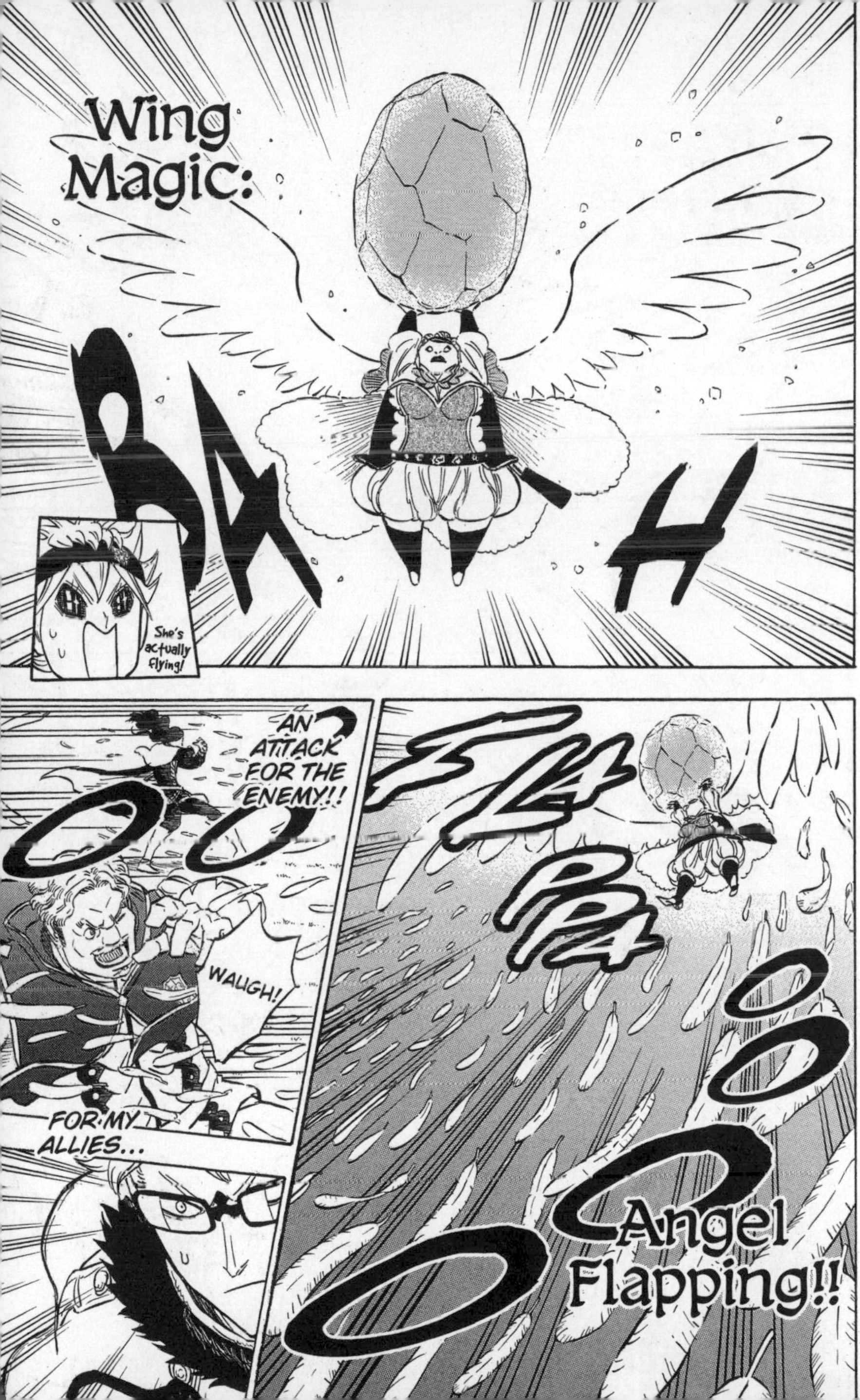
Wing Magic:
She's actually flying!
Angel Flapping!!
AN ATTACK FOR THE ENEMY!!
WAUGH!
FOR MY ALLIES...

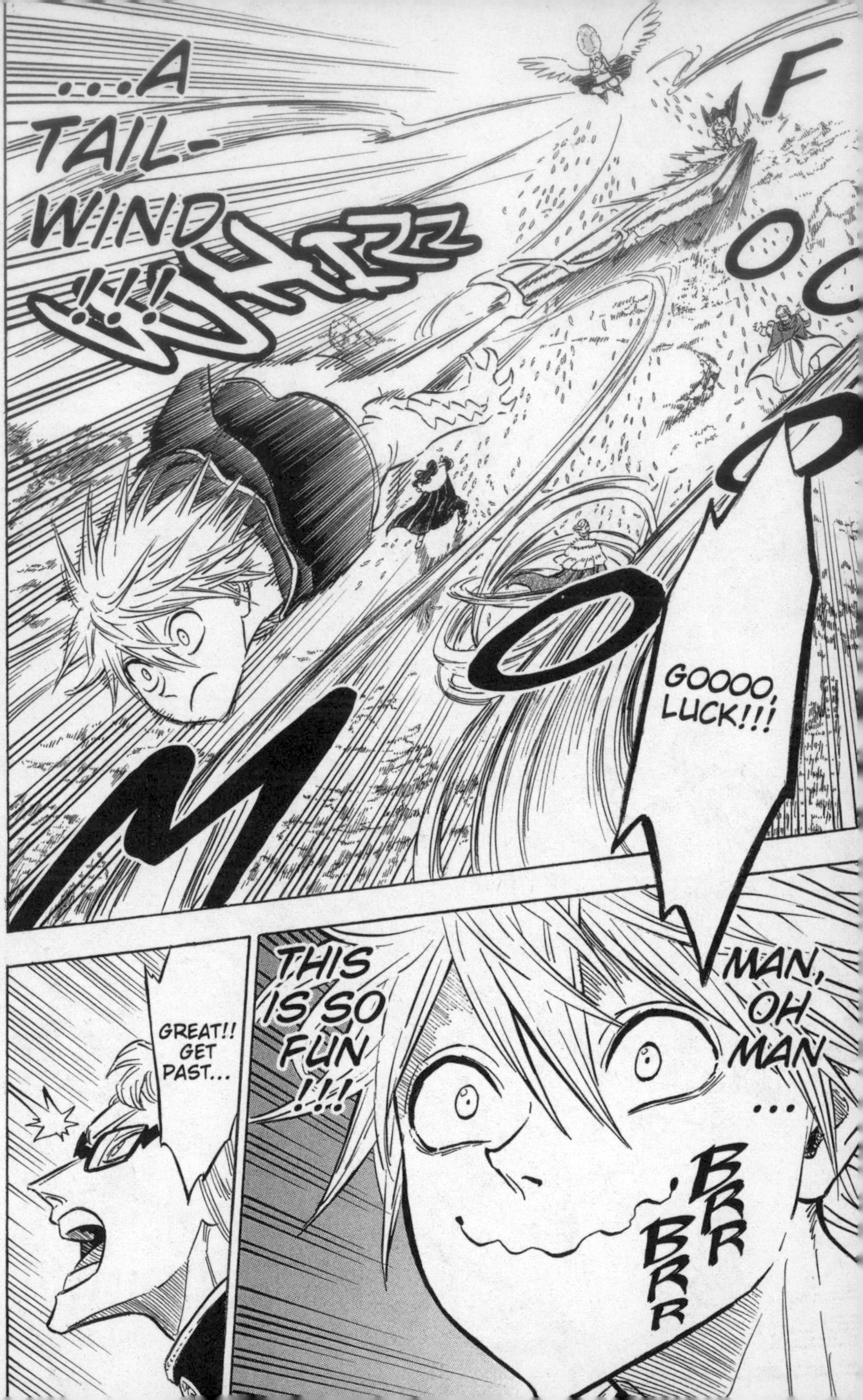
FOOOOM
GOOOO, LUCK!!!
WHIRR
...A TAIL-WIND!!!
MAN, OH MAN...
BRR BRR
THIS IS SO FUN!!!
GREAT!! GET PAST...

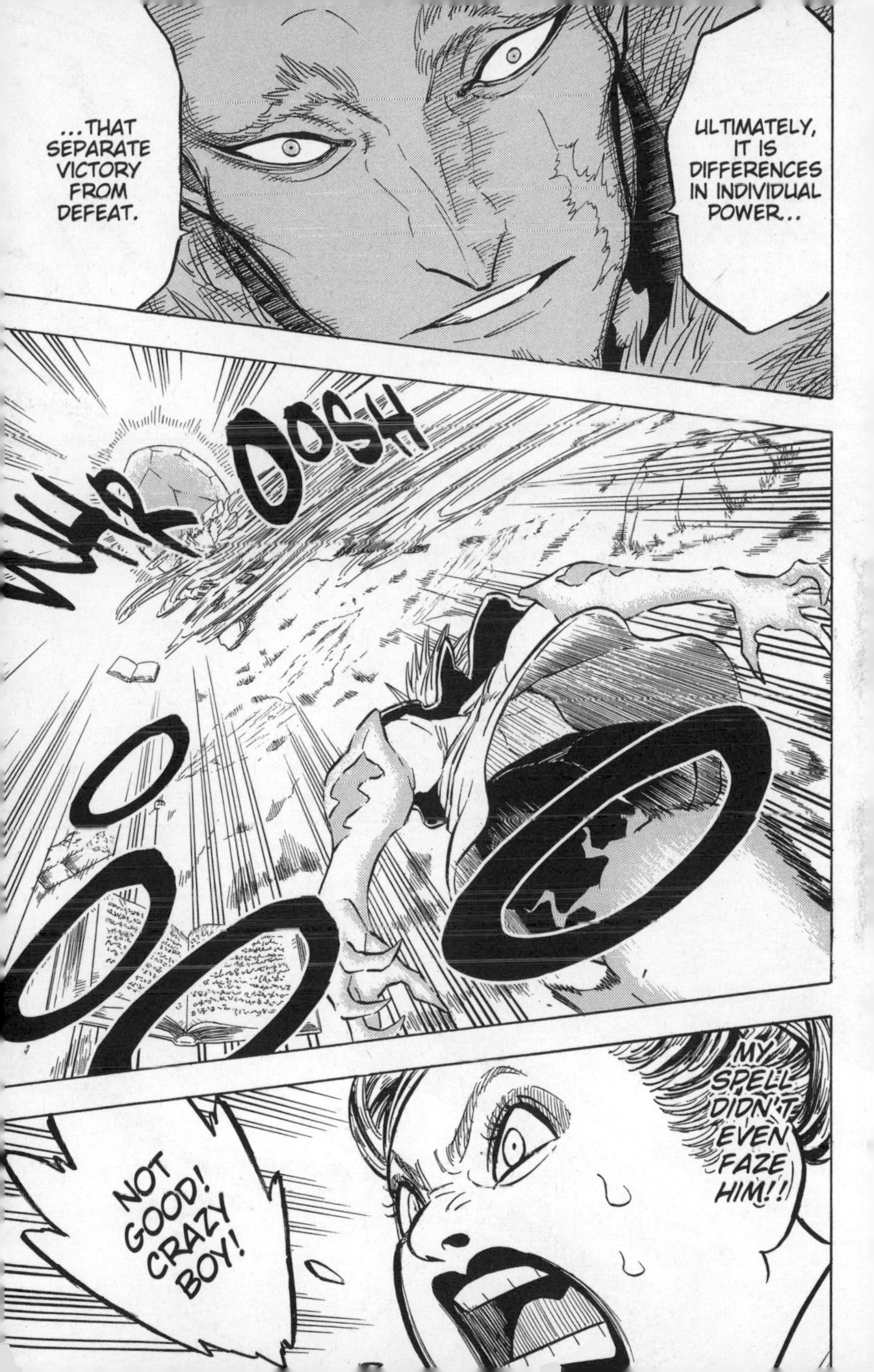
ULTIMATELY, IT IS DIFFERENCES IN INDIVIDUAL POWER...
...THAT SEPARATE VICTORY FROM DEFEAT.
WHOOSH
MY SPELL DIDN'T EVEN FAZE HIM!!
NOT GOOD! CRAZY BOY!

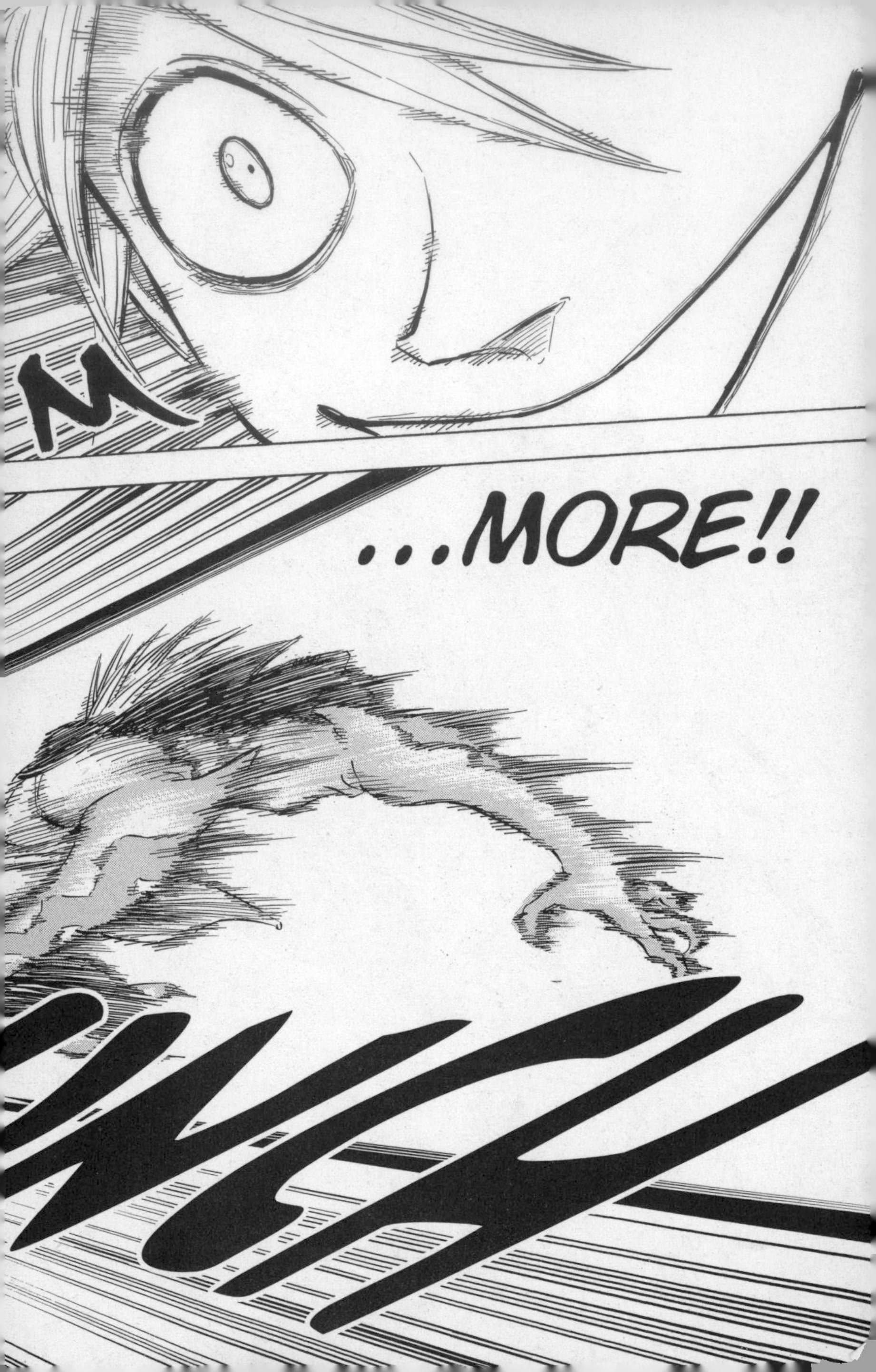
M
...MORE!!

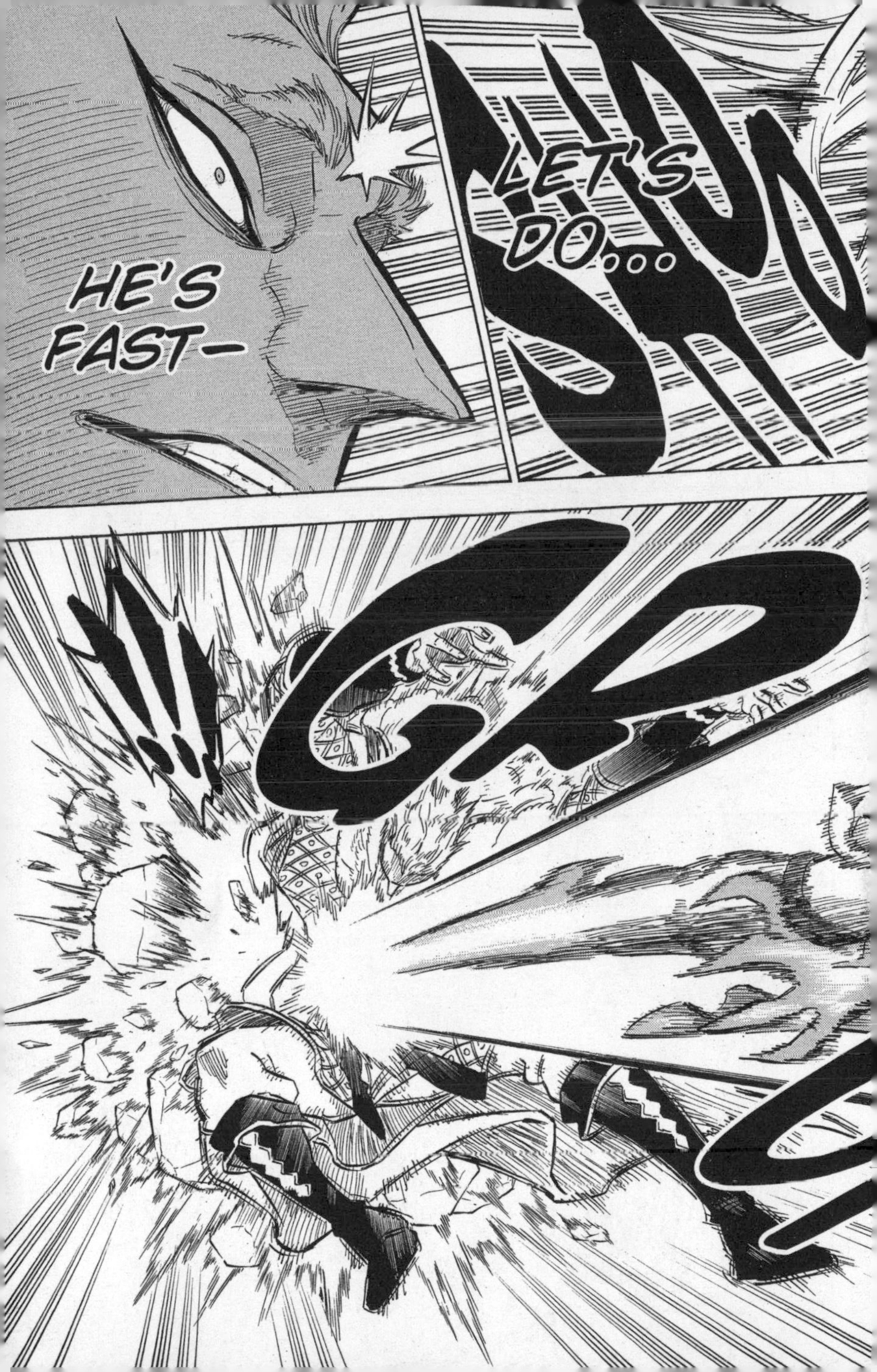
LET'S DO...
HE'S FAST—
!!

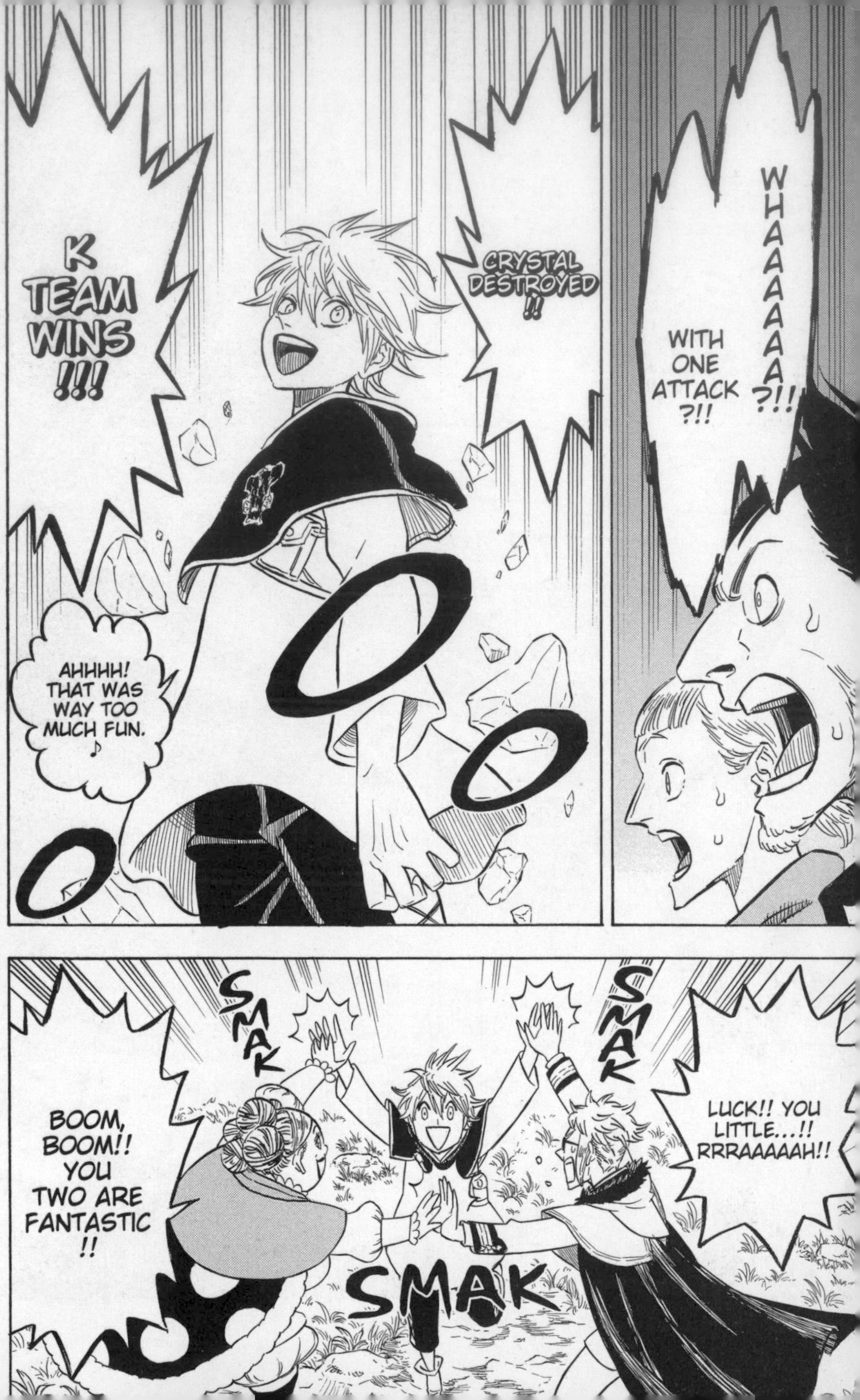
WHAAAAAA?!!
WITH ONE ATTACK?!!
CRYSTAL DESTROYED!!
K TEAM WINS!!!
AHHHH! THAT WAS WAY TOO MUCH FUN. ♪
SMAK
LUCK!! YOU LITTLE...!! RRRAAAAAH!!
SMAK
BOOM, BOOM!! YOU TWO ARE FANTASTIC!!
SMAK

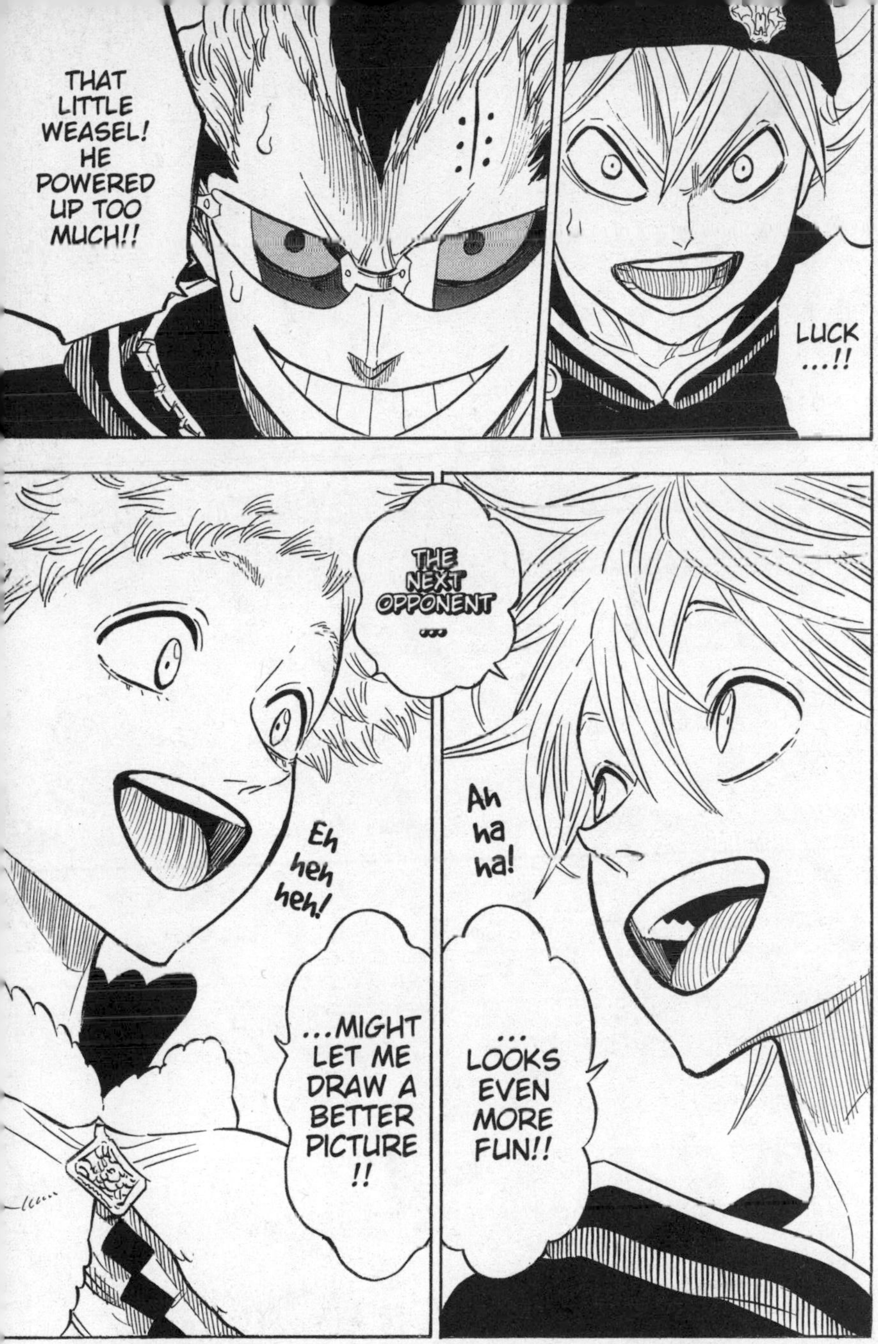
LUCK ...!!
THAT LITTLE WEASEL! HE POWERED UP TOO MUCH!!
THE NEXT OPPONENT ...
Ah ha ha!
... LOOKS EVEN MORE FUN!!
Eh heh heh!
...MIGHT LET ME DRAW A BETTER PICTURE !!

Page 120: Bad Blood

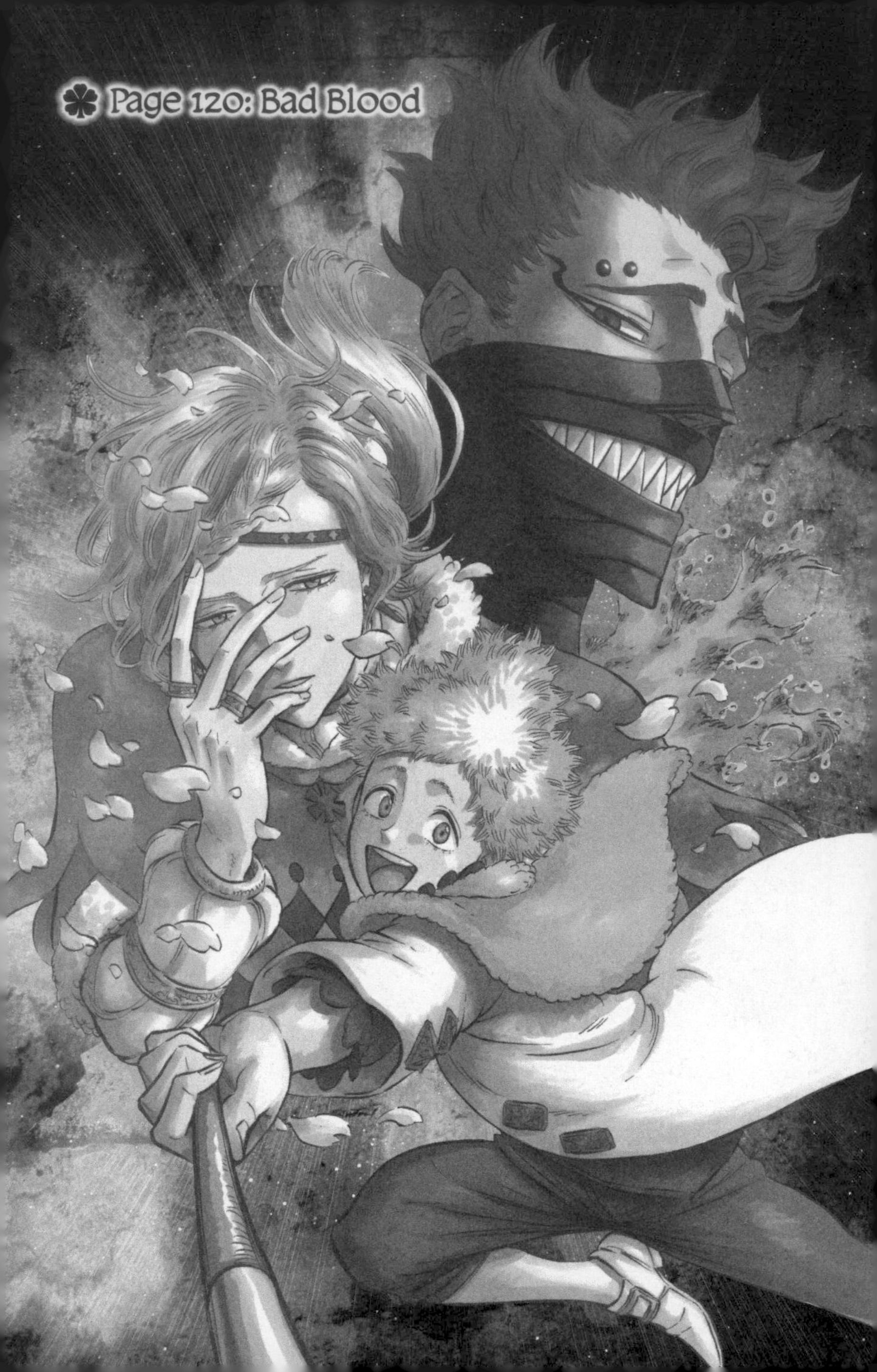

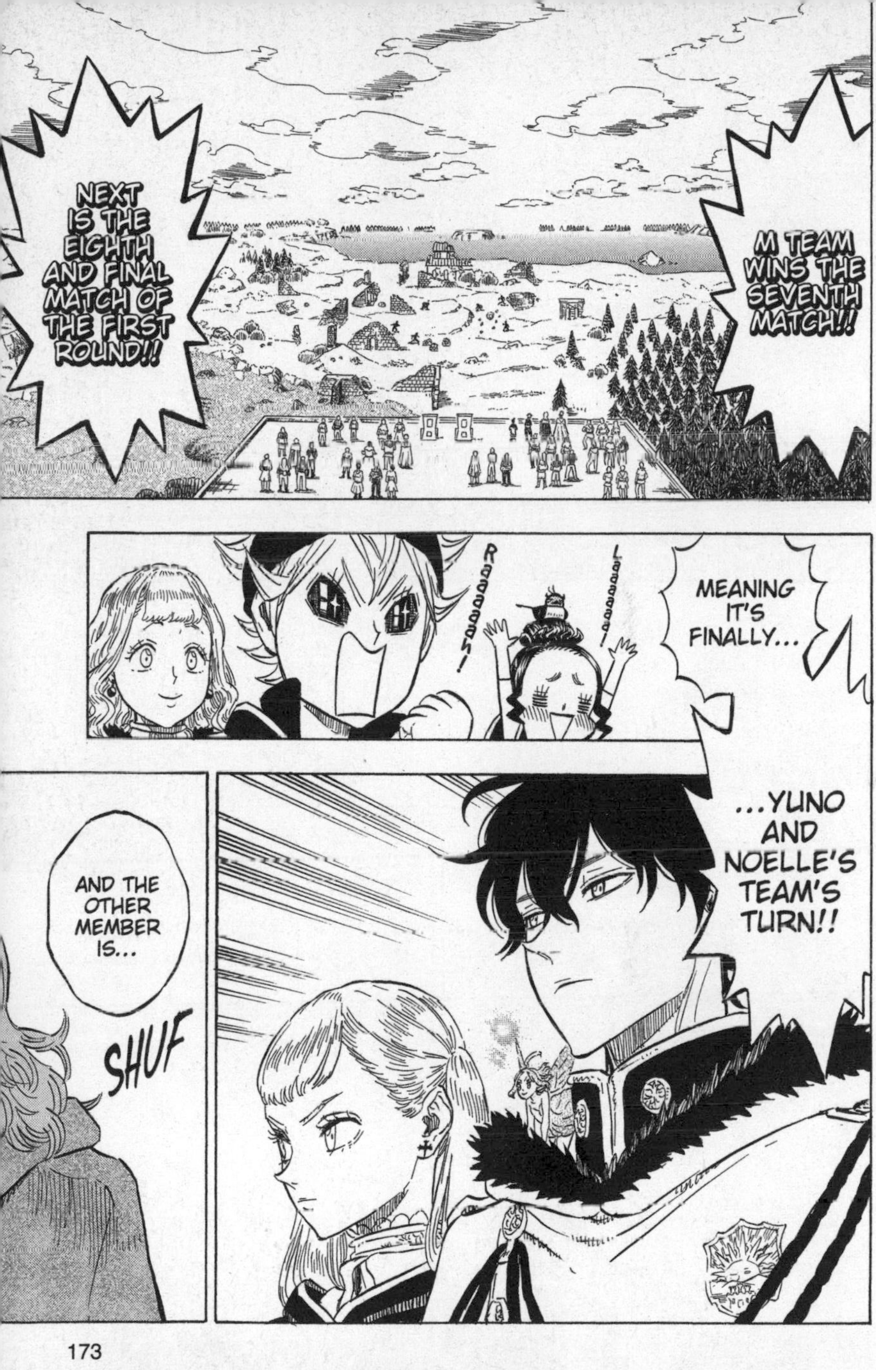
M TEAM WINS THE SEVENTH MATCH!!
NEXT IS THE EIGHTH AND FINAL MATCH OF THE FIRST ROUND!!
MEANING IT'S FINALLY...
Laaaaaaa!
Raaaaaah!
...YUNO AND NOELLE'S TEAM'S TURN!!
AND THE OTHER MEMBER IS...
SHUF

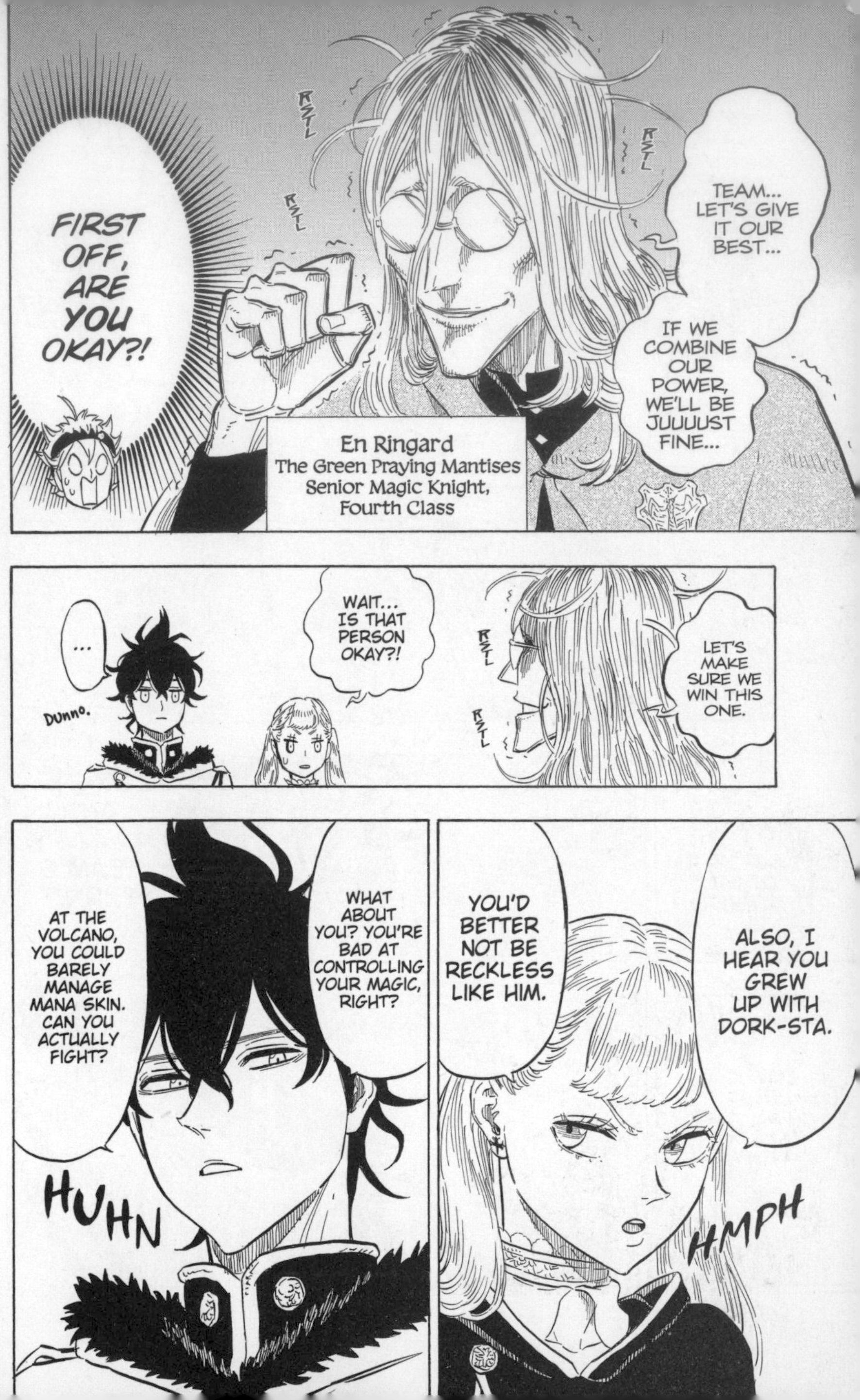
TEAM... LET'S GIVE IT OUR BEST...
IF WE COMBINE OUR POWER, WE'LL BE JUUUUST FINE...
RSTL
RSTL
RSTL
En Ringard
The Green Praying Mantises Senior Magic Knight, Fourth Class
FIRST OFF, ARE YOU OKAY?!
LET'S MAKE SURE WE WIN THIS ONE.
RSTL
RSTL
WAIT... IS THAT PERSON OKAY?!
...
DUNNO.
ALSO, I HEAR YOU GREW UP WITH DORK-STA.
YOU'D BETTER NOT BE RECKLESS LIKE HIM.
HMPH
WHAT ABOUT YOU? YOU'RE BAD AT CONTROLLING YOUR MAGIC, RIGHT?
AT THE VOLCANO, YOU COULD BARELY MANAGE MANA SKIN. CAN YOU ACTUALLY FIGHT?
HUHN

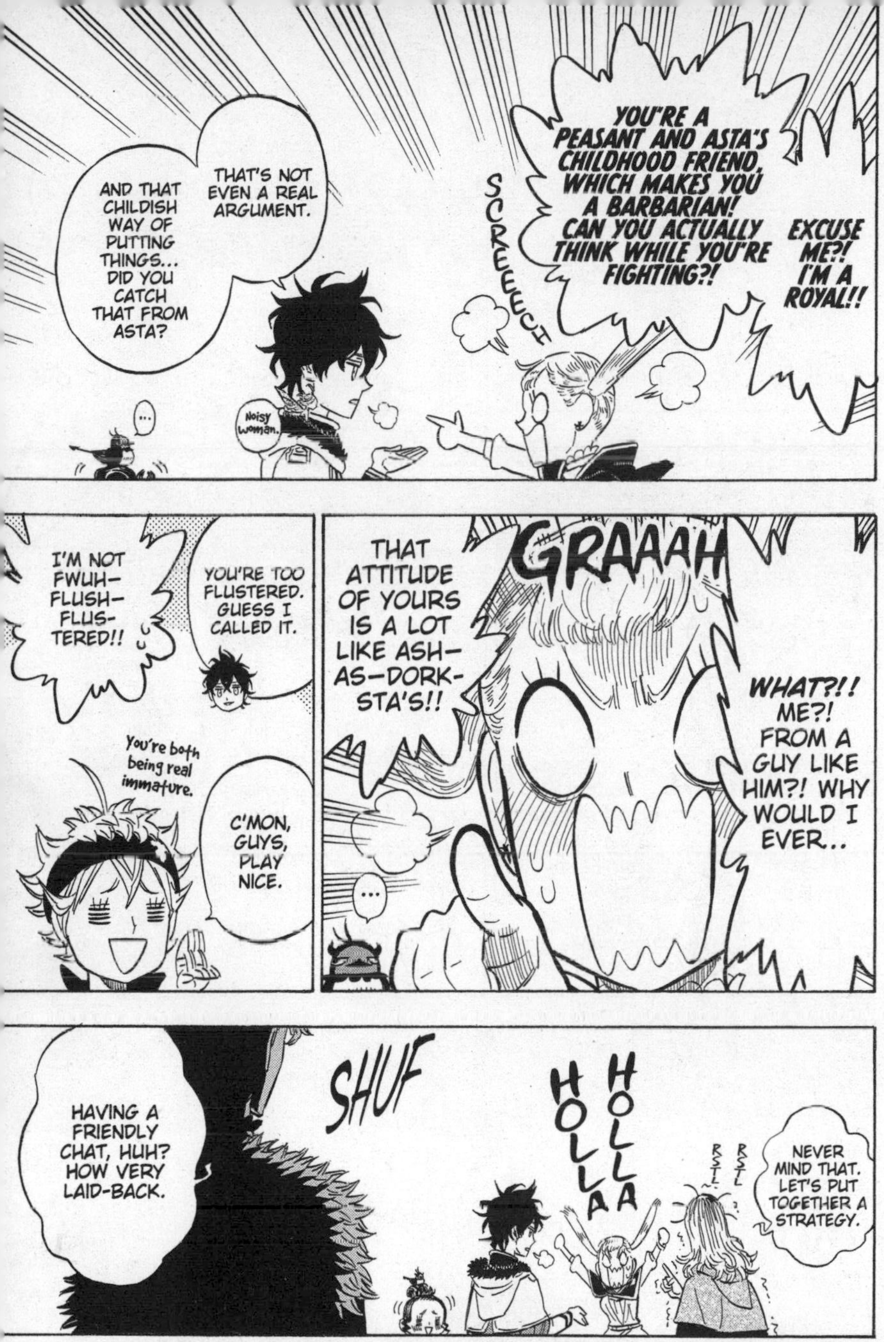
EXCUSE ME?! I'M A ROYAL!!
YOU'RE A PEASANT AND ASTA'S CHILDHOOD FRIEND, WHICH MAKES YOU A BARBARIAN! CAN YOU ACTUALLY THINK WHILE YOU'RE FIGHTING?!
SCREEEECH
THAT'S NOT EVEN A REAL ARGUMENT.
AND THAT CHILDISH WAY OF PUTTING THINGS... DID YOU CATCH THAT FROM ASTA?
Noisy woman.
...
GRAAAH
WHAT?!! ME?! FROM A GUY LIKE HIM?! WHY WOULD I EVER...
THAT ATTITUDE OF YOURS IS A LOT LIKE ASH-AS-DORK-STA'S!!
...
YOU'RE TOO FLUSTERED. GUESS I CALLED IT.
I'M NOT FWUH-FLUSH-FLUS-TERED!!
You're both being real immature.
C'MON, GUYS, PLAY NICE.
NEVER MIND THAT. LET'S PUT TOGETHER A STRATEGY.
RSTL
RSTL
HOLLA
HOLLA
SHUF
HAVING A FRIENDLY CHAT, HUH? HOW VERY LAID-BACK.

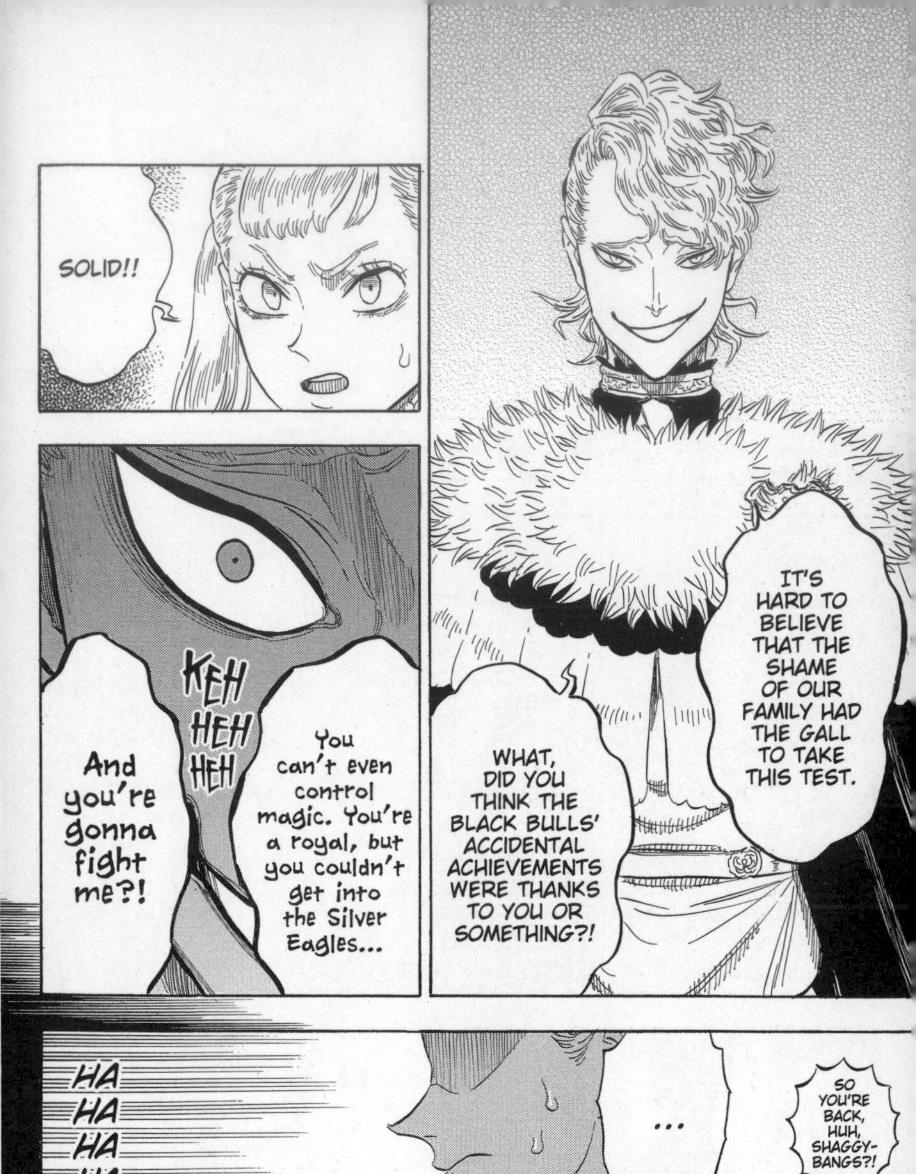
IT'S HARD TO BELIEVE THAT THE SHAME OF OUR FAMILY HAD THE GALL TO TAKE THIS TEST.
WHAT, DID YOU THINK THE BLACK BULLS' ACCIDENTAL ACHIEVEMENTS WERE THANKS TO YOU OR SOMETHING?!
SOLID!!
KEH HEH HEH
You can't even control magic. You're a royal, but you couldn't get into the Silver Eagles...
And you're gonna fight me?!
SO YOU'RE BACK, HUH, SHAGGY-BANGS?!
...
HA HA HA HA HA HA HA!

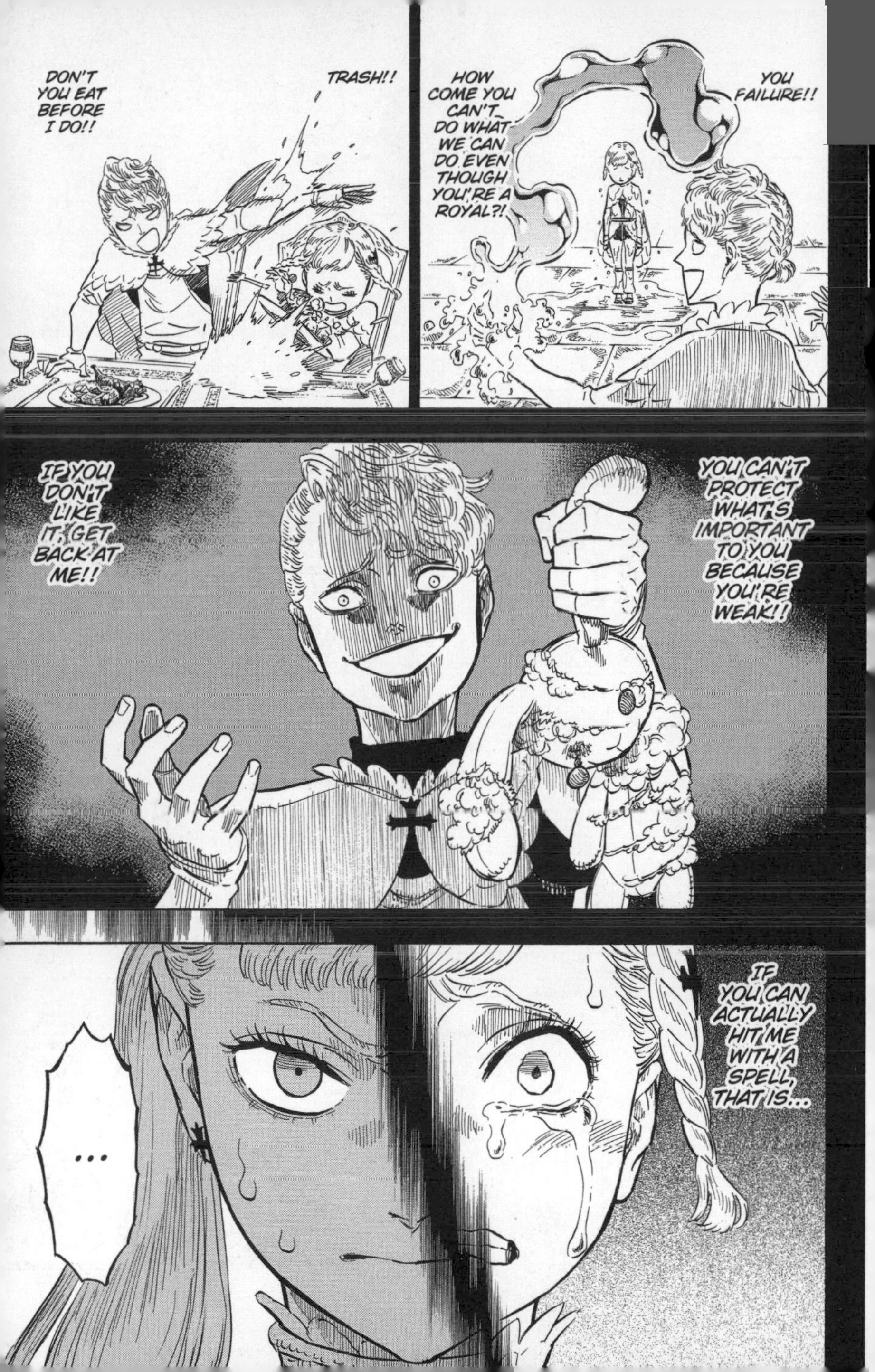
YOU FAILURE!!
HOW COME YOU CAN'T DO WHAT WE CAN DO EVEN THOUGH YOU'RE A ROYAL?!
TRASH!!
DON'T YOU EAT BEFORE I DO!!
YOU CAN'T PROTECT WHAT'S IMPORTANT TO YOU BECAUSE YOU'RE WEAK!!
IF YOU DON'T LIKE IT, GET BACK AT ME!!
IF YOU CAN ACTUALLY HIT ME WITH A SPELL, THAT IS...
...

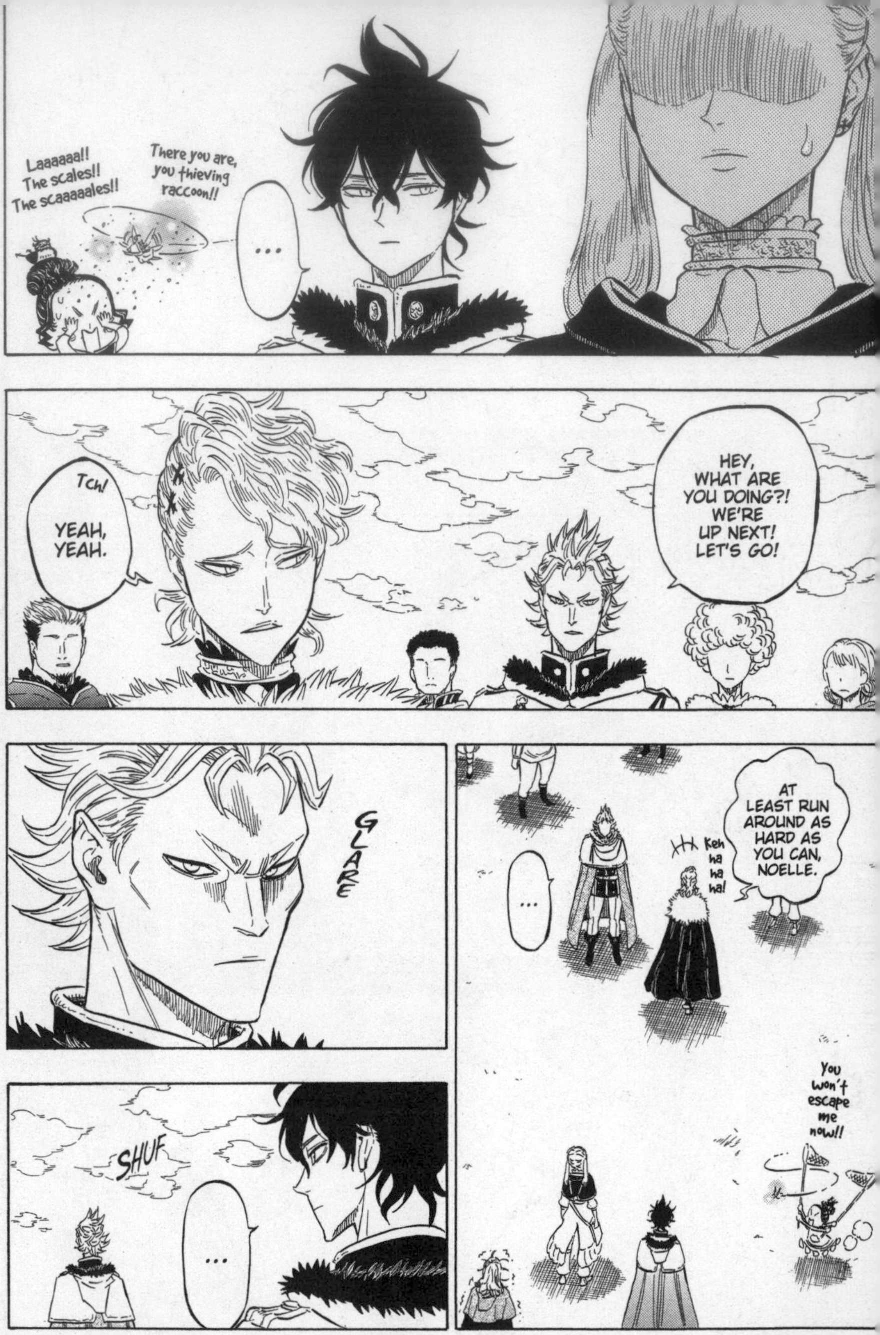
...
There you are, you thieving raccoon!!
Laaaaaa!! The scales!! The scaaaaales!!
HEY, WHAT ARE YOU DOING?! WE'RE UP NEXT! LET'S GO!
Tch! YEAH, YEAH.
AT LEAST RUN AROUND AS HARD AS YOU CAN, NOELLE.
Keh ha ha ha!
...
You won't escape me now!!
GLARE
SHUF
...

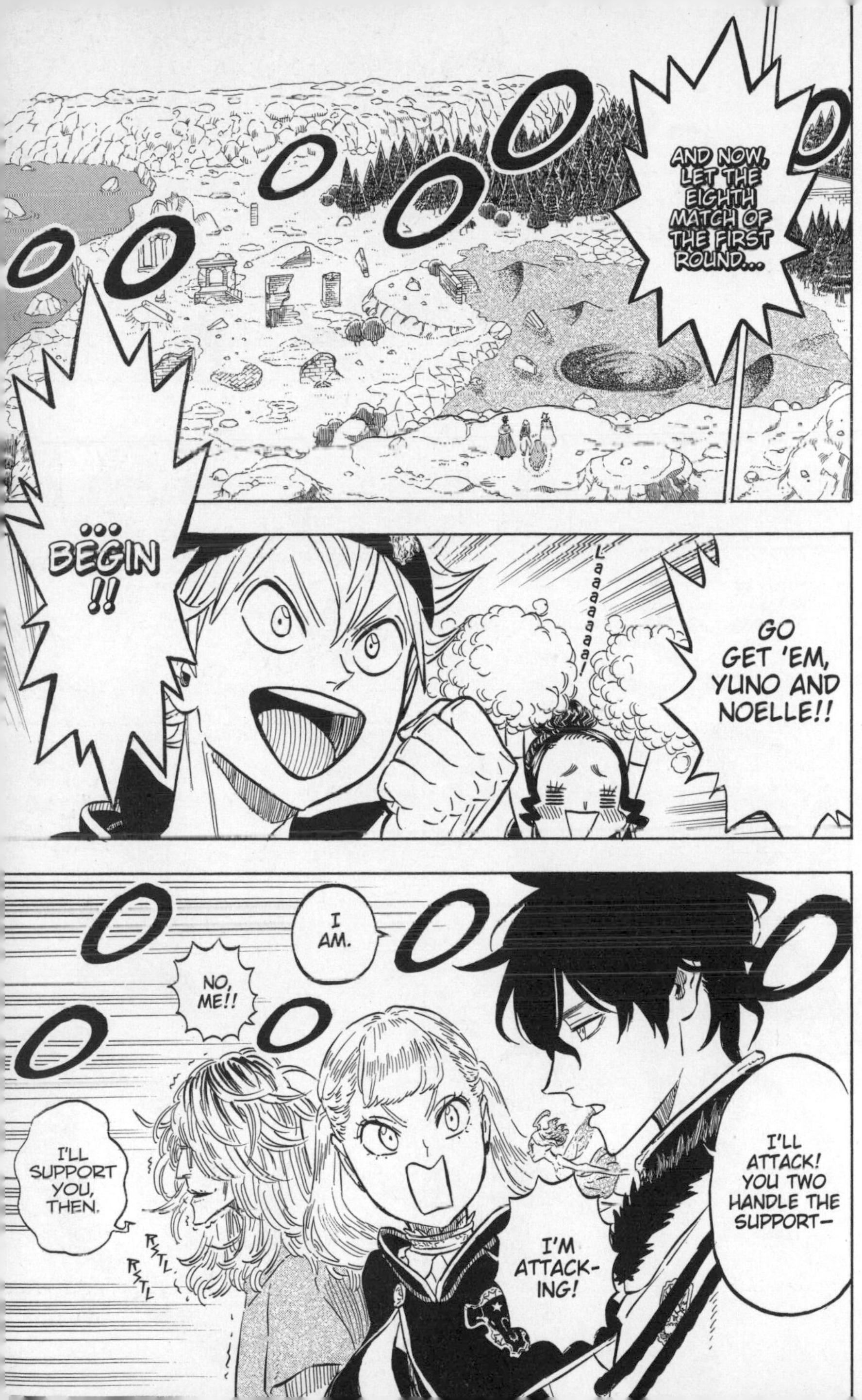
AND NOW, LET THE EIGHTH MATCH OF THE FIRST ROUND...
...BEGIN!!
GO GET 'EM, YUNO AND NOELLE!!
Laaaaaaaa!
I'LL ATTACK! YOU TWO HANDLE THE SUPPORT—
I'M ATTACKING!
I AM.
NO, ME!!
I'LL SUPPORT YOU, THEN.
RSTL
RSTL

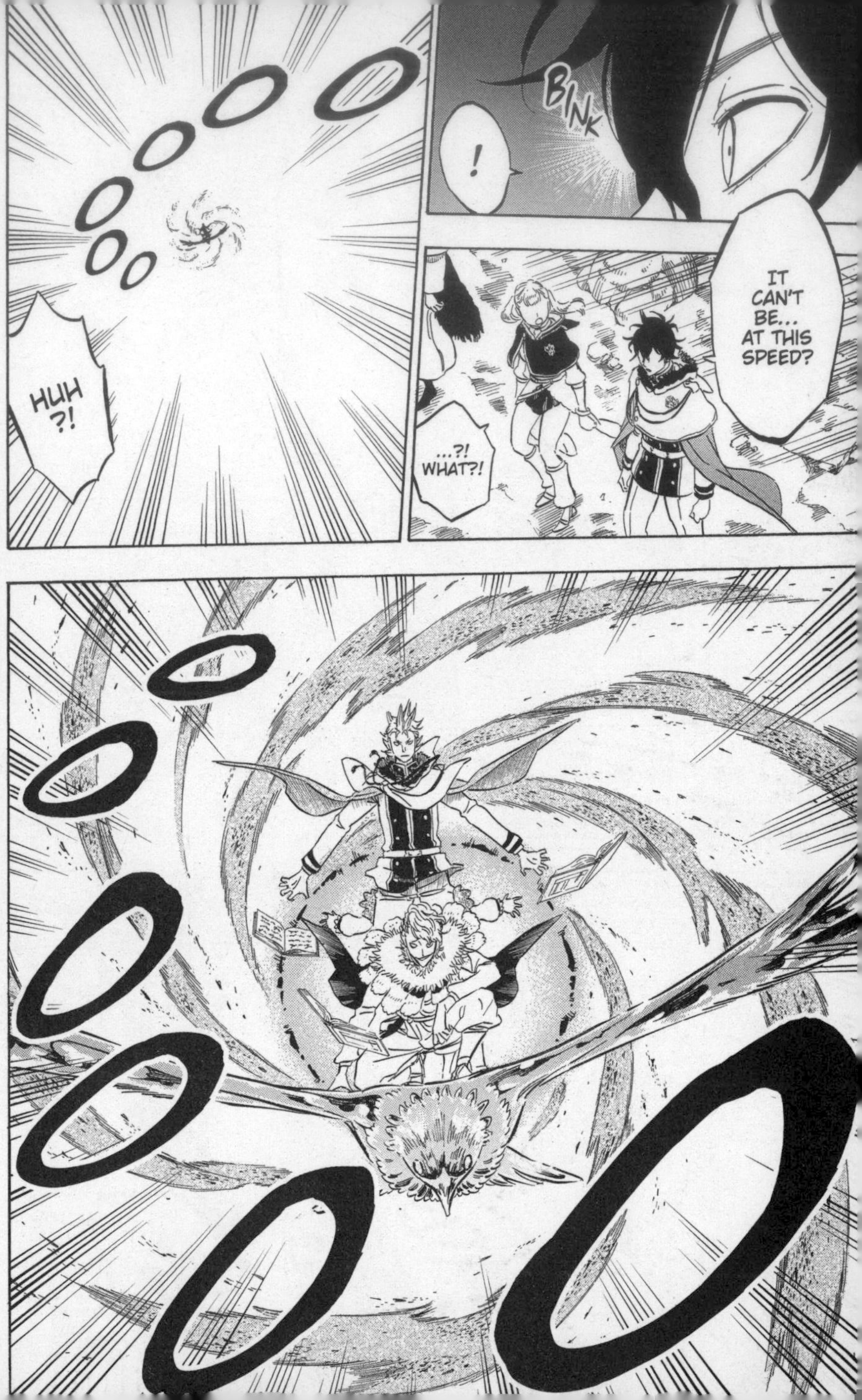
BINK
!
IT CAN'T BE... AT THIS SPEED?
...?! WHAT?!
HUH?!

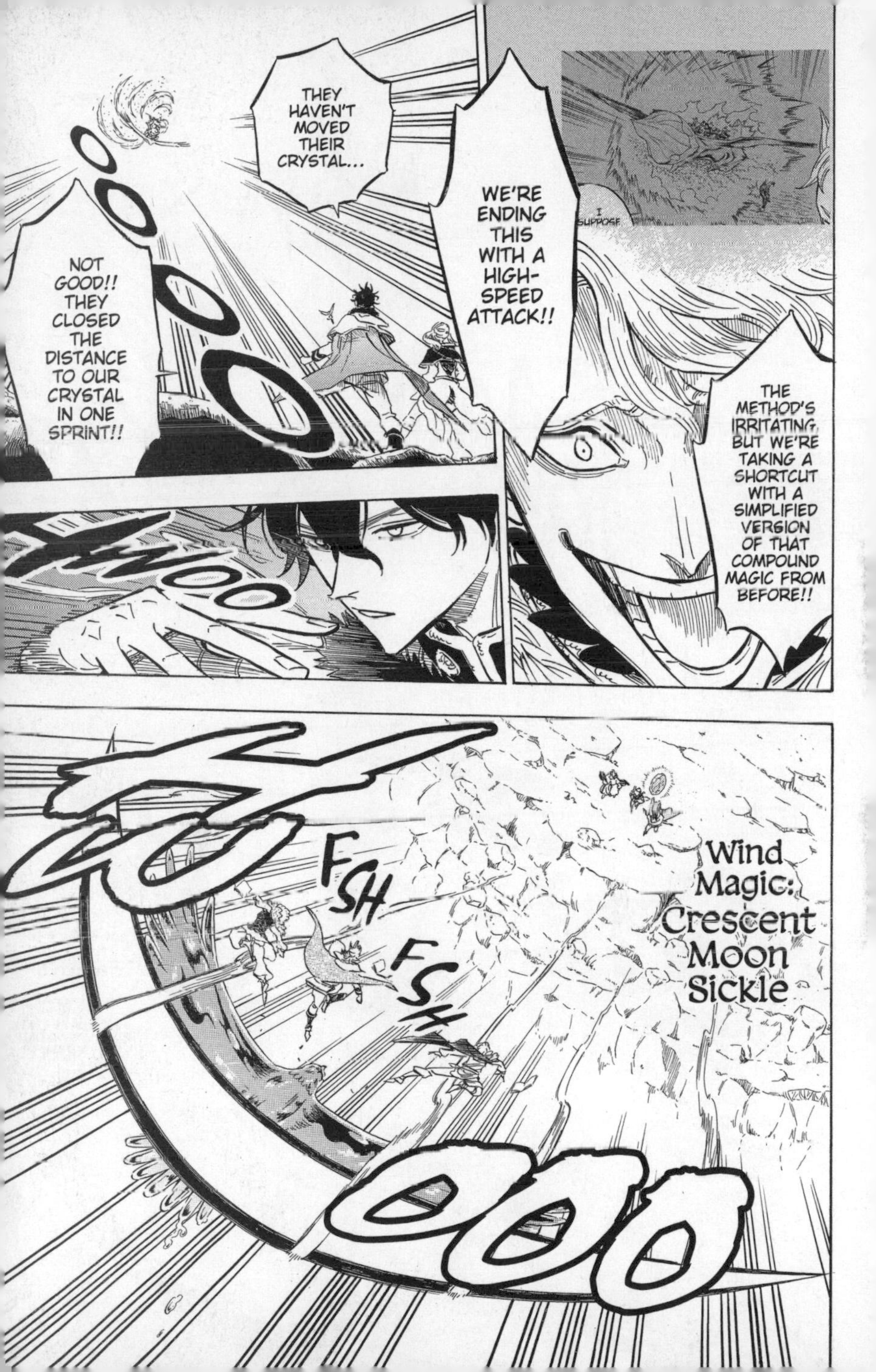
I SUPPOSE
WE'RE ENDING THIS WITH A HIGH-SPEED ATTACK!!
THE METHOD'S IRRITATING, BUT WE'RE TAKING A SHORTCUT WITH A SIMPLIFIED VERSION OF THAT COMPOUND MAGIC FROM BEFORE!!
THEY HAVEN'T MOVED THEIR CRYSTAL...
NOT GOOD!! THEY CLOSED THE DISTANCE TO OUR CRYSTAL IN ONE SPRINT!!
Wind Magic: Crescent Moon Sickle
FSH
FSH

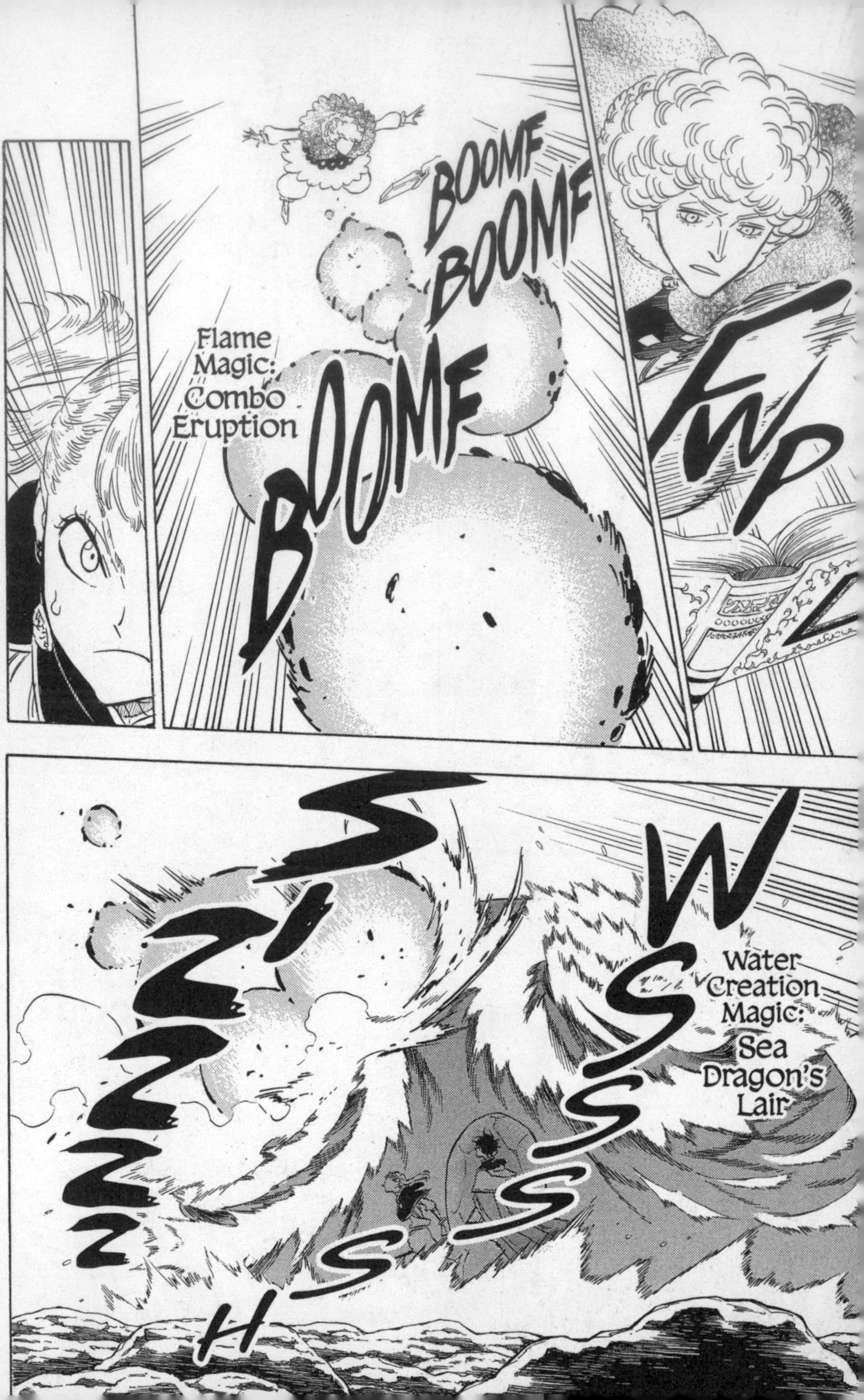
FWIP
BOOMF
BOOMF
BOOMF
Flame Magic: Combo Eruption
Water Creation Magic: Sea Dragon's Lair
WSSSSSH
SIZZZZZZ

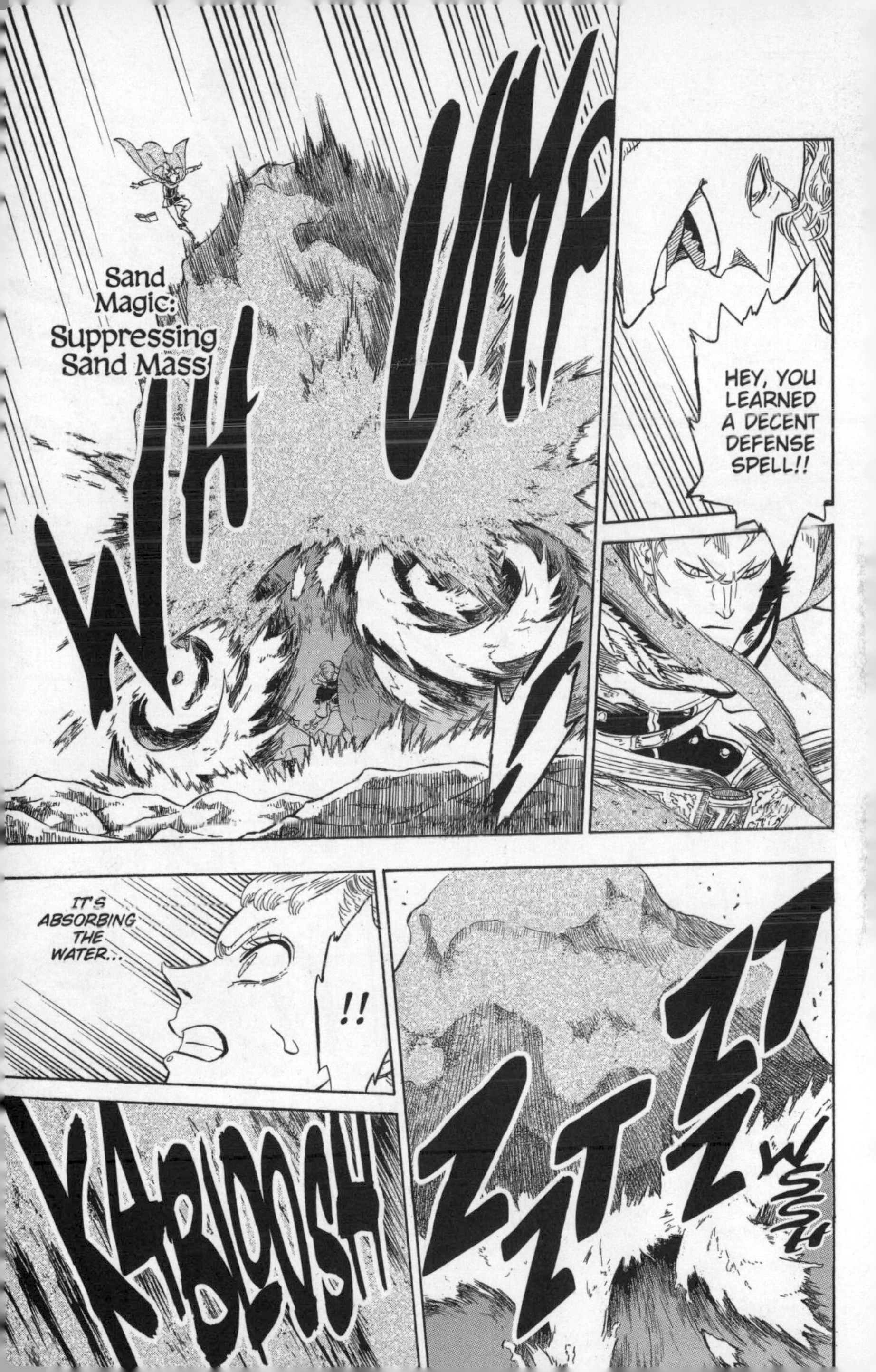
HEY, YOU LEARNED A DECENT DEFENSE SPELL!!
Sand Magic: Suppressing Sand Mass
WHUMF
IT'S ABSORBING THE WATER...
!!
KABLOOSH

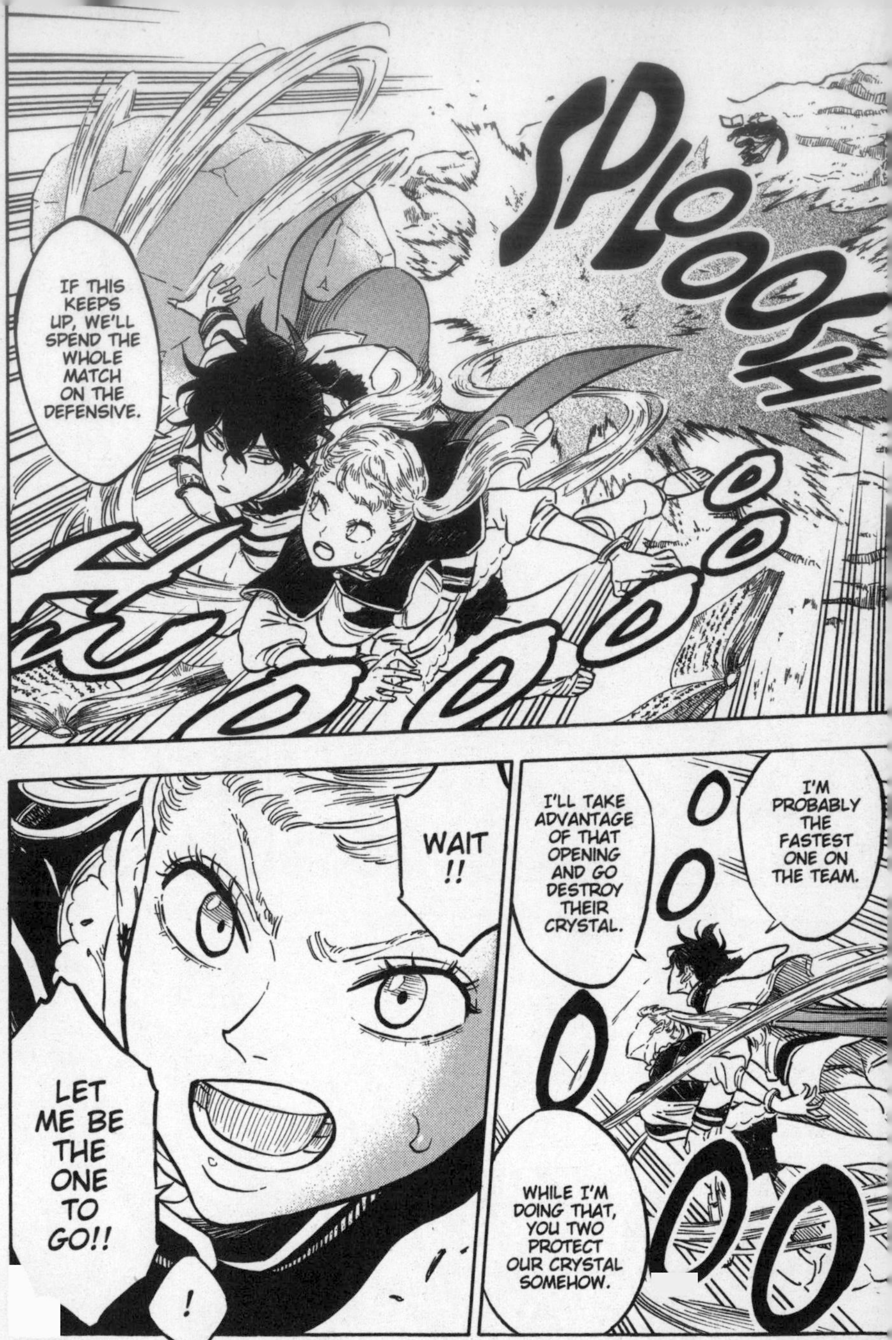
SPLOOOSH
IF THIS KEEPS UP, WE'LL SPEND THE WHOLE MATCH ON THE DEFENSIVE.
WHOOOOOO
I'M PROBABLY THE FASTEST ONE ON THE TEAM.
I'LL TAKE ADVANTAGE OF THAT OPENING AND GO DESTROY THEIR CRYSTAL.
WHILE I'M DOING THAT, YOU TWO PROTECT OUR CRYSTAL SOMEHOW.
WAIT!!
!
LET ME BE THE ONE TO GO!!

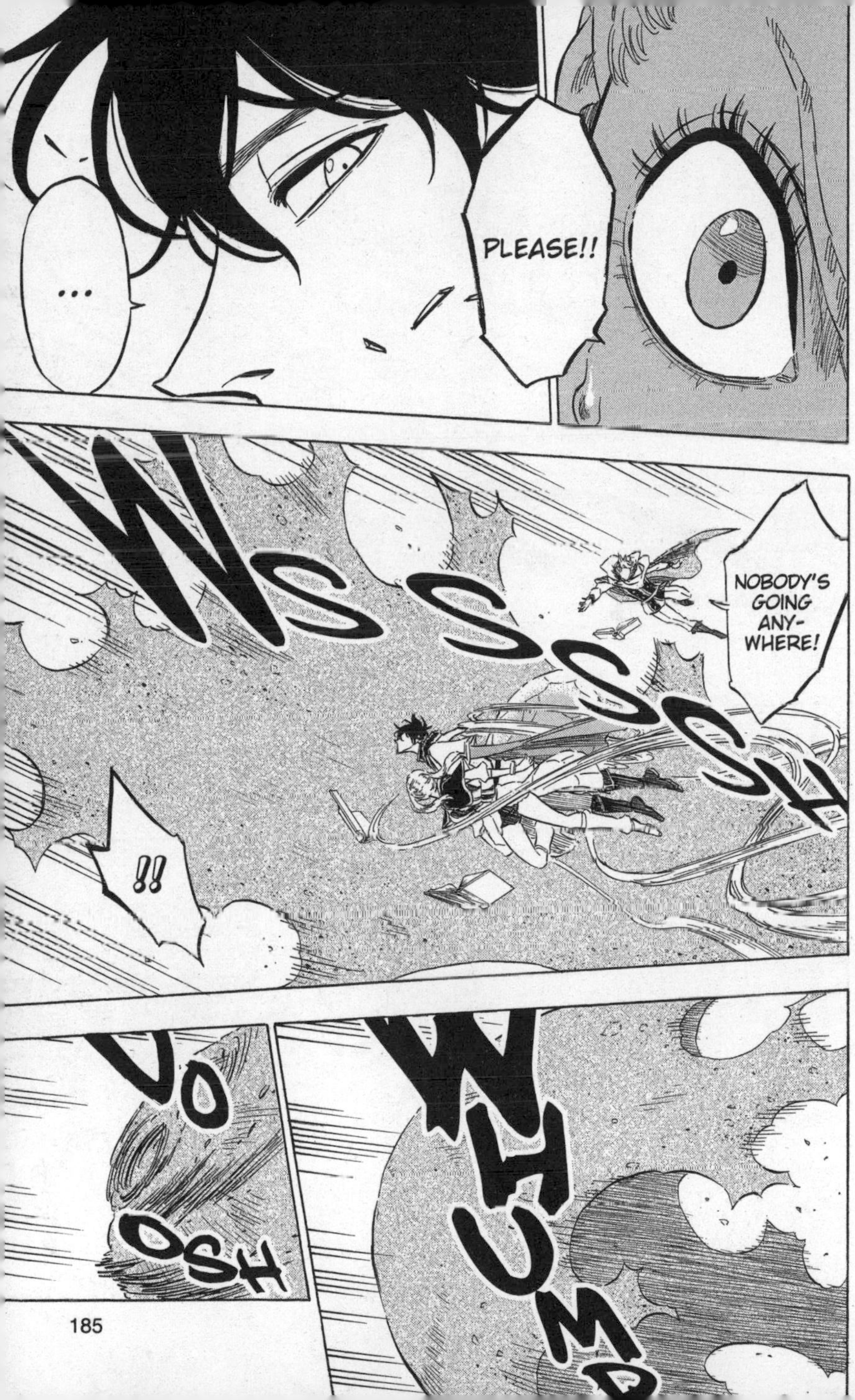
PLEASE!!
...
NOBODY'S GOING ANYWHERE!
WHSSSH
!!
WHUMP
DOOSH

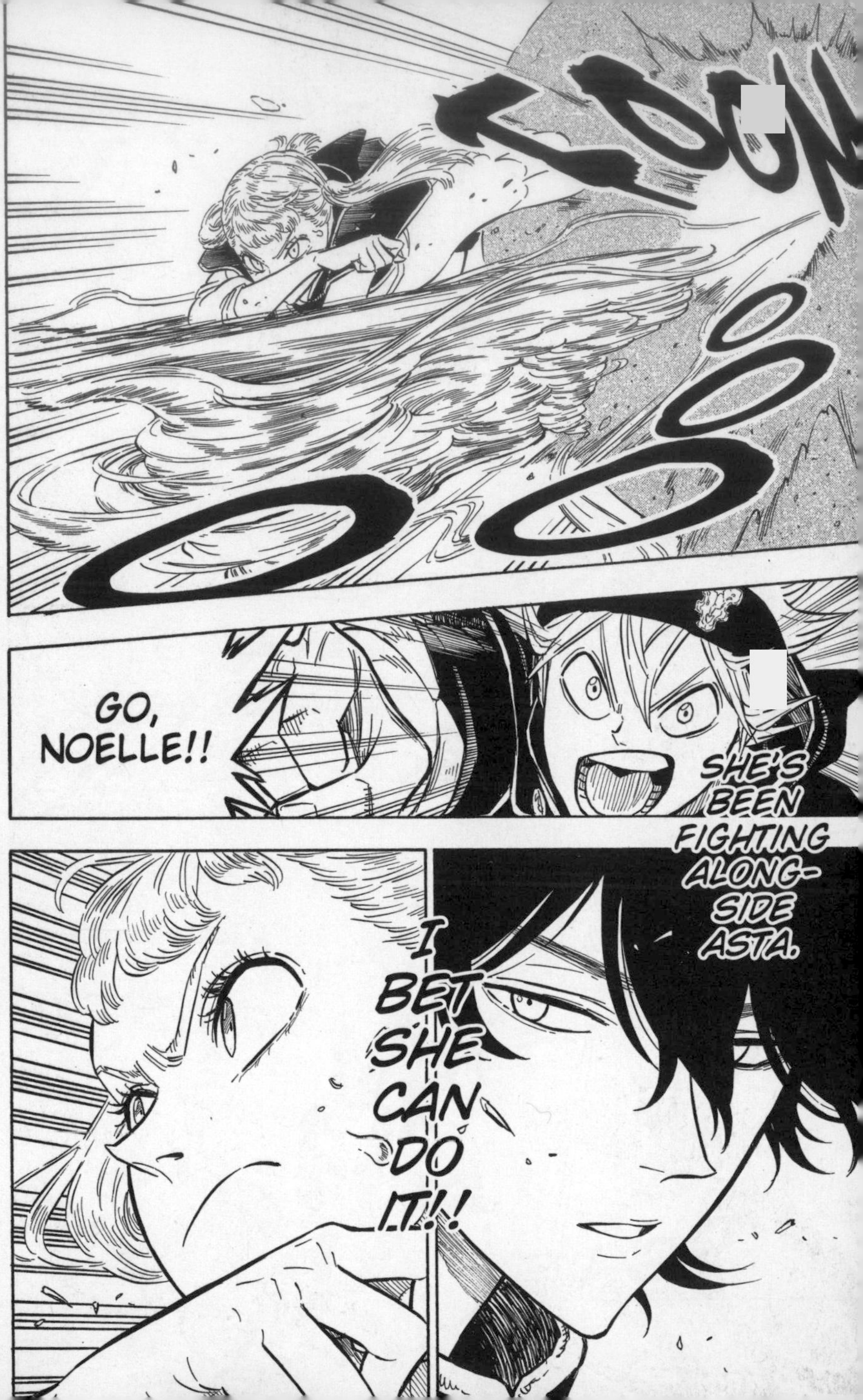
GO, NOELLE!!
SHE'S BEEN FIGHTING ALONG-SIDE ASTA.
I BET SHE CAN DO IT!!

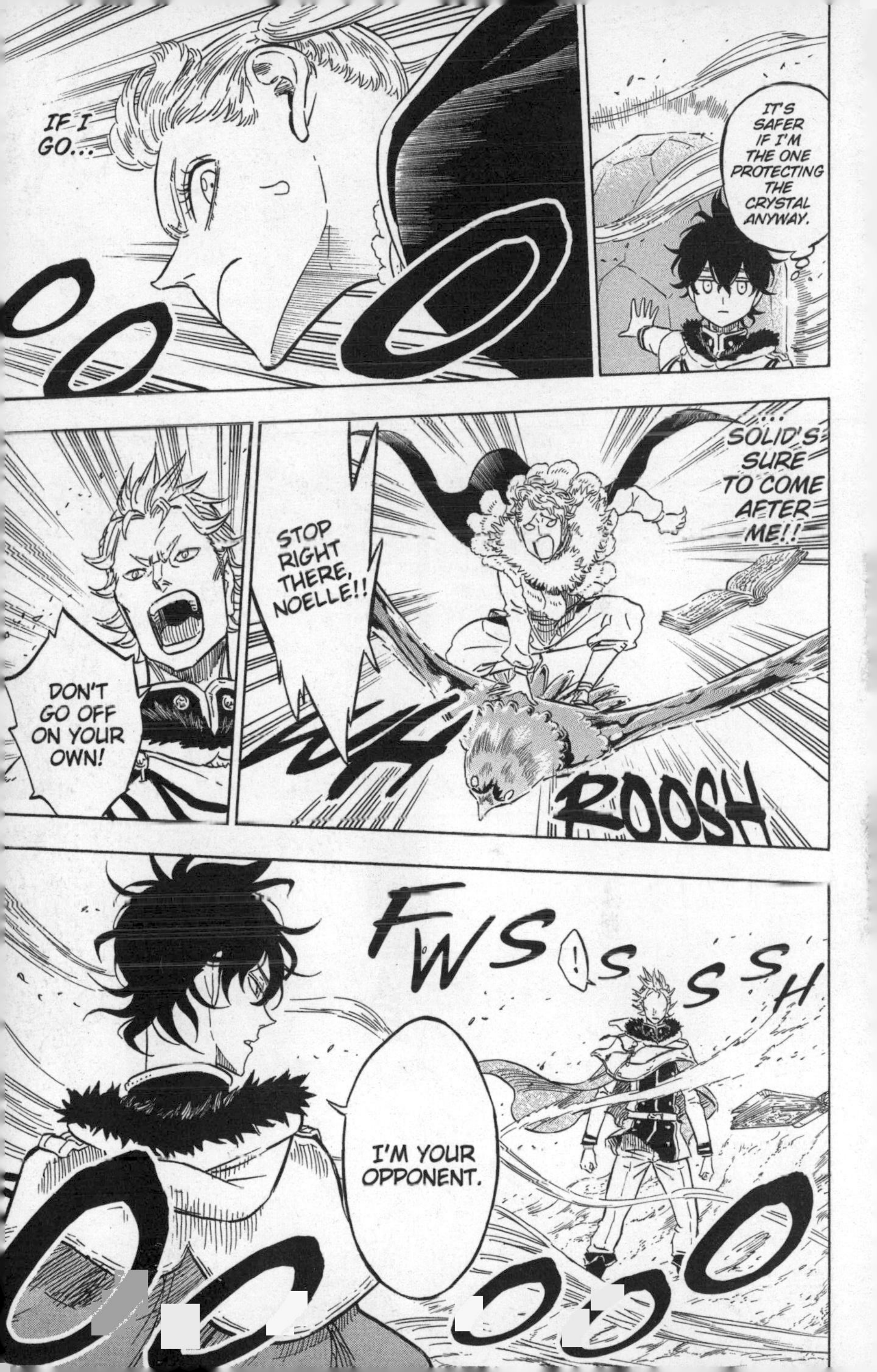
IT'S SAFER IF I'M THE ONE PROTECTING THE CRYSTAL ANYWAY.
IF I GO...
...SOLID'S SURE TO COME AFTER ME!!
STOP RIGHT THERE, NOELLE!!
WHROOSH
DON'T GO OFF ON YOUR OWN!
FWSSSSH
!
I'M YOUR OPPONENT.

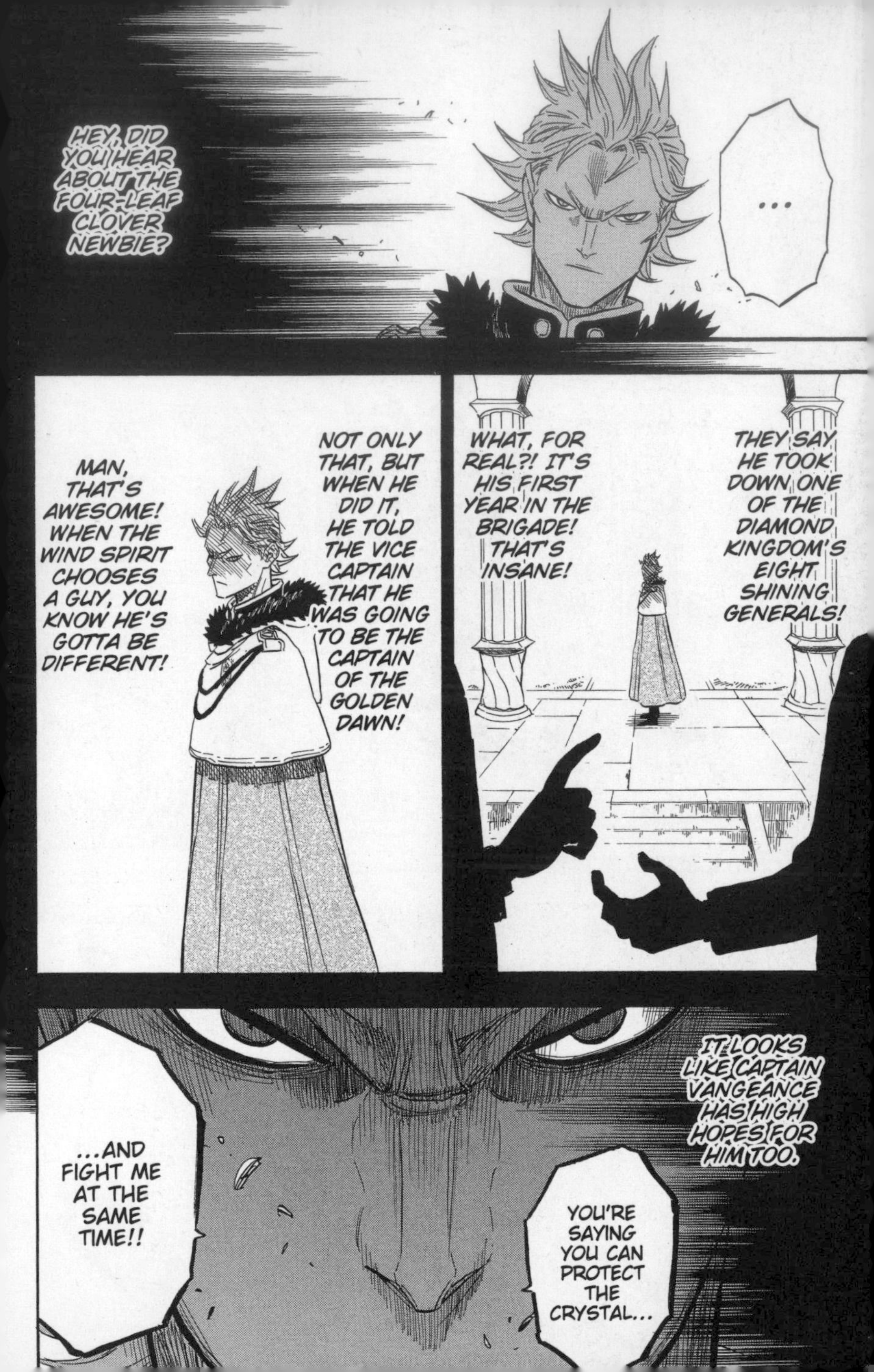
HEY, DID YOU HEAR ABOUT THE FOUR-LEAF CLOVER NEWBIE?
...
THEY SAY HE TOOK DOWN ONE OF THE DIAMOND KINGDOM'S EIGHT SHINING GENERALS!
WHAT, FOR REAL?! IT'S HIS FIRST YEAR IN THE BRIGADE! THAT'S INSANE!
NOT ONLY THAT, BUT WHEN HE DID IT, HE TOLD THE VICE CAPTAIN THAT HE WAS GOING TO BE THE CAPTAIN OF THE GOLDEN DAWN!
MAN, THAT'S AWESOME! WHEN THE WIND SPIRIT CHOOSES A GUY, YOU KNOW HE'S GOTTA BE DIFFERENT!
IT LOOKS LIKE CAPTAIN VANGEANCE HAS HIGH HOPES FOR HIM TOO.
YOU'RE SAYING YOU CAN PROTECT THE CRYSTAL...
...AND FIGHT ME AT THE SAME TIME!!

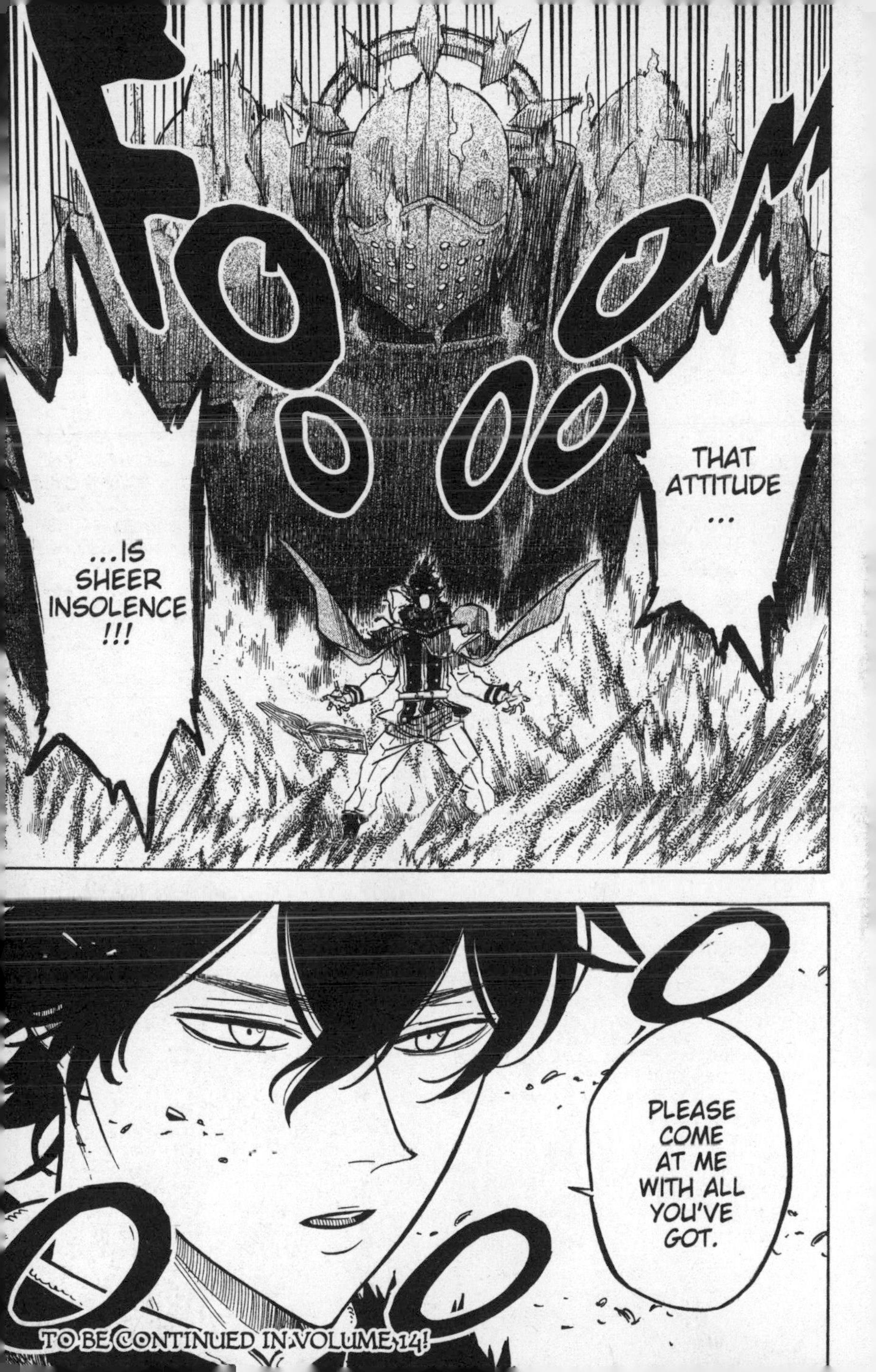
THAT ATTITUDE ...
...IS SHEER INSOLENCE !!!
PLEASE COME AT ME WITH ALL YOU'VE GOT.
TO BE CONTINUED IN VOLUME 14!

The Blank Page Brigade

This volume's topic:
What made you think "Y-you've got to be kidding me!" recently? (Topic submitted by Candy Magician from Niigata Prefecture!)

I took a fall on my motorcycle and dented the frame, and just when I'd gotten it fixed, the battery died, and after I got that changed and finally rode it again, I knocked it over and broke the brake lever.
Suzuki

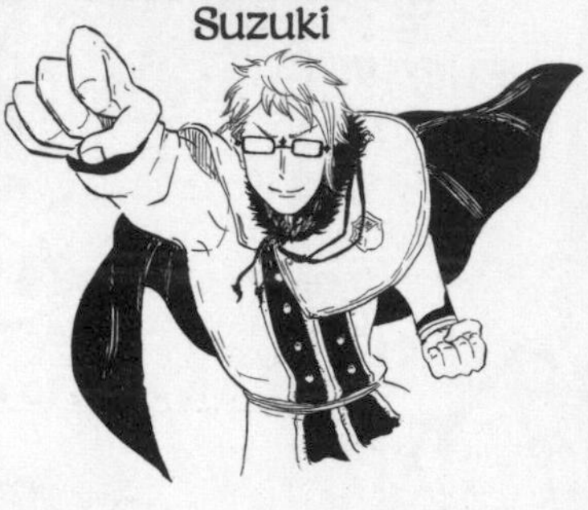

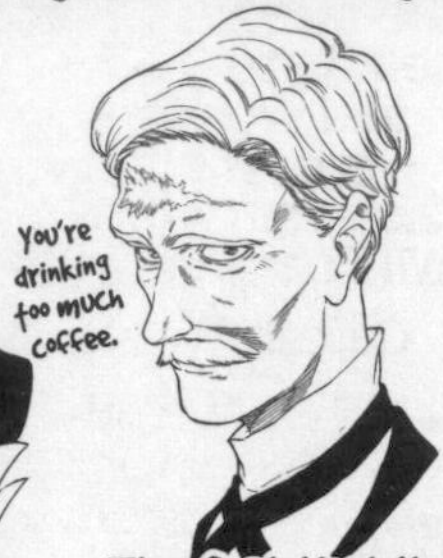
You're drinking too much coffee.

The fact that it seems like my cowlick is growing.
Kazuhiro Wakao

My bookshelf collapsed.
Hayato Gotō

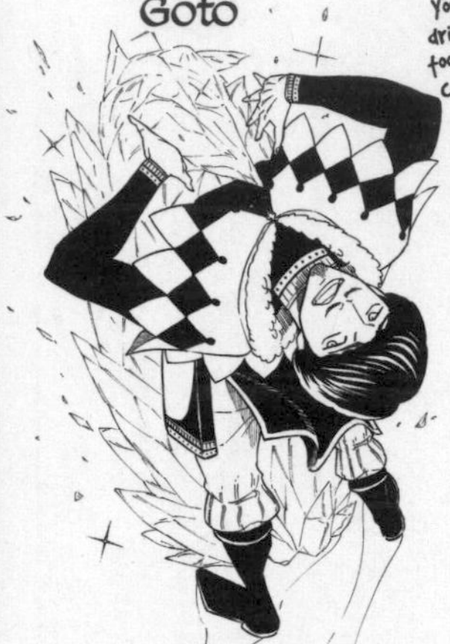

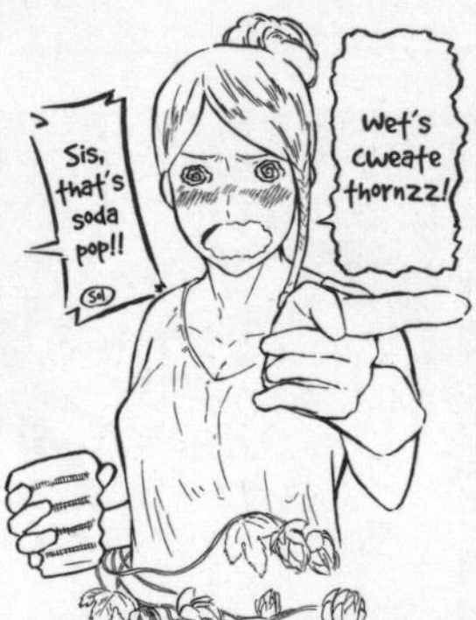
Wet's cweate thornzz!
Sis, that's soda pop!!

The fact that Beyblades these days send components flying everywhere when you lose.
Yōtarō Hayakawa

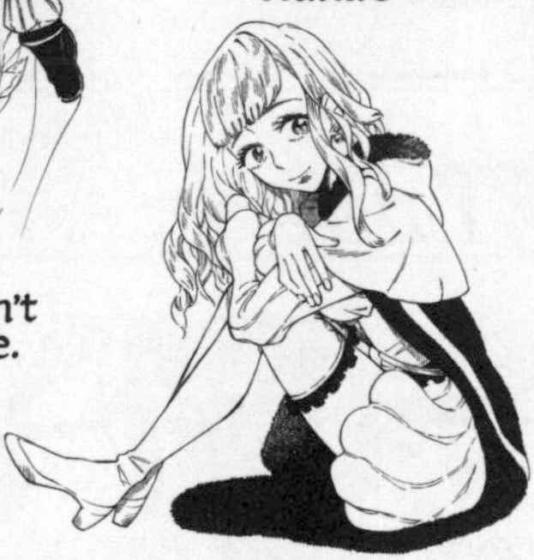

Amelie just won't warm up to me.
Shūtarō Koga

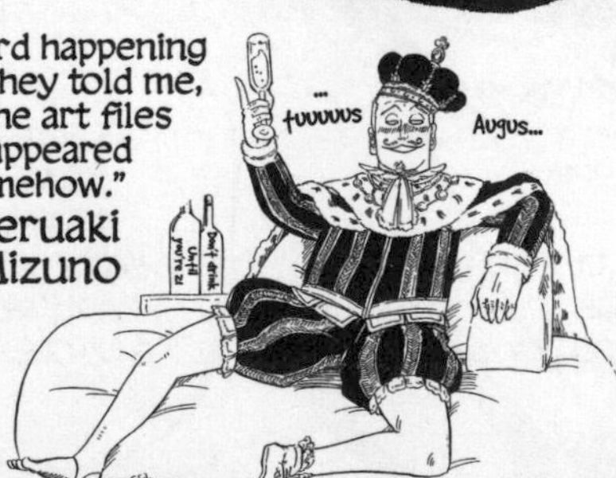
Augus...
... tuuuuus

The weird happening where they told me, "Uh, the art files disappeared somehow."
Teruaki Mizuno

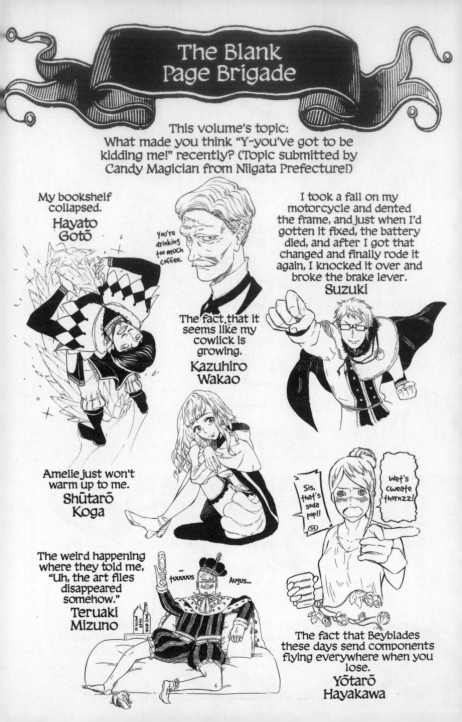

When I went to feed my fish, the lid came off the food container and all the food fell into the tank...

©

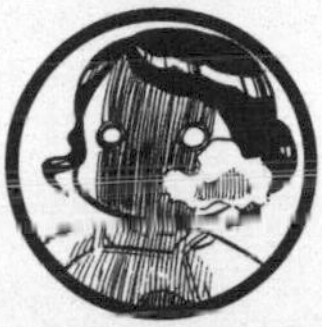

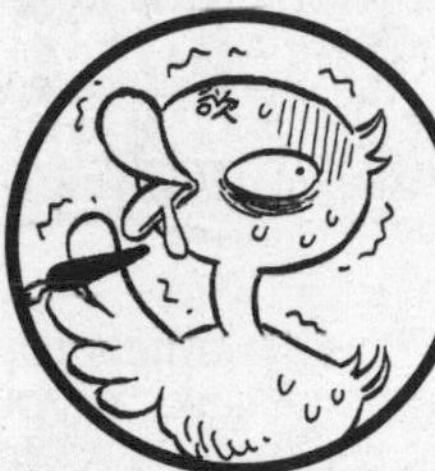

Before I went to bed in the morning, I heard some mystery bird calls outside. I wondered what they were. They were big parakeets. Two of 'em. Wild parakeets...?!

Captain Tabata

The fact that when I buy clothes online they never, ever look good on me.

Editor Katayama

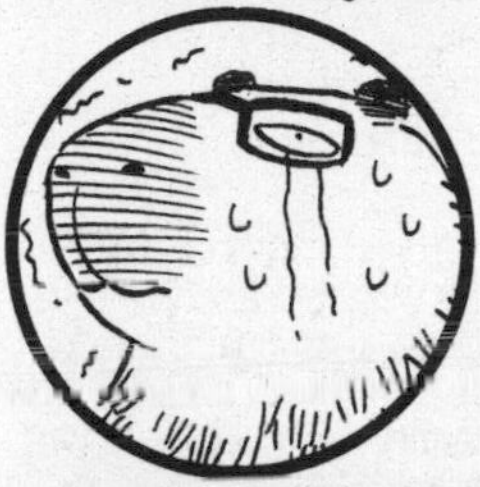

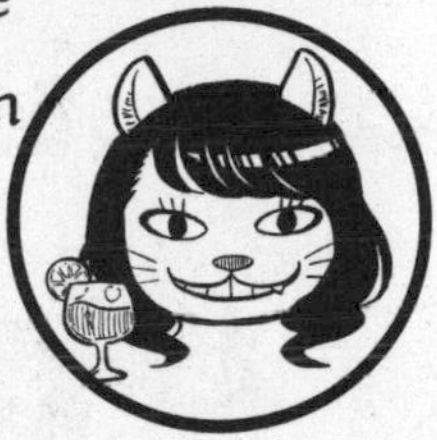

Somewhere along the way, Captain Yami got younger than me.

Designer Iwai

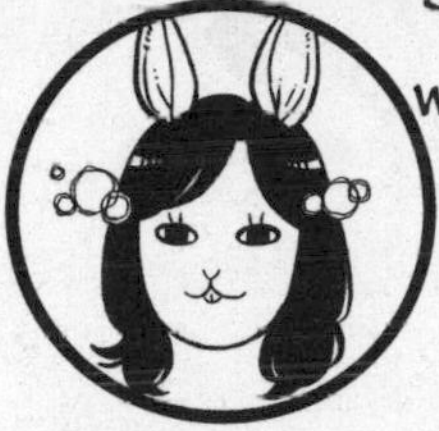

The fact that I didn't realize that one of the comedians I see on TV a lot was one of my college classmates.

Comics Editor Koshimura

AFTERWORD

So the day before this volume goes on sale in Japan (so, "yesterday"), the *Black Clover* anime finally starts!! Woo-hoo!!

Editor Katayama: "They've decided to turn this into an anime!! Congratulations!!"
Me: "Are you serious?! Yessssss!!"
Katayama: "It'll happen a year and a half from now!!"
Me: "A year and a half?!!"

One and a half years later... It feels like it took an awfully long time, and also like it went by in a flash. Ahh, my wife's foil-baked salmon is so good! I'll keep on doing my best!!

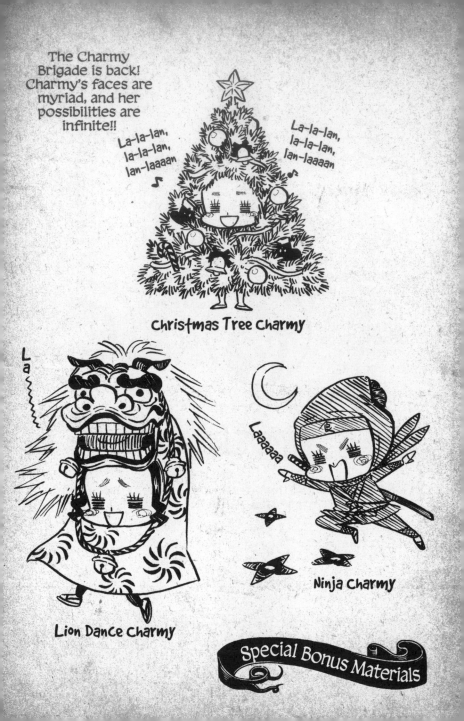

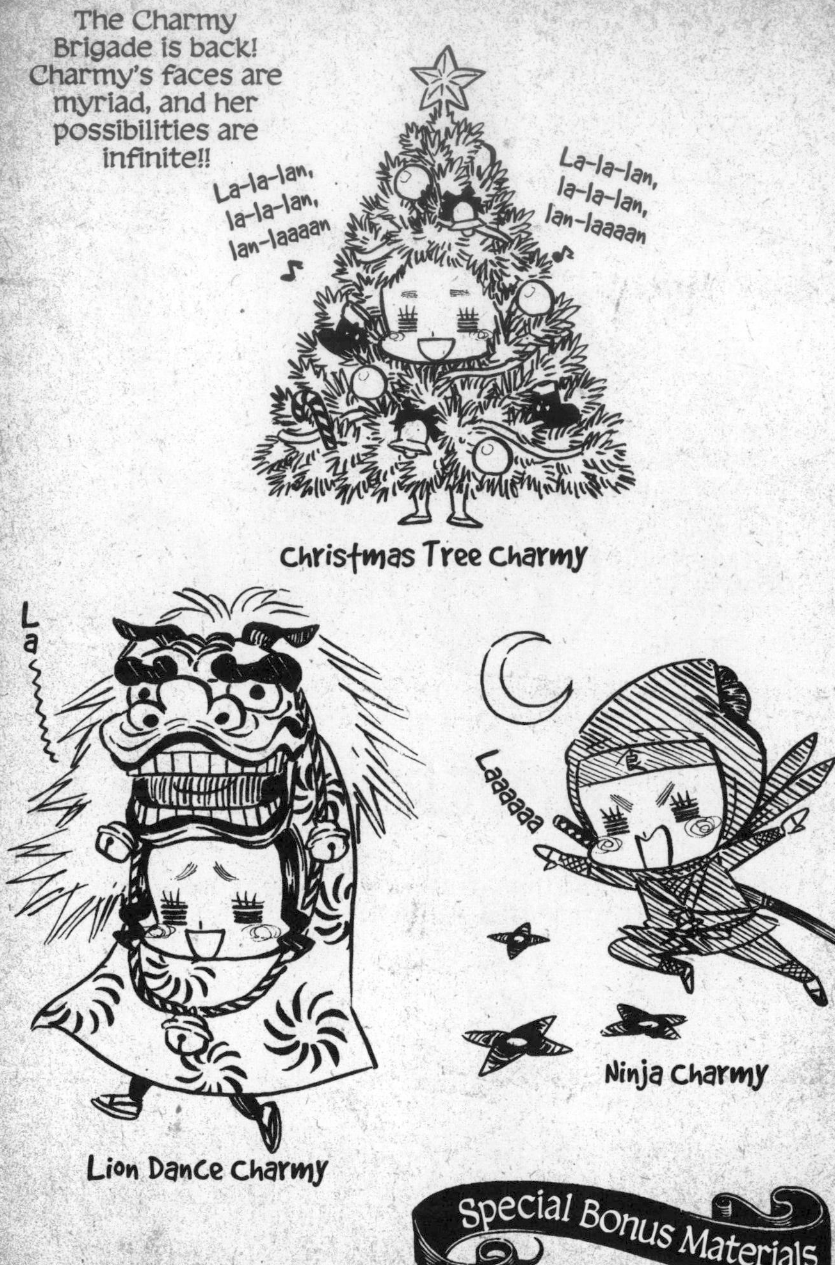
The Charmy Brigade is back! Charmy's faces are myriad, and her possibilities are infinite!!
La-la-lan, la-la-lan, lan-laaaan
La-la-lan, la-la-lan, lan-laaaan
Christmas Tree Charmy
Laaaaaa
Ninja Charmy
La
Lion Dance Charmy
Special Bonus Materials

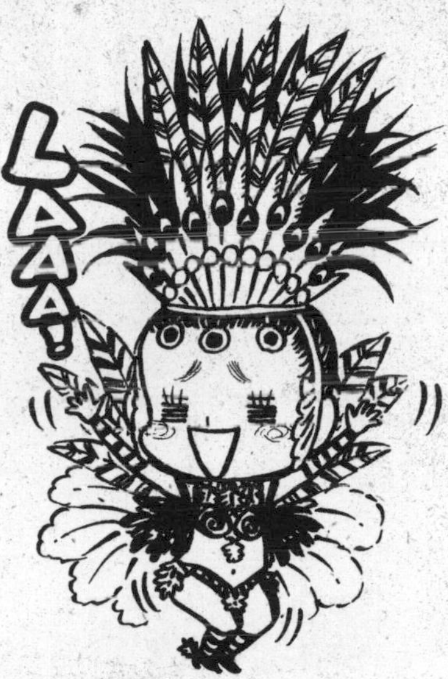
LAAA!

Samba Charmy

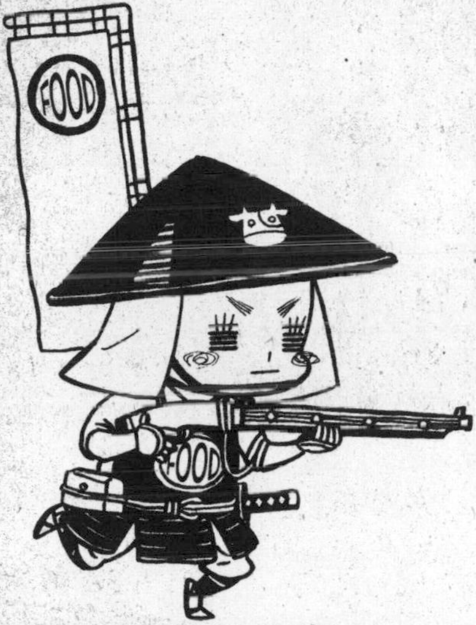
FOOD
FOOD

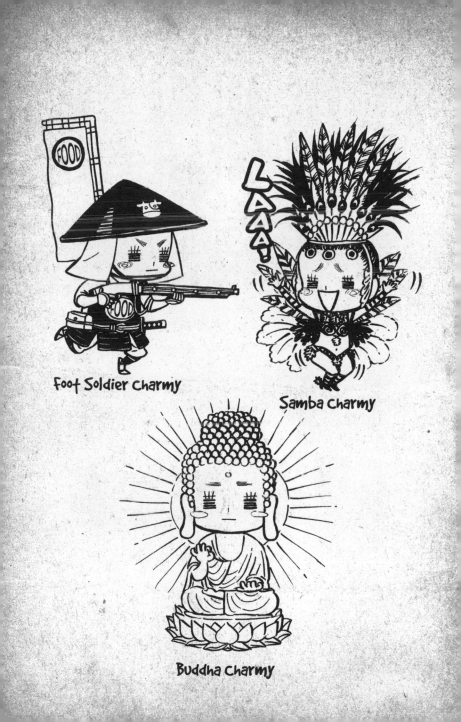

Foot Soldier Charmy

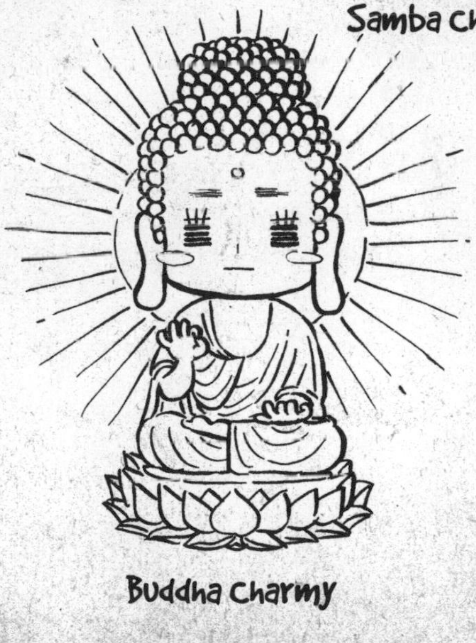

Buddha Charmy

ONE-PUNCH MAN © 2012 by ONE, Yusuke Murata/SHUEISHA Inc.

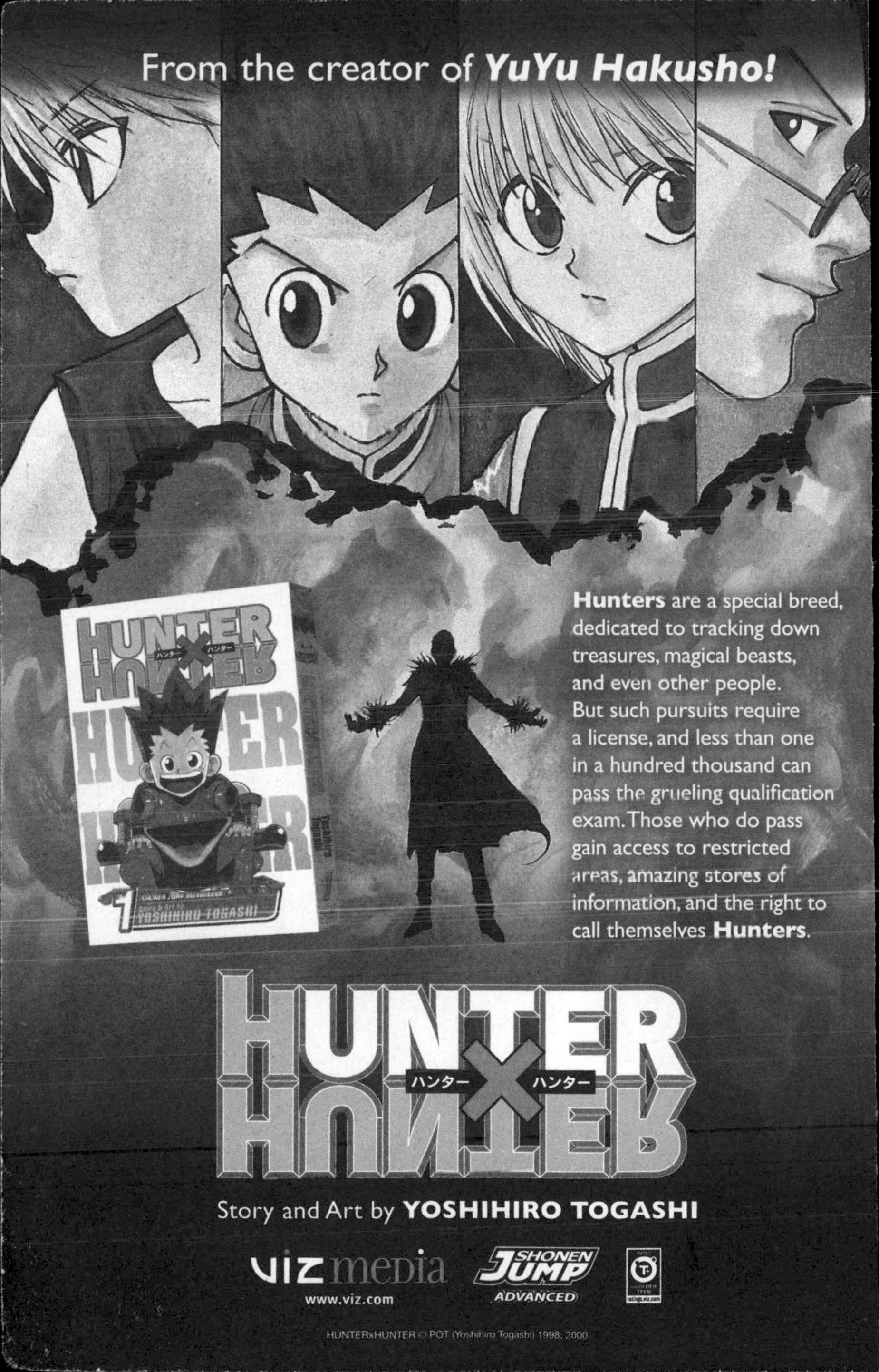
From the creator of YuYu Hakusho!
HUNTER × HUNTER
ハンター ハンター
1
SHONEN JUMP ADVANCED
Story & Art by
YOSHIHIRO TOGASHI
Hunters are a special breed, dedicated to tracking down treasures, magical beasts, and even other people. But such pursuits require a license, and less than one in a hundred thousand can pass the grueling qualification exam. Those who do pass gain access to restricted areas, amazing stores of information, and the right to call themselves Hunters.
HUNTER × HUNTER
ハンター ハンター
Story and Art by YOSHIHIRO TOGASHI
VIZ media
www.viz.com
SHONEN JUMP ADVANCED
ratings.viz.com
HUNTERxHUNTER © POT (Yoshihiro Togashi) 1998, 2000

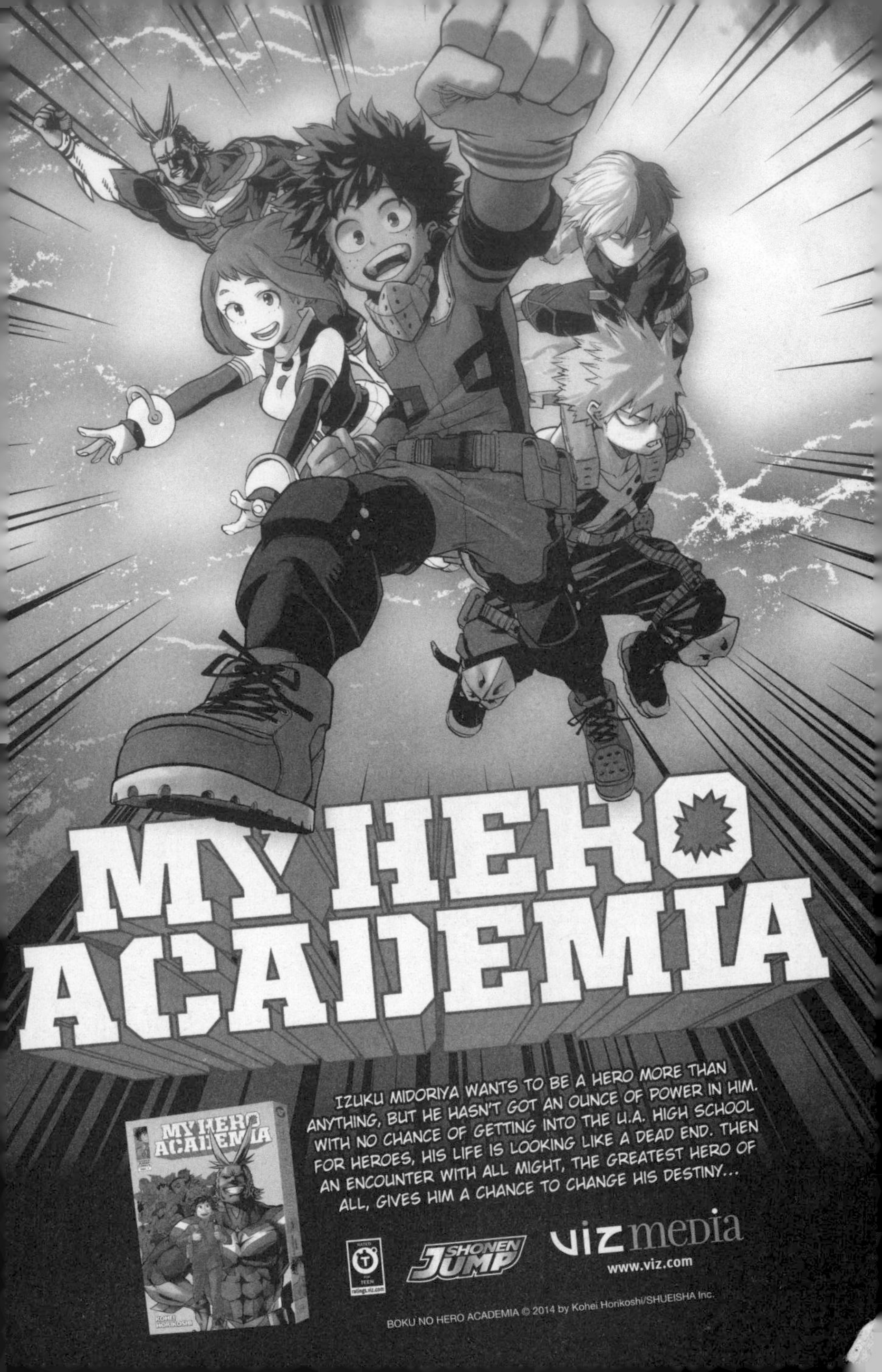

MY HERO ACADEMIA

IZUKU MIDORIYA WANTS TO BE A HERO MORE THAN ANYTHING, BUT HE HASN'T GOT AN OUNCE OF POWER IN HIM. WITH NO CHANCE OF GETTING INTO THE U.A. HIGH SCHOOL FOR HEROES, HIS LIFE IS LOOKING LIKE A DEAD END. THEN AN ENCOUNTER WITH ALL MIGHT, THE GREATEST HERO OF ALL, GIVES HIM A CHANCE TO CHANGE HIS DESTINY...

www.viz.com

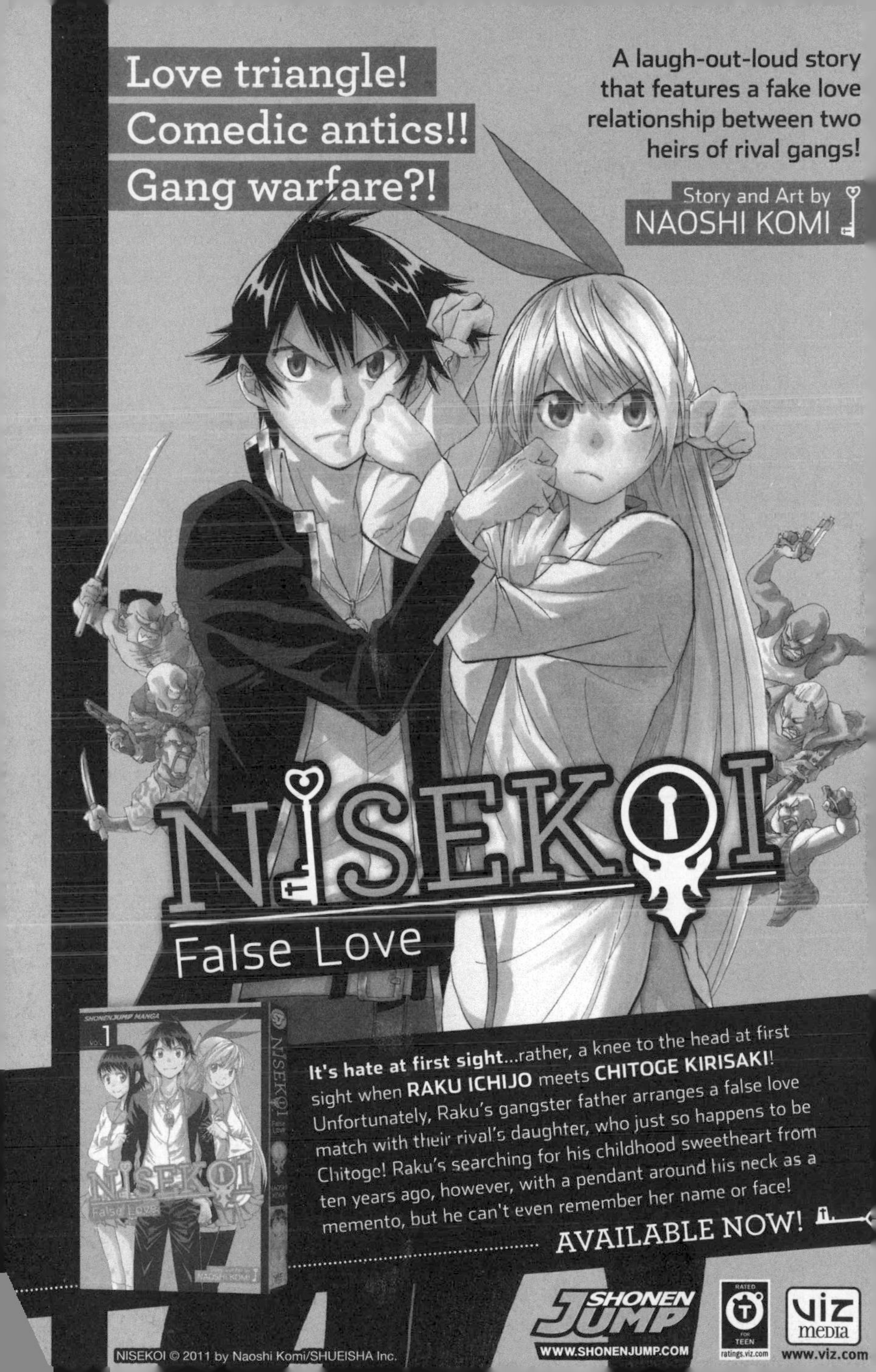
Love triangle!
Comedic antics!!
Gang warfare?!
A laugh-out-loud story that features a fake love relationship between two heirs of rival gangs!
Story and Art by
NAOSHI KOMI
NISEKOI
False Love
SHONEN JUMP MANGA
vol. 1
NISEKOI False Love
NAOSHI KOMI
It's hate at first sight...rather, a knee to the head at first sight when RAKU ICHIJO meets CHITOGE KIRISAKI! Unfortunately, Raku's gangster father arranges a false love match with their rival's daughter, who just so happens to be Chitoge! Raku's searching for his childhood sweetheart from ten years ago, however, with a pendant around his neck as a memento, but he can't even remember her name or face!
AVAILABLE NOW!
SHONEN JUMP
WWW.SHONENJUMP.COM
RATED T FOR TEEN
ratings.viz.com
VIZ media
www.viz.com
NISEKOI © 2011 by Naoshi Komi/SHUEISHA Inc.

ASTRA
LOST IN SPACE

CAN EIGHT TEENAGERS FIND THEIR WAY HOME FROM 5,000 LIGHT-YEARS AWAY?

It's the year 2063, and interstellar space travel has become the norm. Eight students from Caird High School and one child set out on a routine planet camp excursion. While there, the students are mysteriously transported 5,000 light-years away to the middle of nowhere! Will they ever make it back home?!

ASTRA
LOST IN SPACE
Story and Art by KENTA SHINOHARA

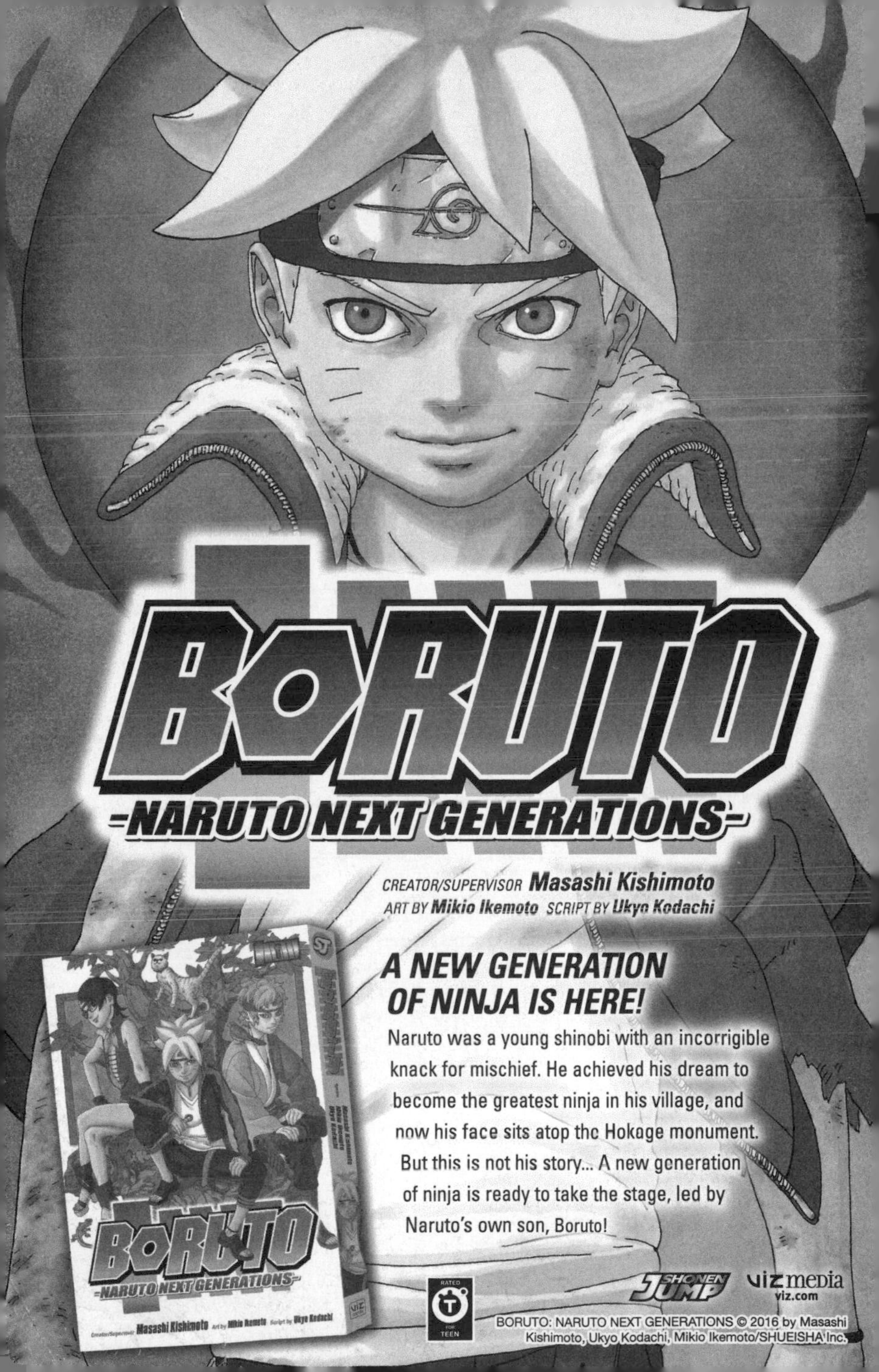
BORUTO
-NARUTO NEXT GENERATIONS-
CREATOR/SUPERVISOR Masashi Kishimoto
ART BY Mikio Ikemoto SCRIPT BY Ukyo Kodachi
A NEW GENERATION OF NINJA IS HERE!
Naruto was a young shinobi with an incorrigible knack for mischief. He achieved his dream to become the greatest ninja in his village, and now his face sits atop the Hokage monument. But this is not his story... A new generation of ninja is ready to take the stage, led by Naruto's own son, Boruto!
BORUTO
-NARUTO NEXT GENERATIONS-
RATED T FOR TEEN
SHONEN JUMP
VIZ media
viz.com
BORUTO: NARUTO NEXT GENERATIONS © 2016 by Masashi Kishimoto, Ukyo Kodachi, Mikio Ikemoto/SHUEISHA Inc.

Stop

YOU'RE READING
THE WRONG WAY!

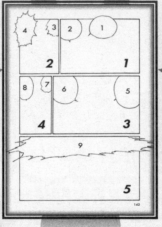

BLACK CLOVER

reads from right to left, starting
in the upper-right corner. Japanese
is read from right to left, meaning
that action, sound effects, and
word-balloon order are completely
reversed from English order.